AF531830

ENCYCLOPAEDIA OF
OPERATING SYSTEM

ENCYCLOPAEDIA
OF
OPERATING SYSTEM

[Volume—Two]

By

Sudhir Kumar

ANMOL PUBLICATIONS PVT. LTD.

NEW DELHI - 110 002 (INDIA)

ANMOL PUBLICATIONS PVT. LTD.
4374/4B, Ansari Road, Daryaganj
New Delhi - 110 002
Phones: 23261597, 23278000
Visit us at: www.anmolpublications.com

Encyclopaedia of Operating System

First Edition, 2004

ISBN 81-261-1792-3 (Set)

PRINTED IN INDIA

Published by J.L. Kumar for Anmol Publications Pvt. Ltd., New Delhi and Printed at Mehra Offset Press, Delhi.

Contents

Vol. 3

Preface

Virtually, an operating system is a program that manages the computer hardware. The components of a computer system are its hardware, software and data. The operating system provides the means for the proper use of these resources in the operation of the computer system. Thus, Operating system is the heart of any computer or we can say operating system is essential part of the computer system. Similarly a course and text on operating system is an essential part of any computer-science education. This field is changing field at breathtakingly rapid rate, as computers are now prevalent in virtually every application, from games for children to the most sophisticated planning tools for governments and multinational firms. Yet the fundamental concepts remain the same and it is clear in all books of operating system.

This work is designed to meet the requirement of introductory course in operating system at the undergraduate and Postgraduate level. It provides a clear description on various concepts that are required for understanding the proper functioning of any operating system.

The hardware text required for an understanding of operating system are included in this book. For coding examples we use predominantly 'C' as well as Java, but the reader can still understand the algorithms without a thorough knowledge of these languages.

The fundamental concepts and algorithms covered in this book are based on the existing commercial operating system in use. The information gathered herein is substantially based on authoritative sources. Our aim is to present these concepts and algorithms in a general setting that is not tied to any particular operating system.

We present a large number of examples that pertain to the most popular operating systems, including Sun Microsystems, Solaris 2, Linux, MS Dos, Windows NT and Windows 2000.

Apart from these some case studies on Unix, and on windows are also included in this work. The entire information is gathered under twenty-seven chapters.

In bringing this text into a book form, I shall be grateful for Mr. J.L. Kumar, Managing Director, Anmol Publications Pvt. Ltd., New Delhi and Mr. J.K. Dawra for their valuable suggestions. Any suggestions for the improvement of the book are also welcome which will be subsequently appended in the revised edition of the book.

— **S.K.**

10

File System Implementation

Some systems combine contiguous allocation with indexed allocation by using contiguous allocation for small files (up to three or four blocks), and automatically switching to an indexed allocation if the file grows large. Since most files are small, and contiguous allocation is efficient for small files, average performance can be quite good.

For instance, the version of the UNIX operating system from Sun Microsystems was changed in 1991 to improve performance in the file-system allocation algorithm. The performance measurements indicated that the maximum disk throughput on a typical workstation (12-MIPS SPARCstation1) took 50 per cent of the CPU and produced a disk bandwidth of only 1.5 MB per second. To improve performance, Sun make changes to allocate space in clusters of size 56 KB whenever possible. (56 KB was the maximum size of a DMA transfer on Suns at that time.) This allocation reduced external fragmentation, and thus seek and latency times. In addition, the disk-reading routines were optimized to read in these large clusters. The inode structure was left unchanged. These changes, plus the use of read-ahead and free-behind resulted in 25 per cent less CPU being used for substantially improved throughput.

Many other optimizations are possible and are in use. Given the disparity between CPU and disk speed, it is not unreasonable to add thousands of extra instructions to the operating system to save just a few disk-head movements. Furthermore, this disparity is increasing over time, to the point where hundreds of thousands of instructions reasonably could be used to optimize head movements.

Free-Space Management

Since disk space is limited, we need to reuse the space from deleted files for new files, if possible. (Write-once optical disks only allow one write to any given sector, and thus such reuse is not physically possible.) To keep track of free disk space, the system maintains a **free-space list.** The free-space list records all *free* disk blocks—those not allocated to some file or directory. To create a file, we search the free-space list for the required amount of space, and allocate that space to the new file. This space is then removed from the free-space list. When a file is deleted, its disk space is added to the free-space list. The free-space list, despite its name, might not be implemented as a list, as we shall discuss.

Bit Vector

Frequently, the free-space list is implemented as a **bit map** or **bit vector.** Each block is represented by 1 bit. If the block is free, the bit is 1; if the block is allocated, the bit is 0.

For example, consider a disk where blocks 2, 3, 4, 5, 8, 9, 10, 11, 12, 13, 17, 18, 25, 26, and 27 are free, and the rest of the blocks are allocated. The free-space bit map would be

001111001111110001100000011100000 ...

The main advantage of this approach is its relatively simplicity and efficiency in finding the first free block, or n consecutive free blocks on the disk. Indeed, many computers supply bit-manipulation instructions that can be used effectively for that purpose. For example, the Intel family starting with the 80386 and the Motorola family starting with the 68020 (processors that have powered PCs and Macintosh systems, respectively) have instructions that return the offset in a word of the first bit with the value 1. In fact, the Apple Macintosh operating system uses the bit-vector method to allocate disk space. To find the first free block, the Macintosh operating system checks sequentially each word in the bit map to see whether that value is not 0, since a 0-valued word has all 0 bits and represents a set of allocated blocks. The first non-0 word is scanned for the first 1 bit, which is the location of the first free block. The calculation of the block number is

$$(\text{number of bits per word}) \times (\text{number of 0-value words}) + \text{offset of first 1 bit.}$$

Again, we see hardware features driving software functionality. Unfortunately, bit vectors are inefficient unless the entire vector is kept in main memory (and is written to disk occasionally for recovery needs). Keeping it in main memory is possible for smaller disks, such as on microcomputers, but no for larger ones. A 1.3-GB disk with 512-byte blocks would need a bit map of over 332 KB to track its free blocks. Clustering the blocks in groups of four reduces this number to over 83 KB per disk.

Linked List

Another approach to free-space management is to link together all the free disk blocks, keeping a pointer to the first free block in a special location on the disk and caching it in memory. This first block contains a pointer to the next free disk block, and so on. In our example we would keep a pointer to block 2, as the first free block. Block 2 would contain a pointer to block 3, which would point to block 4, which would point to block 5, which would point to block 8, and so on. However, this scheme is not efficient; to traverse the list, we must read each block, which requires substantial I/O time. Fortunately, traversing the free list is not a frequent action. Usually, the operating system simply needs a free block so that it can allocate that block to a file, so the first block in the free list is used. The FAT method incorporates free-block accounting into the allocation data structure. No separate method is needed.

Grouping

A modification of the free-list approach is to store the addresses of n free blocks in the first free block. The first $n - 1$ of these blocks are actually free. The last block contains the addresses of another n free blocks, and so on. The importance of this implementation is that the addresses of a large number of frees blocks can be found quickly, unlike in the standard linked-list approach.

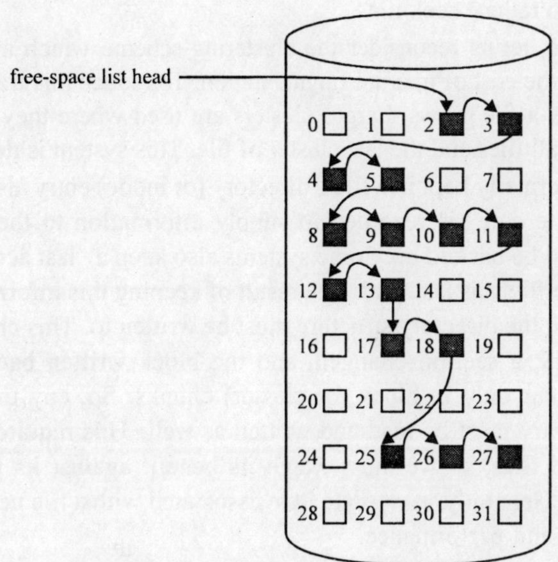

Fig. 10.1. Linked free space list on disk.

Counting

Another approach is to take advantage of the fact that, generally, several contiguous blocks may be allocated or freed simultaneously, particularly when space is allocated with the contiguous-allocation algorithm or through clustering. Thus, rather than keeping a list of *n* free disk addresses, we can keep the address of the first free block and the number *n* of free contiguous blocks that follow the first block. Each entry in the free-space list then consists of a disk address and a count. Although each entry requires more space than would a simple disk address, the overall list will be shorter, as long as the count is generally greater than 1.

Efficiency and Performance

Now that we have discussed the block-allocating and directory-management options, we can further consider their effect on performance and efficient disk use. Disks tend to be a major bottleneck in system performance, since they are the slowest main computer component. In this section, we discuss a variety of techniques used to improve the efficiency and performance of secondary storage.

Efficiency of Disk Space

The efficient use of disk space is heavily dependent on the disk allocation and directory algorithms in use. For instance, UNIX inodes are preallocated on a partition. Even an "empty" disk has a percentage of its space lost to inodes. However, by preallocating the inodes and spreading them across the partition, we improve the file system's performance. This improved performance is a result of the UNIX allocation and free-space algorithms, which try to keep a file's data blocks near that file's inode block to reduce seek time.

As another example, let us reconsider the clustering scheme which aids in file-seek and file-transfer performance at the cost of internal fragmentation. To reduce this fragmentation, BSD UNIX varies the cluster size as a file grows. Larges clusters are used where they can be filled, and small clusters are used for small files and the last cluster of file. This system is descried in Appendix A.

The types of data normally kept in a file's directory (or inode) entry also require consideration. Commonly, a "last write date" is recorded to supply information to the user and to determine whether the file needs to be backed up. Some systems also keep a "last access date," so that a user can determine when the file was last read. The result of keeping this information is that, whenever the file is read, a field in the directory structure must be written to. This change requires the block to be read into memory, a section changed, and the block written back out to disk, because operations on disks occur only in block (or cluster) chunks. So, any time a file is opened for reading, its directory entry must be read and written as well. This requirement can be inefficient for frequently accessed files, so we must weigh its benefit against its performance cost when designing a file system. Generally, *every* data item associated with a file needs to be considered for its effect on efficiency and performance.

As an example, consider how efficiency is affected by the size of the pointers used to access data. Most systems use either 16- or 32-bit pointers throughout the operating system. These pointer sizes limit the length of a file to either 2^{16} (64 KB) or 2^{32} bytes (4 GB). Some systems implement 64-bit pointers to increase this limit to 2^{64} bytes, which is a very large number indeed. However, 64-bit pointers take more space to store, and in turn make the allocation and free-space-management methods (linked lists, indexes, and so on) use more disk space.

One of the difficulties in choosing a pointer size, or indeed any fixed allocation size within an operating system, is planning for the effects of changing technology. Consider that the IBM PC XT had a 10-MB hard drive and an MS-DOS file system that could support only 32 MB. (Each FAT entry was 12 bits, pointing to an 8-KB clusters.) As disk capacities increased, larger disks had to be split into 32-MB partitions, because the file system could not track blocks beyond 32 MB. As hard disks of over 100-MB capacities became common, the disk data structures and algorithms in MS-DOS had to be modified to allow larger file systems. (Each FAT entry was expanded to 16 bits, and later to 32 bits.) The initial file-system decisions were made for efficiency reasons; however, with the advent of MS-DOS Version 4, millions of computer users were inconvenienced when they had to switch to the new, larger file system.

As another example, consider the evolution of Sun's Solaris operating systems. Originally, many data structures were of fixed lengths, allocated at system startup. These structures included the process table and the open-file table. When the process table became full, no more processes could be created. When the file table became full, no more files could be opened. The system would fail to provide services to the users. These table sizes could be increased only by recompiling the kernel and rebooting the system. Since the release of Solaris 2, almost all kernel structures are allocated dynamically, eliminating these artificial limits on system performance. Of course, the algorithms, that manipulate these tables are more complicated, and the operating system is a little slower because it must dynamically allocate and deallocate table entries, but that price is the usual one for more functional generality.

Once the basic file-system algorithms are selected, we can still improve performance in several ways. Most disk controllers include local memory to form an on-board **cache** that is sufficiently large to stores entire tracks at a time. Once a seek is performed, the track is read into the disk cache starting at the sector under the disk head (alleviating latency time). The disk controller then transfers any sector requests to the operating systems. Once blocks make it from the disk controller into main memory, the operating system may cache the blocks there.

Some systems maintain a separate section of main memory of a **disk cache**, where blocks are kept under the assumption that they will be used again shortly. Other systems cache file data using a **page cache.** The page cache used virtual-memory techniques to cache file data as pages rather than as file-system-oriented blocks. Caching file data using virtual addresses is far more efficient that caching through physical disk blocks. Several systems, including Solaris, some new Linux releases, and Windows NT and 2000, use page caching to cache both process pages and file data. This is known as **unified virtual memory.** Solaris used both a block cache and a page cache. The block cache is used for file-system metadata (such as inodes) and the page cache is used for all file-system data.

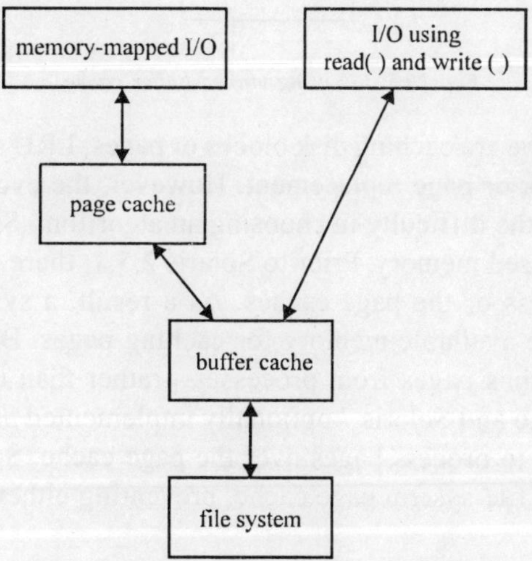

Fig 10.2. I/O without a unified buffer cache.

Some versions of UNIX provide a **unified buffer cache.** Consider the two alternatives of opening and accessing a file. One approach is to use memory-mapping the second is to use the standard system calls read and write. Without a unified buffer cache. In this instance, the read and write system calls go through the buffer cache. The memory mapping call requires using two caches—the page cache and buffer cache. A memory mapping proceeds by reading in disk blocks from the file system and storing them in the buffer cache. Because the virtual memory system cannot interfaces with the buffer cache, the contents of the file in the buffer cache must be copied into the page cache. This situation is known as **double caching** and requires caching file-system data twice. Not only is it wasteful of memory, but it wastes significant CPU and I/O cycles due to the extra data movement within system memory. Also, inconsistencies between the two caches can result in corrupt files. By providing a unified buffer cache both memory mapping and the read and write system calls use the same page cache. This has the benefit of avoiding double caching and it allows the virtual memory system to manage file-system data.

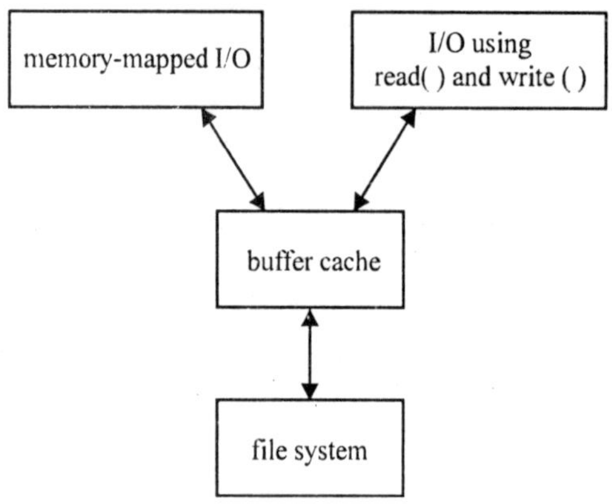

Fig. 10.3. I/O using unified buffer cache.

Regardless of whether we are caching disk blocks or pages, LRU seems a reasonable general-purpose algorithm for block or page replacement. However, the evolution of the Solaris page-caching algorithms reveals the difficulty in choosing an algorithm. Solaris allows processes and the page cache to share unused memory. Prior to Solaris 2.5.1, there was no distinction between allocating pages to a process or the page caches. As a result, a system performing many I/O operations uses most of the available memory for caching pages. Because of the high rates of I/O, the page scanner reclaims pages from processes—rather than the page cache—when free memory runs low. Solaris 2.6 and Solaris 7 optionally implemented *priority paging,* in which the page scanner gives priority to process pages over the page cache. Solaris 8 added a fixed limit between process pages and file-system page cache, preventing either from forcing the other out of memory.

The page cache, the file system, and the disk drivers have some interesting interactions. When data are written to a disk file, the pages are buffered in the cache, and the disk driver sorts its output queue according to disk address. These two actions allow the disk driver to minimize disk-head seeks and to write data at times optimized for disk rotation. Unless synchronous writes are required, a process writing to disk simply writes into the cache, and the system asynchronously writes the data to disk when convenient. The user process sees very fast writes. When data are read from a disk file, the block I/O system does some read-ahead; however, writes are much nearer to asynchronous than are reads. Thus, output to the disk through the file system is often faster than is input for large transfers, counter to intuition.

Synchronous writes occur in the order in which the disk subsystem receives them, and the writes are not buffered. Thus the calling routine must wait for the data to reach the disk drive before it can proceed. **Asynchronous writes** are done the majority of the time. In an asynchronous write the data is stored in the cache and returns control to the caller. Metadata writes, among others, can be synchronous. Operating systems frequently include a flag in the open system call to allow a process to request that writes be performed synchronously. For example, databases use this feature for atomic transactions, to assure that data reaches stable storage in the required order.

Some systems optimize their page cache by using different replacement algorithms, depending on the access type of the file. A file being read or written sequentially should not have its pages replaced in LRU order, because the most recently used page will be used last, or perhaps never again. Instead, sequential access may be optimized by techniques known as free-behind and read-ahead. **Free-behind** removes a page from the buffer as soon as the next page is requested. The previous pages are not likely to be used again and waste buffer spaces. With **read-ahead**, a requested page and several subsequent pages are read and cached. These pages are likely to be requested after the current page is processed. Retrieving this data from the disk in one transfer and caching it saves a considerable amount of time. A track cache on the controller does not eliminate the need for read-ahead on a multiprogrammed system, because of the high latency and overhead of many small transfers from the track cache to main memory.

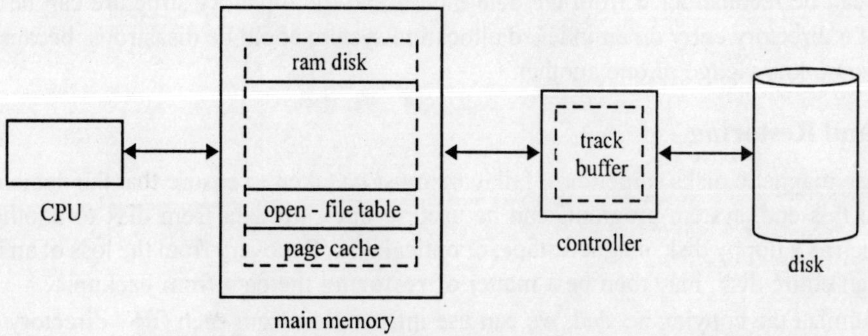

Fig. 10.4. Various disk-caching locations.

Another method of using main memory to improve performance is common on PCs. A section of memory is set aside and treated as a **virtual disk** (or **RAM** disk). In this case, a RAM-disk device driver accepts all the standard disk operations but performs those operations on the memory section, instead of on a disk. All disk operations can then be executed on this RAM disk and, except for the lighting-fast speed, users will not notice a difference. Unfortunately, RAM disk are useful only for temporary storage, since a power failure or a reboot of the system will usually erase them. Commonly, temporary files such as intermediate complier files are stored there.

The differences between a RAM disk and a disk cache is that the contents of the RAM disk are totally user controlled, whereas those of the disk cache are under the control of the operating system. For instance, a RAM disk will stay empty until the user (or programs, at a user's direction) creates files there.

Recovery from Failure

Since files and directories are kept both in main memory and on disk, care must taken to ensure that system failure does not result in loss of data or in data inconsistency.

Consistency Checking

Part of the directory information is kept in main memory (or cache) to speed up access. The directory information in main memory is generally more up to date than is the corresponding information on the disk, because the write of cached directory information to disk does not necessarily occur as soon as the update takes place.

Consider the possible effect of a computer crash. In this case, the table of opened files is generally lost, and with it any changes in the directories of opened files. This event can leave the file system in an inconsistent state: The actual state of some files is not as described in the directory structure. Frequently, a special program is run at reboot time to check for and correct disk inconsistencies.

The **consistency checker** compares the data in the directory structure with the data blocks on disk, and tries to fix any inconsistencies it finds. The allocation and free-space-management algorithms dictate what types of problems the checker can find, and how successful it will be in fixing them. For instance, if linked allocation is used and there is a link from any block to its next block, then the entire file can be reconstructed from the data blocks and the directory structure can be recreated. The loss of a directory entry on an indexed allocation system could be disastrous, because the data blocks have no knowledge of one another.

Backup and Restoring

Because magnetic disks sometimes, fail, care must be taken to ensure that the data are not lost forever. To this end, system programs can be used to **back up** data from disk to another storage devices, such as a floppy disk, magnetic tape, or optical disk. Recovery from the loss of an individual file, or of an entire disk, may then be a matter of **restoring** the data from backup.

To minimize the copying needed, we can use information from each file's directory entry. For instance, if the backup program knows when the last backup of a file was done, and the file's last write data in the directory indicates that the file has not changed since that date, them the file does not need to be copied again. A typical backup schedule may then be as follows:

- **Day 1:** Copy to a backup medium all files from the disk. This is called a **full backup.**
- **Day 2:** Copy to a another medium all files changed since day 1. This is an **incremental backup.**
- **Day 3:** Copy to another medium all files changed since day 2.

.
.
.

- **Day** *N:* Copy to another medium all files changed since day $N-1$. Then go back to Day 1.

The new cycle can have its backup written over the previous set, or onto a new set of backup media. In this manner, we can restore an entire disk by starting restores with the full backup, and continuing through each of the incremental backups. Of course, the larger N is, the more tapes or disks need to be read for a complete restore. An added advantage of this backup cycle is that we can restore any file accidentally deleted during the cycle by retrieving the deleted file from the backup of the previous day. The length of the cycle is a compromise between the amount of backup medium needed and the number of days back from which a restore can be done.

A user may notice that a particular file is missing or corrupted long after the damage was done. For this reason we usually plan to take a full backup from time to time that will be saved "forever," rather than reusing that backup medium. It is a good idea to store these permanent backups far away from the regular backups to protect against hazard, such as a fire that destroys the computer and all the backups too. And if the backup cycle reuses media, one must take care not to reuse the media too many times—if the media wear out, it might not be possible to restore any data from the backups.

Log-Structured File System

Frequently in computer science, algorithms and technologies transition from their original use to other applicable areas. Such is the case with the database log-based-recovery algorithms. These logging algorithms have been applied successfully to the problem of consistency checking. The resulting implementations are known as **log-based transaction-oriented** (or **journaling**) file systems.

Recall that on-disk file-system data structures—such as the directory structures, free-block pointers, free FCB pointers—can become inconsistent due to a system crash. Before the use of log-based techniques in operating systems, changes were usually applied to these structures in place. A typical operation, such as file create, can involve many structural changes within the file system on the disk. Directory structures are modified, FCBs are allocated, data blocks are allocated, and the free counts for all of these blocks are decreased. Those changes can be interrupted by a crash, with the result that the structures are inconsistent. For example, the free FCB count might indicate that an FCB had been allocated, but the directory structure might not point to the FCB. The FCB would be lost were it not for the consistency-check phase.

There are several problems with the approach of allowing the structures to break and repairing them on recovery. One is that the inconsistency may be irreparable. The consistency check may not be able to recover the structures, with the resulting loss of files and even entire directories. Consistency checking can require human intervention to resolve conflicts, and that is inconvenient if no human is available. The system can remain unavailable until the human tells the system how to proceed. Consistency checking also takes system and clock time. Terabytes of data can take hours of clock time to check.

The solution to this problem is to apply log-based-recovery techniques to file-system metadata updates. NTFS and the Veritas File System both use this method, and it is an option of UFS on Solaris 7 and beyond. In fact, it is becoming common on many operating systems.

Fundamentally, all metadata changes are written sequentially to a log. Each set of operations that perform a specific task is a **transaction.** Once the changes are written to this log, they are considered to be committed, and the system call can return to the user process, allowing it to continue execution. Meanwhile, these log entries are replayed across the actual file-system structures. As the changes are made pointer is updated to indicate which actions have completed and which are still incomplete. When an entire committed transaction is completed, it is removed from the log file, which is actually a circular buffer. The log may be in a separate section of the file system, or could even be on a separate disk spindle. It is more efficient, but more complex, to have it under separate read/write heads, thereby decreasing head contention and seek times.

If the system crashes, there will zero or more transactions in the log file. Those transactions were never completed to the file system even though they were committed by the operating system, so they must be completed. The transactions can be executed from the pointer until the work is complete, and the file-system structures remain consistent. The only problems occurs when a transaction has been aborted. That is, it was not committed before the system crashed. Any changes form those transactions that were applied to the file system must be undone, again preserving the consistency of the file system. This recovery is all that is needed after a crash, eliminating all problems with consistency checking.

A side benefit of using logging, on disk metadata updates is that those updates proceed much faster than when they are applied directly to the on-disk data structures. The reason for this improvement is found in the performance advantage of sequential I/O over random I/O. The costly synchronous random metadata writes are turned into much less costly synchronous sequential writes to the log-structured file systems logging area. Those changes in turn are replayed asynchronously via random writes to the appropriate structures. The overall result is a significant gain in performance of metadata-oriented operations, such as file creation and deletion.

NFS (Network File Systems)

Network file systems are commonplace. They typically integrate with the overall directory structure and interface of the client system. NFS is a good example of a widely used, well-implemented client-server network file system. Here, we use it as an example to explore the implementation details of network file systems.

NFS is both an implementation and a specification of a software system for accessing remote files across LANs (or even WANs). NFS is part of ONC+, which most UNIX vendors and some PC operating systems are supporting. The implementation described here is part of the Solaris operating system, which is a modified version of UNIX SVR4, running on Sun workstations and other hardware. It use either the TCP or UDP/IP protocol (depending on the interconnecting network). The specification and the implementation are intertwined in our description of NFS. Whenever detail is needed, we refer to the sun implementation whenever the description is general it applies to the specification also.

Overview of NFS

NFS views a set of interconnected workstations as a set of independent machines with independent file systems. The goal is to allow some degree of sharing among these file systems (on explicit request) in a transparent manner. Sharing is based on a client-server relationship. A machine may be, and often is, both a client and a server. Sharing is allowed between any pair of machines, rather than with only dedicated server machines. To ensure machine independence sharing of a remote file system affects only the client machine and no other machine.

So that a remote directory will be accessible in a transparent manner from a particular machine—say, from *M*1— a client of that machine has to carry out a mount operation first. The semantics of the operation are that a remote directory is mounted over a directory of a local file system. Once the mount operation is completed, the mounted directory looks like an integral subtree of the local file system, replacing the subtree descending from the local directory. The local directory becomes the name of the root of the newly mounted directory. Specification of the remote directory as an argument for the mount operation is done in a non-transparent manner; the location (or host name) of the remote directory has to be provided. However, from then on, users on machine *M*1 can access files in the remote directory in a totally transparent manner.

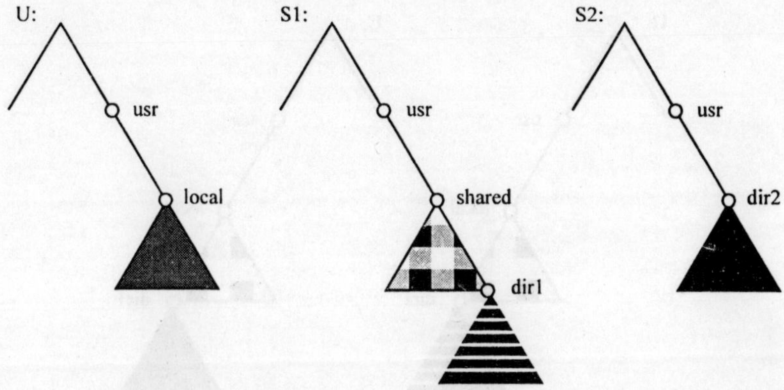

Fig. 10.5. Three independent file systems.

To illustrate file mounting, consider the file system where the triangles represent subtrees of directories that are of interest. The figure shows three independent file systems of machines named *U, S1,* and *S2.* At this point at each machine only the local files can be processed the effects of the mounting of *S1:/usr/shared* over *U:/usr/local* are shown. This figure depicts the view users on *U* haves of their file system. Observe that they can access any file within the *dir*1 directory, for instance, using the prefix*/usr/local/dir*1 on *U* after the mount is complete. The original directory */usr/local* on that machine is no longer visible.

Subject to access-rights accreditation, potentially any file system, or any directory within a file system, can be mounted remotely on top of any local directory. Diskless workstations can even mount their own roots from servers.

Cascading mounts are also permitted in some NFS implementations. That is, a file system can be mounted over another file system that is remotely mounted, not local. A machine is affected by only those mounts that it has itself invoked.

By mounting a remote file system, the client does not gain access to other file systems that were, by chance, mounted over the former file system. Thus, the mount mechanism does not exhibit a transitivity property. We illustrate cascading mounts by continuing our previous example. The figure shows the result of mounting *S2:/usr/dir*2 over *U:/usr/local/dir*1, which is already remotely mounted from *S*1. Users can access files within *dir*2 on *U* using the prefix */usr/local/dir*1. If a shared file system is mounted over a user's home directories on all machines in a network, a user can log in to any workstation and get his home environment. This property permits **user mobility.**

One of the dosign goals of NFS was to operate in a heterogeneous environment of different machines, operating systems, and network architectures. The NFS specification is independent of these media and thus encourages other implementations. This independence is achieved through the use of RPC primitives built on top of an External Data Representation (XDR) protocol used between two implementation-independent interfaces. Hence, if the system consists of heterogeneous machines and file systems that are properly interfaced to NFS, file systems of different types can be mounted both locally and remotely.

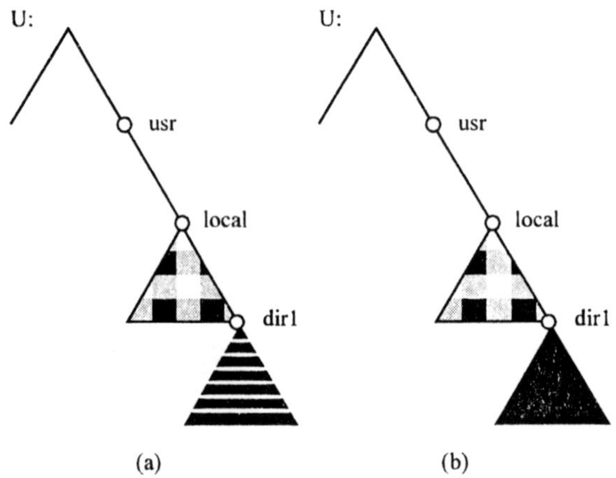

Fig. 10.6. Mounting in NFS. (a) Mounts. (b) Cascading mounts.

The NFS specification distinguishes between the services provided by a mount mechanism and the actual remote-file-access services. Accordingly, two separate protocols are specified for these services: a mount protocol, and a protocol for remote file accesses, **the NFS protocol.** The protocols are specified as sets of RPCs. These RPCs are the building blocks used to implement transparent remote file access.

The Mount Protocol

The **mount protocol** establishes the initial logical connection between a server and a client. In Sun's implementation, each machine has a server process, outside the kernel, performing the protocol functions.

A mount operation includes the name of the remote directory to be mounted and the name of the server machine storing it. The mount request is mapped to the corresponding RPC and is forwarded to the mount server running on the specific server machine. The server maintains an **export list**—the*/etc/dfs/dfstab* in Solaris, which can be edited only by a superuser—which specifies local file systems that it exports for mounting, along with names of machines that are permitted to mount them. The specification can also include access rights, such as read only. To simplify the maintenance of export lists and mount tables, a distributed naming scheme can be used to hold this information and make it available to appropriate clients.

Recall that may directory within an exported file system can be mounted remotely by an accredited machine. Hence, a component unit is such a directory. When the server receives a mount request that conforms to its export list, it returns to the client a **file handle** that serves as the key for further accesses to files within the mounted file system. The file handle contains all the information that the server needs to distinguish an individual file it stores. In UNIX terms, the file handle consists of a file-system identifier and an inode number to identify the exact mounted directory within the exported file system.

The server also maintains a list of the client machines and the corresponding currently mounted directories. This list is used mainly for administrative purposes—for instance, for notifying all clients that the server is going down. Addition and deletion of entries in this list are the only ways that the server state can be affected by the mount protocol.

Usually, a system has a static mounting preconfiguration that is established at boot time (*/etc/* vfstab in Solaris); however, this layout can be modified. In addition to the actual mount procedure, the mount protocol includes several other procedures, such as unmount and return export list.

The Network File System Protocol

The NFS protocol provides a set of RPCs for remote file operations. The procedures support the following operations:

- Searching for a file within a directory
- Reading a set of directory entries
- Manipulating links and directories
- Accessing file attributes
- Reading and writing files

These procedures can be invoked only after a file handle for the remotely mounted directory has been established.

The omission of open and close operations is intentional. A prominent feature of NFS servers is that they are *stateless*. Serves do not maintain information about their clients from one access to another. No parallels to UNIX's open-files table or file structures exist on the server side. Consequently, each request has to provide a full set of arguments, including a unique file identifier and an absolute offset inside the file for the appropriate operations. The resulting design in robust; on special measures need to be taken to recover a server after a crash. File operations need to be idempotent for this purpose. Every NFS request has a sequence number, allowing the server to determine if a request is duplicated or it any are missing.

Maintaining the list of clients that we mentioned seems to violate the statelessness of the server. However, this list is not essential for the correct operation of the client or the server, and hence it does not need to be restored after a server crash. Consequently, it might include inconsistent data and is treated as only a hint.

A single NFS writes procedure call is guaranteed to be atomic, and also is not intermixed with other write calls to the same file. The NFS protocol, however, does not provide concurrency-control mechanisms. A write system call may be broken down into several RPC writes, because each NFS write or read call can contain up to 8 KB of data and UDP packets are limited to 1,500 bytes. As a result, two users writing to the same remote file may get their data intermixed. The claim is that, because lock management is inherently stateful, a service outside the NFS should provide locking (and Solaris does). Users are advised to coordinate access to shared files using mechanisms outside the scope of NFS.

NFS is integrated into the operating system via a VFS. As an illustration of the architecture, let us trace how an operation on an already open remote file is handled. The client initiates the operation by a regular system call. The operating-system layer maps this call to a VFS operation on the appropriate vnode. The VFS layer identifies the file as a remote one and invokes the appropriate NFS procedure. An RPC call is made to the NFS service layer at the remote server. This call is reinjected to the VFS layer on the remote system, which finds that it is local and invokes the appropriate file-system operation. This path is retraced to return the result. An advantage of this architecture is that the client and the server are identical; thus, a machine may be a client, or server or both.

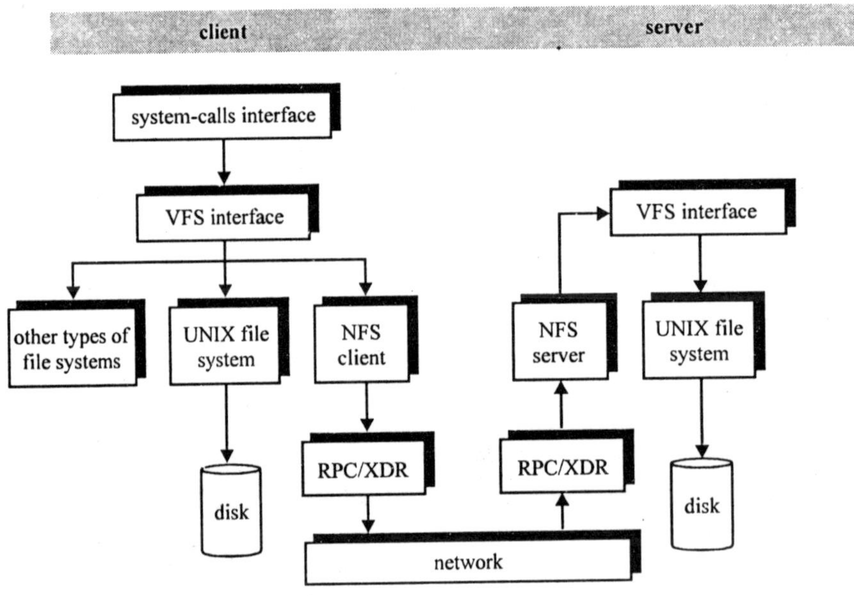

Fig. 10.7. Schematic view of the NFS architecture.

The actual service on each server is performed by several kernel processes that provide a temporary substitute to a lightweight process (or threads) mechanism.

Path-Name Translation

Path-name translation is done by breaking the path into component names and performing a separate NFS lookup call for every pair of component name and directory vnode. Once a mount point is crossed, every component lookup causes a separate RPC to the server. This expensive path-name-traversal scheme is needed, since each client has a unique layout of its logical name space, dictated by the mounts it performed. It would have been much more efficient to hand a server a path name hand to receive a target vnode once a mount point was encountered. At any point, however, there can be another mount point for the particular client of which the stateless server is unaware.

So that lookup is fast, a directory name lookup cache on the client side holds the vnodes for remote directory names. This cache speeds up references to files with the same initial path name.

The directory cache is discarded when attributes returned from the server do not match the attributes of the cached vnode.

Recall that mounting a remote file system on top of another already mounted remote file system (cascading mount) is allowed in some implementations of NFS. However, a server cannot act as an intermediary between a client and another server. Instead, a client must establish a direct client–server connection with the second server by directly mounting the desired directory. When a client has a cascading mount, more than one server can be involved in a path-name traversal. However, each component lookup is performed between the original client and some server. Therefore, when a client does a lookup on a directory on which the server has mounted a file system, the client sees the underlying directory, instead of the mounted directory.

Remote Operations

With the exception of opening and closing files, there is almost a one-to-one correspondence between the regular UNIX system calls for file operations and the NFS protocol RPCs. Thus, a remote file operation can be translated directly to the corresponding RPC. Conceptually, NFS adheres to the remote-service paradigm, but in practice buffering and caching techniques are employed for the sake of performance. No direct correspondence exists between a remote operation and an RPC. Instead, file blocks and file attributes are fetched by the RPCs and are cached locally. Future remote operations use the cached data, subject to consistency constrains.

There are two caches; the file-attribute (inode-information) cache and the file-blocks cache. On a file open, the kernel checks with the remote server whether to fetch or revalidate the cached attributes. The cached file blocks are used only if the corresponding cached attributes are up to date. The attribute cache is updated whenever new attributes arrive from the server. Cached attributes are, by default, discarded after 60 seconds. Both read-ahead and delayed-write techniques are used between the server and the client. Clients do not free delayed-write blocks until the server confirms that the data have been written to disk. In contrast to the system used in Sprite, delayed-write is retained even when a file is opened concurrently, in conflicting modes. Hence, UNIX semantics are not preserved.

Tuning the system for performance makes it difficult to characterize the consistency semantics of NFS. New files created on a machine may not be visible elsewhere for 30 seconds. It is indeterminate whether writes to a file at one site are visible to other sites that have this file open for reading. New opens of that file observe only the changes that have already been flushed to the server. Thus, NFS provides neither strict emulation of UNIX semantics nor the session semantics of Andrew. In spite of these drawbacks, the utility and high performance of the mechanism makes it the most widely used multivendor distributed system in operation.

Summary of the Text

The file system resides permanently on secondary storage, which is designed to hold a large amount of data permanently. The most common secondary-storage medium is the disk.

Physical disks may be segmented into partitions to control media use and to allow multiple, possibly varying, file systems per spindle. These file systems are mounted onto a logical file system architecture to make them available for use. File systems are often implemented in a layered or modular structure. The lower levels deal with the physical properties of storage devices. Upper levels deal with symbolic file names and logical properties of files. Intermediate levels map the logical file concepts into physical device properties.

Every file-system type can have different structures and algorithms. A VFS layer allows the upper layers to deal with each file-system type uniformly. Even remote file systems can be integrated into the system's directory structure and acted on by standard system calls via the VFS interface.

The various files can be allocated space on the disk in three ways: through contiguous, linked, or indexed allocation. Contiguous allocation can suffer from external fragmentation. Direct access is very inefficient with linked allocation. Indexed allocation may require substantial overhead for its index block. These algorithms can be optimized in many ways. Contiguous space may be enlarged through extents to increase flexibility and to decrease external fragmentation. Indexed allocation can be done in clusters of multiple blocks to increase throughput and to reduce the number of index entries needed. Indexing in large clusters is similar to contiguous allocation with extents.

Free-space allocation methods also influence the efficiency of use of disk space, the performance of the file system, and the reliability of secondary storage. The methods used include bit vectors and linked lists. Optimizations include grouping, counting, and the FAT, which places the linked list in one contiguous area.

The directory-management routines must consider efficiency, performance, and reliability. A hash table is the most frequently used method; it is fast and efficient. Unfortunately, damage to the table or a system crash could result in the directory information not corresponding to the disk's contents. A consistency checker—a systems program such as fsck in UNIX, or chkdsk in MS-DOS—can be used to repair the damage. Operating-system backup tools allow disk data to be copied to tape, to recover from data or even disk loss due to hardware failure, operating system bug, or user error.

Network file systems, such as NFS, use client—server methodology to allow users to access files and directories from remote machines as if they were on local file systems. System calls on the client are translated into network protocols, and retranslated into file-system operations on the server. Networking and multiple-client access create challenges in the areas of data consistency and performance.

Due to the fundamental role that file systems play in system operation, their performance and reliability is crucial. Techniques such as log structures and caching help improve the performance, while log structures and RAID improve reliability.

OVERVIEW OF THE MINIX FILE SYSTEM

Like any file system, the MINIX file system must deal with all the issues we have just studied. It must allocate and deallocate space for files, keep track of disk blocks and free space, provide some way to protect files against unauthorized usage, and so on.

In the first part of this chapter, we have repeatedly referred to UNIX rather than to MINIX for the sake of generality, although the external interface of the two is virtually identical. Now we will concentrate on the internal design of MINIX. For information about the UNIX internals.

The MINIX file system is just a big C program that runs in user space. To read and write files, user processes send messages to the file system telling what they want done. The file system does the work and then sends back a reply. The file system is, in fact, a network file server that happens to be running on the same machine as the caller.

This design has some important implication. For one thing, the file system can be modified, experimented with, and tested almost completely independently of the rest of MINIX. For another, it is very easy to move the whole file system to any computer that has a C compiler, compile it there, and use it as a free-standing UNIX-like remote file server. The only changes that need to be made are in the area of how messages are sent and received, which differs from system to system.

In the following sections, we will present an overview of many of the key areas of the file system design. Specifically, we will look at messages, the file system layout, the bit maps, i-nodes, the block cache, directories and paths, file descriptors, file locking, and special files (plus pipes). After studying all of these topics, we will show a simple example of how the pieces fit together by tracing what happens when a user process executes the READ system call.

Messages

The file system accepts 39 types of messages requesting work. All but two are for MINIX system calls. The two exceptions are messages generated by other parts of MINIX. Of the system calls, 31 are accepted from user processes. Six system call message are for system calls which are handled first by the memory manager, which then calls the file system to do a part of the work. Two other messages are also processed by the file system. The messages are shown in Fig 10.8.

The structure of the file system is basically the same as that of the memory manager and all the I/O tasks. It has a main loop that waits for a message to arrive. When a message arrives, its type is extracted and used as an index into a table containing pointers to the procedures within the file system that handle all the types. Then the appropriate procedure is called, it does its work and returns a status value. The file system then sends a reply back to the caller and goes back to the top of the loop to wait for the next message.

File System Layout

A MINIX file system is a logical, self-contained entity with i-nodes, directories, and data blocks. It can be stored on any block device, such as a floppy disk or a (portion of a) hard disk. In all cases, the layout of the file system has the same structure. Figure 10.8 shows this layout for a 360K floppy disk with 128 i-nodes and a 1K block size. Larger file systems, or those with more or fewer i-nodes or a different block size, will have the same six components in the same order, but their relative sizes may be different.

Each file system begins with a **boot block.** This contains executable code. When the computer is turned on, the hardware reads the book block from the boot device into memory, jumps to it, and begins executing its code. The boot block code begins the process of loading the operating system itself. Once the system has been booted, the boot block is not used any more. Not every disk drives can be used as a boot device, but to keep the structure uniform, every block device has a block reserved for boot block code. At worst this strategy wastes one block. To prevent the hardware from trying to boot an unbootable device **magic number** is placed at a known location in the boot block when and only when the executable code is written to the device. When booting from a device, the hardware (actually, the BIOS code) will refuse to attempt to load from a device lacking the magic number. Doing this prevents inadvertently using garbage as a boot program.

The **super-block** contains information describing the layout of the file system. It is illustrated in Fig 10.9. The main function of the super-block is to tell the file system how big the various pieces of the file system are. Given the block size and the number of i-nodes, it is easy to calculate the size of the i-node bit map and the number of blocks of i-nodes. For example, for a 1K block, each block of the bit map has 1K bytes (8K bits), and thus can keep track of the status of up to 8192 i-nodes. (Actually the first block can handle only up to 8191 i-nodes, since there is no 10th inode, but it is given a bit in the bit map, anyway). For 10,000 i-nodes, two bit map blocks are needed. Since i-nodes each occupy 64 bytes, a 1K block holds up to 16 i-nodes. With 128 usable i-nodes, 8 disk blocks are needed to contain them all.

Messages from users	Input parameters	Reply value
ACCESS	File name, access mode	Status
CHDIR	Name of new working directory	Status
CHMOD	File name, new mode	Status
CHOWN	File name, new owner, group	Status
CHROOT	Name of new root directory	Status
CLOSE	File descriptor of file to close	Status
CREAT	Name of file to be created, mode	File descriptor
DUP	File descriptor (for dup2, two fds)	New file descriptor
FCNTL	File descriptor, function code, arg	Depends on function
FSTAT	Name of file, buffer	Status
IOCTL	File descriptor, function code, arg	Status
LINK	Name of file to link to, name of link	Status
LSEEK	File descriptor, offset, whence	New position
MKDIR	File name, mode	Status
MKNOD	Name of dir or special, mode, address	Status
MOUNT	Special file, where to mount, ro flag	Status
OPEN	Name of file to open, r/w flag	File descriptor
PIPE	Pointer to 2 file descriptors (modified)	Status
READ	File descriptor, buffer, how may bytes	#Bytes read
RENAME	File name, file name	Status
RMDIR	File name	Status
STAT	File name, status buffer	Status
STIME	Pointer to current time	Status
SYNC	(None)	Always OK
TIME	Pointer to place where current time goes	Status
TIMES	Pointer to buffer for process and child times	Status
UMASK	Complement of mode mask	Always OK
UMOUNT	Name of special file to unmount	Status

UNLINK	Name of file to unlink	Status
UTIME	File name, file times	Always OK
WRITE	File descriptor, buffer, how many bytes	#Bytes written
Message from MM	**Input Parameter**	**Reply Value**
EXEC	Pid	Status
EXIT	Pid	Status
FORK	Parent pid, child pid	Status
SETGID	Pid, real and effective gid	Status
SETSID	Pid	Status
SETUID	Pid, real and effective uid	Status
Other messages	**Input parameters**	**Reply value**
REVIVE	Process to revive	(No replay)
UNPAUSE	Process to check	(See text)

Fig. 10.8. *File system messages. File name parameters are always pointers to the name. The codes status as reply value means OK or ERROR.*

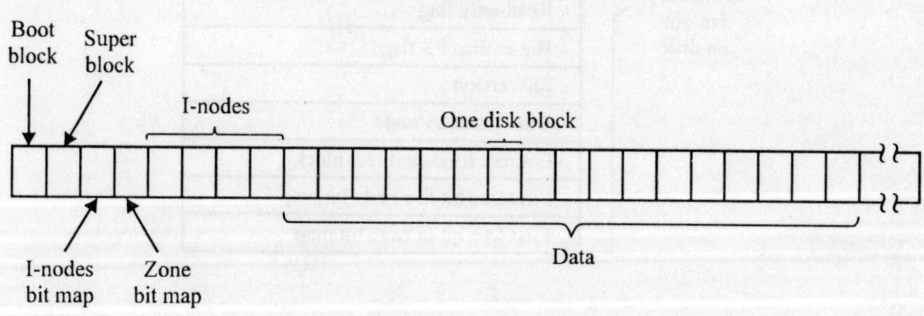

Fig. 10.9. *Disk layout for the simplest disk: a 360K floppy disk, with 128 i-nodes and a 1K block size (i.e., two consecutive 512- byte sectors are treated as a single block.)*

We will explain the difference between zones and blocks in detail later, but for the time being it is sufficient to say that disk storage can be allocated in units (zones) of 1,2,4,8, or in general 2^n blocks. The zone bit map keeps track of free storages in zones, not blocks. For all standard floppy disks used by MINIX the zone and block sizes are the same (1K), so for a first approximation a zone is the same as a block on these devices. Until we come to the details of storage allocation later in the chapter, it is adequate to think "block" whenever you see "zone."

Note that the number of blocks per zone is not stored in the super-block, as it is never needed. All that is needed is the base 2 logarithm of the zone to block ratio, which is used as the shift count to convert zones to blocks and vice versa. For example with 8 blocks per zone, $lgo_2 8 = 3$. so to find the zone containing block 128 we shift 128 right 3 bits to get zone 16.

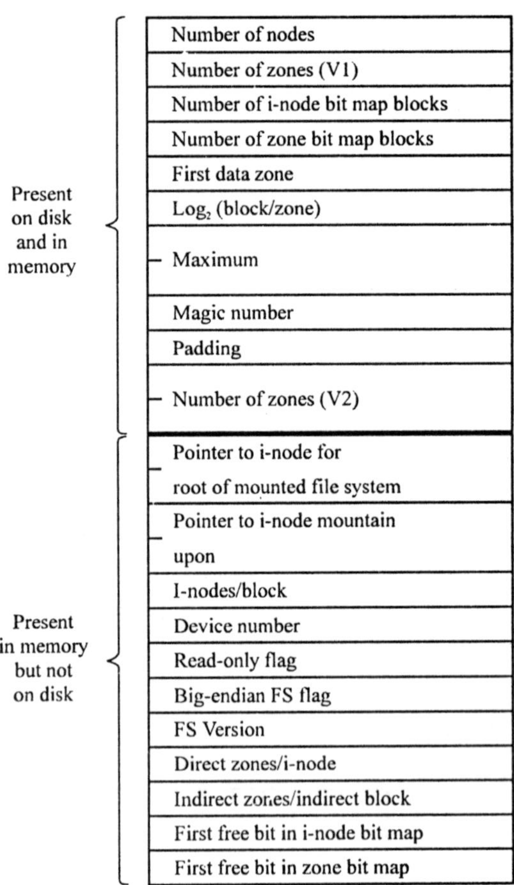

Fig. 10.10. The MINIX super-block.

To zone bit map includes only the data zones (i.e., the blocks used for the bit maps and i-nodes are not in the map), with the first data zone designated zone 1 in the bit map. As with the i-node bit map, bit 0 in the map is unused, so the first block in the zone bit map can map 8191 zones and subsequent blocks can map 8192 zones each. If you examine the bit maps on a newly formatted disk, you will find that both the i-node and zone bit maps haves 2 bits set to 1. One is for the nonexistent 10th i-node or zone; the other is for the i-node and zone used by the root directory on the device, which is placed there when the file system is created.

The information in the super-block is redundant because sometimes it is needed in one form and sometimes in another. With 1K devoted to the super-block, it makes sense to compute this information in all the forms it is needed, rather than having to recomputed it frequently during execution. The zone number of the first data zone on the disk, for example, can be calculated from the block size, zone size, number of i-nodes, and number of zones, but it is faster just to keep it in the super-block. The rest of the super-block is wasted anyhow, so using up another word if it costs nothing.

When MINIX is booted, the super-block for the root device is read into a table is memory. Similarly, as other file systems are mounted, their super-blocks are also brought into memory. The super-block table holds a number of fields not present on the disk. These include flags that allow a device to be specified as read-only or as following a byte-order convention opposite to the standard, and fields to speed access by indicating points in the bit maps below which all bits are marked used. In addition, there is a field describing the device from which the super-block came.

Before a disk can be used as a MINIX file system, it must be given the structure of Fig. 10.9. The utility program *mkfs* has been provided to build file systems. This program can be called either by a command like

mkfs/dev/fd1 1440

to build an empty 1440 block file system on the floppy disk in drive 1, or it can be given a prototype file listing directories and files to include in the new file system. This command also puts a magic number in the super-block to identify the file system as a valid Minix file system. The Minix file system has evolved, and some aspects of the file system (for instance, the size of i-nodes) were different in earlier versions. The magic number identifies the version if *mkfs* that created the file system, so differences can be accomodated. Attempts to mount a file system not in MINIX format, such as an MS-DOS diskette, will be rejected by the MOUNT system call, which checks the super-block for a valid magic number and other things.

Bit Maps

MINIX keeps tracks of which i-nodes and zones are free by using two bit maps. When a file is remove, it is then a simple matter to calculate which block of the bit map contains the bit for the i-node being freed and to find it using the normal cache mechanism. Once the block is found, the bit corresponding to the freed i-node is set to 0. Zones are released from the zone bit map in the same way.

Logically, when a file is to be created, the file system must search through the bit-map blocks one at a time for the first free i-node. This i-node is then allocated for the new file. In fact, the in-memory copy of the super-block has a field which points to the first free i-node, so no search is necessary until after a node is used, when the pointer must be updated to point to the new next free i-node, which will often turn out to be the next one, or a close one. Similarly, when an i-node is freed, a check is made to see if the free i-node comes before the currently-pointed-to one, and the pointer is updated if necessary. If every i-node slot on the disk is full, the search routine returns a 0, which is why i-node 0 is not used (i.e., so it can be used to indicate the search failed). (When *mkfs* creates a new file system, it zeroes i-nodes 0 and sets the lowest bit in the bit map to 1, so the file system will never attempt to allocate it.) Everything that has been said here about the i-node bit maps also applies to the zone bit map; logically it is searched for the first free zone when space is need, but a pointer to the first free zone is maintained to eliminate most of the need for sequential searches through the bit map.

With this background, we can now explain the difference between zones and blocks. The idea behind zones is to help ensure that disk blocks that belong to the same file are located on the same cylinder, to improve performance when the file is read sequentially. The approach chosen is to make it possible to allocates several blocks at a time. If for example, the block size is 1K and the zone size is 4K, the zone bit map keeps track of zones, not blocks. A 20M disk has 5K zones of 4K, hence 5K bits in its zone map.

Most of the file system works with blocks. Disk transfers are always a block at a time, and the buffer cache also works with individual blocks. Only a few parts of the system that keep track of physical disk addresses (e.g.,. the zone bit map and the i-nodes) know about zones.

Some design decision has to be made in developing the MINIX file system. In 1985, when MINIX was conceived, disk capacities were small, and it was expected that many users would have only floppy disks. A decision was made to restrict disk addressed to 16 bits in the V1 file system, primarily to be able to stores many of them in the indirect blocks. With a 16-bit zone number and a 1K zone, only 64K zones can be addressed, limiting disks to 64M. This was an enormous amount of storages in those days, and it was thought that as disks got larger, it would be easy to switch to 2K or 4K zones, without changing the block size. The 16-bit zone number also make it easy to keep the i-node size to 32 bytes.

As MINIX developed, and larger disks became much more common, it was obvious that changes were desirable. Many files are smaller than 1K, so increasing the block size would mean wasting disk bandwidth, reading and writing mostly empty blocks and wasting precious main memory storing them in the buffer cache. The zone size could have been increased, but a larger zone size means more wasted disk space, and it was still desirable to retain efficient operation on small disk. Another reasonable alternatives would have been to have different zone sizes on large and small devices.

Zones also introduce an unexpected problem, best illustrated by a simple example, again with 4K zones and 1K blocks. Suppose that a file is of length 1K, meaning that 1 zone has been allocated for it. The blocks between 1K and 4K contain garbage (residue form the previous owner), but no harm is done because the file size is clearly marked in the i-node as 1K. In fact, the block containing garbage will not be read into the block cache, since reads are done by blocks, not by zones. Reads beyond the end of a file always return a count of 0 and no data.

Now someone seeks to 32768 and writes 1 byte. The file size now changed to 32769. Subsequent seeks to 1K followed by attempts to read the data will now be able to read the previous contents of the block, a major security breach.

The solution is to check for this situation when a write is done beyond the end of a file, and explicitly zero all the not-yet-allocated blocks in the zone that was previously the last one. Although this situation rarely occurs, the code has to deal with it, making the system slightly more complex.

I-nodes

The layout of the MINIX i-node is given in Fig 10.11. It is almost the same as a standard UNIX i-node. The disk zone pointers are 32-bit pointers, and there are only 9 pointers, 7 direct and 2 indirect. The MINIX i-nodes occupy 64 bytes, the same as standard UNIX i-nodes, and there is space available for a 10th (triple indirect) pointer, although its use is not supported by the standard version of the FS. The MINIX i-node access, modification time and i-node change times time are standard, as in UNIX. The last of these is updated for almost every file operation except a read of the file.

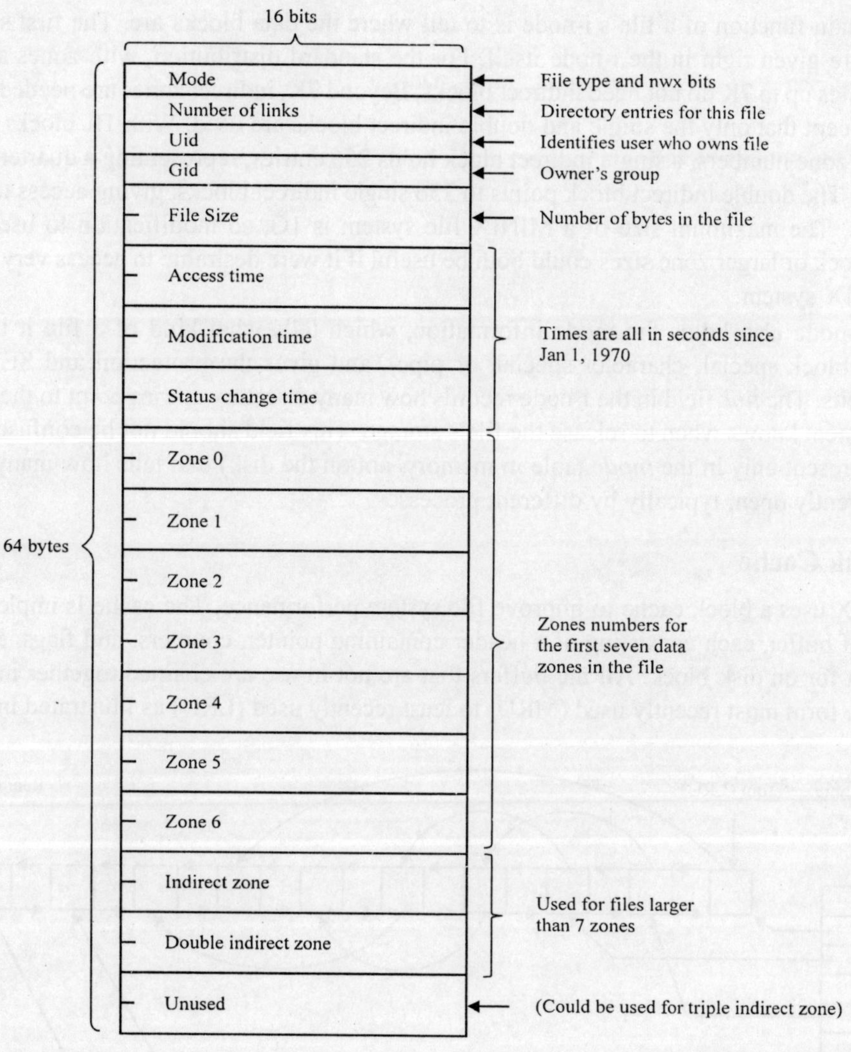

Fig. 10.11. The MINIX i-node.

When a file is opened, its i-node is located and brought into the *i-node* table in memory, where it remains until the file is closed. The *i-node* table has a few additional fields not present on the disk, such as the i-node's device and number, so the file system knows where to rewrite it if is modified while in memory. It also has counter per i-node. If the same file is opened more than once, only one copy of the i-node is kept in memory, but the counter is incremented each time the file is opened and decrements each time the file is closed. Only when the counter finally reaches zero is the i-node removed from the table. If it has been modified since being loaded into memory, it is also rewritten to the disk.

The main function of a file's i-node is to tell where the data blocks are. The first seven zone numbers are given right in the i-node itself. For the standard distribution, with zones and blocks both 1K, files up to 7K do not need indirect blocks. Beyond 7K, indirect zones are needed, using the scheme except that only the single and double indirect blocks are used. With 1K blocks and zones and 32-bit zone numbers, a single indirect block holds 256 entries, representing a quarter megabyte of storage. The double indirect block points to 256 single indirect blocks, giving access to up to 64 megabytes. The maximum size of a MINIX file system is 1G, so modification to use the triple indirect block or larger zone sizes could both be useful if it were desirable to access very large files on a MINIX system.

The i-node also holds the mode information, which tells what kind of a file it is (regular, directory, block special, character special, or pipe), and gives the protection and SETUID and SETGID bits. The *link* field in the i-node records how many directory entries point to the i-node, so the file system knows when to release the file's storage. This field should not be confused with the counter (present only in the *inode* table in memory, not on the disk) that tells how many times the file is currently open, typically by different processes.

The Block Cache

MINIX uses a block cache to improve file system performance. The cache is implemented as an array of buffer, each consisting of a header containing pointer, counters, and flags, and a body with room for on disk block. All the buffers that are not in use are chained together in a double-linked list, form most recently used (MRU) to least recently used (LRU) as illustrated in Fig 10.12

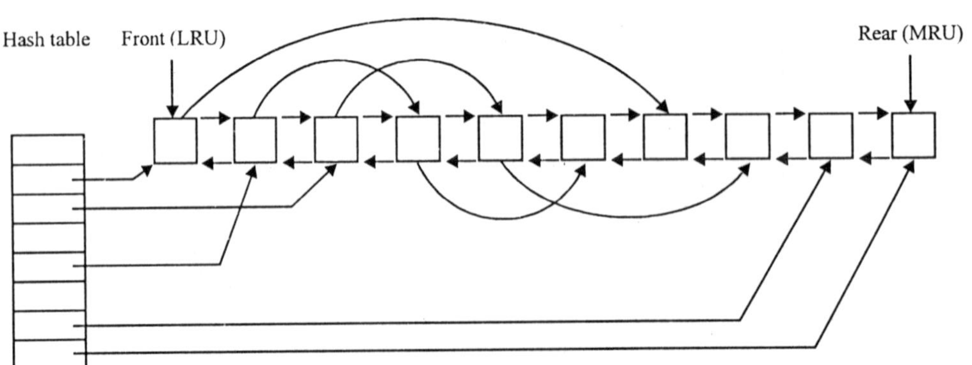

Fig. 10.12. The linked lists used by the block cache.

In addition, to able to quickly determine if a given block is in the cache or not, a hash table is used. All the buffers containing a block that has hash code k are linked together on a single-linked list pointed to by entry k in the hash table. The hash function just extracts the low-order n bits from the block number, so blocks from different devices appear on the same hash chain. Every buffer is on one these chains. When the file system is initialized after MINIX is booted, all buffers are unused, of course, and all are in a single chain pointed to by the 10th hash table entry. At that time all the other hash table entries contain a null pointer, but once the system starts, buffers will be remove from the 10th chain and other chains will be built.

When the file system needs a block, it calls a procedure, *get-block,* which computes the hash code for that block and searches the appropriate list. *Get-block* is called with a device number as well as a block number, and the search compares both numbers with the corresponding fields in the buffer chain. If a buffer containing the block is found, a counter in the buffer header is incremented to show that the block is in use, and a pointer to it is returned. If a block is not found on the hash list, the first buffer on the LRU list can be used: it is guaranteed not to be still in use, and the block in contains may be evicted to free up that buffer.

Once a block has been chosen for eviction, another flag in its header is checked to see if the block has been modified since being read in. If so, it is rewritten to the disk. At this point the block needed is read in by sending a message to the disk task. The file system is suspended until the block arrives at which time it continues and a pointer to the block is returned to the caller.

When the procedure that requested the block has completed its job, it calls another procedure, *put_block,* to free the block. Normally, a block will be used immediately and then released, but since it is possible that additional requests for a block will be made before it has been released, *but_block* decrements the use counter and puts the buffer back onto the LRU list only when the use counter has gone back to zero. While the counter is nonzero, the block remains in limbo.

One or the parameters to *put_block* tells what class of block (e.g., i-nodes, directory, data) is being freed. Depending on the class, two key decisions are made:

1. Whether to put the block on the front or rear of the LRU list.
2. Whether to write the block (if modified) to disk immediately or not

Blocks that are likely to be needed again soon, such as super-blocks, go on the front of the list so they will be claimed the next time a free buffer is needed. All other blocks go on the rear of the list in true LRU fashion.

A modified block is not rewritten until either one of two events occurs:

1. It reaches the front of the LRU chain and is evicted.
2. A SYNC system call is executed.

SYNC does not traverse the LRU chain but instead indexes through the array of buffers in the cache. Even if a buffer has not been released yet, if it has been modified, SYNC will find it and ensure that the copy on disk is updated.

There is an exception, however. A modified super-block is written to disk immediately. In an older version of MINIX a super-block was modified when a file system was mounted, and the purpose of the immediate write was to reduce the chance of corrupting the file system in the event of a crash. Super-blocks are not modified now, so the code to write them immediately is an anachronism. In the standard configuration, no other blocks are written immediately. However, by modifying the default definition of *ROBUST* in the system configuration file, *include/minix/config.h,* the file system can be compiled to mark i-node, directory, indirect, and bit-map blocks so they will be written immediately upon release. This is intended to make the file system more robust; the price paid is slower operation. Whether this will be effective is not clear. A power failure occurring when all blocks haves not been yet been written is going to cause a headache whether it is an i-node or a data block that is lost.

Directories and its Paths

Another important sub-system within the file system is the management of directories and path names. Many system calls, such as OPEN, have a file name as a parameter. What is really needed is the i-node for that file, so it is up to the file system to look up the file in the directory tree and locate its i-node.

A MINIX directory consists of a file containing 16-byte entries. The first 2 bytes form a 16-bit i-node number, and the remaining 14 bytes are the file name. This is the same as the traditional UNIX directory entry. To look up the path */usr/ast/mbox,* the systsem first looks up *usr* in the root directory, then it looks up *ast* in */usr*, and finally it looks up *mbox* in */usr/ast.* The actual lookup proceeds one path component at a time.

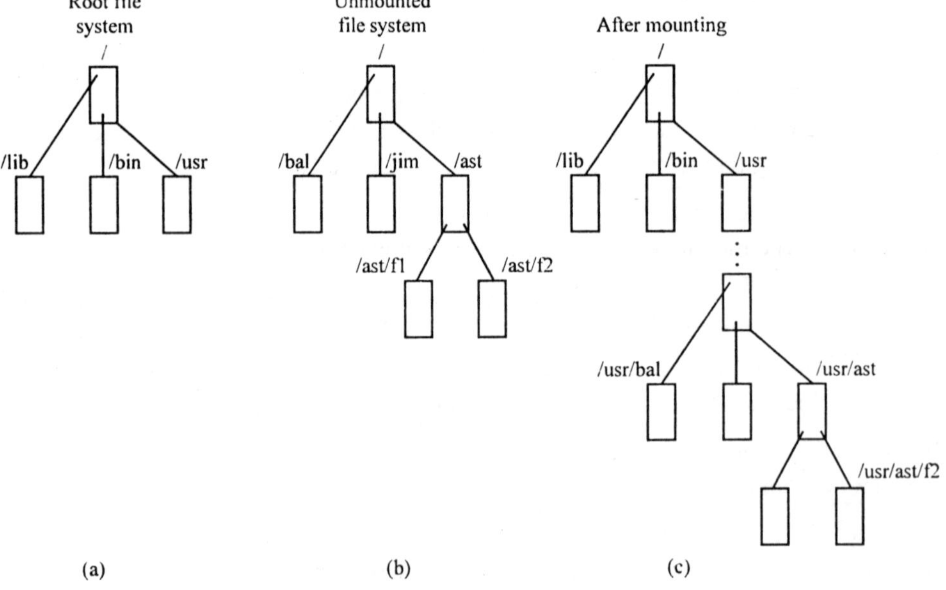

Fig. 10.13. (a) Root file system. (b) An unmounted file system. (c) The result of mounting the file system of (b) on /usr.

The only complication is what happens when a mounted file system is encountered. The usual configuration for MINX and many other UNIX-like systems is to have a small root file system containing the files needed to start the system and to do basic system maintenance, and to have the majority of the files, including users, directories, on a separate device mounted on /usr. This is a good time to look at how mounting is done. When the user types the command.

mount/dev/hd2c/usr

on the terminal, the file system contained on hard disk partition 2 is mounted on to of */usr* in the root file system.

The key to the whole mount business is a flag set in the memory copy of the i-node of */usr* after a successful mount. This flag indicates that the i-node is mounted on. The MOUNT call also loads the super-block for the newly mounted file system into the *super_block* table and sets two pointers in it. Furthermore, it puts the root i-node of the mounted file system in the *inode* table.

In Fig 10.10 we see that super-block in memory contain two fields related to mounted file systems. The first of these, the *i-node-of-the-mountd-file-system,* is set to point to the root i-node of the newly mounted file system. The second, the *i-node-mounted-on,* is set to point to the i-node mounted on, in this case, the i-node for */usr.* These two pointers serve to connect the mounted file system to the root and represent the "glue" that holds the mounted file system to the root [shown as the dots in Fig 10.10 (c)]. This glue is what makes mounted file systems work.

When a path such as */usr/ast/f2* is being looked up, the file system will see a flag in the i-node for */usr* and realize that it must continue searching at the root i-node of the file system mounted on */usr*. The question is: "How does it find this root i-node?"

The answer is straightforward. The system searches all the super-blocks in memory until it finds the one whose *i-node mounted on* field points to */usr.* This must be the super-block for the file system mounted on */usr*. Once it has thes super-block, it is easy to follow the other pointer to find the root i-node for the mounted file system. Now the file system can continue searching. In this example, it looks for *ast* in the root directory of hard disk partition 2.

File Descriptors

Once a file has been opened, a file descriptor is returned to the user process for use in subsequent READ and WRITE calls. In this section we will look at how file descriptors are managed within the file system.

Like the kernel and the memory manager, the file system maintains part of the process table within its address space. Three of its fields are of particular interest. The first two are pointers to the i-nodes for the root directory and the working directory. These pointers are changed by the CHROOT and CHDIR system calls to point to the new root or new working directory, respectively.

The third interesting field in the process table is an array indexed by file descriptor number. It is used to locate the proper file when a file descriptor is presented. At first glance, it might seem sufficient to have the *k*-th entry in this array just point to the i-node for the file belonging to file descriptor *k.* After all, the i-node is fetched into memory when the file is opened and kept there until it is closed, so it is sure to be available.

Unfortunately, this simple plan fails because files can be shard in subtle ways in MINIX (as well as in UNIX). The trouble arises because associated with each file is a 32-bit number that indicates the next byte to be read or written. It is this number, called the **file position,** that is changed by the LSEEK system call. The problem can be stated easily: "Where should the file be stored?"

The first possibility is to put it in the i-node. Unfortunately, if two or more processes have the same file open at the same time, they must all have their own file pointers, since it would hardly do to have an LSEEK by one process affect the next read of a different process. Conclusion: the file position cannot go in the i-node.

What about putting it in the process table? Why not have a second array, paralleling the file descriptor array, giving the current position of each file? This idea does not work either, but the reasoning is more subtle. Basically, the trouble comes form the semantics of the FORK system call. When a process forks, both the parent and the child are required to share a single pointer giving the current position of each open file.

To understand the problem better, consider the case of a shell script whose output has been redirected to a file. When the shell forks off the first program, its file position of standard output is 0. This position is then inherited by the child, which writes, say, 1K of output. When the child terminates, the shared file position must now be 1K.

Now the shell reads some more of the shell script and forks off another child. It is essential that the second child inherit a file position if 1K from the shell, so it will begin writing at the place where the first program left off. If the shell did not share the file position with its children, the second program would overwrite the output from the first ones, instead of appending to it.

As a result, it is not possible to put the file position in the process table. It really must be shared. The solution used in MINIX is to introduce a new, shared table, *filp,* which contains all the file positions. Its use is illustrated in Fig 10.13. By having the file position truly shared, the semantics of FORK can be implemented correctly, and shell scripts work properly.

Although the only thing that the *flip* table really must contain is the shared file position, it is convenient to put the i-node pointer there, too. In this way, all that the file descriptor array in the process table contains is a pointer to a *filp* entry. The *flip* entry also contains the file mode (permission bits), some flags indicating whether the file was opened in a special mode, and a count of the number of processes using it, so the file system can tell when the last process using the entry has terminated, in order to reclaim the slot.

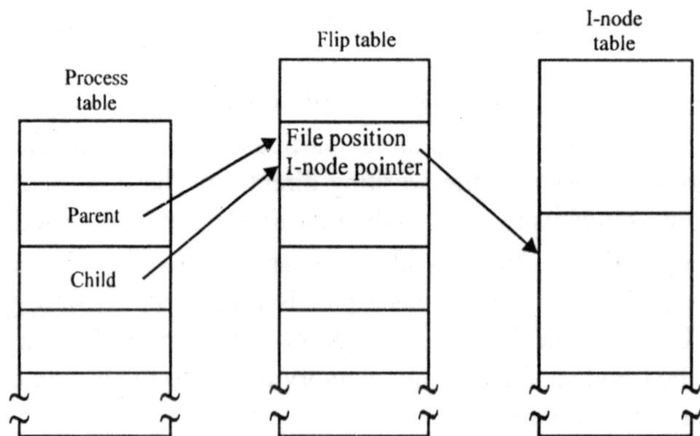

Fig. 10.13. How file positions are shared between a parent and a child.

File Locking

There is yet another aspect of file system management that requires a special table. This is file locking. MINIX supports the POSIX interprocess communication mechanism of **advisory file locking.** This permits any part, or multiple parts, of a file to be marked as locked. The operating system does not enforce locking, but processes are expected to be well behaved and to look for locks on a file before doing anything that would conflict with another process.

The reasons for providing a separate table for locks are similar to the justifications for the *flip* table discussed in the previous section. A single process can have more than one lock active, and different parts of a file may be locked by more than one process (although, of course, the locks cannot overlap), so neither the process table nor the *flip* table is a good place to record locks. Since a file may have more than one lock placed upon it, the i-node is not a good place either.

MINIX uses another table, the *file_lock* table, to record all locks. Each slot in this table has spaces for a lock type, indicating if the file is locked for reading or writing, the process ID holding the lock, a pointer to the i-node of the locked file, and the offsets of the first and last bytes of the locked region.

Pipes and Special Files

Pipes and special files differ from ordinary files in an important way. When a process tries to read or write from a disk file, it is certain that the operation will complete within a few hundred milliseconds at most. In the worst case, two or three disk accesses might be needed, not more. When reading from a pipe, the situation is different: if the pipe is empty, the reader will have to wait until some other process puts data in the pipes, which might take hours. Similarly, when reading from a terminal, a process will have to wait until somebody types something.

As a consequence, the file system's normal rule of handling a requests until it is finished does not work. It is necessary to suspend these requests and restart them later. When a process tries to read or write from a pipe, the file system can check the state of the pipe immediately to see if the operation can be completed. If can be, it is, but if it cannot be, the file system records the parameters of the system call in the process table, so it can restart the process when the time comes.

Note that the file system need not take nay action to have the caller suspended. All it has to do is refrain from sending a reply, leaving the caller blocked waiting for the reply. Thus, after suspending a process, the file system goes back to its main loop to wait for the next system call. As soon as another process modifies the pipe's state so that the suspended process can complete, the file system sets a flag so that next time through the main loop it extracts the suspended process parameters from the process table and executes the call.

This situation with terminals and other characters special files is slightly different. The i-node for each special file contains two numbers, the major device and the minor device. The major device number indicates the device class (e.g., RAM disk, floppy disk, hard disk, terminal). It is used as an index into a file system table that maps it onto the number of the corresponding task (i.e., I/O driver). In effect, the major device determines which I/O driver to call. The minor device number is passed to the driver as a parameter. It specifies which device is to be used, for example, terminal 2 or drive 1.

In some cases, most notably terminal devices, the minor device number encodes some information about a category of devices handled by a task. For instance, the primary MINIX console, */dev/console,* is device 4, 0 (major, minor). Virtual consoles are handled by the same part of the driver software. These are device */dev/ttyc* (4, 1), */dev/ttyc2* (4, 2), and so on. Serial line terminals need different low-level software, and these devices, */dev/tty00,* and */dev/tty01* are assigned device numbers 4, 16 and 4, 17. Similarly, network terminals use pseudo-terminal derivers, and these also need different low-level software. In MINIX these devices, *ttyp0, ttyp1,* etc., are assigned device numbers such as 4, 128 and 4, 129. These pseudo devices each have an associated device, *ptyp0, ptyp1,* etc. the major, minor device number pairs for these are 4,192, 4,193, and so on. These numbers are chosen to make it easy for the driver task to call the low-level functions required for each group of devices. There is no expectation that anyone is going to equip a MINIX system with 192 or more terminals.

When a process reads from a special file, the file system extracts the major and minor device numbers from the file's i-node, and uses the major device number as an index into a file system table to map it onto the corresponding task number. Once it has the task number, the file system sends the task a message, including as parameters the minor device, the operation to be performed, the caller's process number and buffer address, and the number of bytes to be transferred.

If the driver is able to carry out of the work immediately (e.g., a line of input has already been typed on the terminal), it copies the data from its own internal buffers to the user and sends the file system a reply message saying that the work is done. The file system then sends a reply messages to the user, and the call is finished. Note that the driver does not copy the data to the file system. Data from block devices go through the block cache, but data form character special files do not.

On the other hand, if the driver is not able to carry out the work, it records the message parameters in its internal tables, and immediately sends a reply to the file system saying that the call could not be completed. At this point, the file system is in the same situation as having discovered that someone is trying to read from an empty pipe. It records the fact that the processes suspended and waits for the next message.

When the driver has acquired enough data to complete the call, it transfers them to the buffer of the still-blocked user and then sends the file system a message reporting what it has done. All the file system has to do is send a reply message to the user to unblock it and report the number of bytes transferred.

An Example: The READ System Call

As we shall see shortly, most of the code of the file system is devoted to carrying out system calls. Therefore, it is appropriate that we conclude this overview with a brief sketch of how the most important call, READ, works.

When a user program executes the statement

n = read(fd, buffer, nbytes);

to read an ordinary file, the library procedure *read* is called with three parameters. It builds a messages containing these parameters, along with the code for READ as the messages type, sends the message to be file system, and blocks waiting for the reply. When the message arrives, the file system uses the message type as an index into its tables to call the procedure that handles reading.

This procedure extracts the file descriptor from the message and uses it to locate the *flip* entry and then the i-node for the file to be read. The request is then broken up into pieces such that each piece fits within a block. For example, if the current file position is 600 and 1K bytes have been requested, the request is split into two parts, for 600 to 1023, and for 1024 to 1623 (assuming 1K blocks).

For each of these pieces in turn, a check is made to see if the relevant block is in the cache. If the block is not present, the file system picks the least recently used buffer not currently in use and claims it, sending a message to the disk task to rewrite it if it is dirty. Then the disk task is asked to fetch the block to be read.

Once the block is in the cache, the file system sends a message to the system task asking it to copy the data to the appropriate place in the user's buffer (i.e., bytes 600 to 1023 to the start of the buffer, and bytes 1024 to 1623 to offset 424 within the buffer). After the copy has been done, the file system sends a reply message to the user specifying how may bytes have been copied.

When the reply comes back to the user, the library function *read* extracts the reply code and returns it as the function value to the caller.

There is one extra step that is not relay part of the READ call itself. After the file system completes a read and sends a reply, it then initiates a read of the next block, provided that the read is form a block device and certain other conditions are met. Since sequential file reads are common, it is reasonable to expect that the next block in a file will be requested in the next read request, and this makes it likely that the desired block will already be in the cache when it is needed.

Implementation of the MINIX File System

The MINIX file system is relatively large but quite straightforward. Requests to carry out system calls come in, are carried out, and replies area sent. In the following sections we will go through it a file at a time, pointing out the highlights. The code itself contains many comments to aid the reader.

In looking at the code for other parts of MINIX we have generally looked at the main loop of a process first and then looked at the routines that handle the different message types. We will organize our approach to the file system differently. First we will go through the major subsystems (cache management, i-node management, etc.). Then we will look at the main loop and the system calls that operate upon files. Next we will look at system call that operate upon directors. Finally, we will discuss the remaining system calls that fall into neither category.

Header Files and Global Data Structures

Like the kernel and memory manager, various data structures and table used in the file system are defined in header files. Some of these data structures are placed in system-wide header files n *include/* and its subdirectories. For instance, *include/sys/stat.h* defines the format by which system calls can provide i-node information to other programs and the structure of a directory entry is defined in *include/sys/stat.h*. Both of these files are required by POSIX. The file system is affected by a number of definitions contained in the global configuration file *include/minix/config.h,* such as the *ROBUST* macro which defines whether important file system data structures will always be written immediately to the disk, and *NR_BUFS* and *NR_BUF_HASH,* which control the size of the block cache.

File System Headers

The file system's own header files are in the file system source directory *src/fs/*. Many file names will be familiar from studying other parts of the MINIX system. The FS master header file, *fs.h,* is very similar to *src/kernel/kernel.h* and *src/mm/mm.h.* It includes others header files needed by all the C source files in the file system. As in the other parts of MINIX, the file system master header includes the file system's own *const.h, type.h, proto.h,* and *gloh.* We will look at these next.

Const.h, defines some constants, such as table sizes and flags, that are used throughout the file system, MINIX already has a history. An earlier version had a different file system, and for users who want to access files written by the earlier version, support is provided for both the old *V1*and the current *V2* file systems. The super-block of a file system contains a magic number so the operating system can identify the type; the constants ***SUPER_MAGIC*** and *SUPER_V2* define these numbers. Support of old versions is not something one reads about in theoretical texts, but it is always a concern for the implementor of a new version of any software. One must decide how much effort to devote to making life easier of users of the old version. We will see several places in the file system where support for the old version is an issue.

Type.h defines both the old *V1* and new *V2* i-node structures as they are laid out on the disk. The V2 i-node is twice as big as the old one, which was designed for compactness on systems with no hard drive and 360-KB diskettes. The new version provides space for the three time fields which UNIX systems provide. In the *V1* i-node there was only one time field, but a STAT or FSTAT would "fake it" and return a *stat* structure containing all three fields. There is a minor difficulty in providing support for the two file system versions. Older MINIX software expects the *gid_t* type to the an 8_bit quantity, so *d2_gid* must be declared as type *u1/6_t.*

Proto.h provides function prototypes in forms acceptable to either old K&R or newer ANSI Standard C compliers. It is long files, but not of great interest. However, there is one point to note: because there are so many different system calls handled by the file system, and because of the way the file system is organized, the various *do_xxx* functions are scattered through a number of files. *Proto.h* is organized by file and is a handy way to find the file to consult when you want to see the code that handles a particular system call.

Finally, *glo.h* defines global variables. The message buffers for the incoming and reply messages are also hers. The now-familiar trick with the *EXTERN* macro is used, so these variables can be accessed by all parts of the file system. As in the other parts of MINIX the storage spaces will be reserved when *table.c* is compiled.

The file system's part of the process table is contained in *fproch.h.* The *fproc* array is declared with the *EXTERN* macro. It holds the mode mask, pointers to the i-nodes for the current root directory and working directory, the file descriptor array, uid, gid, and terminal number for each process. The process id and the process group id are also found here. These are duplicated in parts of the process table located in the kernel and the memory manager.

Several fields are used to stores the parameters of system calls that may be suspended part way through, such as reads from an empty pipe. The fields *fp_suspended* and *fp_revived* actually require only single bits, but nearly all compliers generate better code for characters than bit fields. There is also a field for the *FD_CLOEXEC* bits called for by the POSIX standard. These are used to indicate that a file should be closed when an EXEC call is made.

Now we come to files that define other tables maintained by the file system. The first, *buf.h.* defines the block cache. The structures here are all declared with *EXTERN.* The array *buf* holds all the buffers, each of which contains a data part, *b,* and a header full of pointers, flags, and counters.

The data part is declared as a union of five types because sometimes it is convenient to refer to the block as a character array, sometimes as a directory, etc.

The proper way to refer to the data part of buffer 3 as a character array is *buf*[3].*b.b_ data because buf[3].b* refers to the union as a whole, form which the *b_ _ data* field is selected. Although this syntax is correct, it is cumbersome. Note that *b_ data* (the field of the union) contains two underscores, whereas *b_data* (the macro) contains just one, to distinguish them.

Each entry points to a list of buffers. Originally all the lists are empty. The macros at the end of *buf.h* define different block types. When a block is returned to the buffer cache after use, one of these values is supplied to tell the cache manager whether to put the block on the front or rear of the LRU list, and whether to writes it to disk immediately or not. The *WRITE_IMMED* bit signals that a block must be rewritten to the disk immediately if it is changed. The super-block is the only structure unconditionally marked with this. What about the other structures marked with *MAYBE_WRITE_IMMED?* This is defined in *include/minix/config.h* to be equal to *WRITE_IMMED* if *ROBUST* is true, or 0 otherwise. In the standard configuration of MINIX. *ROBUST* is defined as 0, and these blocks will be written when data blocks are written.

Finally, in the last line. *HASH_MASK* is defined, based upon the value of *NR_BUF_HASH* configured in *include/minix/config.h. HASH_MASK* is ANDed with a bloc number to determine which entry in *buf_hash* to use as the starting point in a search for a block buffer.

The next file, *dev.h*, defines the *dmap* table. The table itself is declared in *table.c* with initial values, so that version cannot be included in several files. This is why *dev.h* is needed. *Damp* is declared here with *extern,* instead of *EXTERN.* The table provides the mapping between the major derive number and the corresponding task.

File.h contains the intermediate table *flip* (declared as *EXTERN),* used to hold the current file position and i-node pointer. It also tells whether the file was opened for reading, writing, or both, and how many file descriptors are currently pointing to the entry.

The file locking table, *file_lock* (declared as *EXTERN*), is in *lock.h.* The size of the array is determined by *NR_LOCKS,* which is defined as 8 in *const.h.* This number should be increased if it is desired to implement a multiuser data base on a MINIX system.

In *inode.h,* the i-node table *inode* is declared (using *EXTERN)*. It holds i-nodes that are currently in use. As we said earlier, when a file is opened its i-node is read into memory and kept there until the file is closed. The *inode* structure definition provides for information that is kept in memory, but not written to the disk i-node. Notice that there is only one version, and nothing is version-specific here. When the i-node is read in from the disk, differences between *V1* and *V2* file systems are handled. The rest of the file system does not need to know about the file system format on the disk, at least until the time comes to write back modified information.

Most of the fields should be self-explanatory at this point. However, *I-seek* deserves some comment. It was mentioned earlier that, as an optimization, when the file system notices that a file is being read sequentially, it tries to read blocks into the cache even before they are asked for. For randomly accessed files there is no read ahead. When an LSEEK call is made, the field *I-seek* is to inhibit read ahead.

The file *param.h* is analogous to the file of the same name in the memory manager. It defines names for messages fields containing parameters, so the code can refer to, for example, *buffer,* instead of *m.m*1*_p*1*,* which selects one of the fields of the message buffer *m.*

In *super.h*, we have the declaration of the super-block table. When the system is booted, the super-block for the root device is loaded here. As file system are mounted, their super-blocks go here as well. A s with other tables, *super-block* is declared as *EXTERN.*

File System Storage Allocation

The last file we will discuss in this section is not a header. However, as we did when discussing the memory manager, it seems appropriate to discuss *table.c* immediately after reviewing the header files, since they are all included when *table.c* is compiled. Most of the data structures we have mentioned—the block cache, the *flip* table, and so on—are defined with the *EXTERN* macro, as are also the file system's global variables and the file system's part of the process table. In the same way we have seen in other parts of the MINIX system, the storage is actually reserved when *table.c* is compiled. This file also contains two major initialized arrays. *Call_vector* contains the pointers array used in the main loop for determining which procedure handles which system call number. We saw a similar table inside the memory manager.

This table has one row of reach major device, starting at zero. when a device is opened, closed, read, or written, it is this table that provides the name of the procedure to call to handle the operation. All of these procedures are located in the file system's address space. Many of these procedures do nothing, but some call a task to actually request I/O. The task number corresponding to each major device is also provided by the table.

Whenever a new major device is added to MINIX, a line must be added to this table telling what action, if any, is to be taken when the device is opened, closed, read, or written. As a simple example, if a tape drive is added to MINIX, when it special file is opened, the procedure in the table could check to see if the tape drive is already in use. In order to spare users the effort of modifying this table when reconfiguring, a macro, *DT,* is defined to automate the process.

There is a line in the table for each possible major device, and each line is written with the macro. Required devices have a 1 as the value of the *enable* argument to the macro. Some entries are not used, either because a planned driver is not yet ready or because an old driver has been removed. These entries are defined with a value of 0 for *enable.* Entries for devices that may be configured in *include/minix/config.h* use the enabling macro for the device, for instance, *ENABLE_WINI.*

Table Management

Associated with each of the main tables—blocks, i-nodes, super-blocks, and so forth—is a file that contains procedures that manage the table. These procedures are heavily used by the rest of the file system and form the principal interface between tables and the file system. For this reason, it is appropriate to begin our study of the file system code with them.

Block Management

The block cache is managed by the procedures in the file *cache.c.* This file contains the nine procedures listed in Fig. 10.14. This first one, *get_block,* is the standard way the file system gets data blocks. When a file system procedure needs to read a user data blocks, a directory block, a super-block, or nay other kind of block, it calls *get_block,* specifying the device and block number.

Procedure	Function
get_block	Fetch a block for reading or writing
put_block	Return a block previously requested with get_block
alloc_zone	Allocate a new zone (to make a file longer)
free_zone	Release a zone (when a file is removed)
rw_block	Transfer a block between disk and cache
invalidate	Purge all the cache blocks for some device
flushall	Flush all dirty blocks for one device
rw_scattered	Read or write scattered data from or to a device
rm_lru	Remove a block from its LRU chain

Fig. 10.14. *Procedures used for block management.*

When *get_block* is called, it first examines the block cache to see if the requested block is there. If so, it return a pointer to it. Otherwise, it has to read the block in. The blocks in the cache are linked together on *NR_BUF_HASH* linked lists. *NR_BUF_HASH* is a tunable parameter, along with *NR_BUFS*, the size of the block cache. Both of these are set in *include/minix/config.h.* At the end of this section we will say a few words about optimizing the size of the block cache and the hash table. The *HASH_MASK* in *NR_BUF_HASH*— 1. With 256 hash lists, the mask is 255, so all the block on each list have block numbers that end with the same string of 8 bits, that is 00000000, 00000001, ..., or 11111111.

The first step is usually to search a hash chain for a block, although there is a special case, when a hole in a sparse file is being read, where this search is skipped. Otherwise, the next two lines set *bp* to point to the start of the list on which the requested block would be, if it were in the cache, applying *HASH_MASK* to the block number. The loop on the next line searches this list to see if the block can be found. If it is found and is not in use, it is removed from the LRU list. If it is already in use, it is not on the LRU list anyway.

If the block is not on the hash list, it is not in the cache, so the least recently used block from the LRU list is taken. The buffer chosen is removed from its hash chain, since it is about to acquire a new block number and hence belongs on a different hash chain. Doing this with a call to *flushall* rewrites any other dirty blocks for the same device. Blocks that are currently in use are never chosen for eviction, since they are not on the LRU chain. Blocks will hardly ever be found to be in use, however; normally a block is released but *put_block* immediately upon being used.

As soon as the buffer is available, all of the fields, including *b_dev,* are updated with the new parameters, and the block may be read in from the disk. However, there are two occasions when it may not be necessary to read the block from the disk. *Get_block* is called with a parameter *only_search.* This may indicate that this is a prefetch. During a prefetch an available buffer is found, writing the old contents to the disk if necessary, and a new block number is assigned to the buffer, but the *b_dev* field is set to *NO-DEV* to signal there are as yet no valid data in this block. We will see how this is used when we discuss the *rw_scattered* function. *Only_search* can also be used to signal that the file system needs a block just to rewrite all of it. In this case it is wasteful to first read the old version in. In either of these cases the parameters are updated, but the actual disk read is omitted. When the new block has been read n, *get_block* returns to its caller with a pointer to it.

Suppose that these file system needs a directory block temporarily, to look up a file name. It calls *get_block* to acquire the directory block. When it has looked up its file name, it calls *put_block* to return the block to the cache, thus making the buffer available in case it is needed later for a different block.

Put_block takes care of putting thes newly returned block on the LRU list, and in some cases, rewriting it to the disk. A decision is make to put it on the front or rear of the LRU list, depending on *block_type,* a flag provided by the caller telling what kind to of a block it is. Blocks that may be needed again soon go on the rear, so they will stay around for a while. Blocks that are not likely to be needed again soon are put on the front, where they will be reused quickly. Currently, only super-blocks are treated this way.

After the block has been repositioned on the LRU list, another check is made to see if the block should be rewritten to disk immediately. In the standard configuration only super-blocks are marked for immediate writing, but the only times a super-block is modified and needs to be written is when a RAM disk is resized at system initialization. In that case the write is to the RAM disk, and it is unlikely the super-block of a RAM disk will ever need to be read again. Thus, this capability is hardly used. However, the *ROBUST* macro in *include/minix/confg.h* can be edited to mark for immediate writing i-nodes, directory blocks, and other blocks that are essential for the correct functioning of the file system itself.

As a file grows, from time to time a new zone must be allocated to hold the new data. The procedure *alloc_zone* takes care of allocating new zones. It does this by finding a free zone in the zone bit map. There is no need to search through the bit map if this is to be the first zone in a file; the *s_zsearch* field in the super-block, which always points to the first available zone on the device, is consulted. Otherwise an attempt is made to find a zone close to the last existing zone of the current file, in order to keep the zones of a file together. This is done by starting the search of the bit mp at this last zone. The mapping between the bit number in the bit map and the zone number is handled.

When a file is removed, its zones must be returned to the bit map. *Free_zone* is responsible for restrung these zones. All it does is call *free_bit,* passing the zone map and the bit number as parameters. *Free_bit* is also used to return free i-nodes, but then with the i-node map as these first parameter, of course.

Managing the cache requires reading and writing blocks. To provide a simple disk interface, the procedure *rw_block* has been provided. It reads or writes one block. Analogously, *rw_inode* exists to read and write i-nodes.

The next procedure in the file is *invalidate.* It is called when a disk is unmounted, for example, to remove from the cache all the block belonging to the file system just unmounted. If this were not done, then when the device were reused (with a different floppy disk), the file system might find the old blocks instead of the new ones.

Flushall is called by the SYNC system call to flush to disk all dirty buffers belonging to a specific devices. It is called once for each mounted device. It treats the buffer cache as a linear array, so all dirty buffers are found, even ones that are currently in use and are not in the LRU list. All buffers in the cache are scanned, and those that belong to the devices to be flushed and that need to be written are added to an array of pointers, *dirty*. This array is declared as *static* to keep it off the stack. It is then passed to *rw_scattered.*

Rw_scattered receives a device identifier, a pointer to an array of pointers to buffers, the size of the array, and a flag indicating whether to read or write. The first thing it does is sort the array it receives on the block numbers, so the actual read or writ operation will be performed in an efficient order. It is called with the *WRITING* flag only from the *flushall* function described above. In this case the origin of these block numbers is easy to understand. They are buffers which contains data from blocks previously read but now modified. The only call to *rw_scattered* for a read operation is from *rahead* in *read.c.* At this point, we just need to know that before calling *rw_scattered, get_block* has been called repeatedly in prefetch mode, thus reserving a group of buffers. These buffers contain block numbers, but no valid device parameter. This is not a problem, sinces *rw_scattered* is called with a device parameter as one of its arguments.

There is an important difference in the way a device drive may respond to a read (as opposed to a write) request, from *rw_scattered.* A request to write a number of blocks *must* be honored completely, but a request to read a number of blocks may be handled differently by different drivers, depending upon what is most efficient for the particular driver. *Rahead* often calls *rw_scattered* with a request for a list of blocks that may not actually be needed, so the best response is to get as many blocks as can be gotten easily, but not to go wildly seeking all over a device that may have substantial seek time. For instance, the floppy driver may stop at a track boundary, and may other drivers will read only consecutive blocks. When the read is complete, *rw_scattered* marks the blocks read by filling in the device number field in their block buffers.

The last function in Fig 10.14 is *rm_lru.* This function is used to remove a blocks from the LRU list. It is used only by *get_block* in this file, so it is declared *PRIVATE* instead of *PUBLIC* to hide it form procedures outside the file.

Before we leave the block cache, let us say a few words about fine-tuning it. *NR_BUF_HASH* must be a power of 2. if it is larger than *NR_BUFS,* the average length of a hash chain will be less than one. If there is enough memory for a large number of buffers, there is space for a large number of hash chains, so the usual choice is to make *NR_BUF_HASH* the next power of 2 greater than *NR_BUFS.* The listing in the text shows settings of 512 blocks and 1024 hash lists. The optimal size depends upon how the system is used, since that determines how much must be buffered. Empirically it was found that increasing the number of buffers beyond 1024 did not improve performance when recompiling the MINIX systems, so apparently this is large enough to hold the binaries for all complier passes. For some others kind of word a smaller size might be adequate or a larger size might improve performance.

The binary files for the MINIX system on the CD-ROM are compiled with a much smaller block cache. This is because the distribution binary is meant to run on as may machines as possible. It was desired to produce a distribution version of MINIX that could be installed in a system with only 2 MB of RAM memory. A system compiled with a 1024-block cache requires more than 2 MB of RAM. The distributed binary also includes every possible hard disk driver and other drivers that may not be useful in a particular installation. Most users will want to edit *include/minix/config.h* and recompile the system soon after installation, leaving out unnecessary drivers and enlarging the bloc cache as much as possible.

While on the subject of the block cache, we will point out the 64 KB limit on memory segment size on 16-bit Intel processors makes a large cache impossible on these machines. It is possible to configure the file system to use the RAM disk as a secondary cache, to hold blocks that are pushed out of the primary cache. We do not discuss this here because it is not necessary on a 32-bit Intel system when possible, a large primary cache will give the best performance. A secondary cache can be helpful, however, on a machine (such as a 286) that does not have room for a large primary cache within the file system's virtual address space. A secondary cache should perform better than a conventional RAM disk. A cache holds only data that is needed at least once, and if large enough can make a big improvement in system performance. "Large enough" cannot be defined in advance; in can only be measured by seeing if further increases in size result in further increases in performance. The *time* command, which measures the time used in running a program, is a useful tool when trying to optimize a system.

I-node Management

The block cache is not the only table that needs support procedures. The i-node table does, too. Many of the procedures are similar in function to the block management procedures. They are listed in Fig. 10.15.

Procedure	Function
get_inode	Fetch an i-node into memory
put_inode	Return an i-node that is no longer needed
alloc_inode	Allocate a new i-node (for a new file)
wipe_inode	Clear some fields in an i-node
free_inode	Release an i-node (when a file is removed)
update_times	Update time fields in an i-node
rw_inode	Transfer an i-node between memory and disk
old_icopy	Convert i-node contents to write to V1 disk i-node
new_icopy	Convert data read from V1 file system disk i-node
dup_inode	Indicate that someone else is using an i-node

Fig. 10.15a. Procedures used for i-node management.

The procedure *get_inode* is analogous to *get_block*. When any part of the file system needs an i-node, it calls *get-inode* to acquire it. *Get_inode* first searches the *inode* table to see if the i-node is already present. If so, it increments the usages counter and returns a pointer to it. If the i-node is not present in memory, the i-node is loaded by calling *rw_inode*.

When the procedure that needed the i-node is finished with it, the i-node is returned by calling the procedure *put_inode,* which decrements the usage count *i_count.* If the count is then zero, the file is no longer in use, and the i-node can removed from the table. If it is dirty, it is rewritten to disk.

If the *i_link* field is zero, on directory entry is pointing to the file, so all its zones can be freed. Note that the usages cont going to zero and the number of links going to zero and different events, with different causes and different consequences. If the i-node is for a pipe, all the zones must be released even though, the number of links may no be zero. This happens when a process reading from a pipe releases the pipe. There is no sense in having a pipe for one process.

When a new file is created, an i-node must be allocated by *alloc_inode.* MINIX allows mounting of devices in read-only mode, so the super-block is checked to make sure the device is writable. Unlike zones, where an attempt is make to kept the zones of a file close together, any i-node will do. In order to save the time of searching the i-node bit map, advantage is taken of the field in the super-block where the first unused i-node is recorded.

After the i-node has been acquired, *get_inode* is called to fetch the i-node into the table in memory. Then its fields are initialized, partly in line and partly using the procedure *wipe_inode*. This particular division of labor has been chosen because *wipe_inode* is also needed elsewhere in the file system to clear certain i-node fields (but not all of them).

When a file is removed, its i-node is freed by calling *free_inode*. All that happens here is that the corresponding bit in the i-node bit map is set to 0 and the super-block's record of the first unused i-node is updated.

The next function, *update_times*, is called to get the time from the system clock and change the time fields that require updating. *Update_times* is also called by the STAT and FSTAT system calls, so it is declared *PUBLIC.*

The procedure *rw_inode* is analogous to *rw_block.* its job is to fetch an i-node from the disk. It does its work by carrying out the following steps:

1. Calculate which block contains the required i-node
2. Read in the block by calling *get_block.*
3. Extract the i-node and copy it to the *inode* table.
4. Return the block by calling *pur_block.*

Rw_inode is a bit more complex than the basic outline given above, so some additional functions are needed. First, because getting the current time is expensive, any need for a changes to the time fields in the i-node is only marked by setting bits in the i-node's *i_update* field while the i-node is in memory. If this field is nonzero when an i-node must be written, *update_times* is called.

Second, MINIX' history adds a complication: In the old *V1* version of the file system the i-nodes on the disk have a different structure from *V2*. Two functions, *old_icopy* and *new_icopy* take care of the conversions. The first converts between i-node information in memory and the format used by the *V1* filesystem. The second does the same conversion for *V2* filesystem disks. Both of these functions are called only from within this file, so they are declared *PRIVATE.* Each function handles conversions in both directions (disk to memory or memory to disk). MINIX has been implemented on systems which use a different byte order from Intel processors. Every implementation uses the native byte order on its disk; the *sp->native* filed in the super-block identifies which order is used. Both *old_icopy* and *new_icopy* call functions *conv2* and *conv4* to swap byte orders, if necessary.

The procedure *dup_inode* just increments the usages count of the i-node. It is called when an open file is opened again. On the second open, the i-node need not be fetched from disk again.

Super-Block Management

The file *super.c* contains procedures that manage the super-block and the bit maps. There are five procedures in this file, listed in Fig. 10.15

Procedure	Function
alloc_bit	Allocate a bit from the zone or i-node map
free_bit	Free a bit in the zone or i-node map
get_super	Search the super-block table for a device
mounted	Report whether given i-node is on a mounted (or root) f.s.
read_super	Read a super-block

Fig. 10.15b. *Procedures used to manage the super-block and bit maps.*

When an i-node or zone is needed, *alloc_inode* or *alloc_zone* is called, as we have seen above. Both of these call *alloc_bit* to actually search the relevant bit map. The search involves three nested loops, as follows:

1. The outer one loops on all the blocks of a bit map.
2. The middle one loops on all the words of a block.
3. The inner one loops on all the bits of a word.

The middle loop works by seeing if the current word is equal to the one's complement of zero, that is, a complete word full of 1s. If so, it has no free i-nodes or zones, so the next word is tried. When a word with a different value is found, it must have at least one 0 bit in it so, the inner loop is entered to find the free (i.e., 0) bit. If all the blocks have been tried without success, there are no free i-nodes or zones, so the code *NO_BIT* (0) is returned. Searches like this can consume a lot of processor time, but the use of the super-block fields that point to the first unused i-node and zone, passed to *alloc_bit* in *origin,* helps to keep these searches short.

Freeing a bit is simple than allocating one, because no search is needed. *Free_bit* calculates which bit map block contains the bit to free and sets the proper bit to 0 by calling *get_block,* zeroing the bit in memory and then calling *put_block.*

The next procedure, *get_super*, used to search the super-block table for a specific device. For example, when a file system is to be mounted, it is necessary to check that it is not already mounted. This check can be performed by asking *get_super* to find the file system's device. If it does not find the device, then the file system is not mounted.

The next function, *mounted,* is called only when a bloc device is closed. Normally, all cached data for a device are discarded when it is last closed. But, if the device happens to be mounted, this is not desirable. *Mounted* is called with a pointer to the i-node for a device. It just returns *TRUE* if the device is the root device, or if it is a mounted device.

Finally, we have *read_super.* This is partially analogous to *rw_block* and *rw_inode,* but it is called only to read. Writing a super-block is not necessary in the normal operation of the system. *Read_super* checks the version of the file system from which it has just read and performs conversions, if necessary, so the copy of the super-block in memory will have the standard structure even when read from a disk with a different super-block structure.

File Descriptor Management

MINIX contains special procedures to manage file descriptors and the *flip* table. They are contained in the file *filedes.c.* When a files is created or opened, a free file descriptor and a free *flip* slot are needed. The procedure *get_fd* is used to find them. They are not marked as in use, however, because many checks must first be made before it is known for sure that the CREAT or OPEN will succeed.

Get_filp is used to see if a file descriptor is in range, and if so, return its *filp* pointer.

The last procedure in this file is *fund_filp*. It is needed to find out when a process is writing on a broken pipe (i.e., a pipe not open for reading by any other process). It locates potential readers by a brute force search of the *filp* table. If it cannot find one the pipe is broken and the write fails.

File Locking

The POSIX record locking functions are shown in Fig 10.15. A part of a file can be locked for reading and writing, or for writing only, by an FCNTL call specifying at *F_SETLK* or *F_SETLKW* request. Whether a lock exists over a part of a file can be determined using the *F_GETLK* request.

Operation	Meaning
F_SETLK	Lock region for both reading and writing
F_SETLKW	Lock region for writing
F_GETLK	Report if region is locked

Fig 10.15c. *The POSIX advisory record locking operations. These operations are requested by using an FCNTL system call.*

There are only two function in the file *lock.c. Lock_op* is called by the FCNTL system call with a code for one of the operations shown in Fig 10.15. It does some error checking to be sure the region specified is valid. When a lock is being set, it must not conflict with an existing lock, and when a lock is being cleared, an existing lock must not be split in two. When any lock is cleared, the other function in this file, *lock_revive* is called. It wakes up all the processes that are blocked waiting for locks. This strategy is a compromise; it would take extra code to figure out exactly which processes were waiting for a particular lock to be released. Those processes that are still waiting for a locked file will block again when they start. This strategy is based on an assumption that locking will be used infrequently. If a major multiuser data base were to built upon a MINIX system, it might be desirable to reimplement this.

Lock_revive is also called when a locked file is closed, as might happen, for instance if a process is killed before it finishes using a locked file.

The Main Program

The main loop to the file system is contained in the *main.c.* Structurally, it is very similar to the main loop of the memory manager and the I/O tasks. The call to *get_work* waits for the next request message to arrive (unless a process previously suspended on a pipe or terminal can now be handled). It also sets a global variable, *who,* to the caller's process table slot number and another global variable, *fs_call,* to the number of the system call to be carried out.

One back in the main loop, three flags are set: *fp* points to the caller's process table slot, *super_user* tells whether the caller is the super-user or not, and *dont_reply* is initialized to *FALSE.* Then comes the main attraction—the call to the procedure that carries out the system call. The procedure to call is selected by using *fs_call* as an index into the array of procedure pointers, *call_vector.*

When control comes back to the main loop, if *dnot_reply* has been set, the reply is inhibited (e.g., a process has blocked trying to read from an empty pipe). Otherwise a reply is sent. The final statement in the main loop has been designed to detect that a file is being read sequentially and to load the next block into the cache before it is actually requested, to improve performance.

The procedure *get_work* checks to see if any previously blocked procedures have now been revived. If so, these have priority over new messages. Only if there is no internal work to do does the file system call the kernel to get a message.

After a system call has been completed, successfully or otherwise, a reply is sent back to the caller by *reply.* The process may have been killed by a signal, so the status code returned by the kernel is ignored. In this case there is nothing to be done anyway.

Initialization Functions

The rest or *man.c* consists of functions that are used only at system startup. Before the file system enters its main loop, it initializes itself by calling *fs_init* which in turn calls several other function to initialize the block cache, get the boot parameters, load the RAM disk if necessary, and load the root device super-block. The next step is to initialize the file system's part of the process table for all the tasks and servers, up through *init.* Finally, tests are done on some important constants, to see if they make sense, and a message is sent to the memory task with the address of the file system's part of the process table, for use by the *ps* program.

The first function called by *fs_init* is *buf_pool,* which builds the linked lists used by the block cache. Figure 10.9 shows the normal state of the block cache, in which all blocks are linked on both the LRU chain and a hash chain. It may be helpful to see how the situation of Fig 10.9 comes about. Immediately after the cache is initialized by *buf_pool,* all the buffers will be on the LRU chain, and will be linked into the 10th hash chain, as in Fig10.16 (a). When a buffer is requested, and while it is in use, we have the situation of Fig. 10.16 (b), in which we see that a block has been removed from the LRU chain and is now on a different hash chain. Normally, blocks are released and returned to the LRU chain immediately. Figure 10.16 (c) shows the situation after the block has been returned to the LRU chain. Although it is no longer in use, it can be accessed again to provide the same data, if need be, and so it is retained on the hash chain. After the system has been in operation for a while, almost all of the blocks can be expected to have been used and to be distributed among the different hash chains at random.

The next function is *get_boot_parameters.* It sends a message to the system task to ask it for a copy of the boot parameters. They are needed by the following function, *load_ram,* which allocates space for a RAM disk. If the boot parameters specify rootdev = ram

the root device file system is copied from the device named by *ramimagedev* to the RAM disk block by block, starting with the bootblock, with no interpretation of the various file system data structures. If the *ramsize* boot parameter is smaller than the size of the root device file system, the RAM disk is made large enough to hold it. If *ramsize* specifies a size larger than the boot device file system the specified size is allocated and the RAM disk file system is adjusted to use the full size specified. The call to *put_block* is the only time that the file system ever writes a super-block.

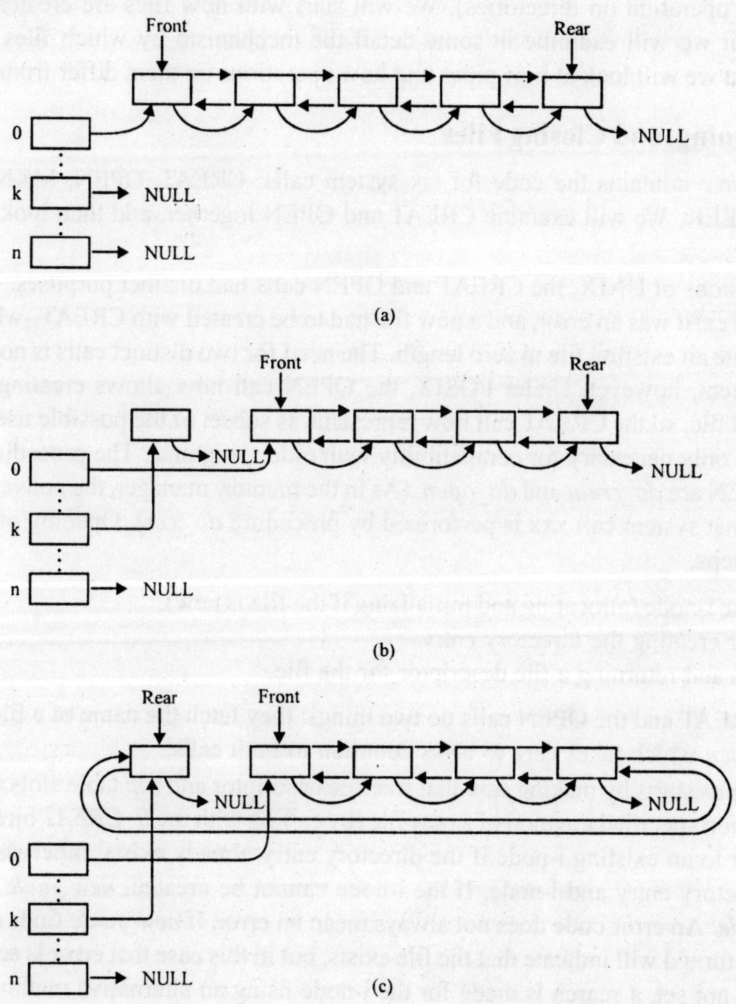

Fig. 10.16. Block cache initialization. (a) Before any buffers have been used. (b) After one block has been requested. (c) After the block has been releases.

Load_ram allocates space for an empty RAM disk if a nonzero *ramsize* is specified. In this case, since no file system structures are copied, the RAM device cannot be used as a file system until it has been initialized by the *mkfs* command. Alternatively, such RAM disk can be used for a secondary cache if support for this is compiled into the file system.

The last function in *main.c* is *load_super*. It initializes the super-block table and reads in the super-block of the root device.

Operations on Individual Files

In this section we will look at the system calls that operate on individual files one at a time (as opposed to, say, operation on directories). We will start with how files are created, opened, and closed. After that we will examine in some detail the mechanism by which files are reads and written. After that we will look at how pipes and how operations on them differ from those on files.

Creating, Opening, and Closing Files

The file *open.c* contains the code for six system calls: CREAT, OPEN, MKNOD, MKDIR, CLOSE, and LSEEK. We will examine CREAT and OPEN together, and then look at each of the others.

In order versions of UNIX, the CREAT and OPEN calls had distinct purposes. Trying to open a file that did not exist was an error, and a new file had to be created with CREAT, which could also be used to truncate an existing file to zero length. The need for two distinct calls is no longer present in a POSIX system, however. Under POSIX, the OPEN call now allows creating a new file or truncating an old file, so the CREAT call now represents as subset of the possible uses of the OPEN call and is really only necessary for compatibility with older programs. The procedures that handle CREAT and OPEN are *do_creat* and *do_open*. (As in the memory manager, the convention is used in the file system that system call xxx is performed by procedure *do_xxx*). Opening or creating a file involves three steps.

1. Finding the i-node (allocating and initializing if the file is new).
2. Finding or creating the directory entry.
3. Setting up and returning a file descriptor for the file.

Both the CREAT and the OPEN calls do two things: they fetch the name of a file and then they call *common_open* which takes care to tasks common to both calls.

Common_open starts by making sure that free file descriptor and *filp* table slots are available. If the calling function specified creation of a new file (by calling with the *0_CREAT* bit set). *New_node* returns a pointer to an existing i-node if the directory entry already exists; otherwise it will create both a new directory entry and i-node. If the i-node cannot be created, *new_node* sets the global variable *err_code*. An error code does not always mean an error. If *new_node* finds an existing file, the error code returned will indicate that the file exists, but in this case that error is acceptable. If the *0_CREAT* bit is not set, a search is made for the i-node using an alternative method, the *eat_path* function in *path.c,* which we will discuss further on. At this point, the important thing to understand is that if an i-node is not found or successfully created, *common_open* will terminate with an error.

If the file is not new, then the file system must test to see what kind of a file it is, what its mode, is, and so on, to determine whether it can be opened. The call to *forbidden* first makes a general check of the *rwx* bits. If the file is a regular file and *common_open* was called with the *0_TRUNC* bit set, it is truncated to length zero and *forbidden* is called again, this time to be sure the file may be written. If the permissions allow, *wipe_inode* and *rw_inode* are called to re-initialize the i-node and write it to the disk. Other file types (directories, special files, and named pipes) are subjected to appropriate tests.

The code of *common_open*, as well as many other file system procedures, contains a large amount of code that checks for various error and illegal combinations. While not glamorous, this code is essential to having an error-free, robust file system. If something is wrong, the file descriptor and *flip* slot previously allocated are deadllocated and the i-node is released. In this case the value returned by *common_open* will be a negative number, indicating an error. If there are no problems the file descriptor, a positive value, is returned.

This is a good place to discuss in more detail the operation of *new_node*, which doe the allocation of the i-node and the entering of the path name into the file system for CREAT and OPEN calls. It is also used for the MKNOD and MKDIR calls, yet to be discussed.

For example, on the call

fd = creat("/usr/ast/foobar", 0755);

last_dir tries to load the i-node for */usr/ast* into the tables and return a pointer to it. If the file does not exist, we will need this i-node shortly in order to add *foobar* to the directory. All the other system calls that add or delete files also use *last_dir* to first open the final directory in the path.

If *new_node* discovers that the file does not exist, it calls *alloc_node* to allocate and load a new i-node, returning a pointer to it. If no free i-nodes are left, *new_node* fails and returns *NIL_INODE.*

If an i-node can be allocated, the operation continues, filling in some of the fields, writing it back to the disk, and entering the file name in the final directory. Again we see that the file system must constantly check for errors, and upon encountering one, carefully release all the resources, such as i-node and blocks that it is holding. If we were prepared to just let MINIX panic when we ran out of, say, i-nodes, rather than undoing all the effects of the current call and returning an error code to the caller, the file system would be appreciably simpler.

As mentioned above, pipes require special treatment. If there is not at least one reader/writer pair for a pipe, *pipe_open* suspends the caller. Otherwise, it calls *release,* which looks through the processes that are blocked on the pipe. If it is successful, the processes are revived.

The MKNOD call is handled by *do_mknod*. This procedure is similar to *do_creat,* except that it just creates the i-node and makes a directory entry for it. In fact, most of the works is done by call to *new_node*. If the i-node already exists, an error code will be returned. This is the same error code that was an acceptable result from *new_node* when it was called by *common_open;* in this case, however, the error code is passed back to the caller, which presumably will act accordingly. The case-by-case analysis we saw in *common_open* is not needed here.

The MKDIR call is handled by the function *do_mkdir.* As with the other system calls we have discussed here, *new_node* plays an important part. Directories, unlike files, always have links and are never completely empty because every directory must contain two entries from the time of its creation: the ".." and ".." entries that refer to the directory itself and to its parent directory. There is a limit to the number of links a file may have, *LINK_MAX* (defined in *include/limits.h* as 127 for the standard MINIX system). Since the reference to a parent directory in a child is a link to parent, the first thing *do_mkdir* does is to see if it is possible to make another link in the parent directory. Once this test has been passed, *new_node* is called. If *new_node* succeeds, then the directory entries for ".." and ".." are made. All of this is straightforward, but there could be failures (for instance, if the disk is full), and to avoid making a mess of things provision is made for undoing the initial stages of the process if it can not be completed.

Closing a file is easier that opening one. The work is done by *do_close.* Pipes and special files need some attention, but for regular files, almost all that needs to be done is to decrement the *filp* counter and check to see if it is zero in which case the i-node is returned with *put_inode.* The final step is to remove any locks and to revive any process that may have been suspended waiting for a lock on the file to be released.

Note that returning an i-node means that is counter in the *inode* table is decremented, so it can be removed from the table eventually. This operation has nothing to do with freeing the i-node (i.e., setting a bit in the bit map saying that it is available). The i-node is only freed when the file has been removed from all directories.

The final procedure in *open.c* is *do_lseek.* When a seek is done, this procedure is called to set the file position to a new value.

Reading a File

Once a file has been opened, it can be read or written. Many functions are used during both reading and writing. These are found in the file *read.c.* We will discuss these first and then proceed to the following file, *write.c,* to look at code specifically used for writing. Reading and writing differ in a number of ways, but they have enough similarities that all that is required of *do_read* is to call the common procedure *read_write* with a flag set to *READING.* We will see in the next section that *do_write* is equally simple.

The special code that is used by the memory manager to have the file system load entire segments in user space for it. Some validity checks follow (e.g., reading from a file opened only for writing) and some variables are initialized. Reads from character special files do not go through the block cache, so they are filtered.

The tests apply only to writes and haves to do with files that may get bigger than the device can hold, or writes that will create a hole in the file by writing *beyond* the end-of-file. As we discussed in the MINIX overview, the presence of multiple blocks per zone causes problems that must be dealt with explicitly. Pipes are also special and are checked for.

The heart of the read mechanism, at least for ordinary files, is the loop starting. This loop breaks the request up into chunks, each of which fits in a singles disk block. A chunk begins at the current position and extends until one of the following conditions is met:

1. All the bytes have been read.
2. A block boundary is encountered.
3. The end-of-file is hit.

These rules mean that a chunk never requires two disk blocks to satisfy it. Figure 10.17 shows three examples of how the chunk size is determined, for chunks sizes of 6, 2, and 1 bytes, respectively.

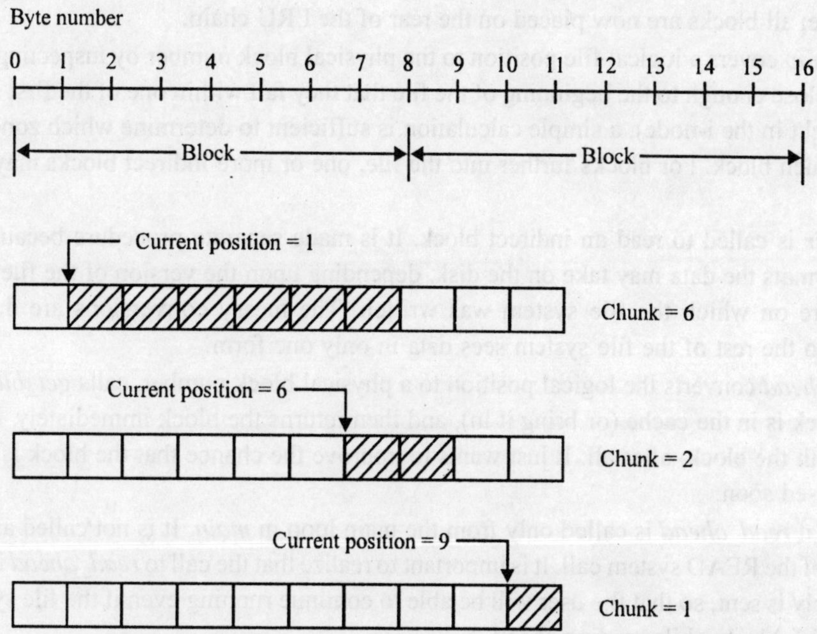

Fig. 10.17. Three examples of how the first chunk size is determined for a 10-byte file. The block size is 8 bytes, and the number of bytes requested is 6. The chunk is shown shaded.

The actual reading of the chunk is done by *rw_chunk.* When control returns, various counters and pointers are incremented, and the next iteration begins. When the loop terminates, the file position and other variables may be updated (e.g., pipe pointers).

Finally, if read ahead is called for, the i-node to read from and the position to read from are stored in global variables, so that after the reply message is sent to the user, the file system can start working on getting the next block. In many cases the file system will block, waiting for the next disk block, during which time the user process will be able to work on the data it just received. This arrangement overlaps processing and I/O and can improve performance substantially.

The procedure *rw_chunk* is concerned with taking an i-node and a file position, converting them into a physical disk block umber, and requesting the transfer of the block (or a portion of it) to the user space. The mapping of the relative file position to the physical disk address is done by *read_map,* which understands about i-nodes and indirect blocks. For an ordinary file, the variables *b* and *dev* contain the physical block number and device number, respectively. The call to *get_block* is where the cache handler is asked to find the block, reading it in if need be.

Once we have a pointer to the block, the call to *sys_copy* takes care of transferring the required portion of it to the user space. The block is then released by *put_block,* so that it can be evicted from the cache later, when the times comes. (After being acquired by *get_block*, it will not be in the LRU queue and it will be not be returned there while the counter in the block's header shows that it is in use, so it will be exempt from eviction; *put_block* decrements the counter and returns the block to the LRU queue when the counter reaches zero.) The code indicates whether a write operation filled the block. However, the value passed to *put_block* in *n* does not affect how the block is placed on the queue; all blocks are now placed on the rear of the LRU chain.

Read_map covers a logical file position to the physical block number by inspecting the i-node. For blocks close enough to the beginning of the file that they fall within one of the first seven zones (the ones right in the i-node), a simple calculation is sufficient to determine which zone is needed, and then which block. For blocks further into the file, one or more indirect blocks may have to be read.

Rd_indir is called to read an indirect block. It is made separate procedure because there are different formats the data may take on the disk, depending upon the version of the file system and the hardware on which the file system was written. The messy conversions are done here, if necessary, so the rest of the file system sees data in only one form.

Read_ahead converts the logical position to a physical block number, calls *get_block* to make sure the block is in the cache (or bring it in), and then returns the block immediately. It cannot do anything with the block, after all. It just wants to improve the chance that the block is around if it should be used soon.

Note that *read_ahead* is called only from the main loop in *main.* It is not called as part of the processing of the READ system call. It is important to realize that the call to *read_ahead* is performed *after* the reply is sent, so that the user will be able to continue running even if the file system has to wait for a disk block while reading ahead.

Read_ahead by itself is designed to ask for just one more block. It calls the last function in *read.c, rahead,* to actually get the job done. *Rahead* works according to the theory that if a little more is good, a lot more is better. Since disks and other storage devices often take a relatively long time to locate the first block requested but then can relatively quickly read in a number of adjacent blocks, it may be possible to get many more blocks read with little additional effort. A perfetch request is made to *get_block* which prepares the blocks cache to receive a number of blocks at once. Then *rw_scattered* is called with a list of blocks. We have previously discussed this; recall that when the device drivers are actually called by *rw_scattered,* each one is free to answer only as much of the request as it can efficiently handle. This all sounds fairly complicated, but the complications make possible a significant speedup of applications which read large amounts of data from the disk.

Figure 10.18 shows the relations between some of the major procedures involved in reading a file, in particular, who calls whom.

Writing a File

The code for writing to files is in *write.c.* Writing a file is similar to reading one, and *do_write* just calls *read_write* with the *WRITING* flag. A major difference between reading and writing is that writing requires allocating new disk blocks. *Write_map* is analogous to *read_map,* only instead of looking up physical block numbers in the i-node and its indirect blocks, it enters new ones there (to be precise, it enters zone numbers, not block numbers).

The code of *write_map* is long and detailed because it must deal with several cases. If the zone to be inserted is close to the beginning of the file, it is just inserted into the i-node on.

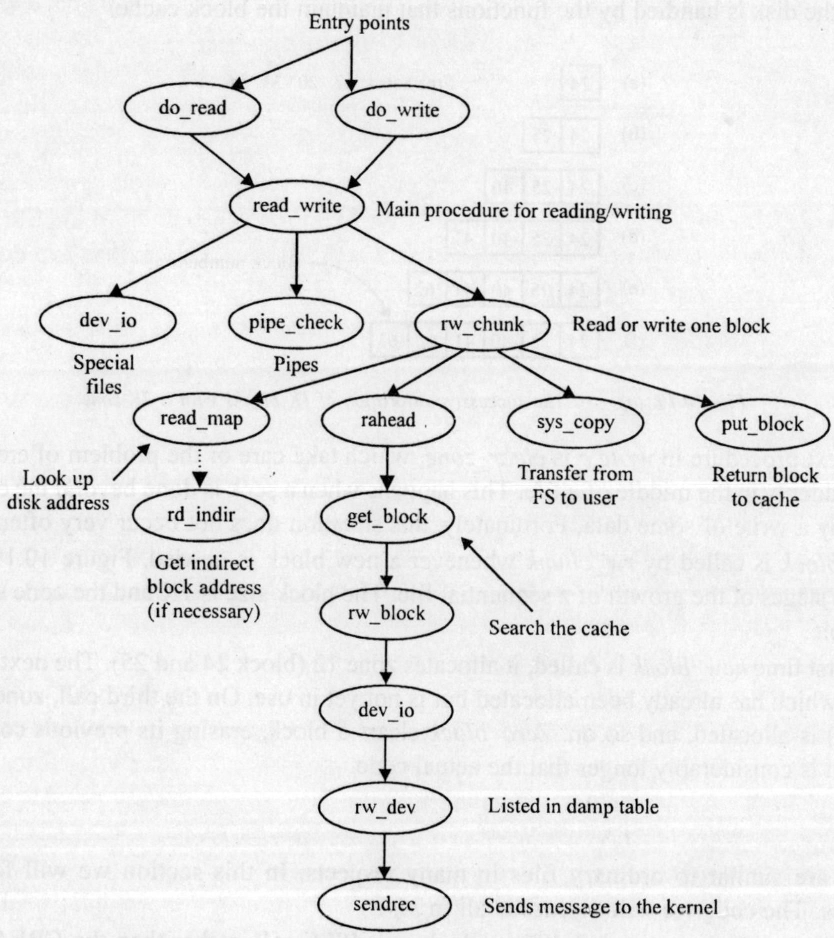

Fig. 10.18. Some of the procedures involved in reading a file.

The worst case is when a file exceeds the size that can be handled by a single-indirect block, so a double-indirect block is now required. Next, a single-indirect block must be allocated and its address put into the double-indirect block. As with reading, a separate procedure, *wr_indir,* is called. If the double-indirect block is acquired correctly, but the disk is full so the single-indirect block cannot be allocated, then the double one must be returned to avoid corrupting the bit map.

Again, if we could just toss in the sponge and panic at this point, the code would be much simpler. However, from the user's point of view it is much nicer that running out of disk space just returns an error from WRITE, rather than crashing the computer with a corrupted file system.

Wr_indir calls one of the conversion routines, *conv2* or *cnv4* to do any necessary data conversion and puts a new zone number into an indirect block. Keep in mind that the name of this function, like the names of many other functions that involve reading and writing, is not literally true. The actual writing to the disk is handled by the functions that maintain the block cache.

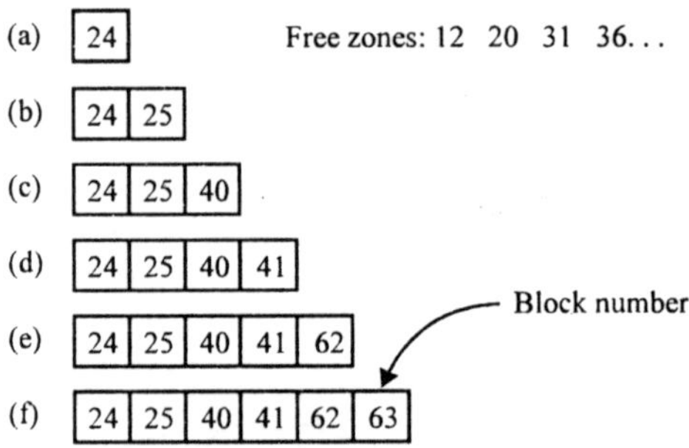

Fig. 10.19. (a) – (f) The successive allocation of 1K blocks with a 2K zone.

The next procedure in *write.c* is *clear_zone*, which take care or the problem of erasing blocks that are suddenly in the middle of a file. This happens when a seek is done beyond the end of a file, followed by a write of some data. Fortunately, this situation does not occur very often.

New_block is called by *rw_chunk* whenever a new block is needed. Figure 10.19 shows six successive stages of the growth of a sequential file. The block size is 1K and the zone size is 2K in this example.

The first time *new_block* is called, it allocates zone 12 (block 24 and 25). The next time it uses block 25, which has already been allocated but is not yet in use. On the third call, zone 20 (blocks 40 and 41) is allocated, and so on. *Zero_block* clears a block, erasing its previous contents. This description is considerably longer that the actual code.

Pipes

Pipes are similar to ordinary files in many respects. In this section we will focus on the differences. The code we will discuss is all in *pipe.c*.

First of all, pipes are created differently, by the PIPE call, rather than the CREAT call. The PIPE call is handled by *do_pipe*. All *do_pipe* really does is allocate an i-node for the pipe and return two file descriptors for it. Pipes are owned by the system, not by the user, and are located on the designated pipe device (configured in *include/minix/config.h*), which could very well be a RAM disk, since pipe data do not have to be preserved permanently.

Reading and writing a pipe is slightly different from reading and writing a file, because a pipe has a finite capacity. An attempt to write to a pipe that is already full will cause the writer to be suspended. Similarly, reading from an empty pipe will suspend the reader. In effect, a pipe has two pointers, the current position (used by readers) and the size (used by writers), to determine where data come from or go to.

The various checks to see if an operation on pipe is possible are carried out by *pipe_check*. In addition to the above tests, which may lead to the caller being suspended, *pipe_check* calls *release* to see if a process previously suspended due to no data or too much data can now be revived.

The act of suspending a process is done by *suspend.* All it does is save the parameters of the call in the process table and set the flag *dont_reply* to *TRUE*, to inhibit the file system's reply message.

The procedure *release* is called to check if a process that was suspended on a pipe can now be allowed to continue. If it finds one, it calls *revive* to set a flag sɔ that the main loop will notice it later.

The last procedure in *pipe.c* is *do_unpause.* When the memory manager is trying to signal a process, it must find out if that process is hanging on a pipe or special file (in which case it must be awakened with an *EINTR* error). Since the memory manager knows nothing about pipes or special files, it sends a message to the file system to ask. That messages is processed by *do_unpause,* which revives the process, if it is blocked. Like *revive, do_unpause* has some similarity to a system call, although it is not one.

Directories and Paths

We have now finished looking at how files are read and written. Our next task is to see how path names and directories are handled.

Converting a Path an I-node

Many system calls (e.g., OPEN, UNLINK, and MOUNT) have path names (i.e., file names) as a parameter. Most of these calls must fetch the i-node for the named file before they can start working on the call itself. How a path name is converted to an i-node is a subject we will now look at in detail.

The parsing of path names is done in the file *path.c.* The first procedure, *eat_path*, accepts a pointer to a path name, parses it, arranges for its i-node to be loaded into memory, and returns a pointer to the i-node. It does its work by calling *last_dir* to get the i-node to the final directory and then calling *advance* to get the final component of the path. If the search fails, for example, because one of the directories along the path does not exist, or exists but is protected against being searched, *NIL_INODE* is returned instead of a pointer to the i-node.

Path names by absolute or relative and may have arbitrarily many components, separated by slashes. These issues are dealt with by *last_dir.* It begins by examining the first character of the path name to see if it is an absolute path or a relative one. For absolute paths, *rip* is set to point to the root i-node; for relative ones, it is set to point to the i-node for the current working directory.

At this point, *last_dir* has the path name and a pointer to the i-node of the directory to look up the first component in. It enters a loop now, parsing the path name, component by component. When it gets to the end, it returns a pointer to the final directory.

Get_name is a utility procedure that extracts components from strings. More interesting is *advance*, which takes as parameters a directory pointer and a string, and looks up the string in the directory. If it finds the string, *advance* returns a pointer to its i-node. This details of transferring across mounted file systems are handled here.

Although *advance* controls the string lookup, the actual comparison of the string against the directory entries is done in *search_dir,* which is the only place in the file system where directory files are actually examined. It contains two nested loops, one to loop over the blocks in a directory, and one to loop over the entries in a block. *Search_dir* is also used to enter and delete names from directories. Figure 10.20 shows the relationships between some of the major procedures used in looking up path names.

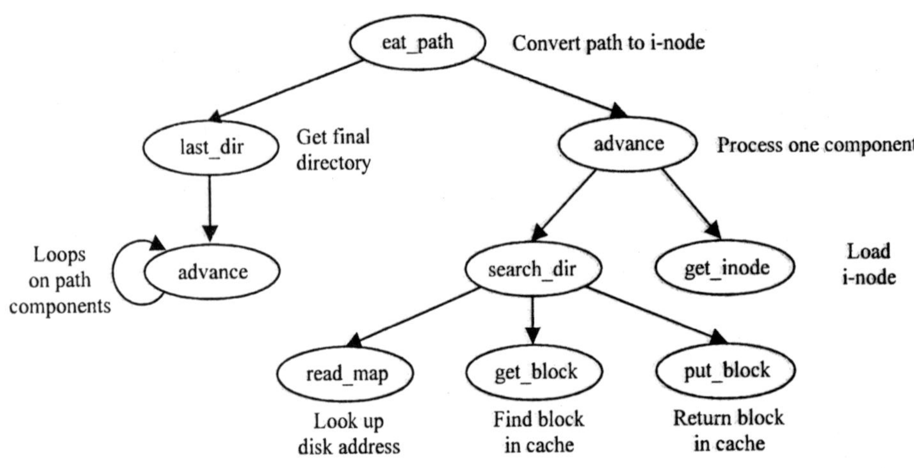

Fig. 10.20. Some of the procedures used in looking up path names.

Mounting File Systems

Two system calls that affect the file system as a whole are MOUNT and UNMOUNT. They allow independent file systems on different minor devices to be "glued" together to form a single, seamless naming tree. Mounting, as we saw in Fig.10.12 is effectively achieved by reading in the root i-node and super-block of the file system to be mounted and setting two pointers in its super-block. One of them points to the i-node mounted on, and the other points to the root i-node of the mounted file system. These pointers hook the file systems together.

The setting of these pointers is done in the file *mount.c* by *do_mount.* The two pages of code that precede setting the pointers are almost entirely concerned with checking for all the errors that can occur while mounting a file system, among them:

1. The special file given is not a block device.
2. The special file is a block device but is already mounted.
3. The file system to be mounted has a rotten magic number.
4. The file system to be mounted is invalid (e.g., no i-nodes).
5. The file to be mounted on does not exist or is a special file.
6. There is no room for the mounted file system's bit maps.
7. There is no room for the mounted file system's super-block.
8. There is no room for the mounted file system's root i-node.

Perhaps it seems inappropriate keep harping on thus point, but the reality of any practical operating system is that a substantial fraction of the code is devoted to doing minor chores that are not intellectually very exciting but are crucial to making a system usable. If a user attempts to mount the wrong floppy disk by accident, say, once a month, and this leads to a crash and a corrupted file system, the user will perceive the system as being unreliable and blame the designer, not himself.

Thomas Edison once made a remark that is relevant here. He said that "genius" is 1 per cent inspiration and 99 per cent perspiration. The difference between a good system and a mediocre one is not the brilliance of the former's scheduling algorithm, but its attention to getting all the details right.

Unmounting a file system is easier then mounting one—there are fewer things that can go wrong. *Do_umount* handles this. The only real issue is making sure that no process has any open files or working directories on the file system to be removed. This check is straightforward: just scan the whole i-node tables to se if any i-nodes in memory belong to the file system to be removed (other than the root i-node). If so, the UNMOUNT call fails.

The last procedure in *mount.c* is *name_to_dev* which takes a special file pathname, gets its i-node, and extracts its major and minor device numbers. These are stored in the i-node itself, in the place where the first zone would normally go. This slot is available because special files do not have zones.

Linking and Unlinking Files

The next file to consider is *link.c,* which deals with linking and unlinking files. The procedure *do_link* is very much like *do_mount* in that nearly all of the code is concerned with error checking. Some of the possible errors that can occur in the call

link(file_name, link_name);

are listed below:

1. *File_name* does not exist or cannot be accessed.
2. *File_name* already has the maximum number of links.
3. *File_name* is a directory (only super-user can link to it).
4. *Link_name* already exists.
5. *File_name* and *link_name* are on different devices.

If no errors are resent, a new directory entry is made with the string *ling_nake* and the i-node number of *file_name.* In the code, *name1* corresponds to *file_name* and *name2* corresponds to *link_name.* The actual entry is made by *searach_dir,* called from *do_link.*

Files and directories are removed by unlinking them. The work of both the UNLINK and RMDIR system calls is done by *do_unlink*. Again, a variety of checks must be made; testing that a file exists and that a directory is not a mount point are done by the common code in *do_unlink,* and then either *remove_dir* or *unlink_file* is called, depending upon the system call being supported. We will discuss these shortly.

The other system call supported in *link.c* is RENAME. UNIX users are familiar with the *mv* shell command which ultimately uses this call; its name reflects another aspect of the call. Not only can it change the name of a file within a directory, it can also effectively move the file from one directory to another, and it can do this atomically, which prevents certain race conditions. The work is done by *do_rename.* There are many conditions that must be tested before this command can be completed, among which are:

1. The original file must exist.
2. The old pathname must not be a directory above the new pathname in the directory tree.
3. Neither . nor .. is acceptable as an old or new name.
4. Both parent directories must be on the same device.
5. Both parent directories must be writable, searchable, and on a writable device.
6. Neither the old nor the new name may be a directory with a file system mounted upon it.

There are some other conditions that must be checked if the new name already exists, most importantly it must be possible to remove the existing file with the new name.

In the code for *do_rename* there are a few examples of design decisions that were taken to minimize the possibility of certain problems. Renaming a file to a name that already exists could fail on a full disk, even though in the end no additional space is used, if the old file were not removed first, and this is what is done. However, if the new file and the old file are to be in different directories, that concern is not relevant, and a new file name is created (in a different directory) before the old one is removed, because from a system integrity standpoint a crash that left two filenames pointing to an i-node would be much les serious than a crash that left an i-node not pointed to by any directory entry. The probability of running out of space during a rename operation is low, and that of a system crash even lower, but in these cases it costs nothing more to be prepared for the worst case.

The remaining functions in *link.c* support the ones that we have already discussed. In addition, the first to them, *truncate,* is called from several other places in the file system. It steps through an i-node one zone at a time, freeing all the zones it finds, as well as the indirect blocks. *Remove_dir* carries out a number of additional tests to be sure the directory can be removed, and then it in turn calls *unlike_file*. If no errors are found, the directory entry is cleared and the link count in the i-node is reduced by one.

Other System Calls

The last group of system calls is a mixed bag of things involving status, directories, protection, time, and other services.

Changing Directories and File Status

The file *stadir.c* contains the code for four system calls: CHDIR, CHROOT, STAT, and FSTAT. In studying *last_dir* we saw how path searches start out by looking at the first character of the path, to see if it is a slash or not. Depending on the results, a pointer is then set to the working directory or the root directory.

Changing from one working directory (or root directory) to another is just a matter of changing these two pointers within the caller's process table. These changes are made by *do_chdir* and *do_chroot*. Both of them do the necessary checking and then cal *change* to open the new directory and replace the old one.

In *do_chdir* the code is into executed on CHDIR calls made by user processes. It is specifically for calls make by the memory manager, to change to a user's directory for the purpose of handling EXEC calls. When a user tries to execute a file, say, *a.out* in this working directory, it is easier for the memory manager to change to that directory than to try to figure out where it is.

The remaining two system calls handled in this file, STAT and FSTAT, are basically the same, except for how the file is specified. The former gives a path name, whereas the latter provides the file descriptor of an open file. The top-level procedures, *do_stat* and *do_fstat,* both call *stat_inode* to do the work. Before calling *stat_inode, do_stat* opens the file to get its i-node. In this way, both *do_stat* and *do_fstat* pass an i-node pointer to *stat_inode.*

All *stat_inode* does is to extract information from the i-node and copy it into a buffer. The buffer must be explicitly copied to user space by calling *sys_copy* because it is too large to fit in a message.

Protection

The MINIX protection mechanism uses the *rwx* bits. Three sets of bits are present for each file: for the owner, for his group, and for others. The bits are set by the CHMOD system call, which is carried out by *do_chmod,* in file *protect.c.*

The CHOWN system call is similar to CHMOD in that both of them change an internal i-node field in some file. The implementation is also similar although *do_chown* can be used to change the owner only by the super-user. Ordinary users can use this call to change the group of their own files.

The UMASK system call allows the user to set a mask (stored in the process table), which then masks out bits in subsequent CREAT system calls. The complete implementation would be only one statement, except that the call must return the old mask value as its result. This additional burden triples the number of lines of code required.

The ACCESS system call makes it possible for process to find out if it can access a file in a specified way (e.g., for reading). It is implemented by *do_access,* which fetches the file's i-node and calls the internal procedure, *forbidden,* to see if the access is forbidden. *Forbidden* checks the uid and gid, as well as the information in the i-node. Depending on what it finds, it selects one of the three *rwx* groups and checks to see if the access is permitted or forbidden.

Read_only is a little internal procedure that the whether the file system on which its i-node parameter is located is mounted read only or read-write. It is needed to prevent writes on file systems mounted read only.

Time

MINIX has several system calls that involve time: UTIME, TIME, STIME, and TIMES. They are summarized in Fig 10.21. Although most of them do not have anything to do with files, it makes sense to include them in the file system because time information is recorded in a file's i-node.

Call	Function
UTIME	Set a file's time of last modification
TIME	Set the current real time in seconds
STIME	Set the real time clock
TIMES	Get the process accounting times

Fig. 10.21. The four system calls involving time.

Associated with each file are three 32-bit numbers. Two of these record the times when the file was last accessed and last modified. The third records when the status of the i-node itself was last changed. The time will change for almost every access to a file except a READ or EXEC. These times are kept in the i-node. With the UTIME system call, the access and modification times can be set by the owner of the file or the super-user. The procedure *do_utime* in file *time.c* performs the system call by fetching the i-node and storing the time in it.

The real time is not maintained by the file system. It is maintained by the clock task within the kernel. Consequently, the only way to get or set the real time is to send a message to the clock task. This is, in fact, what *do_time* and *do_stime* both do. The real time is in seconds, since Jan 1, 1970.

The accounting information is also maintained by the kernel. At each clock tick it charges one tick to some process. This information can be retrieved by sending a messages to the system task, which is what *do_tims* does. The procedure is not named *do_times* because most C compilers add an underscore to the front of all external symbols, and most linkers truncate symbols to eight characters, which would make *do_time* indistinguishable from *do_times*.

Leftovers

The file *misc.c* contains procedures for a few system calls that do not fit in anywhere else. The DUP system call duplicates a file descriptor. In other words, it creates a new file descriptor that points to the same file as its argument. The call has a variant DUP2. Both versions of the call are handled by *do_dup*. This function is included in MINIX to support old binary program. Both of these calls are obsolete. The current version of the MINIX C library will invoke the FCNTL system call when either of these are encountered in a C source file.

Operation	Meaning
F_DUPFD	Duplicate a file descriptor
F_GETFD	Get the close-on-exec flag
F_SETFD	Set the close-on-exec flag
F_GETFL	Get file status flags
F_SETFL	Set file status flags
F_GETLK	Get lock status of a file
F_SETLK	Set read/write lock on a file
F_SETLKW	Set write lock on a file

Fig. 10.22. The POSIX request parameters for the FCNTL system call.

FCNTL, handled by *do_fcntl* is the preferred way to request operations on an open file. Services are requested using POSIX-defined flags described in Fig.10.22. The call is invoked with a file descriptor, a request code, and additional arguments as necessary for the particular request. For instance, the equivalent of the old call

```
dup2 (fd, fd2);
```

would be

```
fcntl (fd, F_DUPFD, fd2);
```

Several of these request set or read a flag; the code consists of just a few lines. For instance, the *F_SETFD* request sets a bit that forces closing of a file when its owner process does an EXEC. The *F_GETFD* request is used to determine whether a file must be closed when an EXEC call is made. The *F_SETFL F_GETFL* requests permit setting flags to indicate a particular file is available in nonblocking mode or for append operations.

Do_fcntl handles file locking, also. A call with the *F_GETLK, F_SETLK,* or *F_SETLKW* command specified is translated into a call to *lock_op,* discussed in an earlier section.

The next system call is SYNC, which copies all blocks and i-nodes that have been modified since being loaded back to the disk. The call is processed by *do_sync*. It simply searches through all the tables looking for dirty entries. The i-nodes must be processed first, since *rw_inode* leaves its results in the block cache. After all dirty i-nodes are written to the block cache, then all dirty blocks are written to the disk.

The system calls FORK, EXEC, EXIST, and SET are really memory manager calls, but the results have to be posted here as well. When a process forks, it is essential that the kernel, memory manager, and file system all know about it. These "system calls" do not come from user processes, but from the memory manager. *Do_fork, do_exit,* and *do_set* record the relevant information in the file system's part of the process table. *Do_exec* search for and closes (using *do_close*) any files marked to be closed-on-exec.

The last function in this file is not really a system call but is handled like one. This is *do_revive.* It is called when a task that was previously unable to complete work that the file system had requested, such as providing input data for a user process, has now completed the work. The file system then revives the process and sends it the reply message.

The I/O Device Interface

I/O in MINIX is done by sending messages to the tasks within the kernel. The file system's interface with these tasks is contained in the file *device.c.* When actual devices I/O is needed, *dev_io* is called from *read_write* to handle character special files, and from *rw_block* for block special files. It builds a standard message and sends it to the specified task. Tasks are called by the line

```
(*dmap[major].dmap_rw)(task, &dev_mess);
```

This call functions via pointers in the *dmap* array defined in *table.c.* The functions that take care of this are all here in *device.c.* While *dev_io* is waiting for a reply from the task, the file system waits. It has no internal multiprogramming. Usually, these waits are quite short though.

Special files may need special processing when they are opened or closed. Exactly what must be done depends upon the type of device. The *dmap* table is also used to determine which functions are called for opening and closing each type of major device. The procedure *dev_opcl* is called for disk devices, whether floppy disks, hard disks, or memory-based devices. The line

```
mess_ptr->PROC_NR = fp – fproc;
```

calculates the process number of the caller. The actual work is done by passing the task number and a pointer to the message to *call_task,* to be discussed below. *Dev_opcl* is also used to close the same devices. In fact, the only difference in the open and close functions at the level of this function is in what happens after the return from *call_task*.

Other functions called via the *dmap* struct include *tty_open* and *tty_close*, which service the serial lines, and *ctty_open* and *ctty_close* which service the console. The last of these, *ctty_close*, is almost a dummy routine, as all it does is to return status *OK* unconditionally.

The SETSID call requires some work by the file system, and this is performed by *do_setsid*. One system call, IOCTL, is handled primarily in *device.c*. This call has been put here because it is closely tied to the task interface. When an IOCTL is done, *do_ioctl* is called to build a message and send it to the proper task.

To control terminal devices one of the functions declared in *include/termios.h* should be used in programs written to the POSIX compliant. The C library will translate such functions into IOCTL calls.

The next function is the only *PRIVATE* functions in this file. This is *find_dev* a little helper procedure that extracts the major and minor device numbers from a full device number.

The actual reading and writing of most devices goes through *call_task*, which directs a message to the appropriate task in the kernel image, by calling *sendrec*. The attempt may fail if the task is trying to revive a process in response to an earlier request. It will likely be a different process from the one on behalf of which the current request is being made. *Call_task* will display a message on the console if an inappropriate message is received. These messages hopefully will not be seen during normal operation of MINIX but could appear during attempts to develop a new device driver.

The device */dev/tty* does not physically exist. It is a fiction to which any user on a multiuser system can refer, without a need to determine which of all possible real terminals is in use. When a message that refers to */dev/tty* must be sent, the next function, *call_ctty*, finds the correct major and minor device and substitutes them into the message before passing the message on a via *call_task*.

Finally, the last function in the file is *no_dev*, which is called from slots in the table for which a device does not exist, for example when a network device is referenced on a machine with no network support. It returns an *ENODEV* status. It prevents crashes when nonexistent devices are accessed.

General Utilities

The file system contains a few general purpose utility procedures that are used in various places. They are collected together in the file *utility.c*.

The first procedure is *clock_time*. It sends messages to the clock task to find out what the current real time is. The next procedure, *fetch_name*, is needed because many system calls have a file name as parameter. If the file name is short, it is included in the message from the user to the file system. If it is long, a pointer to the name in user space is put in the message. *Fetch_name* checks for both cases, and either way, gets the name.

Two functions here handle general classes of errors. *No_sys* is error handler that is called when the file system receives a system call that is not one of its calls. *Panic* prints a message and tells the kernel to throw in the towel when something catastrophic happens.

The last two functions, *conv2* and *conv4,* exist to help MINIX deal with the problem of different byte orders on Intel and Motorola processors. These routines are called when reading from or writing to a disk data structure, such as an i-node or bit map. The byte order in the system that created the disk is recorded in the super-block. If it is different from the order used by the local processor the order will be swapped. The rest of the file system does not need to know anything about the byte order on the disk.

The last file is *putk.c.* It contains two procedures, both of which have to do with printing messages. The standard library procedures cannot be used, because they send messages to the file system. Theses procedures send messages directly to the terminal task. We saw an almost identical pair of functions in the memory manager's version of this file.

Summary of the Case Study

When seen from the outside, a file system is a collection of files and directories, plus operations on them. Files can be read and written, directories can be created and destroyed, and files can be moved from directory to directory. Most modern file systems support a hierarchical directory systems, in which directories many have subdirectories ad infinitum.

When seen from the inside, a file system looks quite different. The file system designers have to be concerned with how storage is allocated, and how the system keeps track of which block goes with which file. We have also seen how different systems have different directory structures. File system reliability and performance are also important issues.

11

I/O Systems

The devices that attach to a computer vary in many aspects. Some devices transfer a character or a block of characters at a time. Some can be accessed only sequentially, others randomly. Some transfer data synchronously, others asynchronously. Some are dedicated, some shared. They can be read-only or read–write. They vary greatly in speed. In many ways they are also the slowest major component of the computer.

Because of all this device variation, the operating system needs to provide a wide range of functionality to applications to allow them to control all aspects of the devices. One key goal of an operating systems I/O subsystem is to provide the simplest interface possible to the rest of the system. Because devices are a performance bottleneck, another key is to optimize I/O for maximum concurrency. We initially describe the myraid variations of I/O devices and the ways in which operating system's control them. Afterwards we discuss the more complicated I/O devices used for secondary and tertiary storage, and we explain the special attention that operating systems must give them.

I/O Systems

The two main jobs of a computer are I/O and processing. In may cases, the main job is I/O and the processing is merely incidental. For instance, when we browse a web page or edit a file, our immediate interest is to read or enter some information, not to compute an answer.

The role of the operating system in computer I/O is to manage and control I/O operations and I/O devices. Although related topics appear in other chapters, here we bring together the pieces to paint a complete picture of I/O. First we describe the basis of I/O hardware because the nature of the hardware interface places requirements on the internal facilities of the operating system. Next, we discuss the I/O services provided by the operating system, and the embodiment of these services in the application I/O interface. Then, we explain how the operating system bridges the gap between the hardware interface and the application interface. We also discuss the UNIX System V STREAMS mechanism, which enables an application to assemble pipelines of driver code dynamically. Finally, we discuss the performance aspects of I/O, and the principles of operating-system design that improve the I/O performance.

Overview of I/O Systems

The control of devices connected to the computer is a major concern of operating-system designers. Because I/O devices vary so widely in their function and speed (consider a mouse, a hard disk, and a CD-ROM jukebox), a variety of methods are needed to control them. These methods form the *I/O subsystem* of the kernel, which separates the rest of the kernel from the complexity of managing I/O devices.

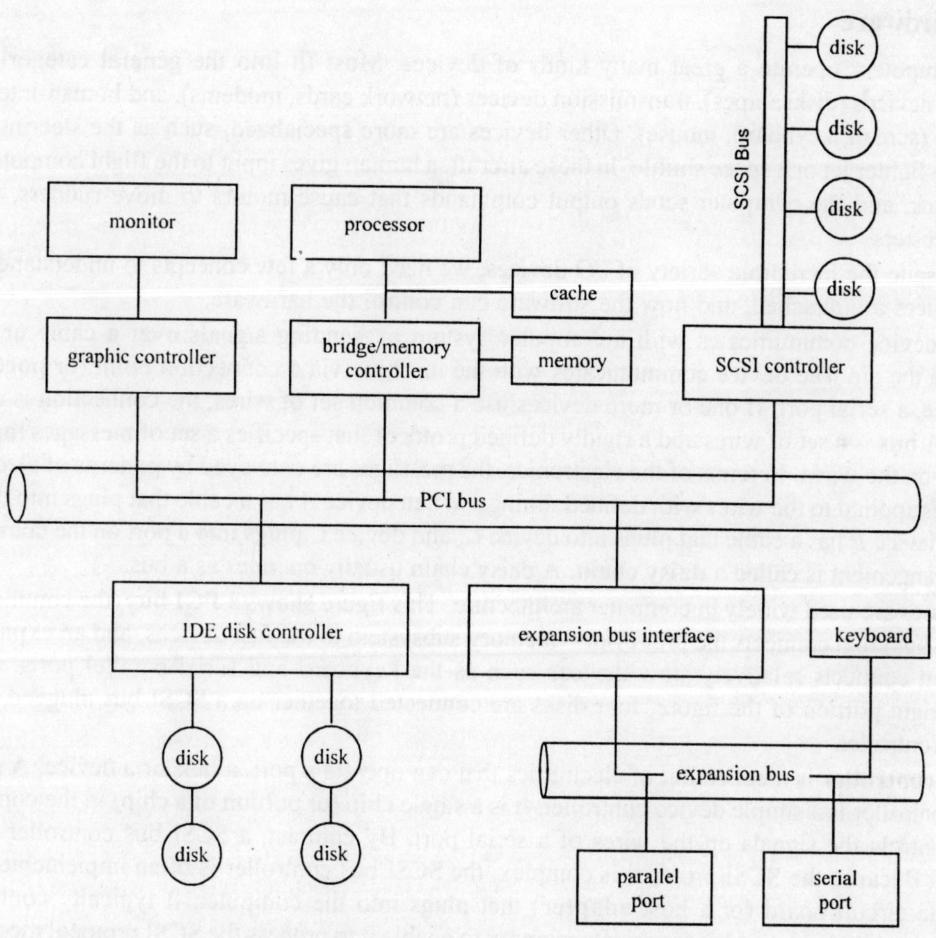

Fig. 11.1. A typical PC bus structure.

I/O-device technology exhibits two conflicting trends. On one hand, we see increasing standardization of software and hardware interfaces. This trend helps us to incorporate improved device generations into existing computers and operating systems. On the other hand, we see an increasingly broad variety of I/O devices. Some new devices are so unlike previous devices that it is a challenge to incorporate them into our computers and operating systems. This challenge is met by a combination of hardware and software techniques. This basic I/O hardware elements, such as ports, buses, and device controllers, accommodate a wide variety of I/O devices. To encapsulate the details and oddities of different devices, the kernel of an operating system is structured to use device-driver modules. The **device drivers** present a uniform device-access interface to the I/O subsystem, much as system calls provide a standard interface between the application and the operating system.

I/O Hardware

Computers operate a great many kinds of devices. Most fit into the general categories of storage devices (disks, tapes), transmission devices (network cards, modems), and human-interface devices (screen, keyboard, mouse). Other devices are more specialized, such as the steering of a military fighter jet or a space shuttle. In these aircraft, a human gives input to the flight computer via a joystick, and the computer sends output commands that cause motors to move rudders, flaps, and thrusters.

Despite the incredible variety of I/O devices, we need only a few concepts to understand how the devices are attached, and how the software can control the hardware.

A device communicates with a computer system by sending signals over a cable or even through the air. The device communicates with the machine via a connection point (or **port**), for example, a serial port. If one or more devices use a common set of wires, the connection is called a *bus*. A **bus** is a set of wires and a rigidly defined protocol that specifies a set of messages that can be sent on the wires. In terms of the electronics, the messages are conveyed by patterns of electrical voltages applied to the wires with defined timings. When device *A* has a cable that plugs into device *B*, and device *B* has a cable that plugs into device *C*, and device *C* plugs into a port on the computer, this arrangement is called a **daisy chain.** A daisy chain usually operates as a bus.

Buses are used widely in computer architecture. This figure shows a **PCI bus** (the common PC system bus) that connects the processor – memory subsystem to the fast devices, and an **expansion bus** that connects relatively slow devices such as the keyboard and serial parallel ports. In the upper-right portion of the figure, four disks are connected together on a SCSI bus plugged into a SCSI controller.

A **controller** is a collection of electronics that can operate a port, a bus, or a device. A serial-port controller is a simple device controller. It is a single chip (or portion of a chip) in the computer that controls the signals on the wires of a serial port. By contrast, a SCSI bus controller is not simple. Because the SCSI protocol is complex, the SCSI bus controller is often implemented as a separate circuit board (or a host **adapter**) that plugs into the computer. It typically contains a processor, microcode, and some private memory to enable it to process the SCSI protocol messages. Some devices have their own built-in controllers. If you look at a disk drive, you will see a circuit board attached to one side. This board is the disk controller. It implements the disk side of the protocol for some kind of connection, SCSI or IDE, for instance. It has microcode and a processor to do many tasks, such as bad-sector mapping, prefetching, buffering, and caching.

How can the processor give commands and data to a controller to accomplish an I/O transfer? The short answer is that the controller has one or more registers for data and control signals. The processor communicates with the controller by reading and writing bit patterns in these registers.

One way that this communication can occur is through the use of special I/O instructions that specify the transfer of a byte or word to an I/O port address. The I/O instruction triggers bus lines to select the proper device and to move bits into or out of a device register. Alternatively, the device controller can support **memory-mapped** I/O. In this case, the device-control registers are mapped into the address space of the processor. The CPU executes I/O requests using the standard data-transfer instructions to read and write the device-control registers.

Some systems use both techniques. For instance, PCs use I/O instructions to control some devices and memory-mapped I/O to control others. The graphics controller has I/O ports for basic control operations, but the controller has a large memory-mapped region to hold screen contents. The process sends output to the screen by writing data into the memory-mapped region. The controller generates the screen image based on the contents of this memory. This technique is simple to use. Moreover, writing millions of bytes to the graphics memory is faster than issuing millions of I/O instructions. But the ease of writing to a memory-mapped I/O controller is offset by a disadvantage. Because a common type of software fault is a write through an incorrect pointer to an unintended region of memory, a memory-mapped device register is vulnerable to accidental modification. Of course, protected memory helps to reduce this risk.

An I/O port typically consists of four registers, called the *status, control, data-in,* and *data-out* registers.

I/O address range (hexadecimal)	Device
000-00F	DMA controller
020-021	interrupt controller
40-043	timer
200-20F	game controller
2F8-2FF	serial port (secondary)
320-32F	hard-disk controller
378-37F	parallel port
3D0-3DF	graphics controller
3F0-3F7	diskette-drive controller
3F8-3FF	serial port (primary)

***Fig. 11.2.** Device I/O port locations on PCs (partial).*

- The *status* registers contains bits that can be ready by the host. These bits indicate states such as whether the current command has completed, whether a byte is available to be read from the data-in register, and whether there has been a device error.
- The *control* register can be written by the host to start a command or to change the mode of a device. For instance, a certain bit in the control register of a serial port chooses between full-duplex and half-duplex communication, another enables parity checking, a third bit sets the word length to 7 or 8 bits, and other bits select one of the speeds supported by the serial port.
- The *data-in* register is read by the host to get input.
- The *data-out* register is written by the host to send output.

The data register are typically 1 to 4 bytes. Some controller have FIFO chips that can hold several bytes of input or output data to expand the capacity of the controller beyond the size of the data register. A FIFO chip can hold a small burst of data until the device or host is able to receive those data.

Polling

The complete protocol for interaction between the host and a controller can be intricate, but the basic *handshaking* notion is simple. We explain handshaking by an example. We assume that 2 bits are used to coordinate the producer-consumer relationship between the controller and the host. The controller indicates its state through the busy bit in the status register. (Recall that to set a bit means to write a 1 into the bit, and to *clear* a bit means to write a 0 into it.) The controller sets the *busy* bit when it is busy working, and clears the *busy* bit when it is ready to accept the next command. The host signals its wishes via the *command-ready* bit in the *command* register. The host sets the *command-ready* bit when a command is available for the controller to execute. For this example, the host writes output through a port, coordinating with the controller by handshaking as follows.

- The host repeatedly reads the *busy* bit until that bit becomes clear.
- The host sets the *write* bit in the *command* register and writes a byte into the *data-out* register.
- The host sets the *command-ready* bit.
- When the controller notices that the *command-ready* bit is set, it sets the *busy* bit.
- The controller reads the command register and sees the write command. It reads the *data-out* register to get the byte, and dose the I/O to the device.
- The controller clears the *command-ready* bit, clears the *error* bit in the status register to indicate that the device I/O succeeded, and clears the *busy* bit to indicate that it is finished.

This loop is repeated for each byte.

In step 1, the host is **busy-waiting** or **polling:** It is in a loop, reading the *status* register over and over until the *busy* bit becomes clear. If the controller and device are fast, this method is a reasonable one. But if the wait may be long, the host should probably switch to another task. How then does the host know when the controller has become idle? For some devices, the host must service the device quickly, or date will be lost. For instance, when data are streaming in on a serial port or from a keyboard, the small buffer on the controller will overflow and data will be lost if the host waits too long before returning to read the bytes.

In many computer architectures, three CPU-instruction cycles are sufficient to poll a device: *read* a device register, *logical-and* to extract a status bit, and *branch* if not zero. Clearly, the basic polling operation is efficient. But polling becomes inefficient when it is attempted repeatedly, yet rarely finds a device to be ready for service, while other useful CPU processing remains undone. In such instances, it may be more efficient to arrange for the hardware controller to notify the CPU when the device becomes ready for service, rather than to require the CPU to poll repeatedly for an I/O completion. The hardware mechanism that enable a device to notify the CPU is called an **interrupt.**

Interrupts

The basic interrupt mechanism works as follows. The CPU hardware has a wire called the **interrupt-request line** that the CPU senses after executing every instruction. When the CPU detects that a controller has asserted a signal on the interrupt request line, the CPU saves a small amount of state, such as the current value of the instruction pointer, and jumps to the **interrupt-handler** routine at a fixed address in memory. The interrupt handler determines the cause of the interrupt, performs the necessary processing, and executes a return from interrupt instruction to return the CPU to the execution state prior to the interrupt. We say that the device controller *raises* an interrupt by asserting a signal on the interrupt request line, the CPU *catches* the interrupt and *dispatches* to the interrupt handler, and the handler *clears* the interrupt by servicing the device.

This basic interrupt mechanism enables the CPU to respond to an asynchronous event, such as a device controller becoming ready for service. In a modern operating system, we need more sophisticated interrupt-handling features. First, we need the ability to defer interrupt handling during critical processing. Second, we need an efficient way to dispatch to the proper interrupt handler for a device, without first polling all the devices to see which one raised the interrupt. Third, we need multilevel interrupts, so that the operating system can distinguish between high-and low-priority interrupts, and can respond with the appropriate degree of urgency. In modern computer hardware, these three features are provided by the CPU and by the **interrupt-controller** hardware.

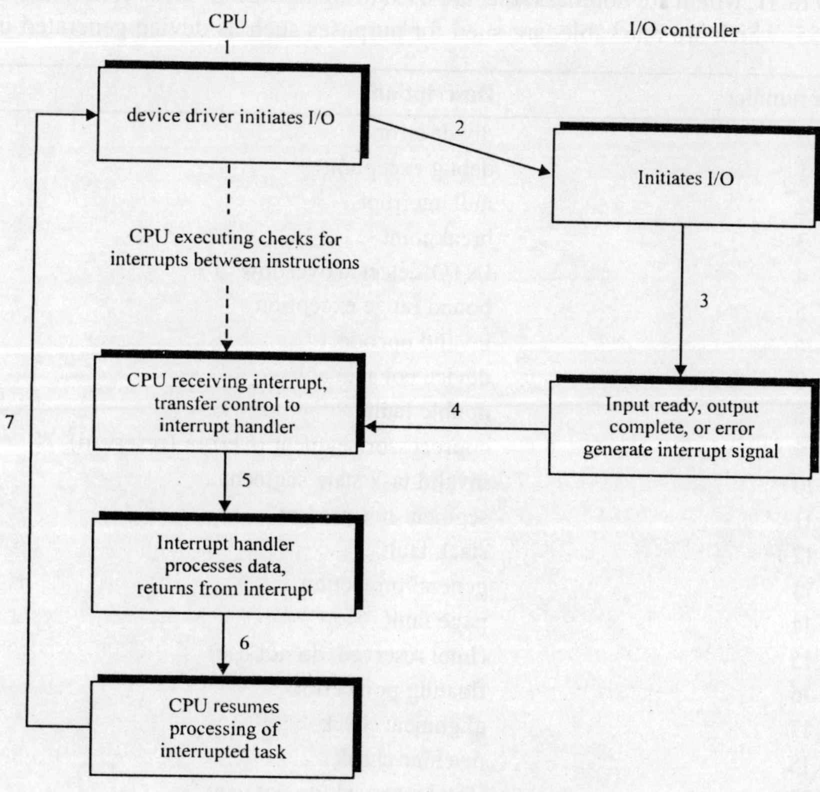

Fig. 11.3. Interrupt-driven I/O cycle.

Most CPUs have two interrupt request lines. One is the **nonmaskable interrupt**, which is reserved for event such as unrecoverable memory errors. The second interrupt line is **maskable:** It can be turned off by the CPU before the execution of critical instruction sequences that must not be interrupted. The maskable interrupt is used by device controllers to request service.

The interrupt mechanism accepts an **address**—a number that selects a specific interrupt-handling routine from a small set. In most architectures, this address is an offset in a table called the **interrupt vector.** This vector contains the memory addresses of specialized interrupt handlers. The purpose of a vectored interrupt mechanism is to reduce the need for a single interrupt handler to search all possible sources of interrupts to determine which one needs service. In practice, however, computers have more devices (and hence, interrupt handlers) than they have address elements in the interrupt vector. A common way to solve this problem is to use the technique of interrupt chaining, in which each element in the interrupt vector points to the head of a list of interrupt handlers. When an interrupt is raised, the handler on the corresponding list are called one by one, until one is found that can service the request. The structure is a compromise between the overhead of a huge interrupt table and the inefficiency of a dispatching to a single interrupt handler.

Figure 11.4 illustrates the design of the interrupt vector for the Intel Pentium processor. The events from 0 to 31, which are nonmaskable, are used to signal various error conditions. The events from 32 to 255, which are maskable, are sued for purposes such as device-generated interrupts.

Vector number	Description
0	divide error
1	debug exception
2	null interrupt
3	breakpoint
4	INTO-detected overflow
5	bound range exception
6	invalid opcode
7	device not available
8	double fault
9	coprocessor segment overrun (reserved)
10	invalid task state segment
11	segment not present
12	stack fault
13	general protection
14	page fault
15	(Intel reserved, do not use)
16	floating-point error
17	alignment check
18	machine check
19-31	(Intel reserved, do not use)
32-255	maskable interrupts

Fig. 11.4. *Intel Pentium processor event-vector table.*

The interrupt mechanism also implements a system of **interrupt priority levels.** This mechanism enables the CPU to defer the handling of low-priority interrupt without masking off all interrupts, and makes it possible for high-priority interrupt to preempt the execution of a low-priority interrupt.

A modern operating system interacts with the interrupt mechanism in several ways. At boot time, the operating system probes the hardware buses to determine what devices are present, and installs the corresponding interrupt handlers into the interrupt vector. During I/O, the various device controllers raise interrupts when they are ready for service. These interrupts signify that output has completed, or that input data are available, or that a failure has been detected. The interrupt mechanism is also used to handle a wide variety of **exceptions**, such as dividing by zero, accessing a protected or nonexistent memory address, or attempting to execute a privileged instruction from user mode. The event that trigger interrupts have a common property: They are occurrences that induce the CPU to execute an urgent, self-contained routine.

An operating system has other good uses for an efficient hardware mechanism that saves a small amount of processor state, and then calls a privileged routine in the kernel. For example, many operating systems use the interrupt mechanism for virtual-memory paging. A page fault is an exception that raises in interrupt. The interrupt suspends the current process and jumps to the pagefault handler in the kernel. This handler saves the sates of the process, moves the process to the wait queue, performs page-cache management, schedules an I/O operation to fetch the page, schedules another process to resume execution, and then returns from the interrupt.

Interrupts can also be used to mange the flow of control within the kernel. For example, consider the processing required to complete a disk read. One steps is to copy data from kernel space to the user buffer. This copying is time consuming but not urgent—it should not block other high-priority interrupt handling. Another step is to start the next pending I/O for that disk drive. This step has higher priority: If the disks are to be used efficiently, we need to start the next I/O as soon as the previous one completes. Consequently, a *pair* of interrupt handlers implements the kernel code that completes a disk read. The high-priority handler records the I/O statues, clears the device interrupt, starts the next pending I/O, and raises a low-priority interrupt to complete the work. Later, when the CPU is not occupied with high-priority work, the low-priority interrupt will be dispatched. The corresponding handler completes the user-level I/O by copying data from kernel buffers to the application space, and then by calling the scheduler to place the application on the ready queue.

A threaded kernel architecture is well suited to implement multiple interrupt priorities and to enforce the precedence of interrupt handling over background processing in kernel and application routines. We illustrate this point with the Solaris kernel. In Solaris, interrupt handlers are executed as kernel threads. A range of high priorities is reserved for these threads. These priorities give interrupt handlers precedence over application code and kernel housekeeping, and implement the priority relationships among interrupt handlers. The priorities cause the Solaris thread scheduler to preempt low-priority interrupt handlers in favor of higher-priority ones, and the threaded implementation enables multiprocessor hardware to run several interrupt handlers concurrently. We describe the interrupt architecture of UNIX and Windows NT in Appendix A respectively.

In summary, interrupts are used throughout modern operating system to handle asynchronous events and to trap to supervisor-mode routines in the kernel. To enable the most urgent work to be done first, modern computers use a system of interrupt priorities. Device controllers, hardware faults, and system calls all raise interrupts to trigger kernel routines. Because interrupts are used so heavily of time-sensitive processing, efficient interrupt handling is required for good system performance.

Direct Memory Access (DMA)

For a device that does large transfers, such as a disk drive, it seems wasteful to use an expensive general-purpose processor to watch status bits and to feed data into a controller register 1 byte at a time—a process termed **programmed I/O (PIO).** Many computers avoid burdening the main CPU with PIO by offloading some of this work to a special-purpose processor called a **direct-memory-access (DMA)** controller. To initiate a DMA transfer, the host writes a DMA command block into memory. This block contains a pointer to the source of a transfer, a pointer to the destination of the transfer and a count of the number of bytes to be transferred. The CPU writes the address of this command block to the DMA controller, then goes on with other work. The DMA controller proceeds to operate the memory bus directly, placing addresses on the bus to perform transfers without the help of the main CPU. A simple DMA controller is a standard component in PCs, and **bus-mastering** I/O boards for the PC usually contain their own high-speed DMA hardware.

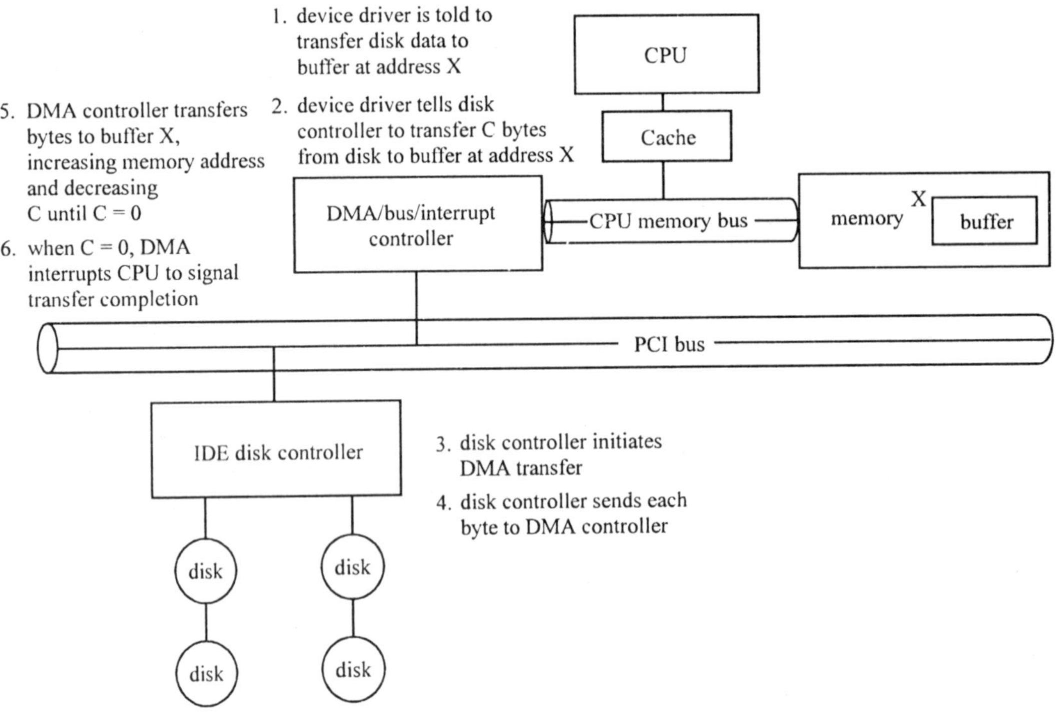

Fig. 11.5. Steps in a DMA transfer.

Handshaking between the DMA controller and the device controller is performed via a pair of wires called DMA-request and DMA-acknowledge. The device controller places a signal on the DMA-request wire when a word of data is available for transfer. This signal causes the DMA controller to seize the memory bus, to place the desired address on the memory-address wires, and to place a signal on the DMA–acknowledge wire. When the device controller receives the DMA–acknowledge signal, it transfers the word of data to memory, and removes the DMA-request signal.

When the entire transfer is finished, the DMA controller interrupts the CPU. When the DMA controller seizes the memory bus, the CPU is momentarily prevented from accessing main memory, although it can still access data items in its primary and secondary cache. Although this **cycle stealing** can slow down the CPU computation, offloading the data-transfer work to a DMA controller generally improves the total system performance. Some computer architectures use physical memory addresses for DMA, but others perform **direct virtual-memory access (DVMA),** using virtual addresses that undergo virtual to physical-memory addresses translation DVMA can perform a transfer between two memory-mapped devices without the intervention of the CPU or the use of main memory.

On protected-mode kernels, the operating generally prevents processes from issuing device commands directly. This discipline protects data from access-control violations, and also protects the system from erroneous use of device controllers that could cause a system crash. Instead, the operating system exports functions that a sufficiently privileged process can use to access low-level operations on the underlying hardware. On kernels without memory protection, processes can access device controllers directly. This direct access can be used to obtain high performance, since it can avoid kernel communication, context switches, and layers of kernel software. Unfortunately, it interferes with system security and stability. The trend in general-purpose operating systems is to protect memory and devices, so that the system can try to guard against erroneous or malicious applications.

Although the hardware aspects of I/O are complex when considered at the level of detail of electronics-hardware designers, the concepts that we have just described are sufficient to understand many I/O aspects of operating systems. Let's review the main concepts:

- A bus
- A controller
- An I/O port and its registers
- The handshaking relationship between the host and a device controller
- The execution of this handshaking in a polling loop or via interrupts
- The offloading of this work to a DMA controller for larges transfers

We gave a basic example of the handshaking that takes place between a device controller and the host. In reality, the wide variety of available devices poses a problem for operating-system implementers. Each kind of device has its own set of capabilities, control-bit definitions, and protocol for interacting with the host—and they are all different. How can the operating system be designed so that new devices can be attached to the computer without the operating system being rewritten? Also, when the devices vary so widely, how can the operating system give a convenient, uniform I/O interface to applications?

Application I/O Interface

In this section, we discuss structuring techniques and interfaces for the operating system that enable I/O devices to be treated in a standard, uniform way. We explain, for instance, how an application can open a file on a disk without knowing what kind of disk it is, and how new disks and other devices can be added to a computer without the operating system being disrupted.

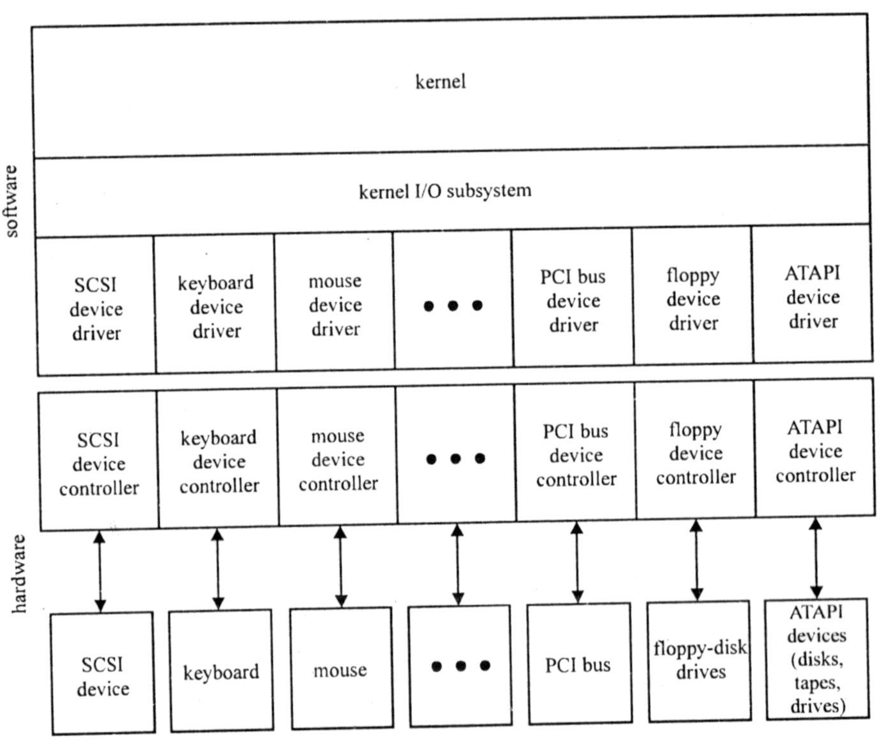

Fig. 11.6. A Kernel I/O structure.

Like other complex software-engineering problems, the approach here involves abstraction, encapsulation, and software layering. Specifically, we can abstract away the detailed differences in I/O devices by identifying a few general kinds. Each general kind is accessed through a standardized set of functions—an **interface.** The differences are encapsulated in kernel modules called device drivers that internally are custom tailored to each device, but that export one of the standard interfaces. Figure 11.6 illustrates how the I/O-related portions of the kernel are structured in software layers.

The purpose of the device-driver layer is to hide the differences among device controllers from the I/O subsystem of the kernel, much as the I/O system calls encapsulate the behaviour of devices in a few generic classes the hide hardware differences from applications. Making the I/O subsystem independent of the hardware simplifies the job of the operating-system developer. It also benefits the hardware manufacture. They either design new devices to be compatible with an existing host controller interface (such as SCSI-2), or they write device drivers to interface the new hardware to popular operating systems. Thus, new peripherals can be attached to a computer without waiting for the operating-system vendor to develop support code.

Unfortunately for device-hardware manufacture, each type of operating system has its own standards for the device-driver interface. A given device may ship with multiple device drivers—for instance, drivers for MS-DOS, Windows 95/98, Windows NT/2000, and Solaris. Devices vary in many dimensions, as illustrated in Figure 11.7.

aspect	variation	example
data-transfer mode	charcater	terminal
	block	disk
access method	sequential	modem
	random	CD-ROM
transfer schedule	synchronous	tape
	asynchronous	keyboard
sharing	dedicated	tape
	sharable	keyboard
device speed	latency	
	seek time	
	transfer rate	
	delay between operations	
I/O direction	read only	CD-ROM
	write only	graphics controller
	read-write	

Fig. 11.7. Characteristics of I/O devices.

- **Character-stream or block:** A character-stream device transfers bytes one by one, whereas a block device transfers a block of bytes as a unit.
- **Sequential or random-access:** A sequential device transfers data in a fixed order determined by the device, whereas the user of a random-access device can instruct the device to seek to any of the available data storage locations.
- **Synchronous or asynchronous:** A synchronous device is one that performs data transfers with predictable response times. An asynchronous device exhibits irregular or unpredictable response times.
- **Sharable or dedicated:** A sharable device can be used concurrently by several processes or threads; a dedicated device cannot.
- **Speed of operation:** Device speeds range from a few bytes per second to a few gigabytes per second.
- **Read-write, read only, or write only:** Some devices perform both input and output, but others support only one data direction.

For the purpose of application access, many of these differences are hidden by the operating system, and the devices are grouped into a few conventional types. The resulting styles of device access have been found to be useful and broadly applicable. Although the exact system calls may differ across operating system, the device categories are fairly standard. The major access conventions include block I/O, character-stream I/O, memory-mapped file access, and network sockets. Operating system also provide special system calls to access a few additional devices, such as a time-of-day clock and a timer. Some operating systems provide a set of system calls for graphical display, video, and audio devices.

Most operating system also have an **escape (or back-door)** that transparently passes arbitrary commands from an application to a device driver. In UNIX, this system calls is ioctl ( ) (for I/O control). The ioctl ( ) system call enables an application to access any functionally that can be implemented by any device driver, without the need to invent a new system call. The ioctl ( ) system call has three arguments. The first is a file descriptor that connects the application to the driver by referring to a hardware device managed by that driver. The second is an integer that selects one of the commands implemented in the driver. The third is a pointer to an arbitrary data structure in memory, thus enabling the application and driver to communicate any necessary control information or data.

Block and Character Devices

The **block-device** interface captures all the aspects necessary for accessing disk drives and other block-oriented devices. The expectation is that the device understands commands such as read ( ) and write ( ), and, if it is a random-access device, it has a seek ( ) command to specify which block to transfer next. Applications normally access such a device through a file-system interface. The operating system itself, and special applications such as database-management systems, may prefer to access a block device as a simple linear array of blocks. This mode of access is some-times called **raw I/O.** We can see that read ( ), write ( ), and seek ( ) capture the essential behaviors of block-storage devices, so that applications are insulated from the low-level differences among those devices.

Memory-mapped file access can be layered on top of block-device drivers. Rather than offering read and write operations, a memory-mapped interface provides access to disk storage via an array of bytes in main memory. The system call that maps a file into memory returns the virtual-memory address of an array of characters that contains a copy of the file. The actual data transfers are performed only when needed to satisfy access to the memory image. Because the transfers are handled by the same mechanism as that used for demand-paged virtual-memory access, memory-mapped I/O is efficient. Memory mapping is also convenient for programmers—access to a memory-mapped file is as simple as reading and writing to memory. Operating systems that offer virtual memory commonly use the mapping interface for kernel services. For instance, to execute a program, the operating system maps the executable into memory, and then transfers control to the entry address of the executable. The mapping interface is also commonly used for kernel access to swap space on disk.

A keyboard is an example of a device that is accessed through a **character-stream** interface. The basic system calls in thin interface enable an application to get ( ) or put ( ) one character. On top of this interface, libraries can be built that offer line-at-a-time access, with buffering and editing services (for example, when a user types a backspace, the preceding character is removed from the input stream). This style of access is convenient for input devices such as keyboards, mice and modems, which produce data for input "spontaneously"—that is, at times that cannot necessarily be predicted by the application. This access style is also good for output devices such as printers or audio boards, which naturally fit the concept of a linear stream of bytes.

Network Devices

Because the performance and addressing characteristics of network I/O differ significantly from those of disk I/O, most operating systems provide a network I/O interface that is different from the read ( ) – write ( ) – seek ( ) interface used for disks. One interface available in many operating systems, including UNIX and Window, NT, is the network **socket** interface.

Think of a wall socket for electricity: Any electrical appliance can be plugged in. By analogy, the system calls in the socket interface enable an application to create a socket, to connect a local socket to a remote address (which plugs this application into a socket created by another application), to listen for any remote application to plug into the local socket, and to send and receive packets over the connection. To support the implementation of servers, the socket interface also provides a function called select ( ) that manages a set of sockets. A call to select ( ) returns information about which sockets have a packet waiting to be received, and which sockets have room to accept a packet to be sent. The use of select ( ) eliminates the polling and busy waiting that would otherwise be necessary for network I/O. These functions encapsulate the essential behaviors of networks, greatly facilitating the creating of distributed applications that can use any underlying network hardware and protocol stack.

Many other approaches to Interprocess communication and network communication have been implemented. For instance, Windows NT provides one interface to the network interface card, and a second interface to the network protocols. In UNIX, which has a long history as a proving ground for network technology, we find half-duplex pipes, full-duplex FIFOs, full–duplex STREAMS, message queues, and sockets. Information on UINX networking.

Clocks and Timers

Most computers have hardware clock and timers that provide three basic functions:

- Give the current time
- Give the elapsed time
- Set a timer to trigger operation *X* at time *T*

These functions are used heavily by the operating system, and also by time-sensitive applications. Unfortunately, the system calls that implement these functions are not standardized across operating systems.

The hardware to measure elapsed time and to trigger operations is called a **programmable interval timer.** It can be set to wait a certain amount of time and then to generate an interrupt. It can be set to do this operation once, or to repeat to process, to generate periodic interrupts. The scheduler used this mechanism to generate an interrupt that will preempt a process at the end of its time slice. The disk I/O subsystem uses it to invoke the flushing of dirty cache buffers to disk periodically, and the network subsystem uses it to cancel operations that are proceeding too slowly because of network congestion or failures. The operating system may also provide an interface for user processes to use timers. The operating system can support more timer requests than the number of timer hardware channels by simulating virtual clocks. To do so, the kernel (or the timer device driver) maintains a list of interrupts wanted by its own routines and by user requests, sorted in earliest-time-first order. It sets the timer for the earliest time. When the timer interrupts, the kernel signals the requester, and reloads the timer with the next earliest time.

On many computers, the interrupt rate generated by the ticking of the hardware clock is between 18 and 60 ticks per second. This resolution is coarse, since a modern computer can execute hundreds of millions of instructions per second. The precision of triggers is limited by the coarse resolution of the timer, together with the overhead of maintaining virtual clocks. And, if the timer ticks are used to maintain the system time-of-day clock, the system clock can drift. In most computers, the hardware clock is constructed from a high-frequency counter. In some computers, the value of this counter can be read from a device register, in which case the counter can be considered to be a high-resolution clock. Although this clock does not generate interrupts, it offers accurate measurements of time intervals.

Blocking and Nonblocking I/O

Another aspect of the system-call interface relates to the choice between blocking I/O and nonblocking (or asynchronous) I/O. When an application issues a **blocking** system call, the execution of the application is suspended. The application is moved from the operating system's run queue to a wait queue. After the system call completes, the application is moved back to the run queue, where it is eligible to resume execution, at which time it will receive the values returned by the system call. The physical actions performed by I/O devices are generally asynchronous—they take a varying or unpredictable amount of time. Nevertheless, most operating systems use blocking system calls for the application interface, because blocking application code is easier to understand than nonblocking application code.

Some user-level processes need **nonblocking** I/O. One example is a user interface that receives keyboard and mouse input while processing and displaying data on the screen. Another example is a video application that reads frames from a file on disk while simultaneously decompressing and displaying the output on the display.

An alternative to a nonblocking system call is an asynchronous system call. An asynchronous call returns immediately, without waiting for the I/O to complete. The application continues to execute its code. The completion of the I/O at some future time is communicated to the application, either through the setting of some variable in the address space of the application, or through the triggering of a signal or software interrupt or a call-back routine that is executed outside the linear control flow of the application. The difference between nonblocking and asynchronous system calls is that a nonblocking read ( ) returns immediately with whatever data are available—the full number of bytes requested, fewer, or none at all. An asynchronous read ( ) call requests a transfer that will be performed in its entirety, but that will complete at some future time.

A good example of nonblocking behavior is the select ( ) system call for network sockets. This system call takes an argument that specifies a maximum waiting time. By setting it to 0, an application can poll for network activity without blocking. But using select ( ) introduces extra overhead, because the select() call only checks whether I/O is possible. For a data transfer, select ( ) must be followed by some kind of read ( ) or write ( ) command. A variation of this approach, found in Mach, is a blocking multiple-read call. It specifies desired reads for several devices in one system call, and return as soon as any one of them completes.

Kernel I/O Subsystem

Kernels provide many services related to I/O. Several services—scheduling, buffering, caching, spooling, device reservation, and error handling—are provided by the kernel's I/O subsystem and build on the hardware and device-driver infrastructure.

I/O Scheduling

To schedule a set of I/O requests means to determine a good order in which to execute them. The order in which applications issue system calls rarely is the best choice. Scheduling can improve overall system performance can share device access fairly among processes, and can reduce the average waiting time for I/O to complete. Here is a simple example to illustrate the opportunity. Suppose that a disk arm is near the beginning of a disk, and that three applications issue blocking read calls to that disk. Application 1 request a block near the end of the disk, application 2 requests one near the beginning, and application 3 requests one in the middle of the disk. The operating system can reduce the distance that the disk arm travels by serving the application in order 2, 3, 1. Rearranging the order of service in this way is the essence of I/O scheduling.

Operating-system developers implement scheduling by maintaining a queue of requests for each device. When an application issues a blocking I/O system call, the request is placed on the queue for that device. The I/O scheduler rearranges the order of the queue to improve the overall system efficiency and the average response time experienced by applications. The operating system may also try to be fair, so that no one application receives especially poor service, or it may give priority service for delay-sensitive requests. For instance, requests from the virtual-memory subsystem may take priority over application requests.

One way that the I/O subsystem improves the efficiency of the computer is by scheduling I/O operations. Another way is by using storage space in main memory or on disk, via techniques called buffering, caching, and spooling.

Buffering

A **buffer** is a memory area that stores data while they are transferred between two devices or between a device and an application. Buffering is done for three reasons. One reason is to cope with a speed mismatch between the producer and consumer of a data stream. Suppose, for example, that a file is being received via modem for storage on the hard disk. The modem is about a thousand times slower that the hard disk. So a buffer is created in main memory to accumulate the bytes received fosr the modem. When an entire buffer of data has arrived, the buffer can be written to disk in a single operation. Since the disk write is not instantaneous and the modem still needs a place to store additional incoming data, two buffers are used. After the modem fills the first buffer, the disk write is requested. The modem then starts to fill the second buffer while the first buffer is written to disk. By the time the modem has filled the second buffer, the disk write from the first one should have completed, so the modem can switch back to the first buffer while the disk writes the second one. This **double buffering** decouples the producer of data from the consumer, thus relaxing timing requirements between them. The need for this decoupling is illustrated in Figures 11.8 which lists the enormous differences in device speeds for typical computer hardware.

A second use of buffering is to adapt between devices that have different data-transfer sizes. Such disparities are especially common in computer networking, where buffers are used widely for fragmentation and reassembly of messages. At the sending side, a large messages is fragmented into small network packets. The packets are sent over the network, and the receiving side places them in a reassembly buffer to form an image of the source data.

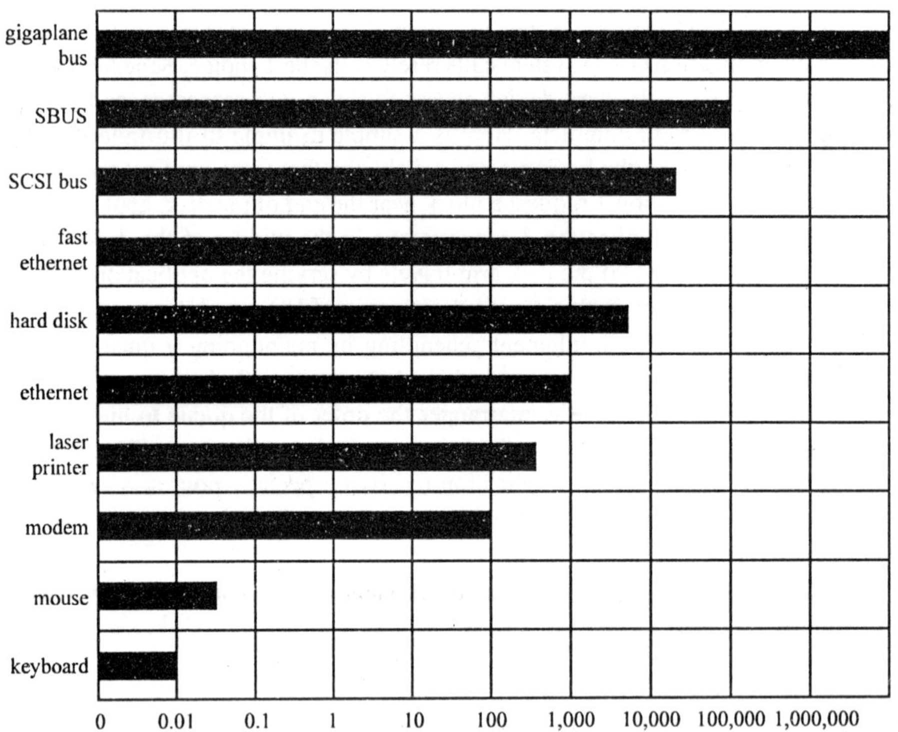

Fig. 11.8. Sun Enterprise 6000 device-transfer rates (logarithmic).

A third use of buffering is to support copy semantics for application I/O. An example will clarify the meaning of "copy semantics." Suppose that an application has a buffer of data that it wishes to write to disk. It calls the write ( ) system call, providing a pointer to the buffer and an integer specifying the number of bytes to write. After the system call returns, what happens if the application changes the contents of the buffer? With **copy semantics,** the version of the data written to disk is guaranteed to be the version at the time of the application system call, independent of any subsequent changes in the application's buffer. A simple way that the operating system can guarantee copy semantics is for the write ( ) system call to copy the application data into a kernel buffer before returning control to the application. The disk write is performed from the kernel buffer, so that subsequent changes to the application buffer have no effect. Copying of data between kernel buffers and application data space is common in operating systems despite the overhead that this operation introduces, because of the clean semantics. The same effect can be obtained more efficiently by clever use of virtual-memory mapping and copy-on-write page protection.

Caching

A **cache** is a region of fast memory that holds copies of data. Access to the cached copy is more efficient than access to the original. For instance, the instructions of the currently running process are stored on disk, cached in physical memory, and copied again in the CPU's secondary and primary caches. The difference between a buffer and a cache is that a buffer may hold the only existing copy of a data item, whereas a cache, by definition, just holds a copy on faster storage of an item that resides elsewhere.

Caching and buffering are distinct functions, but sometimes a region of memory can be used for both purposes. For instance to preserve copy semantics and to enable efficient scheduling of disk I/O, the operating system uses buffers in main memory to hold disk data. These buffers are also used as a cache, to improve the I/O efficiency for files that are shared by applications or that are being written and reread rapidly. When the kernel receives a file I/O request, the kernel first accesses the buffer cache to see whether that region of the file is already available in main memory. If so, a physical disk I/O can be avoided or deferred. Also, disk writes are accumulated in the buffer cache for several seconds, so that large transfers are gathered to allow efficient write schedules. This strategy of delaying writes to improve I/O efficiency is discussed, in the context of remote file access.

Spooling and Device Reservation

A **spool** is a buffer that holds output for a device, such as a printer, that cannot accept interleaved data streams. Although a pointer can serve only one job at a time, several applications may wish to print their output concurrently, without having their output mixed together. The operating system solves this problem by intercepting all output to the printer. Each application's output is spooled to a separate disk file. When an application finishes printing, the spooling system queues the corresponding spool file for output to the printer. The spooling system copies the queued spool files to the printer one at a time. In some operating systems, spooling is managed by a system daemon process. In other operating system, it is handled by an in-kernel thread. In either case, the operating system provides a control interface that enables users and system administrators is display the queue, to remove unwanted jobs before those jobs print, to suspend printing while the printer is serviced, and so on.

Some devices, such as tape drives and printers, cannot usefully multiplex the I/O requests of multiple concurrent applications. Spooling is one way that operating systems can coordinate concurrent output. Another way to deal with concurrent device access is to provide explicit facilities for coordination. Some operating systems (including VMS) provide support for exclusive devices access, by enabling a process to allocate in idle device, and to deallocate that device when it is no longer needed. Other operating systems enforce a limit of one open file handle to such a device. Many operating systems provide functions that enable processes to coordinate exclusive access among themselves. For instance, Windows NT provides system calls to wait until a device object becomes available. It also has a parameter to the open ( ) system call that declares the types of access to be permitted to other concurrent threads. On these systems, it is up to the applications to avoid deadlock.

Error Handling

An operating system that uses protected memory can guard against many kinds of hardware and application errors, so that a complete system failure is not the usual result of each minor mechanical glitch. Devices and I/O transfers can fail in many ways, either for transient reasons, such as a network becoming overloaded, or for "permanent" reasons, such as a disk controller becoming defective. Operating systems can often compensate effectively for transient failures. For instance, a disk read ( ) failure results in a read ( ) retry, and a network send ( ) error results in a resend ( ), if the protocol so specifies. Unfortunately, if an important component experiences a permanent failure, the operating system is unlikely to recover.

As a general rule, an I/O system call will return 1 bit of information about the status of the call, signifying either success or failure. In the UNIX operating system, an additional integer variable named errno is used to return an error code—one of about 100 values—indicating the general nature of the failure (for example, argument out of range, bad pointer, or file not open). By contrast, some hardware can provide highly detailed error information, although many current operating systems are not designed to convey this information to the application. For instance, a failure of a SCSI device is reported by the SCSI protocol in terms of a **sense key** that identifies the general nature of the failure, such as a hardware error or an illegal request; an **additional sense code** that states the category of failure, such as a bad command parameter or a self-test failure; and an **additional sense-code qualifier** that gives even more detail, such as which command parameter was in error, or which hardware subsystem failed its self-test. Further, many SCSI devices maintain internal pages of error-log information that can be requested by the host, but that seldom area.

Kernel Data Structures

The kernel needs to keep state information about the use of I/O components. It does so through a variety of in-kernel data structures, such as the open-file table structure. The kernel uses may similar structures to track network connections, character-device communications, and other I/O activities.

UNIX provides file-system access to a variety of entities, such as user files, raw devices, and the address spaces of processes. Although each of these entities supports a read ( ) operation, the semantics differ. For instance, to read a user file, the kernel needs to probe the buffer cache before deciding whether to perform a disk I/O. To read a raw disk, the kernel needs to ensure that the request size is a multiple of the disk sector size, and is aligned on a sector boundary. To read a process image, it is merely necessary to copy data from memory. UNIX encapsulates these differences within a uniform structure by using an object-oriented techniques. The open-file record, shown in Figure 11.9, contains a dispatch table that holds pointers to the appropriate routines, depending on the type of file.

Some operating systems use object-oriented methods even more extensively. For instance, Windows NT uses a message-passing implementation for I/O. An I/O request is converted into a message that is sent through the kernel to the I/O manager and then to the device driver, each of which may change the message contents. For output, the message contains the data to be written. For input, the message contains a buffer to receive the data. The message-passing approach can add overhead, by comparison with procedural techniques that use shared data structures, but it simplifies the structure and design of the I/O system, and adds flexibility.

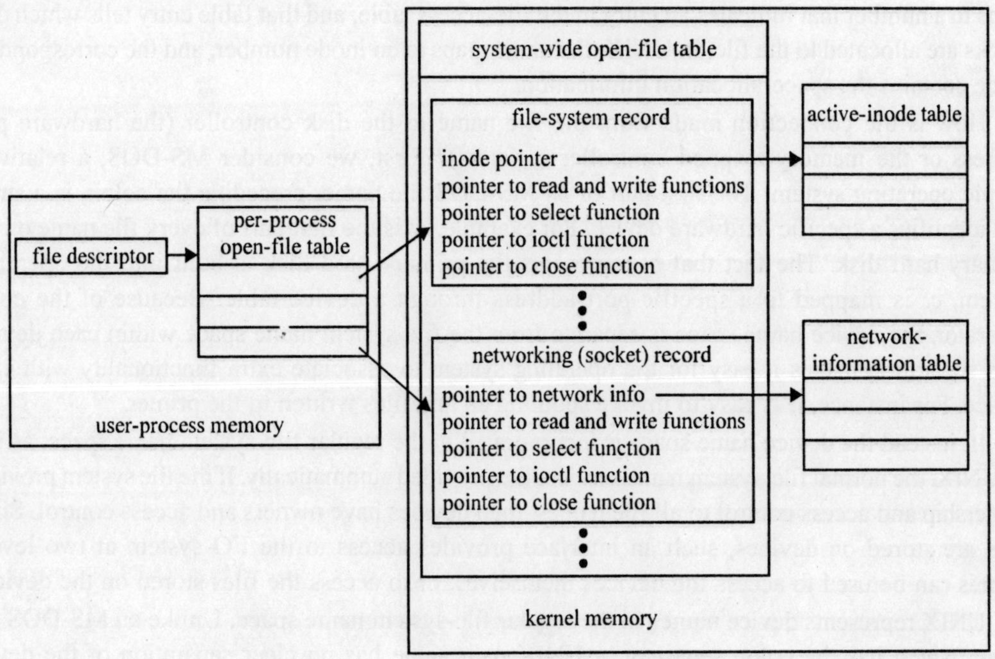

Fig. 11.9. UNIX I/O kernel structure.

In summary, the I/O subsystem coordinates an extensive collection of services that are available to applications and to other parts of the kernel. The I/O subsystem supervises

- The management of the name space for files and devices
- Access control to files and devices
- Operation control (for example, a modem cannot seek ( ))
- File system space allocation
- Device allocation
- Buffering, caching, and spooling
- I/O scheduling
- Device status monitoring, error handling, and failure recovery
- Device driver configuration and initialization

The upper level of the I/O subsystem access devices via the uniform interface provided by the device drivers.

Transforming I/O to Hardware Operations

Earlier, we described the handshaking between a device driver and a device controller, but we did not explain how the operating system connects an application request to a set of network wires or to a specific disk sector. Let us consider the example of reading a file from disk. The application refers to the data by a file name. Within a disk, the file system maps from the file name through the file-system directories to obtain the space allocation of the file. For instance, in MS-DOS, the name maps to a number that indicates an entry in the file-access table, and that table entry tells which disk blocks are allocated to the file. In UNIX, the name maps to an inode number, and the corresponding inode contains the space-allocation information.

How is the connection made from the file name to the disk controller (the hardware port address or the memory-mapped controller registers)? First, we consider MS-DOS, a relatively simple operating system. The first part of an MS-DOS file name, preceding the colon, is a string that identifies a specific hardware device. For example, *c:* is the first part of every file name on the primary hard disk. The fact that *c*: represents the primary hard disk is built into the operating system, *c:* is mapped to a specific port address through a device table. Because of the colon separator, the device name space is separate from the file-system name space within each device. This separation makes it easy for the operating system to associate extra functionality with each device. For instance, it is easy to invoke spooling an any files written to the printer.

If, instead the device name space is incorporated in the regular file-system name space, as it is in. UNIX, the normal file-system name services are provided automatically. If the file system provides ownership and access control to all file names, then devices have owners and access control. Since files are stored on devices, such an interface provides access to the I/O system at two levels. Names can be used to access the devices themselves, or to access the files stored on the devices.

UNIX represents device names in the regular file-system name space. Unlike an MS-DOS file name, which has the colon separator, a UNIX path name has no clear separation of the device portion. In fact, no part of the path name is the name of a device. UNIX has a **mount table** that associates prefixes of path names with specific device names. To resolve a path name, UNIX looks up the name in the mount table to find the longest matching prefix; the corresponding entry in the mount table gives the device name. This device name also has the form of a name in the file-system name space. When UNIX looks up this name in the file-system directory structures, instead of finding an inode number, UNIX finds a <*major, minor*> device number. The major device number identifies a device driver that should be called to handle I/O to this device. The minor device number is passed to the device driver to index into a device table. The corresponding device-table entry gives the port address or the memory-mapped address of the device controller.

Modern operating systems obtain significant flexibility from the multiple stages of lookup tables in the path between a request and a physical device controller. The mechanisms that pass requests between applications and drivers are general. Thus, we can introduce new devices and drivers into a computer without recompiling the kernel. In fact, some operating systems have the ability to load device drivers on demand. At boot time, the system first probes the hardware buses to determine what devices are present, and then the system loads in the necessary drivers, either immediately, or when first required by an I/O request.

Now we describe the typical lifecycle of a blocking read request, as depicted in Figure 11.10. The figure suggests that an I/O operation requires a great many steps that together consume a tremendous number of CPU cycles.

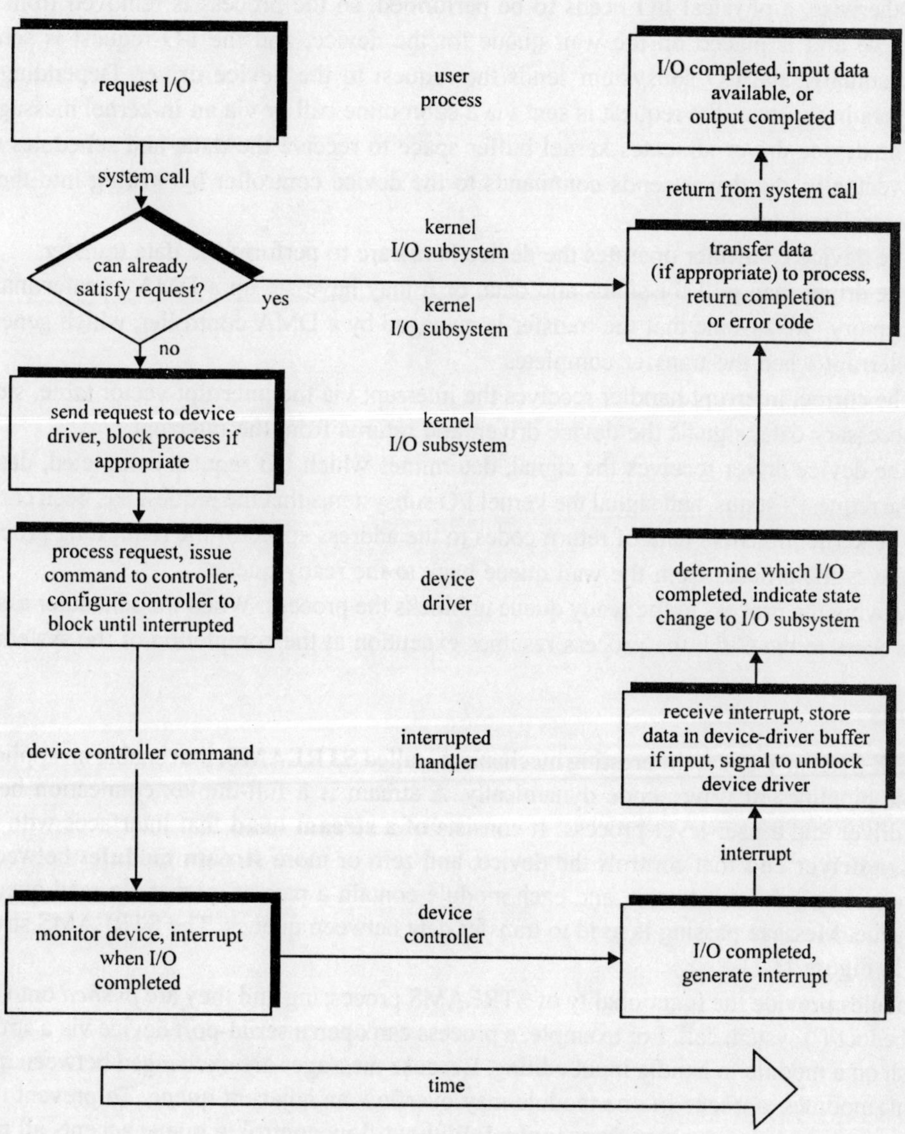

Fig. 11.10. The life cycle of an I/O request.

1. A process issues a blocking read ( ) system call to a file descriptor of a file that has been *opened* previously.
2. The system-call code in the kernel checks the parameters for correctness. In the case of input, if the data are already available in the buffer cache, the data are returned to the process and the I/O request is completed.
3. Otherwise, a physical I/O needs to be performed, so the process is removed from the run queue and is placed on the wait queue for the device, and the I/O request is scheduled. Eventually, the I/O subsystem sends the request to the device driver. Depending on the operating system, the request is sent via a subroutine call or via an in-kernel message.
4. The device driver allocates kernel buffer space to receive the data, and schedules the I/O. Eventually, the driver sends commands to the device controller by writing into the device control registers.
5. The device controller operates the device hardware to perform the data transfer.
6. The driver may poll for status and data, or it may have set up a DMA transfer into kernel memory. We assume that the transfer is managed by a DMA controller, which generates an interrupt when the transfer completes.
7. The correct interrupt handler receives the interrupt via the interrupt-vector table, stores any necessary data, signals the device driver, and returns from the interrupt.
8. The device driver receives the signal, determines which I/O request completed, determines the request's status, and signal the kernel I/O subsystems that the request has been completed.
9. The kernel transfers data of return codes to the address space of the requesting process, and moves the process from the wait queue back to the ready queue.
10. Moving the process to the ready queue unblocks the process. When the scheduler assigns the process to the CPU, the process resumes execution at the completion of the system call.

Streams

UNIX System V has an interesting mechanism, called **STREAMS,** that enable an application to assemble pipelines of driver code dynamically. A stream is a full-duplex connection between a device driver and a user-level process. It consists of a **stream head** that interfaces with the user process, a **driver end** that controls the device, and zero or more **stream modules** between them. The stream head, the driver end, and each module contain a pair of queues—a read queue and a write queue. Message passing is used to transfer data between queues. The STREAMS structure is shown in Figure 11.11.

Modules provide the functionality of STREAMS processing and they are *pushed* onto a stream using the ioctl( ) system call. For example, a process can open a serial-port device via a stream, and can push on a module to handle input editing. Because messages are exchanged between queues in adjacent modules, a queue in one module may overflow an adjacent queue. To prevent this from occurring, a queue may support **flow control.** Without flow control, a queue accepts all messages and immediately sends them on to the queue in the adjacent module without buffering them. A queue supporting flow control buffers messages and does not accept messages without sufficient buffer space. Flow control

is supported by exchanging control messages between queues in adjacent modules.

A user process writes data to a device using either the write ( ) or putmsg ( ) system calls. The write ( ) system call writes raw data to the stream whereas putmsg ( ) allows the user process to specify a message. Regardless of the system call used by the user process, the stream head copies the data into a message and delivers it to the queue for the next module in line. This copying of messages continues until the message is copied to the driver end and hence the device. Similarly, the user process reads data from the stream head using either the read ( ) or getmsg () system calls. If read ( ) is used, the stream head gets a message from its adjacent queue and returns ordinary data (an unstructured byte stream) to the process. If getmsg ( ) is used, a message is returned to the process.

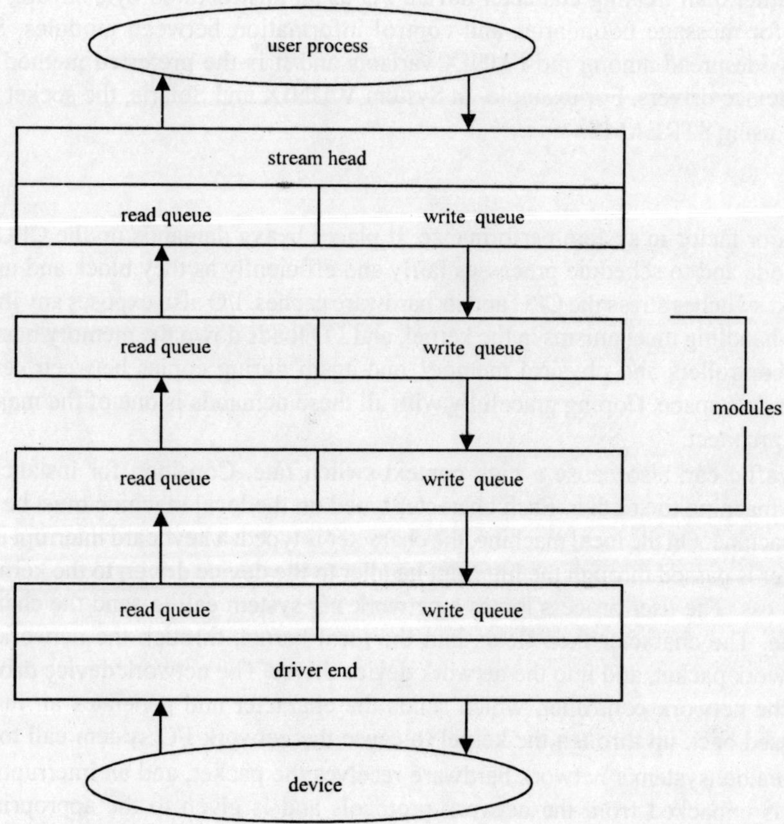

Fig. 11.11. The STREAMS structure.

STREAMS I/O is asynchronous (or non-blocking) with the exception of when the user process communicates with the stream head. When writing to the stream, the user process will block, assuming the next queue uses flow control, until there is room to copy the message. Likewise, the user process will block when reading from the stream until data is available.

The driver end is similar to a stream head or a module in that it has a read and write queue. However, the driver end must respond to interrupts such as one triggered when a frame is ready to be read from a network. Unlike the stream head that may block if it is unable to copy a message to the next queue in line, the driver end must handle all incoming data. Drivers must support flow control as well. However, if a device's buffer is full, a device typically resorts to dropping incoming messages. Consider a network card whose input buffer is full. The network card must simply drop further messages until there is ample buffer space to store incoming messages.

The benefit of using STREAMS is that it provides a framework to a modular and incremental approach to writing device drivers and network protocols.

Modules may be used by different STREAMS and hence by different devices. For example, a networking module may be used by both an Ethernet network card and a token ring network card. Furthermore, rather than treating character device I/O as an unstructured byte stream, STREAMS allow support for message boundaries and control information between modules. Support for STREAMS is widespread among most UNIX variants and it is the preferred method for writing protocols and device drivers. For example, in System V UNIX and Solaris, the socket mechanism is implemented using STREAMS.

Performance

I/O is a major factor in system performance. It places heavy demands on the CPU to execute device-driver code and to schedule processes fairly and efficiently as they block and unblock. The resulting context switches stress the CPU and its hardware caches. I/O also exposes any inefficiencies in the interrupt-handling mechanisms in the kernel, and I/O loads down the memory bus during data copy between controllers and physical memory, and again during copies between kernel buffers and application data space. Coping gracefully with all these demands is one of the major concerns of a computer architect.

Network traffic can also cause a high context-switch rate. Consider, for instance, a remote login from one machine to another. Each character typed on the local machine must be transported to the remote machine. On the local machine, the character is typed; a keyboard interrupt is generated; and the character is passed through the interrupt handler to the device driver, to the kernel, and then to the user process. The user process issues a network I/O system call to send the character to the remote machine. The character then flows into the local kernel, through the network layers that construct a network packet, and into the network device driver. The network device driver transfers the packet to the network controller, which sends the character and generates an interrupt. The interrupt is passed back up through the kernel to cause the network I/O system call to complete.

Now, the remote system's network hardware receives the packet, and an interrupts generated. The character is unpacked from the network protocols and is given to the appropriate network daemon. The network daemon identifies which remote login session is involved, and passes the packet to the appropriate subdaemon for that session. Throughout this flow there are context switches and state switches. Usually, the receiver echoes the character back to the sender; that approach doubles the work.

The Solaris developers reimplemented the **telnet** daemon using in-kernel threads to eliminate the context switches involved in moving each character between daemons and the kernel. Sun estimates that this improvement increased the maximum number of network logins from a few hundred to a few thousand on a large server.

Other systems use separate **front-end processors** for terminal I/O, to reduce the interrupt burden on the main CPU. For instance, a **terminal concentrator** can multiplex the traffic from hundreds of remote terminals into one port on a large computer. An **I/O channel** is a dedicated, special-purpose CPU found in mainframes and in other high-end systems. The job of a channel is to offload I/O work from the main CPU. The idea is that the channels keep the data flowing smoothly, while the main CPU remains free to process the data. Like the device controllers and DMA controllers found in smaller computers, a channel can process more general and sophisticated programs, so channels can be tuned for particular workloads.

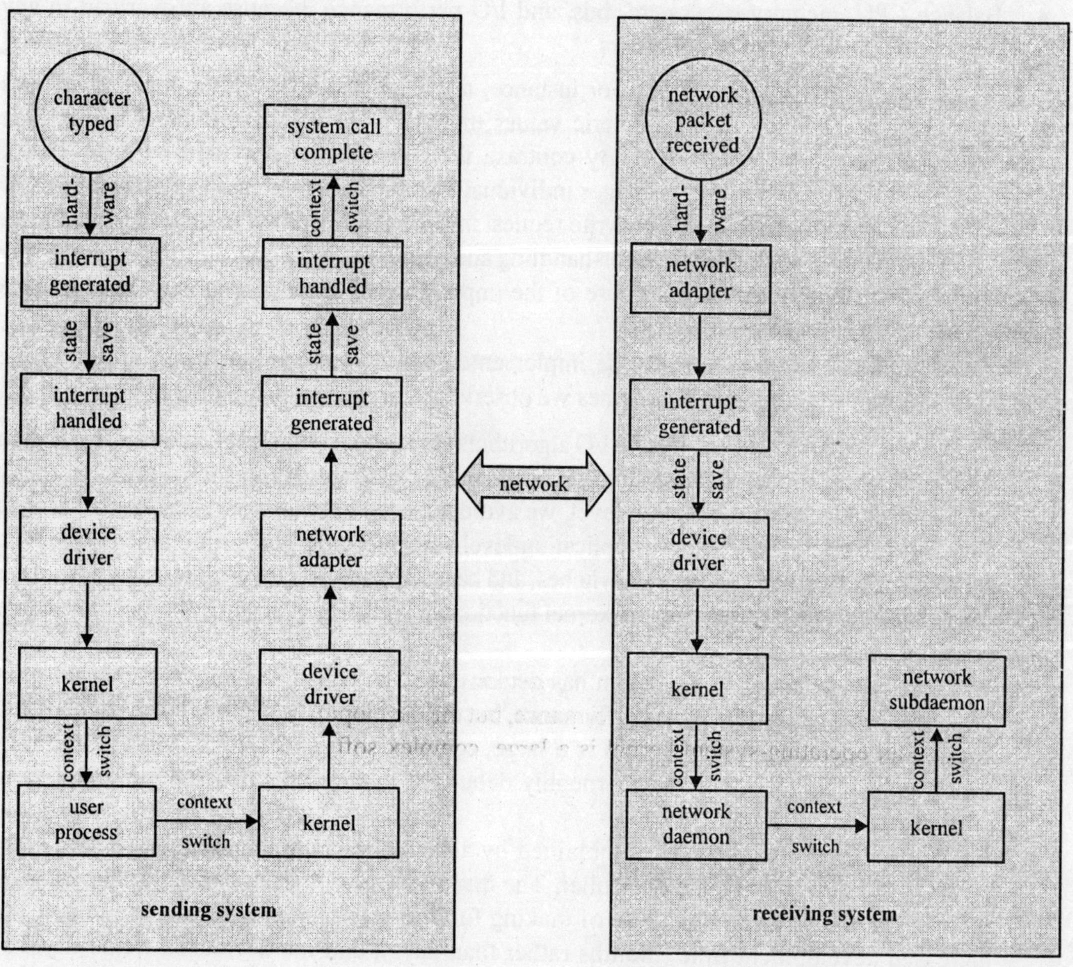

Fig. 11.12. Intercomputer communications.

We can employ several principles to improve the efficiency of I/O:

- Reduce the number of context switches.
- Reduce the number of times that data must be copied in memory while passing between device and application.
- Reduce the frequency of interrupts by using large transfers, smart controllers, and polling (if busy-waiting can be minimized).
- Increase concurrency by using DMA-knowledgeable controllers or channels to offload simple data copying from the CPU.
- Move processing primitives into hardware, to allow their operation in device controllers concurrent with the CPU and bus operation.
- Balance CPU, memory subsystem, bus, and I/O performance, because an overload in any one area will cause idleness in others.

Devices vary greatly in complexity. For instance, a mouse is simple. The mouse movements and button clicks are converted into numeric values that are passed from hardware, through the mouse device driver, to the application. By contrast, the functionality provided by the NT disk device driver is complex. It not only manages individual disk but also implements RAID arrays. To do so, it converts an application's read or write request into a coordinated set of disk I/O operations. Moreover, it implements sophisticated error-handling and data-recovery algorithms, and takes many steps to optimize disk performance, because of the importance of secondary-storage performance to overall system performance.

Where should the I/O functionality be implemented—in the device hardware, in the device driver, or in application software? Sometimes we observe the progression depicted in Figure 11.13.

- Initially, we implement experimental I/O algorithms at the application level, because application code is flexible, and application bugs are unlikely to cause system crashes. Furthermore, by developing code at the application level, we avoid the need to reboot or reload device drivers after every change to the code. An application-level implementation can be inefficient, however, because of the overhead of context switches, and because the application cannot take advantage of internal kernel data structures and kernel functionality (such as efficient in-kernel messaging, threading, and locking).
- When an application-level algorithm has demonstrated its worth, we may reimplement it in the kernel. This can improve the performance, but the development effort is more challenging, because an operating-system kernel is a large, complex software system. Moreover, an in-kernel implementation must be thoroughly debugged to avoid data corruption and system crashes.
- The highest performance may be obtained by a specialized implementation in hardware, either in the device or in the controller. The disadvantages of a hardware implementation include the difficulty and expense of making further improvements or of fixing bugs, the increased development time (months rather than days), and the decreased flexibility. For instance, a hardware RAID controller may not provide any means for the kernel to influence the order or location of individual block reads and writes, even if the kernel has special information about the workload that would enable the kernel to improve the I/O performance.

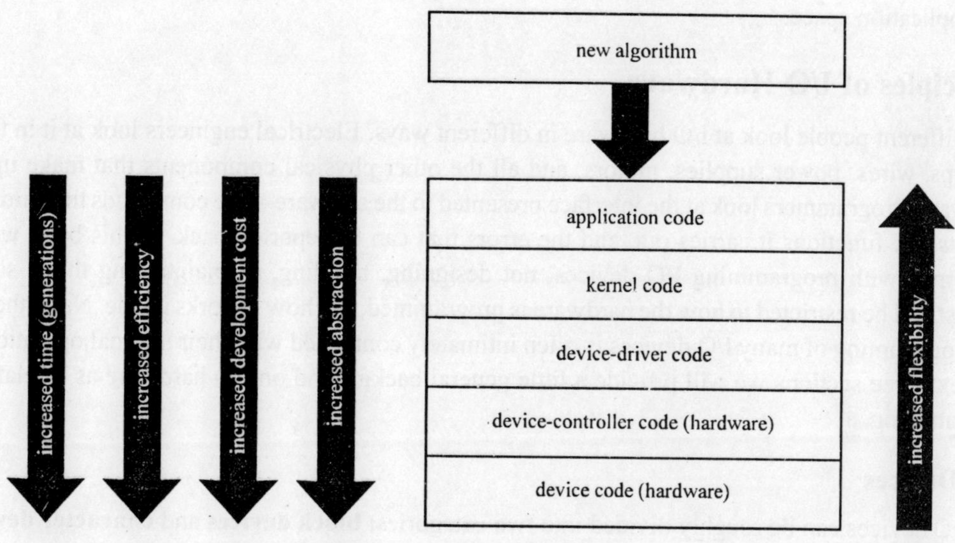

Fig. 11.13. Device-functionality progression.

Summary

The basic hardware elements involved in I/O are buses, device controllers, and the devices themselves. The work of moving data between devices and main memory is performed by the CPU as programmed I/O, or is offloaded to a DMA controller. The kernel module that controls a device is a device driver. The system-call interface provided to applications is designed to handle several basic categories of hardware, including block devices, character devices, memory-mapped files, network sockets, and programmed interval timers. The system calls usually block the process that issues them, but nonblocking and asynchronous falls are used by the kernel itself, and by applications that must not sleep while waiting for an I/O operation to complete.

The kernel's I/O subsystem provides numerous services. Among these are I/O scheduling, buffering, spooling, error handling, and device reservation. Another service is name translation, to make the connection between hardware devices and the symbolic file names used by applications. It involves several levels of mapping that translate from a character string name to a specific device driver and device address, and then to physical addresses of I/O ports or bus controllers. This mapping may occur within the file-system name space, as it does in UNIX, or in a separate device-name space, as it does in MS-DOS.

STREAMS is an implementation and methodology for making drivers reusable and easy to use. Through them, drivers can be stacked, with data passed through them sequentially and bidirectionally for processing.

I/O system calls are costly in terms of CPU consumption, because of the many layers of software between a physical device and the application. These layers imply the overheads of context switching to cross the kernel's protection boundary, of signal and interrupt handling to service the

I/O devices, and of the load on the CPU and memory system to copy data between kernel buffers and application space.

Principles of I/O Hardware

Different people look at I/O hardware in different ways. Electrical engineers look at it in terms of chips, wires, power supplies, motors, and all the other physical components that make up the hardware. Programmers look at the interface presented to the software—the commands the hardware accepts, the functions it carries out, and the errors that can be reported back. In this book we are concerned with programming I/O devices, not designing, building, or maintaining them, so our interest will be restricted to how the hardware is programmed, not how it works inside. Nevertheless, the programming of many I/O devices is often intimately connected with their internal operation. In the next three sections we will provide a little general background on I/O hardware as it relates to programming.

I/O Devices

I/O devices can be roughly divided into two categories: **block devices** and **character devices.** A block device is one that stores information in fixed-size blocks, each one with its own address. Common block sizes range from 512 bytes to 32,768 bytes. The essential property of a block device is that it is possible to read or write each block independently of all the other ones. Disks are the most common block devices.

If you look closely, the boundary between devices that are block addressable and those that are not is not well defined. Everyone agress that a disk is a block addressable device because no matter where the arm currently is, it is always possible to seek to another cylinder and then wait for the required block to rotate under the head. Now consider an 8mm or DAT tape drive used for making disk backups. Its tapes generally contain fixed-size blocks. If the tape drive is given a command to read block *N*, it can always rewind the tape and go forward until it comes to block *N*. This operation is analogous to a disk doing a seek, except that it takes much longer. Also, it may or may not be possible to rewrite one block in the middle of a tape. Even if it were possible to use tapes as random access block devices, that is stretching the point somewhat: they are normally not used that way.

The other type of I/O device is the character device. A character device delivers or accepts a stream of characters, without regard to any block structure. It is not addressable and does not have any seek operation. Printers, network interfaces, mice (for pointing), rats (for psychology lab experiments), and most other devices that are not disk-like can be seen as character devices.

This classification scheme is not perfect. Some devices just do not fit in. Clocks, for example, are not block addressable. Nor do they generate or accept character streams. All they do is cause interrupts at well-defined intervals. Memory-mapped screens do not fit the model well either. Still, the model of block and character devices is general enough that it can be used as a basis for making some of the operating system software dealing with I/O device independent. The file system, for examples, deals just with abstract block devices and leaves the device-dependent part to lower-level software called **device drivers.**

Device Controllers

I/O units typically consist of a mechanical component and an electronic component. It is often possible to separate the two portions to provide a more modular and general design. The electronic component is called the **device controller** or **adapter.** On personal computers, it often takes the form of a printed circuit card that can be inserted into a slot on the computer's **parentboard** (previously incorrectly called a motherboard). The mechanical component is the device itself.

The controller card usually has a connector on it, into which a cable leading to the device itself can be plugged. Many controllers can handle two, four, or even eight identical devices. If the interfaces between the controller and device is a standard interface, either an official standard such as ANSI, IEEE, or ISO, or a de facto one, then companies can make controllers or devices that fit that interface. Many companies, for example, make disk drives that match the IDE (Integrated Drive Electronics) or SCSI (Small Computer System Interface) disk controller interfaces.

We mention this distinction between controller and device because the operating system nearly always deals with the controller, not the device. Most small computers use the single bus model of Fig 11.14, for communication between the CPU and the controllers. Large mainframes often use a different model, with multiple buses and specialized I/O computers called **I/O channels** taking some of the load off the main CPU.

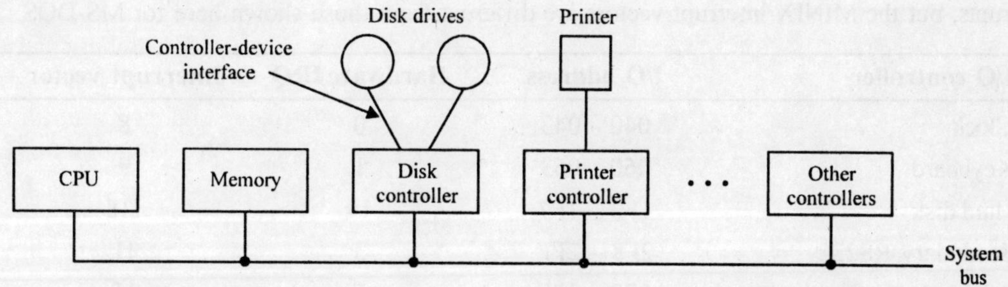

Fig. 11.14. A model for connecting the CPU, memory, controllers, and I/O devices.

The interface between the controller and the device is often a very low-level interface. A disk, for example, might be formatted with 16 sectors of 512 bytes per track. What actually comes off the drive, however, is a serial bit stream, starting with a **preamble,** then the 4096 bits in a sector, and finally a checksum, also called an **Error-Correcting Code (ECC).** The preamble is written when the disk is formatted and contains the cylinder and sector number, the sector size, and similar data, as well as synchronization information.

The controller for a CRT terminal also works as a bit serial device at an equally low level. It reads bytes containing the characters to be displayed from memory and generates the signals used to modulate the CRT beam to cause it to write on the screen. The controller also generates the signals for making the CRT beam do a horizontal retrace after it has finished a scan line, as well as the signals for making it do a vertical retrace after the entire screen has been scanned. If it were not for the CRT controller, the operating system programmer would have to explicitly program the analog scanning of the tube. With the controller, the operating system initializes the controller with a few parameters, such as the number of characters per line and number of lines per screen, and lets the controller take care of actually driving the beam.

Each controller has a few registers that are used for communicating with the CPU. On some computers, these registers are part of the regular memory address space. This scheme is called **memory-mapped I/O.** The 680x0, for example, uses this method. Other computers use a special address space for I/O, with each controller allocated a certain portion of it. The assignment of I/O addresses to devices is made by bus decoding logic associated with the controller. Some manufacturers of so-called IBM PC compatibles use different I/O addresses from those IBM uses. In addition to I/O ports, many controllers use interrupts to tell the CPU when they are ready to have their registers read or written. An interrupt is, in the first place, an electrical event. A hardware Interrupt ReQuest line (IRQ) is a physical input to the interrupt controller chip. The number of such inputs is limited; Pentium-class PCs have only 15 available for I/O devices. Some controllers are hard-wired onto the system parentboard, as is, for instance, the keyboard controller of an IBM PC. In the case of a controller that plugs into the backplane, switches or wire jumpers on the device controller sometimes can be used to select which IRQ the device will use, in order to avoid conflicts (although with some boards, such as Plug 'n play, the IRQs can be set in software). The interrupt controller chip maps each IRQ input to an interrupt vector, which locates the corresponding interrupt service software. Figure 11.15 shows the I/O addresses, hardware interrupts, and interrupt vectors allocated to some of the controllers on an IBM PC, as an example. MINIX uses the same hardware interrupts, but the MINIX interrupt vectors are different from those shown here for MS-DOS.

I/O controller	I/O address	Hardware IRQ	Interrupt vector
Clock	040 – 043	0	8
Keyboard	060 – 063	1	9
Hard disk	1F0 – 1F7	14	118
Secondary RS232	2F8 – 2FF	3	11
Printer	378 – 37F	7	15
Floppy disk	3F0 – 3F7	6	14
Primary RS232	3F8 – 3FF	4	12

Fig. 11.15. *Some examples of controllers, their I/O addresses, their hardware interrupt lines, and their interrupt vectors on a typical PC running MS-DOS.*

The operating system performs I/O by writing commands into the controller's registers. The IMB PC floppy disk controller, for example, accepts 15 different commands, such as READ, WRITE SEEK, FORMAT, and RECALIBRATE. Many of the commands have parameters, which are also loaded into the controller's registers. When a command has been accepted, the CPU can leave the controller alone and go off to do other work. When the command has been completed, the controller causes an interrupt in order to allow the operating system to gain control of the CPU and test the results of the operation. The CPU gets the results and device status by reading one or more bytes of information from the controller's registers.

Principles of I/O Software

Let us turn away from the hardware and now look at how the I/O software is structured. The general goals of the I/O software are easy to state. The basic idea is to organize the software as a series of layers, with the lower ones concerned with hiding the peculiarities of the hardware from the upper ones, and the upper ones concerned with presenting a nice, clean, regular interface to the users. In the following sections we will look at these goals and how they are achieved.

Goals of the I/O Software

A key concept in the design of I/O software is known as **device independence.** What it means is that it should be possible to write programs that can read files on a floppy disk, on a hard disk, or on a CD-ROM, without having to modify the programs for each different device type. One should be able to type a command such as

sort<input>output

and have it work with input coming from a floppy disk, a hard disk, or the keyboard, and the output going to the floppy disk, the hard disk, or even the screen. It is up to the operating system to take care of the problems caused by the fact that these devices really are different and require very different device drivers to actually write the data to the output device.

Closely related to device independence is the goal of **uniform naming.** The name of a file or a device should simply be a string for an integer and not depend on the device in any way. In UNIX, all disks can be integrated together in the file system hierarchy in arbitrary ways so the user need not be aware of which name corresponds to which device. For example, a floppy disk can be **mounted** to top of the directory */usr/ast/backup* so that copying a file to */usr/ast/backup/monday* copies the file to the floppy disk. In this way, all files and devices are addressed the same way: by a path name.

Another important issue for I/O software is error handling. In general, errors should be handled as close to the hardware as possible. If the controller discovers a read error, it should try to correct the error itself if it can. If it cannot, then the device driver should handle it, perhaps by just trying to read the block again. Many errors are transient, such as read errors caused by specks of dust on the read head, and will go away if the operation is repeated. Only if the lower layers are not able to deal with the problem should the upper layers be told about it. In many cases, error recovery can be done transparently at a low level without the upper levels even knowing about the error.

Still another key issue is synchronous (blocking) versus asynchronous (interrupt-driven) transfers. Most physical I/O is asynchronous—the CPU starts the transfer and goes off to do something else until the interrupt arrives. User programs are much easier to write if the I/O operations are blocking—after a READ command the program is automatically suspended until the data are available in the buffer. It is up to the operating system to make operations that are actually interrupt-driven look blocking to the user programs.

The final concept that we will deal with here is sharable versus dedicated devices. Some I/O devices, such as disks, can be used by many users at the same time. No problems are caused by multiple users having open files on the same disk at the same time. Other devices, such as tape drives, have to be dedicated to a single user until that user is finished. Then another user can have the tape drive. Having two or more users writing blocks intermixed at random to the same tape will definitely not work. Introducing dedicated (unshared) devices also introduces a variety of problems. Again, the operating system must be able to handle both shared and dedicated devices in a way that avoids problems.

These goals can be achieved in a comprehensible and efficient way by structuring the I/O software in four layers:

1. Interrupt handlers (bottom).
2. Device drivers.
3. Device-independent operating system software.
4. User-level software (top).

These four layers are (not accidently) the same four layers. In the following sections we will look at each one in turn, starting at the bottom. The emphasis in this chapter is on the device drivers (layer 2), but we will summarize the rest of the I/O software to show how the various pieces of the I/O system fit together.

Interrupt Handlers

Interrupt are an unpleasant fact of life. They should be hidden away, deep in the bowels of the operating system, so that as little of the system as possible knows about them. The best way to hide them is to have every process starting an I/O operation block until the I/O has completed and the interrupt occurs. The process can block itself by doing a DOWN on a semaphore, a WAIT on a conditions variable, or a RECEIVE on a message, for example.

When the interrupt happens, the interrupt procedure does whatever it has to in order to unblock the process that started it. In some system it will do an UP on a semaphore. In others it will do a SIGNAL on a condition variable in a monitor. In still others, it will send a message to the blocked process. In all cases the net effect of the interrupt will be that a process that was previously blocked will now be able to run.

Device Drivers

All the device-dependent code goes in the device drivers. Each device driver handles one device type, or at most, one class of closely related devices. For example, it would probably be a good idea to have a single terminal driver, even if the system supported several different brands of terminals, all slightly different. On the other hand, a dumb, mechanical hardcopy terminal and an intelligent bitmap graphic terminal with a mouse are so different that different drivers should be used.

Earlier in this chapter we looked at what device controllers do. We saw that each controller has one or more device registers used to give it commands. The device drivers issue these commands and check that they are carried out properly. Thus, the disk driver is the only part of the operating system that knows how many registers that disk controller has and what they are used for. It alone knows about sectors, tracks, cylinders, heads, arm motion, interleave factors, motor drives, head settling times, and all the other mechanics of making the disk work properly.

In general terms, the job of a device driver is to accept abstract request from the device-independent software above it and see to it that the request is executed. A typical request is to read block *n*. If the driver is idle at the time a request comes in, it starts carrying out the request immediately. If, however, it is already busy with a request, it will normally enter the new request into a queue of pending requests to be dealt with as soon as possible.

The first step in actually carrying out an I/O request, say, for a disk, is to translate it from abstract to concrete terms. For a disk driver, this means figuring out where on the disk the requested block actually is, checking to see if the drive's motor is running, determining if the arm is positioned on the proper cylinder, and so on. In short, it must decide which controller operations are required and in what sequence.

Uniform interfacing for device drivers
Device naming
Device protection
Providing a device-independent block size
Buffering
Storage allocation on block devices
Allocating and releasing dedicated devices
Error reporting

Fig. 11.16. Functions of the device-independent I/O software.

Once it has determined which commands to issue to the controller, it starts issuing them by writing into the controller's device registers. Some controllers can handle only one command at a time. Other controllers are willing to accept a linked list of commands, which they then carry out by themselves without further help from the operating system.

After the command or commands have been issued, one of two situations will apply. In many cases the device driver must wait until the controller does some work of it, so it blocks itself until the interrupt comes in to unblock it. In other cases, however, the operation finishes without delay, so the driver need not block. As an example of the latter situation, scrolling the screen on some terminals requires just writing a few bytes into the controller's registers. No mechanical motion is needed, so the entire operation can be completed in a few microseconds.

In the former case, the blocked driver will be awakened by the interrupt. In the latter case, it will never go to sleep. Either way, after the operation has been completed, it must check for errors. If everything is all right, the driver may have data to pass to the device-independent software (e.g., a block just read). Finally, it returns some status information for error reporting back to its caller. If any other requests are queued, one of them can now be selected and started. If nothing is queued, the driver blocks waiting for the next request.

Device-Independent I/O Software

Although some of the I/O software is device specific, a large fraction of it is device independent. The exact boundary between the drivers and the device-independent software is system dependent, because some functions that could be done in a device-independent way may actually be done in the drivers, for efficiency or other reasons. The function shown in Fig. 11.16 are typically done in the device-independent software. In MINIX, most of the device-independent software is part of the file system, in layer 3, we will take a quick look at the device-independent software here, to provide some perspective on I/O and show better where the drivers fit in.

The basic function of the device-independent software is to perform the I/O functions that are common to all devices and to provide a uniform interface to the user-level software.

A major issue in an operating system is how objects such as files and I/O devices are named. The device-independent software takes care of mapping symbolic device names onto the proper driver. In UNIX a device name, such as */dev/tty00,* uniquely specifies the i-node for a special file, and this i-node contains the **major device number,** which is used to locate the appropriate driver. The i-node also contains the **minor device number,** which is passed a parameter to the driver to specify the unit to be read or written.

Closely related to naming is protection. How does the system prevent users from accessing devices that they are not entitled to access? In most personal computer systems, there is no protection at all. Any process can do anything it wants to. In most mainframe systems, access to I/O devices by user processes is completely forbidden. In UNIX, a more flexible scheme is used. The special files corresponding to I/O devices are protected by the usual *rwx* bits. The system administrator can then set the proper permissions for each device.

Different disk may have different sector sizes. It is up to the device-independent software to hide this fact and provide a uniform block size to higher layers, for example, by treating several sectors as a single logical block. In this way, the higher layers only deal with abstract devices that all use the same logical block size, independent of the physical sector size. Similarly, some character devices deliver their data one byte at a time (e.g., modems), while others deliver theirs in larger units (e.g., network interfaces). These differences must also be hidden.

Buffering is also an issue, both for block and character devices. For block devices, the hardware generally insists upon reading and writing entire blocks at once, but user processes are free to read and write in arbitrary units. If a user process writes half a block, the operating system will normally keep the data around internally until the rest of the data are written, at which time the block can go out to the disk. For character devices, users can write data to the system faster than it can be output, necessitating buffering. Keyboard input that arrives before it is needed also requires buffering.

When a file is created and filled with data, new disk blocks have to be allocated to the file. To perform this allocation, the operating system needs a list or bit map of free blocks per disk, but the algorithm for locating a free block is device independent and can be done above the level of the driver.

Some devices, such as CD-ROM recorders can be used only by a single process at any given moment. It is up to the operating system to examine requests for device usage and accept or reject them, depending on whether the requested device is available or not. A simple way to handle these requests is to require processes to perform OPENS on the special files for devices directly. If the device is unavailable, the OPEN will fail. Closing such a dedicated device would then release it.

Error handling, by and large, is done by the drivers. Most errors are highly device dependent. So only the driver knows what to do (e.g., retry, ignore it, panic). A typical error is caused by a disk block that has been damaged and cannot be read any more. After the driver has tried to read the block a certain number of times, it gives up and informs the device-independent software. How the error is treated from here on is device independent. If the error occurred while reading a user file, it may be sufficient to report the error back to the caller. However, if it occurred while reading a critical system data structure, such as the block containing the bit map showing which blocks are free, the operating system may have no choice but to print an error message and terminate.

User-Space I/O Software

Although most of the I/O software is within the operating system, a small portion of it consists of libraries linked together with user programs, and even whole programs running outside the kernel. System calls, including the I/O system calls, are normally made by library procedures. When a C program contains the call

```
count = write(fd, buffer, nbytes);
```

the library procedure *write* will be linked with the program and contained in the binary program present in memory at run time. The collection of all these library procedures is clearly part of the I/O system.

While these procedures do little more than put their parameters in the appropriate place for the system call, there are other I/O procedures that actually do real work. In particular, formatting of input and output is done by library procedures. One example from C is *printf,* which takes a format string and possibly some variables as input, builds as ASCII string, and then calls WRITE to output the string. An example of a similar procedure for input is *scanf* which reads input and stores it into variables described in a format string using the same syntax as *printf.* The standard I/O library contains a number of procedures that involves I/O and all run as part of user programs.

Not all user-level I/O software consists of library procedures. Another important category is the spooling system. **Spooling** is a way of dealing with dedicated I/O devices in a multiprogramming system. Consider a typical spooled device: a printer. Although it would be technically easy to let any user process open the character special file for the printer, suppose a process opened it and then did nothing for hours. No other process could print anything.

Instead what is done is to create a special process, called a **daemon,** and a special directory, called a **spooling directory.** To print a file, a process first generates the entire file to be printed and puts it in the spooling directory. It is up to the daemon, which is the only process having permission to use the printer's special file, to print the files in the directory. By protecting the special file against direct use by users, the problem of having someone keeping it open unnecessarily long is eliminated.

Spooling is not only used for printers. It is also used in other situations. For example, file transfer over a network often uses a network daemon. To send a file somewhere, a user puts it in a network spooling directory. Later on, the network daemon takes it out and transmits it. One particular use of spooled file transmission is the Internet electronic mail system. This network consists of millions of machines around the world communicating using many computer networks. To send mail to someone, you call a program such as *send*, which accepts the letter to be sent and then deposits it in a spooling directory for transmission later. The entire mail system runs outside the operating system.

Overview of I/O in MINIX

MINIX I/O is structured as shown in Fig. 3.6. The top four layers of that figure correspond to the four-layered structure of MINIX shown in Fig. 2.26. In the following sections we will look briefly at each of the layers, with the emphasis on the device drivers. Interrupt handling was covered in the previous chapter, and the device-independent I/O will be discussed when we come to the file system.

Interrupt Handlers in MINIX

Many of the device drivers start some I/O device and then block, waiting for a message to arrive. That message is usually generated by the interrupt handler for the device. Other device drivers do not start any physical I/O (e.g., reading from RAM disk and writing to a memory-mapped display), do not use interrupts, and do not wait for a message from an I/O device. In the previous chapter the mechanism by which interrupts generate messages and cause task switches has been presented in great detail, and we will say no more about it here. But interrupt handlers may do more than just generate a message. Frequently they also do some work in processing input and output at the lowest level. We will discuss this in a general way here and then return to the details when we look at the code for various devices.

For disk devices, input and output is generally a matter of commanding a device to perform its operation, and then waiting until the operation is complete. The disk controller does most of the work, and very little is required of the interrupt handler. We saw that the entire interrupt handler for the hard disk task consists of just three lines of code, with the only I/O operation being the reading of a single byte to determine the status of the controller. Our lives would be simple indeed if all interrupts could be handled so easily.

However, there is sometimes more for the low-level handler to do. The message passing mechanism has a cost. When an interrupt may occur frequently but the amount of I/O handled per interrupt is small, it may pay to make the handler itself do somewhat more work and to postpone sending a message to the task until a subsequent interrupt, when there is more for the task to do. MINIX handles interrupts from the clock this way. On many clock ticks there is very little to be done, except for maintaining the time. This can be done without sending a message to the clock task itself. The clock handler increments a variable, appropriately named *_ticks.* The current time is the sum of the time recorded when the clock taks itself last ran plus the value of *pending_ticks.* When the clock task receives a message and wakes up, it adds *pending_ticks* to its main timekeeping variable and then zeroes *pending_ticks.* The clock interrupt handler examines some other variables and sends, a message to the clock task only when it detects the task has actual work to do, such as delivering an alarm or scheduling a new process to execute. It may also send a message to the terminal task.

In the terminal task we see another variation on the theme of interrupt handlers. This task handler several different kinds of hardware, including the keyboard and the RS-232 lines. These each have their own interrupt handler. The keyboard exactly fits the description of a device where there may be relatively little I/O to do in response to each interrupt. On a PC an interrupt occurs each time a key is pressed or released. This includes special keys like the SHIFT and CTRL keys, but if we ignore them for the moment, we can say that on the average half a character is received per interrupt. Since there is not much the terminal task can do with half a character, it makes sense to send it a message only when something worthwhile can be accomplished. We will examine the details later; for now we will just say that the keyboard interrupt handler does the low-level reading of data from the keyboard and then filters out events it can ignore, such as the release of an ordinary key. (The release of a special key, for instance, the SHIFT key, cannot be ignored.). Then codes representing all nonignored events are placed in a queue for later processing by the terminal task itself.

The keyboard interrupt handler differs form the simple paradigm we have presented of the interrupt handler that sends a message to its associated task, because the interrupt handler sends no message at all. Instead, when it adds a code to the queue, it modifies a variable, *tty_timeout,* that is read by the clock interrupt handler. When an interrupt does not change the queue, *tty_timeout* is not changed either. On the next clock tick the clock handler sends a message to the terminal task if there have been changes to the queue. Other terminal-type interrupt handlers, for instance those for the RS-232 lines, work the same way. A message to the terminal task will arrive soon after a character is received, but a message is not necessarily generated for each character when characters are arriving rapidly. Several characters may accumulated and then be processed in response to a single message. Moreover, all terminal devices are checked each time a message is received by the terminal task.

Device Drivers in MINIX

For each class of I/O device present in a MINIX system, a separate I/O task (device driver) is present. These drivers are full-fledged processes, each with its own state, registers, stack, and so on. Device drivers communicate with each other (where necessary) and with the file system using the standard message passing mechanism used by all MINIX processes. Simple device drivers are written as single source files, such as *clock.c.* For other drivers, such as the drivers for the RAM disk, the hard disk, and the floppy disk, there is a source file to support each type of device, as well as a set of common routines in *driver.c* to support all of the different hardware types. In a sense this divides the device driver level of Fig. 3.6 into two sublevels. This separation of the hardware-dependent and hardware-independent parts of the software makes for easy adaptation to a variety of different hardware configurations. Although some common source code is used, the driver for each disk type runs as a separate process, in order to support rapid data transfers.

The terminal driver source code is organized in a similar way, with hardware-independent code in *tty.c* and source code to support different devices, such as memory-mapped consoles, the keyboard, serial lines, and pseudo terminals in separate files. In this case, however, a single process supports all of the different device types.

For groups of devices such as disk devices and terminals, for which there are several source files, there are also header files. *Driver.h* supports all the block device drivers. *Tty.h* provides common definitions for all the terminal devices.

The main difference between device drivers and other processes is that the device drivers are linked together in the kernel, and thus all share a common address space. As a result, if several device drivers use a common procedure, only one copy will be linked into the MINIX binary.

This design is highly modular and moderately efficient. It is also one of the few places where MINIX differs from UNIX in an essential way. In MINIX a process reads a file by sending a message to the file system process. The file system, in turn, may send a message to the disk driver asking it to read the needed block. This sequence (slightly simplified from reality) is shown in Fig. 11.17 (a). By making these interaction via the message mechanism, we force various parts of the system to interface in standard ways with other parts. Nevertheless, by putting all the device drivers in the kernel address space, they have easy access to the process table and other key data structures when needed.

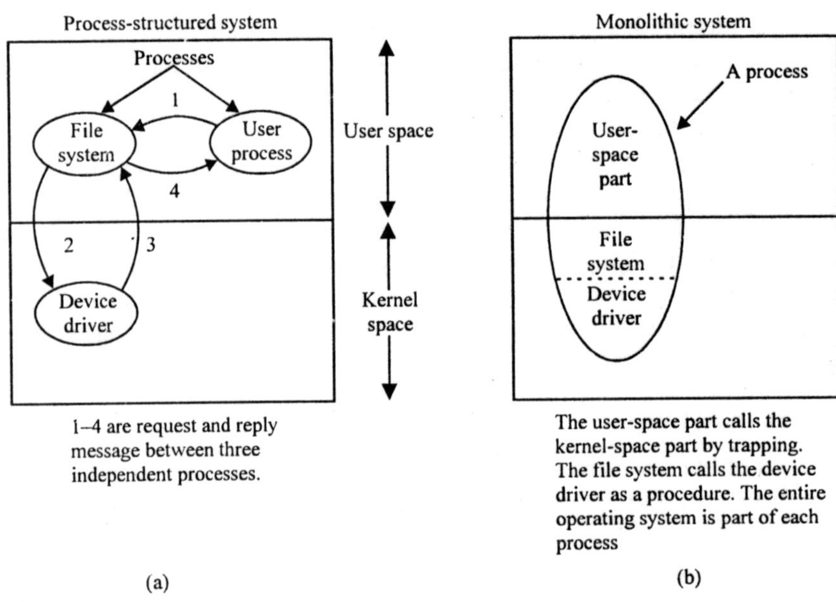

Fig. 11.17. Two ways of structuring user-system communication.

In UNIX all processes have two parts: a user-space part and a kernel-space part, as shown in Fig 11.17 (b). When a system call is made, the operating system switches from the user-space part to the kernel-space part in a somewhat magical way. This structure is a remnant of the MULTICS design, in which the switch was just an ordinary procedure call, rather than a trap followed by saving the state of the user-part, as it is in UNIX.

Device drivers in UNIX are simply kernel procedures that are called by the kernel-space part of the process. When a driver needs to wait of an interrupt, it calls a kernel procedure that puts it to sleep until some interrupt handler wakes it up. Note that it is the user process itself that is being put to sleep here, because the kernel and user parts are really different parts of the same process.

Among operating system designers, arguments about the merits of monolithic system, as in UNIX, versus process-structured system, as in MINIX, are endless. The MINIX approach is better structured (more modular), has cleaner interfaces between the pieces, and extends easily to distributed systems in which the various process run on different computers. The UNIX approach is more efficient, because procedure calls are much faster than sending messages. MINIX was split into many processes because we believe that with increasingly powerful personal computers available, cleaner software structure was worth making the system slightly slower. Be warned that many operating system designers do not share this belief.

In this chapter, drivers of RAM disk, hard disk, clock, and terminal are discussed. The standard MINIX configuration also includes drivers for floppy disk and printer, which are not discussed in detail. In the MINIX software distribution contains source code for additional drivers for RS-232 serial lines, a SCSI interface, CD-ROM, Ethernet adapter, and sound card. There may be included by recompiling MINIX.

All of these tasks interface with other parts of the MINIX system in the same way: request messages are sent to the tasks. The messages contain a variety of fields used to hold the operation code (e.g., READ and WRITE) and its parameters. A task attempts to fulfil a request and returns a reply messages.

For block devices, the fields of the request and reply messages are shown in Fig. 11.17. The request message includes the address of a buffer area containing data to be transmitted or in which received data are expected. The reply includes status information so the requesting process can verify that its request was properly carried out. The fields for the character devices are basically similar but can vary slightly from task to task. Messages to the clock task, for example, contain times, and messages to the terminal task can contain the address of a data structure which specifies all of the many configurable aspects of a terminal, such as the characters to use for the intraline editing functions erase-character and kill-line.

The function of each task is to accept request from other processes, normally the file system, and carry them out. All the block device tasks have been written to get a message, carry it out, and send a reply. Among other things, this decision means that these tasks are strictly sequential and do not contain any internal multiprogramming, to keep them simple. When a hardware request has been issued, the task does a RECEIVE operation specifying that it is interestd only in accepting interrupt messages, not new requests for work. Any new request messages are just kept waiting until the current work has been done (rendezvous principle). The terminal task is slightly different, since a single task services several devices. Thus, it is possible to accept a new request for input from the keyboard while a request to read from a serial line is still being fulfilled. Nevertheless, for each device a request must be completed before beginning a new one.

Request

Field	**Type**	**Meaning**
m.m_type	int	Operation requested
m.DEVICE	int	Minor devices to use
m.PROC_NR	int	Process requesting the I/O
m.COUNT	int	Byte count or ioctl code
m.POSITION	long	Position on device
m.ADDRESS	char*	Address within requesting process

Replies

Field	**Type**	**Meaning**
m.m_type	int	Always TASK_REPLY
m.REP_PROC_NR	int	Same as PROC_NR in request
m.REP_STATUS	int	Bytes transferred or error number

Fig. 11.18. Fields of the messages sent by the file system to the block device drivers and fields of the replies sent back.

The main program for each block device driver is structurally the same and is outlined in Fig 11.19. When the system first comes up, each of the drivers is started up in turn to give each a chance to initialize internal tables and similar things. Then each driver task blocks by trying to get a message. When a message comes in, the identity of the caller is saved, and a procedure is called to carry out the work, with a different procedure invoked for each operation available. After the work has been finished, a reply is sent back to the caller, and the tasks then goes back to the top of the loop to wait for the next request.

Each of the *dev< xxx* procedures handles one of the operations of which the deriver is capable. It returns a status code telling what happened. The status code, which is included in the reply message as the field *REP_STATUS,* is the count of bytes transferred (zero or positive) if all went well, or the error number (negative) if something went wrong. This count may differ from the number of bytes requested. When the end of a file is reached the number of bytes available may be less than number requested. On terminals at most one line is returned, even if the count requested is larger.

```
message mess;                  /*message buffer */
void io_task() {
initialize( );                 /* only done once, during system init. */
while (TRUE) {
receive (ANY, &mess);          /* wait for a request for work */
caller = mess.source;          /* process from whom message came */
switch(mess.type) {
case READ:          rcode = dev_read(&mess); break;
case WRITE:         rcode = dev_write(&mess); break;
/* Other cases go here, including OPEN, CLOSE, and IOCTL */
default:            rcode = ERROR;
}
mess.type = TASK_REPLY;
mess.status = rocde;           /* result code */
send(caller, &mess);           /* send reply message back to caller */
}
}
```

Fig 11.19. Outline of the main procedure of an I/O task.

Device-Independent I/O Software in MINIX

In MINIX the file system process contains all the device-independent I/O code. The I/O system is so closely related to the file system that they were merged into one process. They could, however, easily be added to the relevant device drivers should the need arise in the future.

In addition of handling the interface with the drivers, buffering, and block allocation, the file system also handles protection and the management of i-nodes, directories, and mounted file systems.

User-level I/O Software in MINIX

The general model outlined earlier in this chapter also applies here. Library procedures are available for making system calls and for all the C functions required by the POSIX standard. Such as the formatted input and output functions *printf* and *scanf.* The standard MINIX configuration contains one spooler daemon, *lpd,* which spools and prints files passed to it by the *lp* command. The standard MINIX software distribution contains a number of daemons that support various network functions. Network operations require some operating system support that is not part of MINIX in the configuration described in this book, but MINIX can easily be recompiled to add the network server. It runs at the same priority as the memory manager and the file system, and like them, it runs as a user process.

Deadlock Handling in MINIX

True to its heritage, MINIX follows the same path as UNIX respect to deadlocks: it just ignores the problem altogether. MINIX contains no dedicated I/O devices, although if someone wanted to hang an industry standard DAT tape drive on a PC, making the software for it would not pose any special problems. In short, the only place deadlocks can occur are with the implicit shared resources, such as process table slots, i-node table slots, and so on. None of the known deadlock algorithms can deal with resources like these that are not requested explicitly.

Actually, the above is not strictly true. Accepting the risk that user processes could deadlock is one thing, but within the operating system itself a few places do exist where considerable care has been taken to avoid problems. The main one is the interaction between the file system and the memory manager. The memory manager sends messages to the file system to read the binary file (executable program) during an EXEC system call, as well as in other contexts. If the file system is not idle when the memory manager is trying to send to it, the memory manager will be blocked. If the file system should then try to send a message to the memory manger, it too would discover that the rendezvous fails and would block, leading to a deadlock.

This problem has been avoided by constructing the system in such a way that the file system never sends *request* messages to the memory manager, just *replies,* with one minor exception. The exception is that upon starting up, the file system reports the size of the RAM disk to the memory manager, which is guaranteed to be waiting for the message.

It is possible to lock devices and files even without operating system support. A file name can serve as a truly global variable, whose presence or absence can be noted by all other processes. A special directory. */usr/spool/locks/,* is usually present on MINIX systems, as on most UNIX systems, where processes can create **lock files,** to mark any resources they are using. The MINIX file system also supports POSISX-style advisory file locking. But neither of these mechanisms is enforceable. They depend upon the good behavior of processes, and there is nothing to prevent a program from using a resource that is locked by another process. This is not exactly the same thing as preemption of the resource, because it does not prevent the first process from attempting to continue its use of the resource. In other words, there is no mutual exclusion. The result of such an action by an ill-behaved process is likely to be a mess, but no deadlock results.

Block Devices in MINIX

In the following sections we will return to the device drivers, the main topic of this chapter, and study several of them in detail. MINIX supports several different block devices, so we will begin by discussing common aspects of all block devices. Then we will discuss the RAM disk, the hard disk, and the floppy disk. Each of these is interesting for a different reason. The RAM disk is a good example to study because it has all the properties of block devices in general except the actual I/O—because the "disk" is actually just a portion of memory. This simplicity makes it a good place to start. The hard disk shows what a real disk driver looks like. One might expect the floppy disk to be easier to support than the hard disk, but, in fact, it is not. We will not discuss all the details of the floppy disk, but we will point out several of the complications to be found in the floppy disk driver.

Following the discussion of block drivers, we will discuss other driver classes. The clock is important because every system has one, and because it is completely different from all the other drivers. It is also of interest as an exception to the rule that all devices are either block or character devices, because it does not fit into either category. Finally, we will discuss the terminal driver, which is important on all systems, and, furthermore, is a good example of a character device driver.

Each of these sections describes the relevant hardware, the software principles behind the driver, an overview of the implementation, and the code itself. This structure makes the sections useful reading even for those readers who are not interested in the details of the code itself.

Overview of Block Device Drivers in MINIX

We mentioned earlier that the main procedures of all I/O tasks have a similar structure. MINIX always has at least three block device tasks (the RAM disk driver, the floppy disk driver, and one of several possible hard disk drivers) compiled into the system. In addition, a CD-ROM task and a SCSI (Small Computer Standard Interface) driver may be compiled in, if support for such devices is needed. Although the driver of reach of these executes as an independent process, the fact that they are all compiled as part of the kernel executable makes it possible to share a considerable amount of the code, especially the utility procedures.

Each block device deriver has to do some initialization, of course. The RAM disk driver has to reserve some memory, the hard disk driver has to determine the parameters of the hard disk hardware, and so on. All of the disk drivers are called individually for hardware-specific initialization, but after doing whatever may be necessary, each driver then calls the function containing the common main loop. This loop is executed forever: there is no return to the caller. Within the main loop a message is received, a function to perform the operation needed by each message is called, and then a reply message is generated.

The common main loop called by each disk driver task is not just a copy of a library function compiled into each driver. There is only one copy of the main loop code in the MINIX binary. The technique used is to have each of the individual drivers pass to the main loop a parameter consisting of a pointer to a table of the addresses of the functions that driver will use for each operation and then call these functions indirectly. This technique also makes it possible for drivers to share functions.

```
code = (*entry_points->dev_read))&mess);
```

are indirect function calls. A different *dev_read* function is called by each driver, even though each driver is executing the same main loop. But some other operations, for example CLOSE, are simple enough that more than one device can call the same function.

```
message mess;                    /*message buffer */
void shared_io_task(struct driver_table *entry_points) {
/*initialization is done by each task before calling this */
while (TRUE) {
receive (ANY, &mess);
caller = mess.source;
switch(mess.type) {
case READ:        rcode = (*entry_points->dev_read)(&mess); break;
case WRITE:       rcode = (*entry_points->dev_write)(&mess); break;
/*Other cases go here, including OPEN, CLOSE, and IOCTL */
default:          rcode = ERROR;
}
mess.type = TASK_REPLY;
mess.status = rcode;             /* result code */
send(caller, &mess);
}
}
```

Fig. 11.20. A shared I/O task main procedure using indirect calls.

There is only one copy of the executable code in memory for the main loop of the block device drivers, but it is executed as the main loop of there or more distinct processes. Each of these processes is probably at a different point in the code at a given instant, and each is operating upon its own set of data and has its own stack.

There are six possible operations that can be requested of any device driver. These correspond to the possible values that can be found in the m.m_type field of the message of Fig. 11.18. They are:

1. OPEN
2. CLOSE
3. READ
4. WRITE
5. IOCTL
6. SCATTERED_IO

Most of these operations are probably familiar to readers with programming experience. At the device driver level most operations are related to system calls with the same name. For instance, the meanings of *READ* and *WRITE* should be clear. For each of these operations, a block of data is transferred from the device to the memory of the process that initiated the call, or vice versa. A *READ* operation normally does not result in a return to the caller until the data transfer is complete, but an operating system may buffer data transferred during a *WRITE* for actual transfer to the destination at a later time, and return to the caller immediately. That is fine as far as the caller is concerned; it is then free to reuse the buffer from which the operating system has copied the data to write. *OPEN* and *CLOSE* for a device have similar meanings to the way the OPEN and CLOSE system calls apply to operations on files: an *OPEN* operation should verify that the device is accessible, or return an error message if not, and a *CLOSE* should guarantee that any buffered data that were written by the caller is completely transferred to their final destination on the device.

The *IOCTL* operation may not be so familiar. Many I/O devices have operational parameters which occasionally must be examined and perhaps changed. *IOCTL* operations do this. A familiar example is changing the speed of transmissions or the parity of a communications line. For block devices, *IOCTL* operations are less common. Examining for changing the way a disk device is partitioned is done using an *IOCTL* operation in MINIX (although it could just as well have been done by reading and writing a block of data).

The *SCATTERED_10* operation is no doubt the least familiar of these. Except with exceedingly fast disk devices (for example, the RAM disk), satisfactory disk I/O performance is difficult to obtain if all disk requests are for individual blocks, one at a time. A *SCATTERED_10* request allows the file system to make a request to read or write multiple blocks. In the case of a *READ* operation, the additional blocks may not have been requested by the process on whose behalf the call is made; the operating system attempts to anticipate future requests for data. In such a request not all the transfers requested are necessarily honored by the device driver. The request for each block may be modified by a flag bit that tells the device driver that the request is optional. In effect the file system can say, "It would be nice to have all these data, but I do not really need them all right now." The device can do what is best for it. The floppy disk driver, for instance, will return all the data blocks it can read from a single track, effectively saying, "I will give you these, but it takes too long to move to another track; ask me again later for the rest."

When data must be written, there is no question of its being optional whether or not to write a particular block. Nevertheless, the operating system may buffer a number of write requests in the hope that writing multiple blocks can be done more efficiently than handling each request as it comes in. In a *SCATTERED_IO* request, whether for reading or writing, the list of blocks requested is sorted, and this makes the operation more efficient than handling the requests randomly. In addition, making only one call to the driver to transfer multiple blocks reduces the number of messages sent within MINIX.

Common Block Device Driver Software

Definitions that are needed by all the block device drivers are located in *driver.h.* The most important thing in this file is the *driver* structure, which is used by each driver to pass a list of the address of the functions it will use to perform each part of its job. Also defined here is the *device* structure which holds the most important information about partitions, the base address, and the size, in-byte units. This format was chosen so no conversions are necessary when working with memory-based devices, maximizing speed of response. With real disks there are so many other factors delaying access that converting to sectors is not a significant inconvenience.

The main loop and shared functions of all the block driver tasks are in *driver.c.* After doing whatever hardware-specific initialization may be necessary, each driver calls *driver_task,* passing a *driver* structure as the argument to the call. After obtaining the address of a buffer to use for DMA operations the main loop is entered. This loop is executed forever; there is no return to the caller.

The file system is the only process that is supposed to send a message to a driver task. A leftover interrupt from the hardware is ignored, any other misdirected message results only in printing a warning on the screen. This seems innocuous enough, but of course the process that sent the erroneous message is probably permanently blocked waiting for a reply. In the switch in the main loop, the first three message types, *DEV_OPEN, DEV_CLOSE,* and *DEV_IOCTL,* result in indirect calls using addresses passed in the *driver* structure. The *DEV_READ, DEV_WRITE,* and *SCATTERED-IO* messages result in direct calls to *do_rdwt* or *do_vrdwt.* However, the *driver* structure is passed as an argument by all the calls from within the switch, whether direct or indirect, so all the called routines can make further use of it as needed.

After doing whatever is requested in the message, some sort of cleanup may be necessary, depending upon the nature of the device. For a floppy disk, for instance, this might involve starting a timer to turn off the disk drive motor if another request does not arrive soon. An indirect call is used for this as well. Following the cleanup, a reply message is constructed and sent to the caller.

The first thing each task does after entering the main loop is to call *init_buffer* which assigns a buffer for use in DMA operations. The same buffer is used by all the driver tasks, if they use it all—some drivers do not use DMA. The initializations for each entry after the first are redundant but do not harm. It would be more cumbersome to code a test to see whether the initialization should be skipped.

That this initialization is even necessary at all is due to a quirk of the hardware of the original IBM PC, which requires that the DMA buffer not cross a 64k boundary. That is, a 1K DMA buffer may begin at 64510, but not at 64514 because a buffer starting at the latter address extends just beyond the 64K boundary at 65536.

This annoying rule occurs because the IBM PC used an old DMA chip, the Intel 8237A, which contains a 16-bit counter. A bigger counter is needed because DMA uses absolute addresses, not addresses relative to a segment register. On older machines that can address only 1M or memory, the low-order 16 bits of the DMA address are loaded into the 8237A, and the high-order 4 bits are loaded into a 4-bit latch. Newer machines user an 8-bit latch and can address 16M. When the 8237A goes from 0xFFFF to 0x0000, it does not generate a carry into the latch, so the DMA address suddenly jumps down by 64K in memory.

A portable C program cannot specify an absolute memory location for a data structure, so there is no way to prevent the compiler from placing the buffer in an unusable location. The solution is to allocate an array of bytes twice as large as necessary at *buffer* and to reserve a pointer *tmp_buf* to use for actually accessing this array. *Init_buffer* makes a trial setting of *tmp_buf* pointing to the beginning of *buffer*, then tests to see if that allows enough space before a 64K boundary is hit. If the trial setting does not provide enough space, *tmp_buf* is incremented by the number of bytes actually required. Thus some space is always wasted at one end or the other of the space allocated in *buffer,* but there is never a failure due to the buffer falling on a 64K boundary.

Newer computers of the IBM PC family haves better DMA controllers, and this code could be simplified, and a small amount of memory reclaimed, if one could be sure that one's machine were immune to this problem. If you are considering this, however, consider how the bug will manifest itself if you are wrong. If a 1K DMA buffer is desired, the chance is 1 in 64 that there will be a problem on a machine with the old DMA chip. Every time the kernel source code is modified in a way that changes the size of the compiled kernel, there is the same probability that the problem will manifest itself. Most likely, when the failure occurs next month or next year, it will be attributed to the code that was last modified. Unexpected hardware "features" like this can cause weeks of time spent looking for exceedingly obscure bugs (all the more so when, like this one, the technical reference manual says nary a work about them).

Do_rdwt is the next function in *driver.c.* It, in turn, may call three device-dependent functions pointed to by the *dr_prepare, dr_schedule,* and *dr_finish* fields in the *driver* structure. In what follows we will use the C language notation **function_pointer* to indicate we are talking about the function pointed to by *function_pointer.*

After checking to see that the byte count in the request is positive, *do_rdwt* calls **dr_prepare.* This should succeed, since **dr_prepare* can fail only if an invalid device is specified in an OPEN operation . Next, a standard *iorequest_s* structure is filled in. Then comes another indirect call, this time to **dr_schedule.* As we will see in the discussion of disk hardware in the next section, responding to disk requests in the order they are received can be inefficient, and this routine allows a particular device to handle requests in the way that is best for the device. The indirection here masks much possible variation in the way individual devices perform. For the RAM disk, *dr_schedule* points to a routine that actually performs the I/O, and the next indirect call, to **dr_finish,* is a do-nothing operation. For a real disk, *dr_finish* points t a routine that carries out all of the pending data transfers requested in all previous calls to **dr_schedule* since the last call to **dr_finish.* As we will see, however, in some circumstances the call to **dr_finish* may not result in a transfer of all data requested.

In whichever call does an actual data transfer, the *io_nbytes* count in the *iorequest_s* structure is modified, returning a negative number if there was an error or a positive number indicating the difference between the number of bytes in the original request and the number successfully transferred. It is not necessarily an error if no bytes are transferred; this indicates that the end of the device has been reached. Upon returning to the main loop, the negative error code is returned in the reply message *REP_STATUS* field if there was an error. Otherwise the bytes remaining to be transferred are subtracted from the original request in the *COUNT* field of the message, and the result (the number actually transferred) is returned in *REP_STATUTS* in the reply message from *driver_task.*

The next function, *do_vrdwt,* handles all scattered I/O requests. A message that requests a scattered I/O request uses the *ADDRESS* field to point to an array of *iorquest_s* type structures, each of which specifies the information needed for one request: the address of the buffer, the offset on the device, the number of bytes, and whether the operation is a read or a write. All the operations in one request will be for either reading or writing, and they will be sorted into block order on the device. There is more work to do than for the simple read or write performed by *do_rdwt,* since the array of requests must be copied into the kernel's space, but once this has been done, the same three indirect calls to the device-dependent **dr_prepare, *dr_finish* routines are made. The difference is that the middle call, to **dr_schedule,* is done in a loop, once for each request, or until an error occurs. After termination of the loop, **dr_finish* is called once, and then the array of requests is copied back where it came from. The *io_bytes* field of each element in the array will have been changed to reflect the number of bytes transferred, and although the total is not passed back directly in the reply message that *driver_back* constructs, the caller can extract the total from this array.

In a scattered I/O read request, not all the transfers requested in the call to **dr_schedule* are necessarily honored when the final call to **dr_finish* is make, as we discussed in the previous section. The *io_request* field in the *iorequest_s* structure contains a flag bit that tells the device driver if a request for that block is optional.

The next few routines in *driver.c* are for general support of the above operations. A **dr_name* call can be used to return the name of a device. For a device with no specific name the *no_name* function retrieves the device's name from the table of tasks. Some devices may not require a particular service, for instance, a RAM disk does not require that anything special be done upon a *DEV_CLOSE* request. The *do_nop* function fills in here, returning various codes depending upon the kind of request. The following functions, *nop_finish*, and *nop_cleanup,* are similar dummy routines for devices that need no **dr_finish* or **dr_cleanup* services.

Some disk device functions require delays, for example, to wit for a floppy disk motor to come up to speed. Thus *driver.c* is a good places for the next function, *clock_mess,* used to send messages to the clock task. It is called with the number of clock ticks, to wait and the address of a function to call when the timeout period is complete.

Finally, *do_diocntl,* carries out DEV_IOCTL request for a block device. It is an error if any *DEV_IOCTL* operation other than reading *(DIOGETP)* or writing *(DIOSETP)* partition information is requested. *Do_dicontl* calls the device's **dr_prepare* function to verify the device is valid and to get a pointer the *device* structure that describes the partition base and size in byte units. On a request to read, it calls the device's **dr_geometry* function to get the last cylinder, head, and sector information about the partition.

The Driver Library

The files *drvlib.h* and *drvlib.c* contain system-dependent code that supports disk partitions on IBM PC compatible computers.

Partitioning allows a single storage device to be divided up into subdevices. It is most commonly used with hard disks, but MINIX provides support for partitioning floppy disks, as well. Some reasons to partition a disk device are:

1. Disk capacity is cheaper per unit in large disks. If two or more operating system with different file systems are used, it is more economical to partition a single large disk than to install multiple smaller disks for each operating system.
2. Operating system may have limits to the device size they can handle. The version of MINIX discussed here can handle a 1-GB file systems, but older versions are limited to 256 MB. Any disk space beyond that is wasted.
3. Two or more different file systems may be used by an operating system. For example, a standard file system may be used for ordinary files and a differently structured file system may be used for virtual memory swap space.
4. It may be convenient to put a portion of a system's files on a separate logical device. Putting the MINIX root file system on a small device makes it easy to back up and facilitates copying it to a RAM disk at boot time.

Support for disk partitions is platform specific. This specificity is not related to the hardware. Partition support is device independent. But if more than one operating system is to run on a particular set of hardware, all must agree on a format for the partition table. On IBM PCs the standard is set by the MS-DOS *fdisk* command, and other OSs, such as MINIX, OS/2, and Linux, use this format so they can coexist with MS-DOs. When MINIX is ported to another machine type, it makes sense to use a partition table format compatibe with other operating systems used on the new hardware. Thus the MINIX source code to support partitions on IBM computers is put in *drvlib.c,* rather than being included in *driver.c,* to make it easier to port MINIX to different hardware.

The basic data structure inherited from the firmware designers is defined in *include/ibm/partition.h,* which is included by a #include statement in *drvlib.h.* This includes information on the cylinder-head-sector geometry of each partition, as well as codes identifying the type of file system on the partition and an active flag indication if it is bootable. Most of this information is not needed by MINIX once the file system is verified.

The *partition* function is called when a block device is first opened. Its arguments include a *driver* structure, so it can call device-specific functions, an initial minor device number, and a parameter indication whether the partitioning style is floppy disk, primary partition, or subpartition. It calls the device-specific **dr_prepare* function to verify the device is valid and to get the base address and the size into a device structure of the type mentioned in the previous section. Then it calls *get_part_table* to determine if a partition table is present and, if so, to read it. If there is no partition table, the work is done. Otherwise the minor device number of the first partition is computed, using the rules for numbering minor devices that apply to the style of partitioning specified in the original call. In the case of primary partitions the partition table is sorted so the order of the partitions is consistent with that used by other operating systems.

At this point another call is made to **dr_prepare,* this time using the newly calculated device number of the first partition. If the subdevice is valid, then a loop is made over all the entries in the table, checking that the values read from the table on the device are not of the range obtained earlier for the base and size of the device. If there is a discrepancy, the table in memory is adjusted to conform. This may seem paranoid, but since partition tables may be written by different operating systems, a programmer using another system may have cleverly tried to use the partition table for something unexpected or there could be garbage in the table on disk for some other reason. We put the most trust in the numbers we calculate using MINIX. Better safe than sorry.

Still within the loop, for all partitions on the device, if the partition is identified as a MINIX partition, *partition* is called recursively to gather subpartition information. If a partition is identified as an extended partition, the next function in the file, *extpartition,* is called instead.

Extpartition really has nothing to do with the MINIX operating system, so we will not discuss its details. MS-DOS used extended partitions, which are just another mechanism for creating subpartitions. In order to support MINIX commands that can read and write MS-DOS files, we need to know about these subpartitions.

Get_part_table calls *do_rdwt* to get the sector on a device (or subdevice) where a partition table is located. The offset argument is zero if it is called to get a primary partition of nonzero for a subpartition. It checks for the magic number (0xAA55) and returns true or false status to indicate whether a valid partition table was found. If a table is found, it copies it to the table address that was passed as an argument.

Finally, *sort* sorts the entries in a partition table by lowest sector. Entries that are marked as having no partition are excluded from the sort, so they come at the end, even though they may have a zero value in their low sector field. The sort is a simple bubble sort; there is no need to use a fancy algorithm to sort a list of four items.

RAM Disks

Now we will get back to the individual block device drivers and study several of them in detail. The first one we will look at is the RAM disk driver. It can be used to provide access to any part of memory. Its primary used is to allow a part of memory to be reserved for use like an ordinary disk. The does not provide permanent storage, but once files have been copied to this are they can be accessed extremely quickly.

In a system such as MINIX, which was designed to work even on computers with only one floppy disk, the RAM disk has another advantage. By putting the root device on the RAM disk, the one floppy disk can be mounted and unmounted at will, allowing for removable media. Putting the root device on the floppy disk would make it impossible to save files on floppies, since the root device (the only floppy) cannot be unmounted. In addition, having the root device on the RAM disk makes the system highly flexible: any combination of floopy disks or hard disks can be mounted on it. Although most computers now have hard disks, except computers used in embedded systems, the RAM disk is useful during installation, before the hard disk is ready for use by MINIX, or when it is desired to use MINIX temporarily without doing a full installation.

RAM Disk Hardware and Software

The idea behind a RAM disk is simple. A block devices is a storage medium with two commands: write a block and read a block. Normally these blocks are stored on rotating memories, such as floppy disks or hard disks. A RAM disk is simpler. It just uses a preallocated portion of the main memory for storing the blocks. A RAM disk has the advantage of having instant access (no seek or rotational delay), making it suitable for storing programs or data that are frequently accessed.

As an aside, it is worth briefly pointing out a difference between systems that support mounted file systems and those they do not (e.g., MS-DOS and WINDOWS). With mounted file systems, the root device is always present and in a fixed location, and removable file system, (i.e., disks) can be mounted in the file tree to form an integrated file system. Once everything has been mounted, the user need not worry at all about which device a file is on.

In contrast, with systems like MS-DOS, the user must specify the location of each file, either explicitly as in *B: \DIR\FILE* or using certain defaults (current device, current director, and so on). With only one or two floppy disks, this burden is manageable, but on a large computer system, with dozens of disks, having to keep track of devices all the time would be unbearable. Remember that UNIX runs on systems ranging from an IBM PC, through workstations and supercomputers up to the Cray-2; MS-DOS runs only on small systems.

Figure 11.21, shows the idea behind a RAM disk. The RAM disk is split up into *n* blocks, depending on how much memory has been allocated for it. Each block is the same size as the block size used on the real disk. When the driver receives a message to read or write a block, it just computes where in the RAM disk memory the requested block lies and reads from it or writes to it, instead of from or to a floppy or hard disk. The transfer is done by calling as assembly language procedure that copies to or from the user program at the maximum speed of which the hardware is capable.

A RAM disk driver may support several areas of memory used as RAM disk, each distinguished by a different minor device number. Usually these areas are distinct, but in some situations it may be convenient to have them overlap, as we shall see in the next section.

Overview of the RAM Disk Driver in MINIX

The RAM disk driver is actually four closely related drivers in one. Each message to it specifies a minor device as follows:

0: /dev/ram 1:/dev/mem 2: /dev/kmem 3: /dev/null

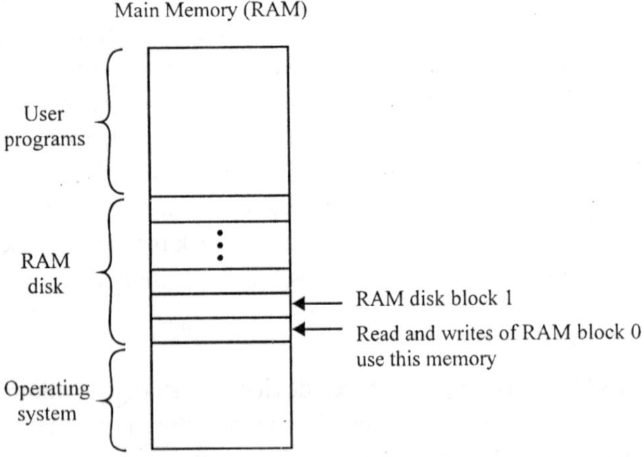

Fig. 11.21. A RAM disk.

The first special file listed above, */dev/ram*, is a true RAM disk. Neither its size nor its origin is built into the driver. They are determined by the file system when MINIX is booted. By default a RAM disk of the same size as the root file system image device is created, so the root file system can be copied to it. A boot parameter can be used to specify a RAM disk larger than the root file system, or if the root is not to be copied to the RAM, the specified size may be nay value that fits in memory and leaves enough memory for system operation. Once the size is known a block of memory big enough is found and removed from the memory pool even before the memory manager begins its work. This strategy makes it possible to increase or reduce the amount of RAM disk present without having to recompile the operating system.

The next two minor devices are used to read and write physical memory and kernel memory, respectively. When */dev/mem* is opened and read, it yields the contents of physical memory locations starting at absolute address zero (the real-mode interrupt vectors). Ordinary user programs never do this, but a system program concerned with debugging the system might need this facility. Opening */dev/mem* and writing on it will change the interrupt vectors. Needless to say, this should only be done with the greatest of caution by an experienced user who knows exactly what he is doing.

The special file */dev/kmem* is like */dev/mem,* except that byte 0 of this file is byte 0 of the kernel's data memory, a location whose absolute address varies, depending on the size of the MINIX kernel code. It too is used mostly for debugging and very special programs. Note that the RAM disk areas covered by these two minor devices overlap. If you know exactly how the kernel is placed in memory, you can open */dev/mem*, seek to the beginning of the kernel's data area, and see exactly the same thing as reading from the beginning of */dev/kmen.* But, if you recompile the kernel, changing its size, or if in a subsequent version of MINIX the kernel is moved somewhere else in memory, you will have to seek a different amount in */dev/mem* to see the same thing you see at the start of */dev/kmem.* Both of these special files should be protected to prevent everyone except the super-user from using them.

The last file in this group, */dev/null,* is a special file that accepts data and throws them away. It is commonly used in shell commands when the program being called generates output that is not needed. For example,

```
a.out>/dev/null
```

runs the program *a.out* but discards its output. The RAM disk driver effectively treats this minor device as having zero size, so no data are ever copied to or from it.

The code for handling */dev/ram, /dev/mem,* and */dev/kmen* is identical. The only difference among them is that each one corresponds to a different portion of memory, indicated by the arrays *ram_origin* and *ram_limit,* each indexed by minor device number.

Implementation of the RAM Disk Driver in MINIX

As with other disk drivers the main loop of the RAM disk is in the file *driver.c.* The device-specific support for memory devices is in *memory.c.* The array *m_geom* holds the base and size of each of the four memory devices. The *driver* structure *m_dtab* defines the memory device calls that will be made from the main loop. Four of the entries in this table are do-little or do-nothing routines in *driver.c,* a sure clue that the operation of a RAM disk is not terribly complicated. The main procedure *mem_task* calls one function to do some local initialization. After that, it calls the main loop, which gets messages, dispatches to the appropriate procedure, and sends the replies. There is no return to *mem_task* upon completion.

On a read or write operation the main loop makes three calls: one to prepare a device, one to schedule the I/O operations, and one to finish the operation. For a memory device a call to *m_prepare* is the first of these. It checks that a valid minor device has been requested and then returns the address of the structure that holds the base address and size of the requested RAM area. The second call is for *m_schedule.* This does all the work. For memory devices the name of this function is a misnomer; by definition, any location is a accessible as any other in random access memory, and thus there is no need to do any scheduling, as there would be with a disk having a moving arm.

The RAM disk's operation is so simple and fast there is never any reason to postpone a request, and the first thing done by this function is to clear the bit that may be set by a scattered I/O call to indicate completion of an operation is optional. The destination address passed in the message points to a location in the caller's memory space, and the code converts this into an absolute address in the system memory and then checks that it is a valid address.

A memory device does not need a third step to finish a read or write operation, and the corresponding slot in *m_dtab* is a call to *nop_finish.*

Opening a memory device is done by *m_do_open*. The main job is done by calling *m_prepare* to check that a valid device is being referenced. In the case of a reference to */dev/mem* or */dev/kmem,* a call to *enable_iop* (in the file *protect.c*) is made to change the CPU's current privilege level. This is not necessary to access memory. It is a trick to deal with another problem. Recall that Pentium-class CPUs implement for privilege levels. User programs are at the least privileged level. Intel processors also have an architectural feature that is not present in many other systems, a separate set of instructions to address I/O ports. On these processors I/O ports are treated separately from memory. Normally, an attempt by a user process to execute an instruction that addresses an I/O port causes a general protection exception. However, there are valid reasons for MINIX to allow users to write programs that can access ports, especially on small systems. Thus *enable_iop* changes the CPU's I/O Protection Level (IOPL) bits to permit this. The effect is to allow a process permitted to open */dev/mem* or */dev/kmem* the additional privilege of access of I/O ports. On an architecture where I/O devices are addressed as memory locations, the *rwx* bits for these devices automatically cover access to I/O. If this feature were hidden, it might be considered a security flaw, but now you know about it. If you plan to use MINIX to control a bank security system, you might want to recompile the kernel without this function.

The next function, *m_init,* is called only once, when *mem_task* is called for the first time. It sets up the base address and size of */dev/kmem* and it also sets the size of */dev/mem* to 1 MB 16 MB, or 4 GB-1, depending upon whether MINIX is running in 8088, 80286, or 80386 mode. These sizes are the maximum sizes supported by MINIX and do not have anything to do with how much RAM is installed in the machine.

The RAM disk supports several IOCTL operations in *m_ioctl.* The *MIOCRAMSIZE* is a convenient way for the file system to set the RAM disk size. The *MIOCSPSINFO* operation is used by both the file system and the memory manager to set the addresses of their parts of the process table into the *psinfo* table, where the utility program *ps* can retrieve it using a *MIOCGPSINFO* operation. *Ps* is a standard UNIX program whose implementation is complicated by MINIX's microkernel structure, which puts the process table information needed by the program in several different places. The IOCTL system call is a convenient way to handle this problem. Otherwise a new version of *ps* would have to be compiled each time a new version of MINIX were compiled.

That last function in *memory.c* is *m_geometry.* Memory devices do not have a geometry of cylinders, tracks, and sectors per track like mechanical disk drives, but in case the RAM disk is asked it will oblige by pretending it does.

Disks

The RAM disk is a good introduction to disk drivers (because it is so simple), but real disks present a number of issues that we have not yet touched upon. In the following sections we will fist say a few words about disk hardware and then take a look at disk drivers in general and the MINIX hard disk driver in particular. We will not examine the floppy disk driver in detail, but we will go over some of the ways a floppy disk driver differs from a hard disk driver.

Disk Hardware

All real disks are organized into cylinders, each one containing as many tracks as there are heads stacked vertically. The tracks are divided into sectors, with the number of sectors around the circumference typically being 8 to 32 on floppy disks, and up to several hundred on some hard disks. The simplest designs have the same number of sectors on each track. All sectors contain the same number of bytes, although, a little thought will make it clear that sectors close to the outer rim of the disk will be physically longer than those close to the hub. The time to read or write each sector will be sector will be same, however. The data density is obviously higher on the innermost cylinders, and some disk designs require a change in the drive current to the read-write heads for the inner tracks. This is handled by the disk controller hardware and is not visible to the user (or the implementor of an operating system).

The difference in data density between inner and outer tracks means a sacrifice in capacity, and more sophisticated systems exist. Floppy disk designs that rotate at higher speeds when the heads are over the outer tracks have been tried. This allows more sectors on those tracks, increasing disk capacity. Such disks are not supported by any system for which MINIX is currently available, however. Modern large hard drives also have more sectors per track on outer tracks than on inner tracks. These are **IDE (Integrated Drive Electronics)** drives, and the sophisticated processing done by the drive's built-in electronics masks the details. To the operating system they appear to have a simple geometry with the same number of sectors on each track.

The drive and controller electronics are as important as the mechanical hardware. The main element of the controller card that is plugged into the computer's backplane is a specialized integrated circuit, really a small microcomputer. For a hard disk the controller card circuit may be simpler than for a floppy disk, but this is because the hard drive itself has a powerful electronic controller built in. A device feature that has important implications for the disk driver is the possibility of a controller doing seeks on two or more drives at the same time. These are known as **overlapped seeks.** While the controller and software are waiting for a seek to complete on one drive, the controller can initiate a seek on another drive. Many controllers can also read or write on one drive while seeking on one or more other drives, but a floppy disk controller cannot read or write on two drives at the same time. (Reading or writing requires the controller to move bits on a microsecond time scale, so one transfer uses up most of its computing power.) The situation is different for hard disk with integrated controllers, and in a system with more than one of these hard drives they can operate simultaneously, at least to the extent of transferring between the disk and the controller's buffer memory. Only one transfer between the controller and the system memory is possible at once, however. The ability to perform two or more operations at the same time can reduce the average access time considerably.

Figure 11.22, compares parameters of double-sided, double-density diskettes, the standard storage medium for the original IBM PC, with parameters of a typical medium-capacity hard drive such as might be found on a Pentium-based computer. MINIX uses 1K blocks, so with either of these disk formats the block used by the software consist of two consecutive sectors, which are always read or written together as unit.

One thing to be aware of in looking at the specification of modern hard disks is that the geometry specified, and used by the driver software, may be different than the physical format. The hard disk described in Fig. 11.22, for instance, is specified with "recommended setup parameters" of 1048 cylinders, 16 heads, and 63 sectors per track. The controller electronics mounted on the disk converts the logical head and sector parameters supplied by the operating system to the physical ones used by the disk. This is another example of a compromise designed to maintain compatibility with older systems, in this case old firmware. The designers of the original IBM PC only allotted a 6-bit field for the BIOS ROM's sector count, and a disk that has more than 63 physical sectors per track must work with an artificial set disk parameters. In this case the vendor's specifications state that there are really four heads, and thus it would appear that there are really 252 sectors per track, as indicated in the figure. This is an over-simplification, because disks like these have more sectors on the outermost tracks than on the inner tracks. The disk described in the figure does have four physical heads, but there are actually slightly over 3000 cylinders. The cylinders are grouped in a dozen zones which gave from 57 sectors per track in the innermost zones to 105 cylinders per track on the outermost cylinders. These numbers are not to be found in the disk's specifications, and the translations done by the drive's electronics make it unnecessary for us to know such details.

Parameter	IBM 360-KB floppy disk	WD 540-MB hard disk
Number of cylinders	40	1048
Tracks per cylinder	2	4
Sectors per track	9	252
Sectors per disk	720	1056384
Bytes per sector	512	512
Bytes per disk	368640	540868608
Seek time (adjacent cylinders)	6 msec	4 msec
Seek time (average case)	77 msec	11 msec
Rotation time	200 msec	13 msec
Motor stop/start time	250 msec	9 sec
Time to transfer 1 sector	22 msec	53 μsec

Fig. 11.22. Disk parameters for the original IBM PC 360-KB floppy disk and a Western Digital WD AC2540 540-MB hard disk.

Disk Software

In this section we will look at some issues related to disk drivers in general. First, consider how long it takes to read or write a disk block. The time required is determined by three factors:

1. The seek time (the time to move the arm to the proper cylinder).
2. The rotational delay (the time for the proper sector to rotate under the head).
3. The actual data transfer time.

For most disks, the seek time dominates the other two times, so reducing the mean seek time can improve system performance substantially.

Disk devices are prone to errors. Some kind of error check, a checksum or a cyclic redundancy check, is always recorded along with the data in each sector on a disk. Even the sector addresses recorded when the disk is formatted have check data. Floppy disk controller hardware can report when an error is detected but the software must then decide what to do about it. Hard disk controllers often take on much of this burden.

Particularly with hard disks, the transfer time for consecutive sectors within a track can be very fast. Thus reading more data than is requested and caching them in memory can be very effective in speeding disk access.

Disk Arm Scheduling Algorithms

If the disk driver accepts requests one at a time and carries them out in that order, that is, First-Come, First-Served (FCFS), little can be done to optimize seek time. However, another strategy is possible when the disk is heavily loaded. It is likely that while the arm is seeking on behalf of one request, other disk requests may be generated by other processes. Many disk drivers maintain a table, indexed by cylinder number, with all the pending requests for each cylinder chained together in a linked list headed by the table entries.

Given this kind of data structure, we can improve upon the first-come, first-served scheduling algorithm. To see how, consider a disk with 40 cylinders. A request comes in to read a block on cylinder 11. While the seek to cylinder 11 is in progress, new requests come in for cylinders 1, 36, 16, 34, 9, and 12, in that order. They are entered into the table of pending requests, with a separate linked list for each cylinder. The requests are shown in Fig. 11.23.

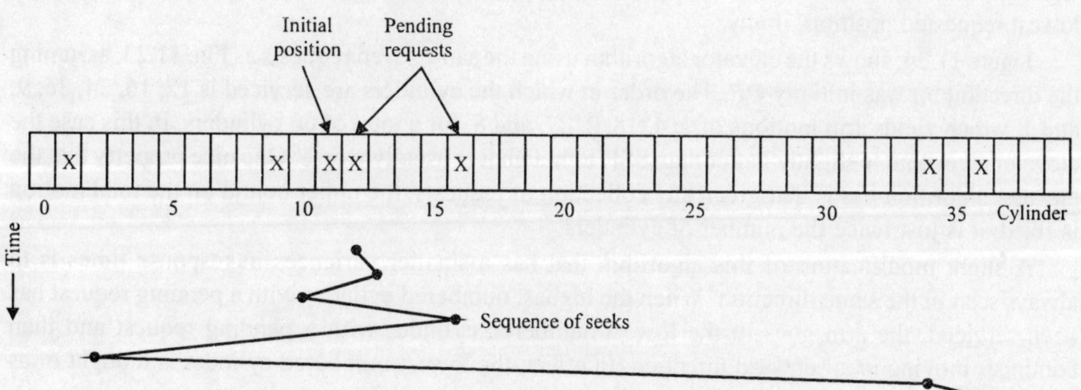

Fig. 11.23. Shortest Seek First (SSF) disk scheduling algorithm.

When the current request (for cylinder 11) is finished, the disk driver has a choice of which request to handle next. Using FCFS, it would go next to cylinder 1, then to 36, and so on. This algorithm would require arm motions to 10, 35, 20, 18, 25, and 3, respectively, for a total of 111 cylinders.

Alternatively, it could always handle the closest request next, to minimize seek time. Given the request of Fig 11.23, the sequence is 12, 9, 16, 1, 34, and 36 as shown as the jagged line at the bottom of Fig 11.23. With this sequence, the arm motions are 1,3, 7, 15, 33, and 2, for a total of 61 cylinders. This algorithm, **Shortest Seek First (SSF),** cuts the total arm motion almost in half compared to FCFS.

Unfortunately, SSF has a problem. Suppose more requests keep coming in while the requests of Fig 11.23, are being processed. For example, if, after going to cylinder 16, a new request for cylinder 8 is present, that request will have priority over cylinder 1. if a request for cylinder 13 then comes in, the arm will next go to 13, instead of 1. With a heavily loaded disk, the arm will tend to stay in the middle of the disk most of the time, so requests at either extreme will have to wait until a statistical fluctuation in the load causes there to be no request near the middle. Requests far from the middle may get poor service. The goals of minimal response time and fairness are in conflict here.

Tall buildings also have to deal with this trade-off. The problem of scheduling an elevator in a tall building is similar to that of scheduling a disk arm. Requests come in continuously calling the elevator to floors (cylinders) at random. The microprocessor running the elevator could easily keep track of the sequence in which customers pushed the call button and service them using FCFS. It could also use SSF.

However, most elevators use a different algorithm to reconcile the conflicting goals of efficiency and fairness. They keep moving in the same direction until there are no more outstanding requests in that direction, then they switch directions. This algorithm, known both in the disk world and the elevator world as the **elevator algorithm,** requires the software to maintain 1 bit: the current direction bit, *UP* or *DOWN*. When a request finishes, the disk or elevator driver checks the bit. If it is *UP*, the arm or cabin is moved to the next highest pending request. If no requests are pending at higher positions, the direction bit is reversed. When the bit is set of *DOWN*, the move is to the next lowest requested position, if any.

Figure 11.24, shows the elevator algorithm using the same seven requests as Fig. 11.23, assuming the direction bit was initially *UP*. The order in which the cylinders are serviced is 12, 16, 34, 36, 9, and 1, which yields arm motions of 1, 4, 18, 2, 27, and 8, for a total of 60 cylinders. In this case the elevator algorithm is slightly better than SSF, although it is usually worse. One nice property that the elevator algorithm has is that given any collection of requests, the upper bound on the total motion is fixed: it is just twice the number of cylinders.

A slight modification of this algorithm that has a smaller variances in response times is to always scan in the same direction. When the highest numbered cylinder with a pending request has been serviced, the arm goes to the lowest-numbered cylinder with a pending request and then continues moving in an upward direction. In effect, the lowest-numbered cylinder is thought of as being just above the highest-numbered cylinder.

Some disk controllers provide a way for the software to inspect the current sector number under the head. With such a controller, another optimization is possible. If two or more requests for the same cylinder are pending, the driver can issue a request for the sector that will pass under the head next. Note that when multiple tracks are present in a cylinder, consecutive requests can be for different tracks with no penalty. The controller can select any of its heads instantaneously, because head selection involves neither arm motion nor rotational delay.

With a modern hard disk, the data transfer rate is so much faster than that of a floppy disk that some kind of automatic caching is necessary. Typically any request to read a sector will cause that sector and up to the rest of the current track to be read, depending upon how much space is available in the controller's cache memory. The 540M disk described in Fig 11.23, has a 64K or 128K cache. The use of the cache is determined dynamically by the controller. In this its simplest mode, the cache is divided into two sections, one for reads and one for writes.

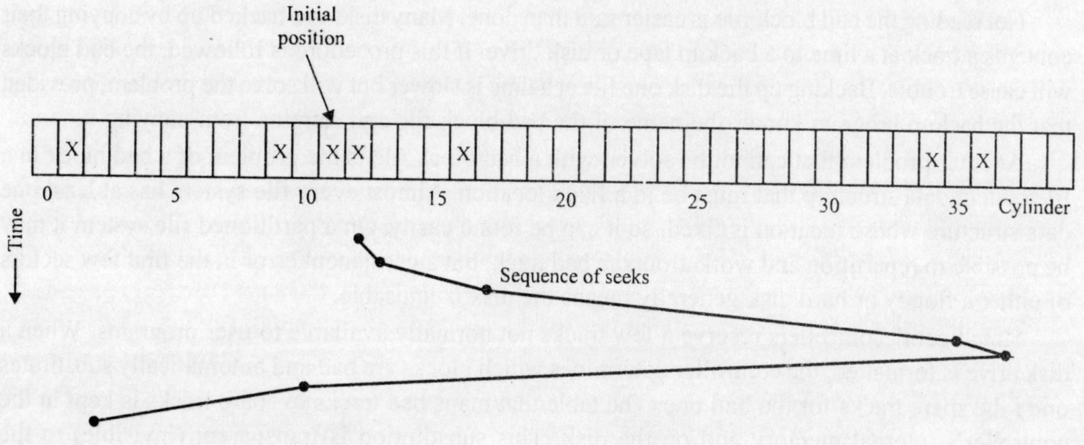

Fig. 11.24. The elevator algorithm for scheduling disk requests.

Error Handling

RAM disks do not have to worry about seek or rotational optimization: at any instant all blocks can be read or written without any physical motion. Another area in which RAM disks are simpler than real disks is error handling. RAM disks always work; real ones do not always work. They are subject to a wide variety of errors. Some of the more common ones are:

1. Programming error (e.g., request for nonexistent sector).
2. Transient checksum error (e.g., caused by dust on the head).
3. Permanent checksum error (e.g., disk block physically damaged).
4. Seek error (e.g., the arm sent to cylinder 6 but it went to 7).
5. Controller error (e.g., controller refuses to accept commands).

It is up to the disk driver to handle each of these as best it can.

Programming error occur when the driver tells the controller to seek to a nonexistent cylinder, read from a nonexistent sector, use a nonexistent head, or transfer to or from nonexistent memory. Most controllers check the parameters given to them and complain if they are invalid. In theory, these errors should never occur, but what should the driver do if the controller indicates that one has happened? For a home-grown system, the best thing to do is stop and print a message like "Call the programmer" so the error can be tracked down and fixed. For a commercial software product in use at thousands of sites around the world, this approach is less attractive. Probably the only thing to do is terminate the current disk request with an error and hope it will not recur too often.

Transient checksum errors are caused by specks of dust in the air that get between the head and the disk surface. Most of the timer they can be eliminated by just repeating the operation a few times. If the error persists, the block has to be marked as a **bad block** and avoided.

One way to avoid bad blocks is to write a very special program that takes a list of bad blocks as input and carefully hand crafts a file containing all the bad blocks. Once this file has been made, the disk allocator will think these blocks are occupied and never allocate them. As long as no one ever tries to read the bad block file, no problems will occur.

Not reading the bad block file is easier said than done. Many disks are backed up by copying their contents a track at a time to a backup tape or disk drive. If this procedure is followed, the bad blocks will cause trouble. Backing up the disk one file at a time is slower but will solve the problem, provided that the backup program knows the name of the bad block file and refrains from copying it.

Another problem that cannot be solved with a bad block file is the problem of a bad block in a file system data structure that must be in a fixed location. Almost every file system has at least one data structure whose location is fixed, so it can be found easily. On a partitioned file system it may be possible to repartition and work around a bad track, but a permanent error in the first few sectors of either a floppy or hard disk generally means the disk is unusable.

"Intelligent" controllers reserve a few tracks not normally available to user programs. When a disk drive is formatted, the controller determines which blocks are bad and automatically substitutes one f the spare tracks for the bad one. The table that maps bad tracks to spare tracks is kept in the controller's internal memory and on the disk. This substitution is transparent (invisible) to the driver, except that its carefully worked out elevator algorithm may perform poorly if the controller is secretly using cylinder 800 whenever cylinder 3 is requested. The technology of manufacturing disk recording surfaces is better than it used to be, but it is still not perfect. However, the technology of hiding the imperfections from the user has also improved. On hard disk such as the one described in Fig 11.23, the controller also manages new errors that may develop with use, permanently assigning substitute blocks when it determines that an error is unrecoverable. With such disks the driver software rarely sees any indication that there any bad blocks.

Seek errors are caused by mechanical problems in the arm. The controller keeps track of the arm position internally. To perform a seek, it issues a series of pulses to the arm motor, one pulse per cylinder, to move the arm to the new cylinder. When the arm gets to its destination, the controller reads the actual cylinder number (written when the drive was formatted). If the arm is in the wrong place, a seek error has occurred.

Most hard disk controllers correct seek error automatically, but many floppy controller (including the IBM PCs) just set an error bit and leave the rest to the driver. The driver handles this error by issuing a RECALIBRATE command, to move the arm as far out as it will go and reset the controller's internal idea of the current cylinder to 0. Usually this solves the problem. If it does, not, the drive must be repaired.

As we have seen, the controller is really a specialized little computer, complete with software, variables, buffers, and occasionally, bugs. Sometimes an unusual sequence of events such as an interrupt on one drive occurring simultaneously with a RECALIBRATE command for another drive will trigger a bug and cause the controller to go into a loop or lose track of what it was doing . Controller designers usually plan for the worst and provide a pin on the chip which, when asserted, forces the controller to forget whatever it was doing and reset itself. If all else fails, the disk driver can set a bit to invoke this signal and reset the controller. If that does not help, all the driver can do is print a message and give up.

Track-at-a-Time Caching

The time required to seek to a new cylinder is usually much more than the rotational delay, and always much more than the transfer time. In other words, once the driver has gone to the trouble of moving the arm somewhere, it hardly matters whether it reads one sector or a whole track. This effect is especially true if the controller provides rotational sensing, so the driver can see which sector is currently under the head and issue a request for the next sector, thereby making it possible to read a track in one rotation time.

Some disk drivers take advantage of this property by maintaining a secret track-at-a-time cache, unknown to the device-independent software. If a sector that is in the cache is needed, no disk transfer is required. A disadvantage of track-at-a-time caching (in addition to the software complexity and buffer space needed) is that transfers from the cache to the calling program will have to be done by the CPU using a programmed loop, rather than letting the DMA hardware do the job.

Some controllers take this process a step further, and do track-at-a-time caching in their own internal memory, transparent to the driver, so that transfer between the controller and memory can use DMA. If the controller works this way, there is little point in having the disk driver do it as well. Note that both the controller and the driver are in a good position to read and write entire tracks in one command, but that the device-independent software cannot, because it regards a disk as a linear sequence of blocks, without regard to how they are divided up into tracks and cylinders.

Overview of the Hard Disk Driver in MINIX

The hard disk driver is the first part of MINIX we have looked at that has to deal with a wide range of different types of hardware. Before we discuss the details of the driver, we will briefly consider some of the problems hardware differences can cause. The "IBM PC" is really a family of different computers. Not only are different processors used in different members of the family, there are also some major differences in the basic hardware. The earliest members of the family, the original PC and the PC-XT, used an 8-bit bus, appropriate for the 8-bit external interface of the 8088 processor. The next generation, the PC-AT, used a 16-bit bus, which was cleverly designed so older 8-bit peripherals could still be used. Newer 16-bit peripherals generally cannot be used on older PC-XT systems, however. The AT bus was originally designed for systems using the 80286 processor, and many systems based on the 80386, 80486, and Pentium use the AT bus. However, since these newer processors have a 32-bit interface, there are now several different 32-bit bus systems available, such as Intel's PCI bus.

For every bus there is a different family of **I/O adapters,** which plug into the system parentboard. All the peripherals for a particular bus design must be compatible with the standards for that design but need not be compatible with older designs. In the IBM PC family, as in most other computer systems, each bus design also comes with firmware in the Basic I/O System Read-Only Memory (the BIOS ROM) which is designed to bridge the gap between the operating system and the peculiarities of the hardware. Some peripheral devices may provide extensions to the BIOS in ROM chips on the peripheral cards themselves. The difficulty faced by an operating system implementor is that the BIOS in IBM-type computers was designed for an operating system, MS-DOS, that does not support multiprogramming and that runs in 16-bit real mode, the lowest common denominator of the various modes of operation available from the 80x86 family of CPUs.

The implementor of a new operating system for the IBM PC is thus faced with several choices. One is whether to use the driver support for peripherals in the BIOS or to write new drivers from scratch. This was not a hard choice in the original design of MINIX, since the BIOS was in many ways not suitable to the needs of MINIX. Of course, in order to get started, the MINIX boot monitor uses the BIOS to do the initial loading of the system, whether from hard disk or floppy disk—there is no practical alternative to doing it this way. Once we have loaded the system, including our own I/O drivers, we can do much better than the BIOS.

The second choice then must be faced: without the BIOS support how are we going to make our drivers adapt to the varied kinds of hardware on different systems? To make the discussion concrete, consider that there are at least four fundamentally different types of hard disk controllers that we might find on a system which is otherwise suitable for MINIX: the original 8-bit XT-type controller, the 16-bit AT-type controller, and two different controllers for two different types of IBM PS/2 series computers. There are several possible ways to deal with this:

1. Recompile a unique version of the operating system for each type of hard disk controller we need to accommodate.
2. Compile several different hard disk drivers into the kernel and have the kernel automatically determine at startup time which one to use.
3. Compile several different hard disk drivers into the kernel and provide a way for the user to determine which one to use.

As we shall see, these are not mutually exclusive.

The first way is really the best way in the long run. For use on a particular installation there is no need to use up disk and memory space with code for alternative drivers that will never be used. However, it is a nightmare for the distributor of the software. Supplying four different startup disks and advising users on how to use them is expensive and difficult. Thus, one of the other alternatives is advisable, at least for the initial installation.

The second method is to have the operating system probe the peripherals, by reading the ROM on each card or writing and reading I/O ports to identify each card. This is feasible on some systems but does not work well on IBM-type systems because there are too many nonstandard I/O devices available. Probing I/O ports to identify one device may, in some cases, activate another device which seizes control and disables the system. This method complicates the startup code for each device, and yet still does not work very well. Operating systems that do use this method generally have to provide some kind of override, typically a mechanism such as we use with MINIX.

The third method, use in MINIX, is to allow compilation of several drivers, with one of them being the default. The MINIX boot monitor allows various **boot parameters** to be read at startup time. These can be entered by hand, or stored permanently on the disk. At startup time, if a boot parameter of the form

hd = xt

is found, this forces use of the XT hard disk driver. If no hd boot parameter is found, the default driver is used.

There are two other things MINIX does to try to minimize problems with multiple hard disk drivers. One is that there is, after all, a driver that interfaces between MINIX and the ROM BIOS hard disk support. This driver is almost guaranteed to work on any system and can be selected by use of an

hd = bios

boot parameter. Generally, this should be a last resort, however. MINIX runs in protected mode on systems with an 80286 or better processor, but the BIOS code always run in real (8086) mode. Switching out of protected mode and back again whenever a routine in the BIOS is called is very slow.

The other strategy MINIX uses in dealing with drivers is to postpone initialization until the last possible moment. Thus, if on some hardware configuration none of the hard disk drivers work, we can still start MINIX from a floppy disk and do some useful work. MINIX will have no problems as long as no attempt is made to access the hard disk. This may not seem like a major breakthrough in user friendliness, but consider this: if all the drivers try to initialize immediately on system startup, the system can be totally paralyzed by improper configuration of some device we do not need anyway. By postponing initialization of each driver until it is needed, the system can continue with whatever does work, while the user tries to resolve the problems.

As an aside, we learned this lesson the hard way: earlier versions of MINIX tried to initialize the hard disk as soon as the system was booted. If no hard disk was present, the system hung. This behavior was especially unfortunate because MINIX will run quite happily on a system without hard disk, albeit with restricted storage capacity and reduced performance.

In the discussion in this section and the next, we will take as our model the AT-style hard disk driver, which is the default driver in the standard MINIX distribution. This is a versatile driver that handles hard disk controllers from the ones used in the earliest 80286 system to modern **EIDE (Extended Integrated Drive Electronics)** controllers that handle gigabyte capacity hard disks. The general aspects of hard disk operation we discuss in this section apply to the other supported drivers as well.

The main loop of the hard disk task is the same shared code we have already discussed, and the standard six kinds of requests can be made. A *DEV_OPEN* request can entail a substantial amount of work, as there are always partitions and may be subpartitions on a hard disk. These must be read when a device is opened, (i.e., when it is first accessed). Some hard disk controllers can also support CD-ROM drives, which have removable media, and on a *DEV_OPEN* the presence of the medium must be verified. On a CD-ROM a *DEV_CLOSE* operation also has meaning: it requires that the door be unlocked and the CD-ROM ejected. There are other complications of removable media that are more applicable to floppy drives, so we will discuss these in a later section. For the hard disk, the *DEV_IOCTL* operation is used to set a flag to mark that the medium should be ejected upon a *DEV_CLOSE*. This feature is useful for CD-ROMs. It is also used to read and write partition tables, we noted as earlier.

The *DEV_READ, DEV_WRITE,* and *SCATTERED_IO* requests are each handled in there phases, prepare, schedule, and finish, as we saw previously. The hard disk, unlike the memory devices, makes a real distinction between the schedule and finish phases. The hard disk driver does not use SSF r the elevator algorithm, but it does do a more limited form of scheduling, gathering requests for consecutive sectors. Requests normally come from the MINIX file system and are for multiples of blocks of 1024 bytes, but the driver is able to handle requests for any multiple of a sector (512 bytes). As long as each request is for a starting sector immediately following the last sector requested, each request is appended to a list of requests. The list is maintained as an array, and when it is full, or when a list of requests. The last is maintained as an array, and when it is full, or when a nonconsecutive sector is requested, a call is make to the finish routine.

In a simple *DEV_READ* or *DEV_WRITE* request, more than a single block may be requested, but each call to the schedule routine is immediately followed by a call to the finish routine, which ensures the current request list is fulfilled. In the case of a *SCATTERED_I/O* request, there may be multiple calls to the schedule routine before the finish routine is called. As long as they are for consecutive blocks of data, the list will be extended until the array becomes full. Recall that in a *SCATTERED_IO* request a flag can signify that a request for a particular block is optional. The hard disk driver, like the memory driver, ignores the *OPTIONAL* flag and delivers all data requested.

The rudimentary scheduling performed by the hard disk driver, postponing actual transfers while consecutive block are being requested, should be seen as the second step of a potential three-step processes of scheduling. The file system itself, by using scattered I/O, can implement something similar to Teory's version of the elevator algorithm—recall that in a scattered I/O request the list of requests is sorted on the bock number. The third step in scheduling takes place in the controller of a modern hard disk, like the one described in Fig 11.23. Such controllers are "smart" and can buffer large quantities of data, using internally programmed algorithms to retrieve data is the most efficient order, irrespective of the order of receipt of the requests.

Implementation of the Hard Disk Driver in MINIX

Small hard disks used on microcomputers are sometimes called "winchester" disks. There are several different stories about the origin of the name. It was apparently an IBM code name for the project that developed the disk technology in which the read/write heads fly on a thin cushion of air and land on the recording medium when the disk stops spinning. One explanation of the name is that an early model had two data modules, a 30-Mbyte fixed and a 30-Mbyte removable one. Supposedly this reminded the developers of the Winchester 30-30 firearm which figures in may tables of the United States' western frontier. Whatever the origin of the name, the basic technology remains the same, although today's typical microcomputer disk is much smaller and the capacity is much larger than the 14-inch disks that were typical of the early 1970s when the winchester technology was developed.

The file *wini.c* has the job of hiding the actual hard disk driver used from the rest of the kernel. This allows us to follow the strategy discussed in the previous section, compiling several hard disk drivers into a single kernel image, and selecting the one to use at boot time. Later, a custom installation can be recompiled with only the one driver actually needed.

Wini.c contains one data definition, *hdmap*, an array that associates a name with the address of a function. The array is initialized by the compiler with as many elements as are needed for the number of hard disk drivers enabled in *include/minix/config.h.* The array is used by the function *winchester_task,* which is the name entered in the *task_tab* table used when the kernel is first initialized. When *winchester_task* is called, it tries to find an *hd* environment variable, using a kernel function that works similarly to the mechanism used by ordinary C programs, reading the environment created by the MINIX boot monitor. If no *hd* value is defined, the first entry in the array is used; otherwise, the array is searched for a matching name. The corresponding function is then called indirectly. In the rest of this section we will discus the *at_winchester_task,* which is the first entry in the *hdmap* array in the standard distribution of MINIX.

The AT-style driver is in *at_wini.c*. This is a complicated driver for a sophisticated device, and there are several pages of macro definitions specifying controller registers, status bits and commands, data structures, and prototypes. As with other block device drivers, a *driver* structure, *w_dtab*, is initialized with pointers to the functions that actually do the work. Most of them are defined in *at_wini.c*, but as the hard disk requires no special cleanup operation, its *dr_cleanup* entry points to the common *nop_cleanup* in *driver.c,* shared with other drivers that have no special cleanup requirement. The entry function, *at_winchester_task*, calls a procedure that does hardware-specific initialization and then calls the main loop in *driver.c.* This runs forever, dispatching calls to the various functions pointed to by the *driver* table.

Since we are now dealing with real electromechanical storage devices, there is a substantial amount of work to be done to initialize the hard disk driver. Various parameters about the hard disk are kept in the *wini* array. As part of the policy of postponing initialization steps that could fail until the first time they are truly necessary, *init_params,* which is called during kernel initialization, does not do anything that requires accessing the disk device itself. The main things it does is to copy some information about the hard disk logical configuration into the *wini* array. This is information that is retrieved by the ROM BIOS from the CMOS memory that Pentium-class computers use to preserve basic configuration data. The BIOS actions take place when the computer is first turned on, before the first part of the MINIX loading process begins. It is not necessarily fatal if this information cannot be retrieved; if the disk is a modern one, the information can be retrieved directly from the disk.

After the call to the common main loop, nothing may happend for a while until an attempt is made to access the hard disk. Then a message requesting a *DEV_OPEN* operation is received and *w_do_open* is indirectly called. In turn, *w_do_open* calls *w_prepare* to determine if the device requested is valid, and then *w_identify* to identify the type of device and initialize some more parameters in the *wini* array. Finally a counter in the *wini* array is used to test whether this is first time the device has been opened since MINIX was started. After being examined, the counter is incremented. If it is the first *DEV_OPEN* operation, the *partition* function (in *drvlib.c*) is called.

The next function, *w_prepare,* accepts an integer argument, *device,* which is the minor device number of the drive or partition to be used, and returns a pointer to the *device* structure that indicates the base address and size of the device. In C the use of an identifier to name a structure does not preclude use of the same identifier to name a variable. Whether a device is a drive, a partition, or a subpartition can be determined from the minor device number. Once *w_prepare* has completed its job, none of the other functions used to read or write the disk need to concern themselves with partitioning. As we have seen, *w_prepare* is called when a *DEV_OPEN* request is made: it is also one phase of the prepare/schedule/finish cycle used by all data transfer requests. In that context its initialization of *w_count* to zero is important.

Software-compatible AT-type disks have been in use for quite a while, and *w_identify* has to distinguish between a number of different designs that have been introduced over the years. The first step is to see that a readable and writeable I/O port exists where one should exists on all disk controllers in this family. If this condition is met, the address of the hard disk interrupt handler is installed in the interrupt descriptor table and the interrupt controller is enable to respond to that interrupt. Then an *ATA_IDENTIFY* command is issued to the disk controller. If the result is *OK*, various pieces of information are retrieved, including a string that identifies the model of the disk, and the physical cylinder, head, and sector parameters for the device. (Note that the "physical" configuration reported may not be the true physical configuration, but we have no alternative to accepting what the disk drive claims.) The disk information also indicates whether or not the disk is capable of **Linear Block Addressing (LBA).** If it is, the driver can ignore the cylinder, head, and sector parameters and can address the disk using absolute sector numbers, which is much simpler.

As we mentioned earlier, it is possible that *init_params* may not recover the logical disk configuration information from the BIOS tables. If that happens, the code tries to create an appropriate set of parameters based on what it reads from the drive itself. The idea is that the maximum cylinder, head, and sector numbers can be 1023, 255, and 63 respectively, due to the number of bits allowed for these fields in the original BIOS data structures.

If the *ATA_IDENTIFY* command fails, it may simply mean that the disk is an older model that does not support the command. In this case the logical configuration values previously read by *init_params* are all we have. If they are valid, they are copied to the physical parameter fields of *wini;* otherwise an error is returned and the disk is not usable.

Finally, MINIX uses a *u32_t* variable to count addresses in bytes. The size of device the driver can handle, expressed as a count of sectors, must be limited if the product of cylinders × heads × sectors is too large. Although at the time of writing this code devices of 4-GB capacity were rarely found on machines that one might expect to be used of MINIX, experience has taught that software should be written to test for limits such as this, unnecessary as such tests may appear at the time the code is written. The base and size of the whole drive are then entered into the *wini* array, and *w_specify* is called, twice if necessary, to pass the parameters to be used back to the disk controller. Finally, the name of the device (determined by *w_name*) and the identification string found by *identify* (if it is an advanced device) or the cylinder head and sector parameters reported by the BIOS (if an old device) are printed on the console.

W_name returns a pointer to a string containing the device name, which will be either "at-hd0," "at-hd5," "at-hd10," or "at-hd 15." *W_specify* in addition to passing the parameters to the controller, also recalibrates the drive (if it is an older model), by doing a seek to cylinder zero.

Now we are ready to discuss the functions called in satisfying a data transfer request. *W_prepare,* which we have already discussed, is called first. Its initialization of the variable *w_count* to zero is important here. The next function called during a transfer is *w_schedule.* It sets up the basic parameters: where the data are to come from, where they are to go to, the count of bytes to transfer, and whether the transfer is a read or write. The bit that may be present in a *SCATTERED_IO* request to indicate an optional transfer is reset in the operation code to be passed to the controller, but note that it is retained in the *io_request* field of the *iorequest_s* structure. For the hard disk an attempt is made to honor all requests, but, as we will see, the driver may later decide not to do so if there have been errors. The last thing in the setup is to check that the request does not go beyond the last byte on the device and to reduce the request if it does. At this point the first sector to be read can be calculated.

The process of scheduling begins in earnest. If there are already requests pending (tested by seeing if *w_count* is greater than zero), and if the sector to read next is not consecutive with the last one requested, then *w_finish* is called to complete the previous requests. Otherwise, *w_nextblock,* which holds the sector number of the next sector, is updated, and the loop is entered to add new sector requests to the array of requests. Within maximum allowable number of requests has been reached. The limit is kept in a variable, *max_count*, since, as we will see later, it is sometimes helpful to be able to adjust the limit. Here again, a call to *w_finish* may result.

As we have seen, there are two places within *w_prepare* where a call to *w_finish* may be made. Normally *w_prepare* terminates without calling *w_finish,* but whether or not it is called from within *w_prepare, w_finish* is always called eventually from the main loop in *driver.c.* If it has just been called, it may have no work, so there is a test to check this. If there are still requests in the request array, the main part of *w_finish* is entered.

As one might expect, since there may be a considerable number of requests queued, the main part of *w_finish* is a loop. Before entering the loop, the variable *r* is preset to a value signifying an error, to force reinitialization of the controller. If a call to *w_specify* succeeds the *command* structure, *cmd* is initialized to do a transfer. This structure is used to pass all the required parameters to the function that actually operates the disk controller. The *cmd.precomp* parameter is used by some drives to compensate for differences in the performance of the magnetic recording medium with differences in speed of passage of the medium under the disk heads as they move from outer to inner cylinders. It is always the same for a particular drive and is ignored by many drives. *Cmd.count* receives the number of sectors to transfer, masked to a quantity that fits in an 8-bit byte, since that is the size of all the command and status registers of the controller. The code specifies the first sector to transfer, either as a 28-bit logical block number, or as cylinder, head, and sector parameters. In either case the same fields in the *cmd* structure are used.

Finally, the command itself, read or wirte, is loaded and *com_out* is called to initiate the transfer. The call to *com_out* may fail if the controller is not ready or does not become ready within a preset timeout period. In this case the count of errors is incremented and the attempt is aborted if *MAX_ERRORS* is reached. Otherwise, the

```
continue;
```

statement causes the loop to start over again at line 10665.

If the controller accepts the command passed in the call to *com_out*, it may be a while before the data are available, so (assuming the command is *DEV_READ*) *w_intr_wait* is called. We will discuss this function in detail later, but for now just note that it calls *receive,* so at this point the disk task blocks.

Some time later, more or less, depending upon whether a seek was involved, the call to *w_intr_wait* will return. This driver does not use DMA, although some controllers support it. Instead, programmed I/O is used. If there is no error returned from *w_intr_wait,* the assembly language function *port_read* transfers *SECTOR_SIZE* bytes of data from the controller's data port to their final destination, which should be a buffer in the file system's block cache. Next, various addresses and counts are adjusted to account for the successful transfer. Finally, if the count of bytes in the current request goes to zero, the pointer to the array of requests is advanced to point to the next request.

In the case of a *DEV_WRITE* command, the first part, setting up the command parameters and sending the command to the controller, is the same as for a read, except for the command operation code. The order of subsequent events is different for a write, however. First there is wait for the controller to signal it is ready to receive data. *Waitfor* is a macro, and normally will return very quickly. We will say more about it later; for now we will just note that the wait will time out eventually, but that long delays are expected to be extremely rare. Then the data are transferred from memory to the controller data port using *port_write,* and at this point *w_intr_wait* is called and the disk task blocks.

Finally, if there have been errors in reading or writing, they must be dealt with. If the controller informs the driver that the error was due to a bad sector, there is no point in trying again, but other types of errors are worth a retry, at least up to a point. That point is determined by counting the errors and giving up if *MAX_ERRORS* is reached. When *MAX_ERRORS/2* is reached, *w_need_reset* is called to force reinitialization when the retry is made. However, if the request was originally an optional one (made by a *SCATTERED_IO* request), no retry is attempted.

Whether *w_finish* terminates without errors or because of an error, the variable *w_command* is always set to *CMD_IDLE.* This allows other functions to determine that the failure was not because of a mechanical or electrical malfunction of the disk itself causing failure to generate an interrupt following an attempted operation.

The disk controller is controlled through a set of registers, which could be memory mapped on some systems, but on a **IBM** compatible appear as I/O ports. The registers used by a standard IBM-AT class hard disk controller are shown in Fig. 11.25.

This is our first encounter with I/O hardware, and it may be helpful to mention some ways I/O ports may behave differently from memory addresses. In general, input and output registers that happen to have the same I/O port address are not the same register. Thus, the data written to a particular address cannot necessarily be retrieved by a subsequent read operation. For example, the last register address shown in Fig. 11.25, shows the status of the disk controller when read and is used to issue commands to the controller when written to. It is also common that the very act of reading or writing an I/O device register causes an action to occur, independently of the details of the data transferred. This is true of the command register on the AT disk controller. In use, data are written to the lower-numbered registers to select the disk address to be read from or written to, and then the command register is written last with an operation code. The act of writing the operation code into the command register starts the operation.

It is also the case that the use of some registers of fields in the registers may vary with different modes of operation. In the example given in the figure, writing a 0 or a 1 to the LBA bit, bit 6 of register 6, selects whether CHS (Cylinder-Head-Sector) or LBA (Linear Block Addressing) mode is used. The data written to or read from registers 3, 4, and 5, and the low four bits of register 6 are interpreted differently according to the setting of the LBA bit.

Now let us look at how a command is sent to the controller by calling *com_out*. Before changing any registers, the status register is read to determine that the controller is not busy. This is done by testing the *STATUS_BSY* bit. Speed is important here, and normally the disk controller is ready or will be ready in a short time, so busy waiting is used. On line 10779 *waitfor* is called to test *STATUS_BSY.* To maximize the speed of response, *waitfor* is a macro, it makes the required test once, avoiding an expensive function call on most calls, when the disk is ready. On the rare occasions when a wait is necessary, it then calls *w_waitfor,* which executes the test in a loop until it is true or a predefined timeout period elapses. Thus the returned value will be true with the minimum possible delay if the controller is ready, true after a delay if it is temporarily unavailable, or false if it is not ready after the timeout period. We will have more to say about the timeout when we discuss *w_waitfor* itself.

Register	Read Function	Write Function
0	Data	Data
1	Error	Write Precompensation
2	Sector Count	Sector Count
3	Sector Number (0-7)	Sector Number (0-7)
4	Cylinder Low (8-15)	Cylinder Low (8-15)
5	Cylinder High (16-23)	Cylinder High (16-23)
6	Select Drive/Head (24-27)	Select Drive/Head (24-27)
7	Status	Command

(a)

7	6	5	4	3	2	1	0
1	LBA	1	D	HS3	HS2	HS1	HS0

LBA: 0 = Cylinder/Head/Sector Mode
1 = Logical Block Addressing Mode
D: 0 = master drive
1 = slave drive
HSn: CHS mode: Head Select in CHS mode
LBA mode: Block select bits 24 - 27

(b)

Fig. 11.25. *(a) The control registers of an IDE hard disk controller. The numbers in parentheses are the bits of the logical block address selected by each register in LBA mode. (b) The fields of the Select Drive/Head register.*

A controller can handle more than one drive, so once it is determined that the controller is ready, a byte is written to select the drive, head, and mode of operation and then *waitfor* is called again. A disk drive sometimes fails to carry out a command or to properly return an error code—it is, after all, a mechanical device that can stick, jam, or break internally—and as insurance a message is sent to the clock task to schedule a call to a wakeup routine. Following this, the command is issued by first writing all the parameters to the various registers and finally writing the command code itself to the command register. The latter step and the subsequent modification of the *w_command* and *w_status* variables is a critical section, so the entire sequence is bracketed by calls to *lock* and *unlock* which disable and then reenable interrupts.

The next several function are short. We noted that *w_need_reset* is called by *w_finish* when the failure count hits half of *MAX_ERRORS.* It is also called when timeouts occur while waiting for the disk to interrupt or become ready. The action of *w_need_reset* is just to mark the *state* variable for every drive in the *wini* array to force initialization on the next access.

W_do_close has very little to do for a conventional hard disk. When support is added for CD-ROMs or other removable devices, this routine will have to be extended to generate a command to unlock the door or eject the CD, depending upon what the hardware supports.

Com_simple is called to issue controller commands that terminate immediately without a data transfer phase. Commands that fall into this category include those that retrieve the disk identification, setting of some parameters, and recalibration.

When *com_out* calls the clock task to prepare for a possible rescue after a disk controller failure, it passes the address of *w_timeout* as the function for the clock task to awaken when the timeout period expires. Usually the disk completes the requested operation and when the timeout occurs, *w_command* will be found to have the value *CMD_IDLE,* meaning the disk completed its operation, and *w_timeout* can then terminate. If the command does not complete and the operation is a read or write, it may help to reduce the size of I/O requests. This is done in two steps, first reducing the maximum number of sectors that can be requested to 8, and then to 1. For all timeouts a message is printed, *w_need_reset* is called to force re-initialization of all drives on the next attempted access, and *interrupt* is called to deliver a message to the disk task and simulate the hardware-generated interrupt that should have occurred at the end of the disk operation.

When a reset is required, *w_reset* is called. This function makes use of a function provided by the clock driver, *milli_dealy*. After an initial delay to give the drive time to recover from previous operations, a bit in the disk controller's control register is **strobed**—that is, brought to a logical 1 level for a definite period, then returned to the logical 0 level. Following this operation, *waitfor* is called to give the drive a reasonable period to signal it is ready. In case the reset does not succeed, a message is printed and an error status returned. It is left to the caller to decide what to do next.

Commands to the disk that involve data transfer normally terminate by generating an interrupt, which sends a message back to the disk task. In fact, an interrupt is generated for each sector read or written. Thus, after issuing such a command, *w_intr_wait* will always be called. In turn, *w_intr_wait* calls *receive* in a loop, ignoring the contents of each message, waiting for an interrupt that sets *w_status* to "not busy." Once such a message is received, the status of the request is checked. This is another critical section, so *lock* and *unlock* are used here to guarantee that a new interrupt will not occur and change *w_status* before the various steps involved are complete.

We have seen several places where the macro *waitfor* is called to do busy waiting on a bit in the disk controller status register. After the initial tests, the *waitfor* macro calls *w_waitfor* which calls *milli_start* to begin a timer and then enters a loop that alternately checks the status register and the timer. If a timeout occurs, *w_need_reset* is called to set things up for a reset of the disk controller the next time its services are requested.

The *TIMEOUT* parameter used by *w_waitfor* is defined as 32 seconds. A similar parameter, *WAKEUP*, used to schedule wakeups from the clock task, is set to 31 seconds. These are very long periods of time to spend busy waiting, when you consider that an ordinary process only gets 100 msec to run before it will be evicted. But, these numbers are based upon the published standard for interfacing disk devices to AT-class computers, which states that up to 31 seconds must be allowed for a disk to "spin up" to speed. The fact is, of course, that this is a worst-case specification, and that on most systems spin up will only occur at power-on time, or possibly after long periods of inactivity. MINIX is still being developed. It is possible that a new way of handling timeouts may be called for when support for CD-ROMs (or other devices which must spin up frequently) is added.

W_handler is the interrupt handler. The address of this function is put into the Interrupt Descriptor Table by *w_identify* when the hard disk task is first activated. When a disk interrupt occurs the disk controller status register is copied to *w_status* and then the *interrupt* function in the kernel is called to reschedule the hard disk task. When this occurs, of course, the hard disk task is already blocked as a result of a previous call to *receive* from *w_intr_wait* after initiation of a disk operation.

The last function in *at_wini.c* is *w_geometry.* It returns the logical maximum cylinder, head, and sector values of the selected hard disk device. In this case the numbers are real ones, not made up as they were for the RAM disk driver.

Floppy Disk Handling

The floppy disk driver is longer and more complicated than the hard disk driver. This may seem paradoxical, since floppy disk mechanisms would appear to be simpler than those of hard disks, but the simpler mechanism has a simpler controller that requires more attention from the operating system, and the fact that the medium is removable adds some complications. In this section we will describe some of the thing an implementor has to consider in dealing with floppy disks. However, we will not go into the details of the MINIX floppy disk driver code. The most important parts are similar to those for the hard disk.

One of the things we do not have to worry about with the floppy driver is the multiple types of controller to support that we had to deal with in the case of the hard disk driver. Although the high-density floppy disks currently used were not supported in the design of the original IBM PC, the floppy disk controllers of all computers in the IBM PC family are supported by a single software driver. The contrast with hard disk situation is probably due to lack of pressure to increase floppy disk performance. Floppy disks are rarely used as working storage during operation of a computer system; their speed and data capacity are too limited compared to those of hard disks. Floppy disks remain important for distribution of new software and for backup, so almost all small computer systems are equipped with at least one floppy drive.

The floppy disk driver does not use the SSF or the elevator algorithm. It is strictly sequential, accepting a request and carrying it out before even accepting another request. In the original design of MINIX it was felt that, since MINIX was intended for use on personal computer, most of the time there would be only one process active, and the chance of a disk request arriving while another was being carried out was small. Thus there would be little to gain from the considerable increase in software complexity that would be required for queueing requests. It is even less worthwhile now, since floppy disks are rarely used for anything but transferring data into or out of a system with a hard disk.

That said, even though there is no support in the driver software for reordering requests, the floppy driver, like any other block driver, can handle a request for scattered I/O, and just like the hard disk driver, the floppy driver collects requests in an array and continues to collect such requests as long as sequential sectors are requested. However, in the case of the floppy driver the array of requests is smaller than for the hard disk, limited to the maximum number of sectors per track on a floppy diskette. In addition, the floppy driver pays attention to the *OPTIONAL* flag in scattered I/O requests and does not proceed to a new track if all current requests are optional.

The simplicity of the floppy disk hardware is responsible for some of the complications in floppy disk driver software. Cheap, slow, low-capacity floppy drives do not justify the sophisticated integrated controllers that are part of modern hard drives, so the driver software has to deal explicitly with aspects of disk operation that are hidden in the operation of a hard drive. As an example of a complication caused by the simplicity of floppy drives, consider positioning the read/write head to a particular track during a *SEEK* operation. No hard disk has ever required the driver software to explicitly call for a *SEEK*. For a hard disk the cylinder, head, and sector geometry visible to the programmer may not correspond to the physical geometry, and, in fact, the physical geometry may be quite complicated, with more sectors on outer cylinders than on inner ones. This is not visible to the user, however. Hard disks may accept Logical Block Addressing (LBA), addressing by the absolute sector number on the disk, as an alternative to cylinder, head, and sector addressing. Even if addressing is done by cylinder, head, and sector, any geometry that does not address nonexistent sectors may be used, since the integrate controller on the disk calculates where to move the read/write heads and does a seek operation when required.

For a floppy disk, however, explicit programming of *SEEK* operations is needed. In case a *SEEK* fails, it is necessary to provide a routine to perform a *RECALIBRATE* operation, which forces the heads to cylinder 0. This makes it possible for the controller to advance them to a desired track position by stepping the heads a known number of times. Similar operation are necessary for the hard drive, of course, but the drive controller handles them without detailed guidance from the device driver software.

Some characteristics of a floppy disk drive that complicate its driver are:

1. Removable media;
2. Multiple disk formats.
3. Motor control.

Some hard disk controllers provide for removable media, for instance, on a CD-ROM drive, but the drive controller is generally able to handle any complications without much support in the device driver software. With a floppy disk, however, the built-in support is not there, and yet it is needed more. Some of the most common uses for floppy disks—installing new software or backing up files—are likely to require switching of disks in and out of the drives. It can cause grief if data that were intended for one diskette are written onto another diskette. The device driver should do what it can to prevent this, although this is not always possible, as not all floppy drive hardware allows determination of whether the drive door has been opened since the last access. Another problem that can be caused by removable media is that a system can become hung up if an attempt is made to access a floppy drive that currently has no diskette inserted. This can be solved if an open door can be detected, but since this is not always possible some provision must be made for a timeout and an error return if an operation on a floppy disk does not terminate in a reasonable time.

Removable media can be replaced with other media, and in the case of floppy disks there are many different possible formats. MINIX hardware supports both 3.5-inch and 5.25-inch disk drives and the diskettes can be formatted in a variety of ways to hold from 360 KB up to 1.2 MB (on a 5.25-inch diskette) or 1.44 MB (on a 3.5-inch diskette). MINIX supports seven different floppy disk formats. There are two possible solutions to the problem this causes, and MINIX allows for both of them. One way is to refer to each possible format as a distinct drive and provide multiple minor devices. MINIX does this, and in the device directory you will find fourteen different devices defined, ranging from */dev/pc0,* a 360K 5.25-inch diskette in the first drive, to */dev/PS1,* a 1.4M 3.5-inch diskette in the second drive. Remembering the different combinations is cumbersome, and a second alternatives is provided. When the first floppy disk drive is addressed as */dev/fd0,* or the second as */dev/fd1*, the floppy disk driver tests the diskette currently in the drive when it is accessed, in order to determine the format. Some formats have more cylinders, and others have more sectors per track than other formats. Determination of the format of a diskette is done by attempting to read the higher numbered sectors and tracks. By a process of elimination the format can be determined. This does, of course, take time, and a disk with bad sectors could be misidentified.

The final complication of the floppy disk driver is motor control. Diskettes cannot be read or written unless they are revolving. Hard disk are designed to run for thousands of hours on end without wearing out, but leaving the motors on all the time causes a floppy drive and diskette to wear out quickly. If the motor is not already on when a drive is accessed, it is necessary to issue a command to start the drive and then to wait about a half second before attempting to read or write data. Turning the motors on or off is slow, so MINIX leaves a drives motor on for a few seconds after a drive is used. If the drive is used again within this interval, the timer is extended for another few seconds. If the drive is not used in this interval, the motor is turned off.

Clocks

Clocks (also called **timers**) are essential to the operation of any timesharing system for a variety of reasons. They maintain the time of day and prevent one process from monopolizing the CPU, among other things. The clock software can take the form of a device driver, even though a clock is neither a block devices, like a disk, nor a character device, like a terminal. Our examination of clocks will follow the same pattern as in the previous sections: first a look at clock hardware and software in general, and then a closer look at how these ideas are applied in MINIX.

Clock Hardware

Two types of clocks are commonly used in computers, and both are quite different from the clocks and watches used by people. The simpler clocks are tied to the110- or 220- volt power line, and cause an interrupt on every voltage cycle, at 50 or 60 Hz.

The other kind of clock is built out of three components: a crystal oscillator, a counter, and a holding register, as shown in Fig. 11.26. When a piece of quartz crystal is properly cut and mounted under tension, it can be make to generate a periodic signal of very high accuracy, typically in the range of 5 to 100 MHz, depending on the crystal chosen. At least one such circuit is usually found in any computer, providing a synchronizing signal to the computer's various circuits. This signal is fed into the counter to make it count down to zero. When the counter gets to zero, it causes a CPU interrupt.

Programmable clocks typically have several modes of operation. In **one-shot mode,** when the clock is started, it copies the value of the holding register into the counter and then decrements the counter at each pulse from the crystal. When the counter gets to zero, it causes an interrupt and stops until it is explicitly started again by the software. In **square-wave mode,** after getting to zero and causing the interrupt, the holding register is automatically copied into the counter, and the whole process is repeated again indefinitely. These periodic interrupts are called **clock ticks.**

The advantage of the programmable clock is that its interrupt frequency can be controlled by software. If a 1-MHz crystal is used, then the counter is pulsed every microsecond. With 16-bit registers, interrupts can be programmed to occur at intervals from 1 microsecond to 65.536

milliseconds. Programmable clock chips usually contain two or three independently programmable clocks and have many other options as well (e.g., counting up instead of down, interrupts disabled and more).

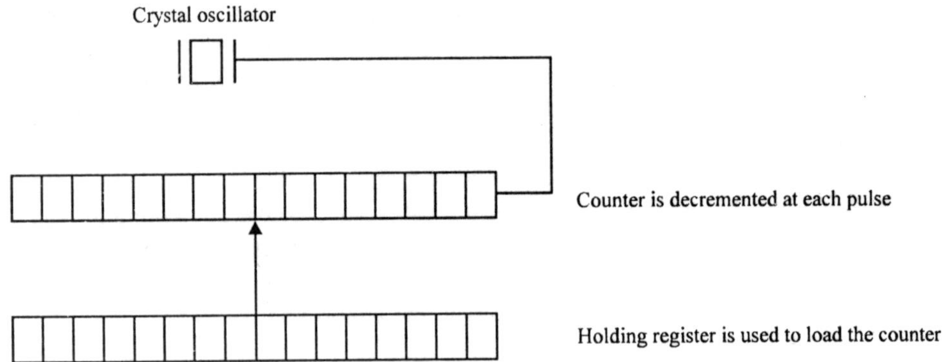

Fig. 11.26. A programmable clock.

To prevent the current time from being lost when the computer's power is turned off, most computers have a battery-powered backup clock, implemented with the kind of low-power ciruitry used in digital watches. Th battery clock can be read at startup. If the backup clock is not present, the software may ask the user for the current date and time. There is also a standard protocol for a networked system to get the current time from a remote host. In any case the time is then translated into the number of clock ticks since 12 A.M. **Universal Coordinated Time (UTC)** on Jan. 1, 1970, as UNIX and MINIX do, or since some other benchmark. At every clock tick, the real time is incremented by one count. Usually utility programs are provided to manually set the system clock and the backup clock and to synchronize the two clocks.

Clock Software

All the clock hardware does is generate interrupts at known intervals. Everything else involving time must be done by the software, the clock driver. The exact duties of the clock driver vary among operating systems, but usually include most of the following:

1. Maintaining the time of day.
2. Preventing processes from running longer than they are allowed to.
3. Accounting for CPU usage.
4. Handling the ALARM system call made by user processes.
5. Providing watchdog timers of parts of the system itself.
6. Doing profiling, monitoring, and statistics gathering.

The first clock function, maintaining the time of day (also called the **real time**) is not difficult. It just requires incrementing a counter at each clock tick, as mentioned before. The only thing to watch out for is the number of bits in the time-of-day counter. With a clock rate of 60 Hz, a 32-bit counter will overflow in just over 2 years. Clearly the system cannot store the real time as the number of ticks sine Jan. 1, 1970 in 32 bits.

Three approaches can be taken to solve this problem. The first way is to use a 64-bit counter, although doing so makes maintaining the counter more expensive since it has to be done many times a second. The second way is to maintain the time of day in seconds, rather than in ticks, using a subsidiary counter to count ticks until a whole second has been accumulated. Because 2^{32} seconds is more than 136 years, this method will work until well into the twenty-second century.

The third approach is to count in ticks, but to do that relatives to the time the system was booted, rather than relative to a fixed external moment. When the backup clock is read or the user types in the real time, the system boot time is calculated from the current time-of-day value and stored in memory in any convenient form. Later, when the time of day is requested, the stored time of day is added to the counter to get the current time of day. All three approaches are shown in Fig. 11.27.

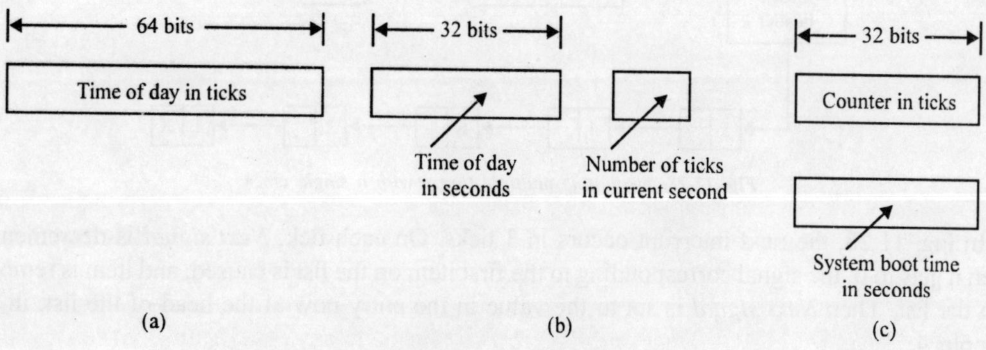

Fig. 11.27. Three ways to maintain the time of day.

The second clock function is preventing processes from running too long. Whenever a process is started, the scheduler should initialize a counter to the value of that process' quantum in clock ticks. At every clock interrupt, the clock driver decrements the quantum counter by 1. When it gets to zero, the clock driver calls the scheduler to set up another process.

The third clock function is doing CPU accounting. The most accurate way to do it is to start a second timer, distinct from the main system timer, whenever a process is started. When that process is stopped, the timer can be read out to tell how long the process has run. To do things right, the second timer should be saved when an interrupt occurs and restored afterward.

A less accurate, but much simpler, way to do accounting is to maintain a pointer to the process table entry for the currently running process in a global variable. At every clock tick, a field in the current process' entry is incremented. In this way, every clock tick is "charged" to the process running at the time of the tick. A minor problem with this strategy is that if many interrupts occur during a process' run, it is still charged for a full tick, even though it did not get much work done. Properly accounting for the CPU during interrupts is too expensive and is never done.

In MINIX and many other systems, a process can request that the operating system give it a warning after a certain interval. The warning is usually a signal, interrupt, message, or something similar. One application requiring such warnings is networking, in which a packet not acknowledged within a certain time interval must be retransmitted. Another application is computer-aided instruction, where a student not providing a response within a certain time is told the answer.

If the clock driver had enough clocks, it could set a separate clock for each request. This not being the case, it must simulate multiple virtual clocks with a single physical clock. One way is to maintain a table in which the signal time for all pending timers is kept, as well as a variable giving the time of the next one. Whenever the time of day is updated, the driver checks to see if the closest signal has occurred. If it has, the table is searched for the next one to occur.

If many signals are expected, it is more efficient to simulate multiple clocks by chaining all the pending clock requests together, sorted on time, in a linked list, as shown in Fig. 11.28. Each entry on the list tells how many clock ticks following the previous one to wait before causing a signal. In this example, signals are pending for 4203, 4207, 4213, 4215, and 4216.

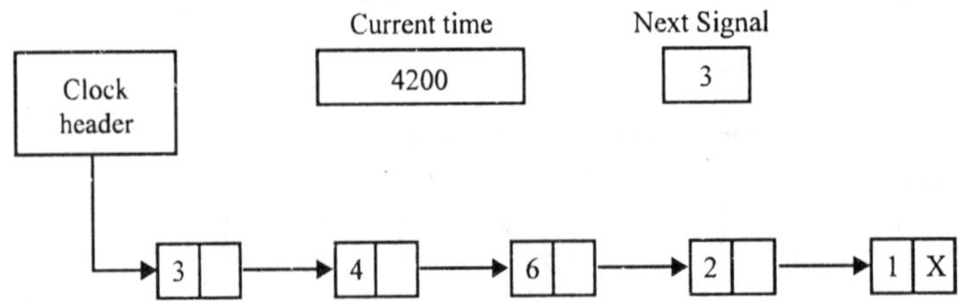

Fig. 11.28. Simulating multiple timers with a single clock.

In Fig. 11.28, the next interrupt occurs in 3 ticks. On each tick, *Next signal* is decremented. When it gets to 0, the signal corresponding to the first item on the list is caused, and item is removed from the list. Then *Next signal* is set to the value in the entry now at the head of the list, in this example, 4.

Note that during a clock interrupt, the clock driver has several things to do—increment the real time, decrement the quantum and check for 0, do CPU accounting, and decrement the alarm counter. However, each of these operations has been carefully arranged to be very fast because they have to be repeated many times a second.

Parts of the operating system also need to set timers. These are called **watchdog timers.** When studying the hard disk driver, we saw that a wakeup call is scheduled each time the disk controller is sent a command, so an attempt at recovery can be made if the command fails completely. We also mentioned that floppy disk drivers have to wait for the disk motor to get up to speed and must shut down the motor if no activity occurs for a while. Some printers with a movable the print head can print at 120 character/sec (8.3 msec/character) but cannot return the print head to the left margin in 8.3 msec, so the terminal driver must delay after typing a carriage return.

The mechanism used by the clock driver to handle watchdog timers is the same as for user signals. The only difference is that when a timer goes off, instead of causing a signal, the clock driver calls a procedure supplied by the caller. The procedure is part of the caller's code, but since all the drivers are in the same address space, the clock driver can call it anyway. The called procedure can do whatever is necessary, even causing an interrupt, although within the kernel interrupts are often inconvenient and signals do not exist. That is why the watchdog mechanism is provide.

The last thing in our lit is profiling. Some operating systems provide a mechanism by which a user program can have the system build up a histogram of its program counter, so it can see where it is spending its time. When profiling is a possibility, at every tick the driver checks to see if the current process is being profiled, and if so, computers the bin number (a range of addresses) corresponding to the current program counter. It then increments that bin by one. This mechanism can also be used to profile the system itself.

Overview of the Clock Driver in MINIX

The MINIX clock driver is contained in the file *clock.c*. The clock task accepts these six message types, with the parameters shown:

1. HARD_INT
2. GET_UPTIME
3. GET_TIME
4. SET_TIME (new time in seconds)
5. SET_ALARM (process number, procedure to call, delay)
6. SET_SYN_AL (process number, delay)

HARD_INT is the message sent to the driver when a clock interrupt occurs and there is work to do, such as when an alarm must be sent or a process has run too long.

GET_UPTIME is used to get the time in ticks since boot time, *GET_TIME* returns the current real time as the number of seconds elapsed since Jan. 1, 1970 at 12:00 A.M., and *SET_TIME* sets the real time. It can only be invoked by the super-user.

Internal to the clock driver, the time is kept track of using the method of Fig.11.27 (c). When the time is set, the driver computes when the system was booted. It can make this computation because it has the current real time and it also knows how many ticks the system has been running. The system stores the real time of the boot in a variable. Later, when *GET_TIME* is called, it converts the current value of the tick counter to seconds and adds it to the stored boot time.

SET_ALARM allows a process to set a timer that goes off in a specified number of clock ticks. When a user process does an ALARAM call, it sends a message to the memory manager, which then sends this message to the clock driver. When the alarm goes off, the clock driver sends a message back to the memory manager, which then takes care of making the signal happen.

SET_ALARM is also used by tasks that need to start a watchdog timer. When the timer goes off, the procedure provided is simply called. The clock driver has no knowledge of what the procedure does.

SET_SYN_AL is similar to *SET_ALARM,* but is used to set a **synchronous alarm.** A synchronous alarm sends a message to a process, rather than generating a signal or calling a procedure. The synchronous alarm task handles dispatching messages to the processes that require them. Synchronous alarms will be discussed in detail later.

The clock task uses no major data structures, but there are several variables used to keep track of time. Only one is a global variable, *last_ticks,* defined it *glo.h.* This variable is provided for the use of any driver that may be added to MINIX in the future that might disable interrupts long enough that one of more clock ticks could be lost. It currently is not used, but if such a driver were to be written the programmer could cause *lost_ticks* to be incremented to compensate for the time during which clock interrupts were inhibited.

Obviously, clock interrupts occur very frequently, and fast handling of the clock interrupt is important. MINIX achieves this by doing the bare minimum amount of processing on most clock interrupts. Upon receipt of an interrupt the handler sets a local variable, *ticks,* to *lost_ticks* + 1 and then uses this quantity to update accounting times and *pending_ticks* and resets *lost_ticks* to zero. *Pending_ticks* is a *PRIVATE* variable, declared outside of all function definitions, but known only to function defined in *clock.c.* Another *PRIVATE* variable, *sched_ticks,* is decremented on each tick to keep track of execution time. The interrupt handler sends a message to the clock task only if an alarm is due or an execution quantum has been used. This scheme results in the interrupt handler returning almost immediately on most interrupts.

When the clock task receives any message, it adds *pending_ticks* to the variable *realtime* and then zeroes *pending_ticks. Realtime,* together with the variable *boot_time* allows the current time of day to be computed. These are both *PRIVATE* variables, so the only way for any other part of the system to get the time is by sending a message to the clock task. Although at any instant *realitme* may be inaccurate, this mechanism ensures it is always accurate when needed. If your watch is correct when you look at it, does it matter if it is incorrect when you are not looking?

To handle alarms, *next_alarm* records the time when the next signal or watchdog call may happen. The driver has to be careful here, because the process requesting the signal may exit or be killed before the signal happens. When it is time for the signal, a check is maked to see if it is still needed. If it is not needed, it is not carried out.

Each user process is allowed to have only one outstanding alarm timer. Executing an ALARM call while the timer is still running cancels the first timer. Therefore, a convenient way to store the timers is to reserve one word in the process table entry for each process for its timer, if any. For tasks, the function to be called must also be stored somewhere, so an array, *watch_dog,* has been provided for this purpose. A similar array, *syn_table,* stores flags to indicate for each process if it is due to receive a synchronous alarm.

The overall logic of the clock driver follows the same pattern as the disk drivers. The main program is an endless loop that gets messages, dispatches on the message type, and then sends a reply (except for *CLOCK_TICK*). Each message type is handled by a separate procedure, following our standard naming convention of naming all the procedures called from the main loop *do_xxx,* where *xxx* is different for each one, of course. As an aside, unfortunately, many linkers truncate procedure names to seven or eight characters, so the names *so_set_time* and *do_set_alarm* are potentially in conflict. The latter has been renamed *do_setalarm.* This problem occurs throughout MINIX and is usually solved by mangling one of the names.

The Synchronous Alarm Task

There is a second task to be discussed in this section, the **synchronous alarm task.** A synchronous alarm is similar to an alarm, but instead of sending a signal or calling a watchdog function when the timeout period expires, the synchronous alarm task sends a message. A signal may arrive or a watchdog task may be called without any relation to what part of a task is executing, so alarms of these types are **asynchronous.** In contrast, a message is received only when the receiver has executed a *receive* call.

The synchronous alarm mechanism was added to MINIX to support the network server, which, like the memory manager and the file server, runs as a separate process. Frequently there is a need to set a limit on the time a process may be blocked while waiting for input. For instance, in a network, failure to receive an acknowledgement of a data packet within a definite periods is probably due to a failure of transmission. A network server can set a synchronous alarm before it tries to receive a message and blocks. Since the synchronous alarm is delivered as a message, it will unblock the server eventually if no message is received from the network. Upon receiving any message the server must first reset the alarm. Then by examining the type or origin of the message, it can determine a packet has arrived or if it has been unblocked by a timeout. If it is the latter, then the server can try to recover usually by resending the last unacknowledged packet.

A synchronous alarm is faster than an alarm sent using a signal, which requires several messages and a considerable amount of processing. A watchdog function is fast, but is only useful for tasks compiled into the same address space as the clock task. When a process is waiting for a message, a synchronous alarm is more appropriate and simpler than either signals or watchdog functions, and it is easily handled with little additional processing.

The Clock Interrupt Handler

As described earlier, when a clock interrupt occurs, *realtime* is not updated immediately. The interrupt service routine maintains the *pending_ticks* counter and does simple jobs like charging the current tick to a process and decrementing the quantum timer. A message is sent to the clock task only when more complicated jobs must be done. This is something of a compromise with the ideal of MINIX tasks that communicate totally by messages, but it is a practical concession to the reality that servicing clock ticks consumes CPU time. On a slow machine it was found that doing it this way resulted in a 15% increase in system speed relative to an implementation that sent a message to the clock task on every clock interrupt.

Millisecond Timing

As another concession to reality, a few routines are provided in *clock.c* that provide millisecond resolution timing. Delays as short as a millisecond area needed by various I/O devices. There is no practical way to do this using alarms and the message passing interface. The functions here are meant to be called directly by tasks. The technique used is the oldest and simplest I/O technique: polling. The counter that is used for generating the clock interrupts is read directly, as rapidly as possible, and the count is converted to milliseconds. The caller does this repeatedly until the desired time has elapsed.

Summary of Clock Services

Figure 11.28 summarizes the various services provided by *clock.c.* There are several ways to access the clock, and several ways the request can be honored. Some services are available to any process, with results returned in a message.

Uptime can be obtained by a function call from the kernel or a task, avoiding the overhead of a message. An alarm can be requested by a user process, with the eventual result being a signal, or by a task, causing activation of a watchdog function. Neither of these mechanisms can be used by a server process, but a server can ask for a synchronous alarm. A task or the kernel can request a delay using the *milli_delay* function, or it can incorporate calls to *milli_elapsed* into a polling routine, for instance, while waiting for input from a port.

Implementation of the Clock Driver in MINIX

When MINIX starts up, all the drivers are called. Most of them just try to get a message and block. The clock driver, *clock_task,* does that too, but first it calls *init_clock* to initialize the programmable clock frequency to 60Hz. When any message is received, it ads *pending_ticks* to *realtime* and then resets *pending_ticsk* before doing anything else. This operation could potentially conflict with a clock interrupt, so calls to *lock* and *unlock* are used to prevent a race. Otherwise the main loop of the clock driver is essentially the same as the other drivers: a message is received, a function to do the required work is called, and a reply message is sent.

Service	Access	Response	Clients
Gettime	System call	Message	Any process
Uptime	System call	Message	Any process
Uptime	Function call	Function value	Kernel or task
Alarm	System call	Signal	Any process
Alarm	System call	Watchdog activation	Task
Synchronous alarm	System call	Message	Server process
Milli_delay	Function call	Busy wait	Kernel or task
Milli_elapsed	Function call	Function value	Kernel or task

Fig. 11.29. The clock code supports a number of time-related services.

Do_clocktick is not called on each tick of the clock, so its name is not an exact description of its function. It is called when the interrupt handler has determined there might be something important to do. First a check is made to see if a signal or watchdog timer has gone off. If one has, all the alarm entries in the process table are inspected. Because ticks are not processed individually, several alarms may go off in one pass over the table. It is also possible that the process that was to receive the next alarm has already exited. When a process is found whose alarm is less than the current time, but no zero, the slot in the *watch_dog* array corresponding to that process is checked. In the C programming language a numeric value also has a logical value, so the test returns *TRUE* is a valid address is stored in the *watch_dog* slot, and the corresponding function is called indirectly. If a **null pointer** is found the test evaluates to *FLASE* and *cause_sig* is called to send a *SIGALRM* signal. The *watch_dog* slot is also used when a synchronous alarm is needed. In that case the address stored is the address of *cause_alarm*, rather then the addres of a watchdog function belonging to a particular task. For sending a signal we could have stored the address *cause_sig* but then we would have had to have written *cause_sig* differently, to expect no arguments and get the target process number from a global variable. Alternatively, we could have required all watchdog processes to expect an argument they do not need.

We will discuss *cause_sig* when we discuss the system task in a subsequent section. Its job is to send a message to the memory manager. This requires a check to see if the memory manager is currently waiting for a message. If so, it sends a message telling about the alarm. If the memory manager is busy, a note is make to inform it at the first opportunity.

While looping through the process table inspecting the *p_alarm* value for each process, *next_alarm* is updated. Before starting the loop it is set to a very large number, and then, for each process whose alarm value is nonzero after sending alarms or signals, a comparison is made between the process alarm and *next_alarm,* which is set to the smaller value.

After processing alarms, *do_clocktick* goes on to see if it is time to schedule another process. The execution quantum is maintained in the *PRIVATE* variable *sched_ticks,* which is normally decremented by the clock interrupt handler on every clock tick. However, on those ticks when *do_clocktick* is activated, it is not decremented by the handler, allowing *do_clocktick* itself to do this and test for a zero result. *Sched_ticks* is not reset whenever a new process is scheduled (because the file system and memory manager are allowed to run to completion). Instead it is rest after every *SCHED_RATE* ticks. The comparison is to make sure that the current process has actually run at least one full scheduler tick before taking the CPU away from it.

The next procedure, *do_getuptime*, is just one line: it puts the current value of *realitme* (the number of ticks since boot) into the proper field in the message to be returned. Any process can find the elapsed time this way, but the message overhead is a big price to ask of tasks, so a related function, *get_uptime*) is provided that can be called directly by tasks. Since it is not invoked via a message to the clock task, it has to add pending ticks to the current *realtime* itself. *Lock* and *unlock* are necessary here to prevent a clock interrupt occurring while *pending_ticks* is being accessed.

To get the current real time, *do_get_time* computes the current real time from *realtime* and *boot_time* (the system boot time in seconds). *Do_set_time* is its complement. It computes a new value for *boot_time* based on the given current real time and number of ticks since booting.

The procedures *do_setalarm* and *do_setsyn_alrm* are so similar we will discuss them together. Both extract the parameters that specify the process to be signaled and the time to wait from the message. *Do_setalarm* also extracts a function to call, although a few lines farther on it replaces this value with a null pointer if the target process is a user process and not a task. We have already seen how this pointer is later tested in *do_cloctick* to determine whether the target should get a signal or a call to watchdog. The time remaining to the alarm (in seconds) is also calculated by both functions and set into the return message. Both then call *common_setalarm* to finish up. In the case of the *do_setsyn_alarm* call, the function parameter passed to *common_setalarm* is always *cause_alarm.*

Common_setalarm finishes the work started by either of the two functions just discussed. Then it stores the alarm time in the process table and the pointer to the watchdog procedure (which may also be a pointer to *cause_alarm* or a null pointer) in the *watch_dog* array. Then it scans the entire process table to find the next alarm, just as is done by *do_clocktick.*

Cause_alarm is simple; it sets to *TRUE* an entry in the *syn_table* array corresponding to the target of the synchronous alarm. If the synchronous alarm task is not alive, it is sent a message to wake it up.

Implementation of the Synchronous Alarm Task

The synchronous alarm task, *syn_alarm_task*, follows the basic model of all tasks. It initializes and then enters an endless loop in which it receives and sends messages. The initialization consists of declaring itself alive by setting the variable *syn_al_alive* to *TRUE* and then declaring that it has nothing to do by setting all the entries in *syn_table* to *FALSE.* There is a slot in *syn_table* for each slot in the process stable. In begins its outer loop by declaring it has completed its work and then enters an inner loop where it check all slots in *syn_table.* If it finds an entry indicating a synchronous alarm is expected, it resets the entry, sends a message of type *CLOCK_INT* to the appropriate process, and declares its work not complete. At the bottom of its outer loop it does not pause to wait for any new messages unless its *work_done* flag is set. A new message is not needed to tell it there is more work to do, since *cause_alarm* writes directly into *syn_table*. A message is needed only to wake it up after it has run out of work. The effect is that it cycles very rapidly as long as there are alarms to be delivered.

In fact, this task is not used by the distribution version of MINIX. If you recompile MINIX to add networking support, it will be used by the network server, however, which needs exactly this kind of mechanism to enforce rapid timeouts if packets are not received when expected. In addition to the need for speed, a server cannot be sent a signal, since servers must run forever, and the default action of most signals is to kill the target process.

Implementation of the Clock Interrupt Handler

The design of the clock interrupt handle is a compromise between doing very little (so the processing time will be minimized) and doing enough to make expensive activations of the clock task infrequent. It changes a few variables and tests a few others. *Clock_handler* starts off by doing system accounting. MINIX keeps track of both user time and system time. User time is charged against a process if it is running when the clock ticks. System time is charged if the file system or memory manager is running. The variable *bill_ptr* always points to the last user process scheduled (the two serve do not count). The billing is done. After billing is finished, the most important variable maintained by *clock_handler*, *pending_ticks,* is incremented.

The real time must be known for testing whether *clock_handler* should wake up the tty or send a message to the clock task, but actually updating *realtime* itself is expensive, because this operation must be done using locks. To avoid this, the handler calculates its own version of the real time in the local variable *now.* There is a small chance that the result will be incorrect once in a while, but the consequences of such an error would not be serious.

The rest of the handler's work depends upon various tests. The terminal and the printer both need to be awakened from time to time. *Tty_timeout* is a global variable, maintained by the terminal task, which holds the next time the tty should be awakened. For the printer several variables which are *PRIVATE* within the printer module need to be checked, and they are tested in the call to *pr_restart,* which returns quickly even in the worst case of the printer being hung up. A test is made that activates the clock task if an alarm is due or if it is time to schedule another task. The latter test is complex, a logical AND of three simpler tests. The

```
interrupt(CLOCK);
```

code result in a *HARD_INT* message to the clock task.

In discussing *do_clocktick* we noted that it decrements *sched_ticks* and tests for zero to see if the execution quantum has expired. Testing whether *sched_ticsk* is equal to one is part of the complex test we mentioned above: if the clock task is not activated, it is still necessary to decrement *sched_ticks* within the interrupt handler and, if it reaches zero, reset the quantum. If this occurs, it is also time to note that the current process was active at the start of the new quantum: this is done by the assignment of the current value of *bill_ptr* to *prev_ptr*.

Time Utilities

Finally, *clock.c* contains some functions that provide various kinds of support. Many of these are hardware specific and will need to be replaced for a port of MINIX to non-Intel hardware. We will only describe the function of these, without going into details of their internals.

Init_clock is called by the timer task when it runs for the first time. It sets the mode and time delay of the timer chip to produce clock tick interrupts 60 times per second. Despite the fact that the "CPU speed" one sees in advertisements for PCs has increased from 4.77 Mhz for the original IBM PC to over 200 Mhz for modern systems, the constant *TIMER_COUNT,* used to initialize the timer, is the same no matter what PC model MINIX is run on. Every IBM compatible PC, no matter how fast its processor runs, provides a 14.3 Mhz signal for use by various devices that need a time reference. Serial communications lines and the video display also need such a timing reference.

The complement of *init_clock* is *clock_stop.* It is not really necessary, but it is a concession to the fact that MINIX users may want to start another operating system at times. It simply resets the timer chip parameters to the default mode of operation that MS-DOS and other operating systems may expect the ROM BIOS to have provided when they first start.

Milli_delay is provided for use by any task that needs very short delays. It is written in C without any hardware-specific references, but it uses a technique one might expect to find only in a low-level assembly language routine. It initializes a counter to zero and then rapidly polls it until a desired value is reached, we said that this technique of busy waiting should generally be avoided, but the necessities of implementation can require exceptions to general rules. The initialization of the counter is done by the next function, *milli_start* which simply zeroes two variables. The polling is done by calling the last function, *milli_elapsed,* which accesses the timer hardware. The counter that is examined is the same one used to count down clock ticks, and thus it can underflow and be reset to its maximum value before the desired delay is complete. *Milli_elapsed* corrects for this.

Terminals

Every general purpose computer has one or more terminals used to communicate with it. Terminals come in an extremely large number of different forms. It is up to the terminal driver to hide all these differences, so that the device-independent part of the operating system and the user programs do not have to be rewritten for each kind of terminal. In the following sections we will follow our now-standard approach of first discussing terminal hardware and software in general, and then discussing the MINIX software.

Terminal Hardware

From the operating system's point of view, terminals can be divided into three broad categories based on how the operating system communicates with them. The first category consists of memory-mapped terminals, which consist of a keyboard and a display, both of which are hardwired to the computer. The second category consists of terminals that interface via a serial communication line using the RS-232 standard, most frequently over a modem. The third category consists of terminals that are connected to the computer via a network. This taxonomy is shown in Fig.11.29.

Memory-Mapped Terminals

The first broad category of terminals named in Fig. 11.29, consists of memory-mapped terminals. These are an integral part of the computers themselves. Memory-mapped terminals are interfaced via a special memory called a **video RAM,** which forms part of the computer's address space and is addressed by the CPU the same way as the rest of memory.

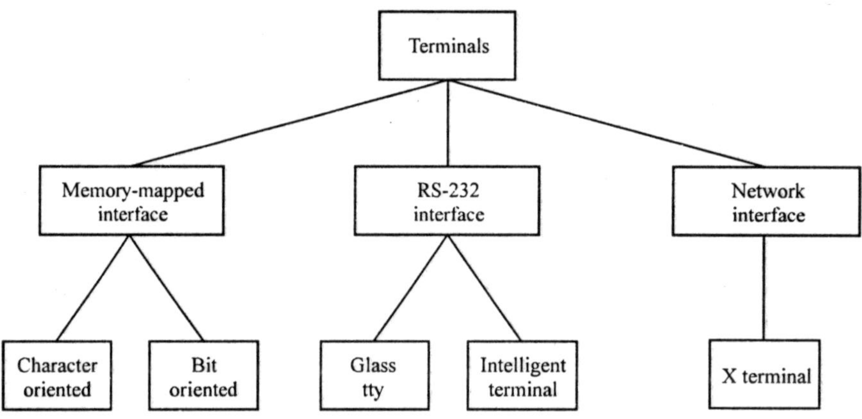

Fig. 11.30. Terminal types.

Also on the video RAM card is a chip called a **video controller.** This chip pulls character codes out of the video RAM and generates the video signal used to drivers the display (monitor). The monitor generates a beam of electrons that scans horizontally across the screen, painting lines on it. Typically the screen has 480 to 1024 lines from top to bottom, with 640 to 1200 points per line. These points are called **pixels**. The video controller signal modulates the electron beam, determining whether a given pixel will be light or dark. Color monitors have three beams, for red, green, and blue, which are independently modulated.

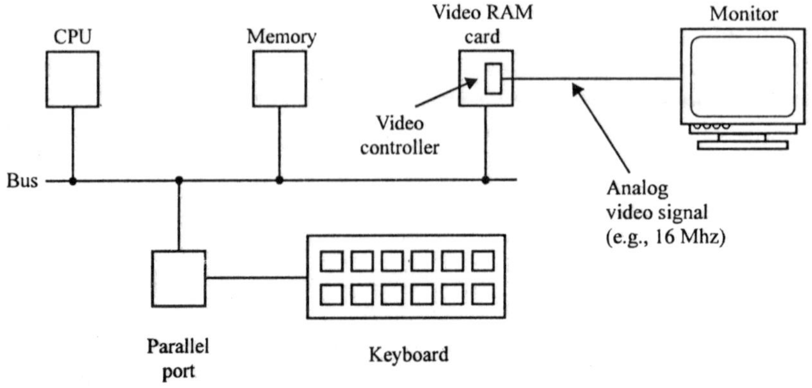

Fig. 11.31. Memory-mapped terminals write directly into video RAM.

A simple monochrome display might fit each character in a box 9 pixels wide by 14 pixels high (including the space between characters), and have 25 lines of 80 characters. The display would then have 350 scan lines of 720 pixels each. Each of these frames is redrawn 45 to 70 times a second. The video controller could be designed to fetch the first 80 characters from the video RAM, generate 14 scan lines, fetch the next 80 characters from the video RAM, generate the following 14 scan lines, and so on. In fact, most fetch each character one per scan line to eliminate the need for buffering in the controller. The 9-by-14 bit patterns for the characters are kept in a ROM used by the video controller. (RAM may also be used to support custom fonts.) The ROM is addressed by a 12-bit address, 8 bits from the character code and 4 bits to specify a scan line. The 8 bits in each byte of the ROM control 8 pixels; the 9th pixel between characters is always blank. Thus $14 \times 80 = 1120$ memory references to the video RAM are needed per line of text on the screen. The same number of references are made to the character generator ROM.

The IBM PC has several modes for the screen. In the simplest one, it uses a character-mapped display for the console. In Fig.11.31 (a) we see a portion of the video RAM. Each character on the screen of Fig.11.31 (b) occupies two characters in the RAM. The low-order character is the ASCII code for the character to be displayed. The high-order character is the attribute byte, which is used to specify the color, reverse video, blinking, and so on. The full screen of 25 by 80 characters requires 4000 bytes of video RAM in this mode.

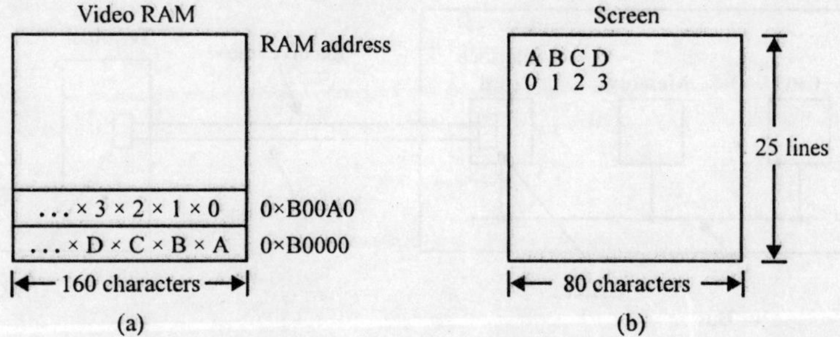

Fig.11.32. (a) A video RAM image for the IBM monochrome display. (b) The corresponding screen. The ×s are attribute bytes.

Bit-map terminals use the same principle, except that each pixel on the screen is individually controlled. In the simplest configuration, for a monochrome display, each pixel has a corresponding bit in the video RAM. At the other extreme, each pixel is represented by a 24-bit number, with 8 bits each for red, green, and blue. A 768 × 1024 color display with 24 bits per pixel requires 2 MB of RAM just to hold the image.

With a memory-mapped display, the keyboard is completely decoupled from the screen. It may be interfaced via a serial or parallel port. On every key action the CPU is interrupted, and the keyboard driver extracts the character typed by reading an I/O port.

On the IBM PC, the keyboard contains an embedded microprocessor which communicates through a specialized serial port with a controller chip on the motherboard. An interrupt is generated whenever a key is struck and also when one is released. Furthermore, all that the keyboard hardware provides is the key number, not the ASCII code. When the *A* key is struck, the key code (30) is put in an I/O register. It is up to the driver to determine whether it is lower case, upper case, CTRL-A,

ALT-A, CTRL-ALT-A, or some other combination. Since the driver can tell which keys have been struck but not yet released (e.g., shift), it has enough information to do the job. Although this keyboard interface puts the full burden on the software, it is extremely flexible. For example, user programs may be interested in whether a digit just typed came from the top row of keys or the numeric key pad on the side. In principle, the driver can provide this information.

RS-232 Terminals

RS-232 terminals are devices containing a keyboard and a display that communicate using a serial interface, one bit at a time. These terminals use a 9-pin or 25-pin connector, of which one pin is used for transmitting data, one pin is for receiving data, and one pin is ground. The other pins are for various control functions, most of which are not used. To send a character to an RS-232 terminal, the computer must transmit it 1 bit at a time, prefixed by a start bit, and followed by 1 or 2 stop bits to delimit the character. A parity bit which provides rudimentary error detection may also be inserted preceding the stop bits, although this is commonly required only for communication with mainframe systems. Common transmission rates are 9600, 19,200, and 38,400 bps. RS-232 terminals are commonly used to communicate with a remote computer using a modern and a telephone line.

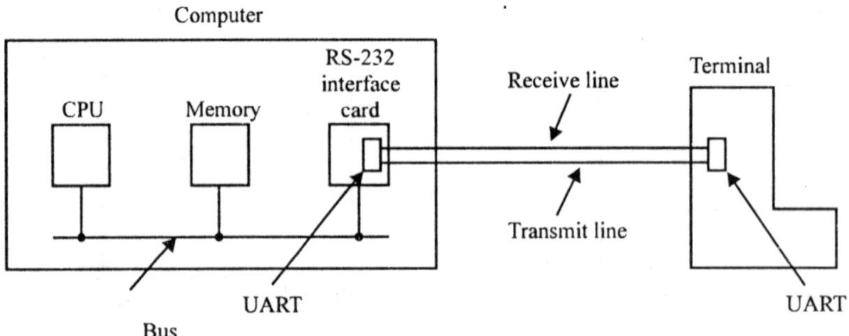

Fig. 11.33. An RS-232 terminal communicates with a computer over a communication line, one bit at a time. The computer and the terminal are completely independent.

Since both computers and terminals work internally with whole characters but must communicate over a serial line a bit at a time, chips have been developed to do the character-to-serial and serial-to-character conversions. They are called **UARTs** (Universal Asynchronous Receiver Transmitters). UARTs are attached to the computer by plugging RS-232 interface cards into the bus as illustrated in Fig. 11.33, RS-232 terminals are gradually dying off, being replaced by PCs and X terminals, but they are still encountered on older mainframe systems, especially in banking, airline reservation, and similar applications.

To print a character, the terminal driver writes the character to the interface card, where it is buffered and then shifted out over the serial line one bit at a time by the UART. Even at 38,400 bps, it takes just over 250 microsec to send a character. As a result of this slow transmission rate, the driver generally outputs a character to the RS-232 card and blocks, waiting for the interrupt generated by the interface when the character has been transmitted and the UART is able to accept another character. The UART can simultaneously send and receive characters, as its name implies. An interrupt is also generated when a character is received, and usually a small number of input characters can be buffered. The terminal driver must check a register when an interrupt is received to determine the cause of the interrupt. Some interface cards have a CPU and memory and can handle multiple lines, taking over much of the I/O load from the main CPU.

RS-232 terminals can be subdivided into categories, as mentioned above. The simplest ones were hardcopy (printing) terminals. Characters typed on the keyboard were transmitted to the computer. Characters sent by the computer were typed on the paper. These terminals are obsolete and rarely seen any more.

Dumb CRT terminal work the same way, only with a screen instead of paper. These are often called "glass ttys" because they are functionally the same as hardcopy ttys. (The term "tty" is an abbreviation for Teletype® a former company that pioneered in the computer terminal business; "tty" has come to mean any terminal.) Glass ttys are also obsolete.

Intelligent CRT terminals are in fact miniature, specialized computers. They have a CPU and memory and contain software, usually in ROM. From the operating system viewpoint, the main difference between a glass tty and an intelligent terminal is that the latter understands certain escape sequences. For example, by sending the ASCII ESC character (033), followed by various other characters, it may be possible to move the cursor to any position on the screen, insert text in the middle of the screen, and so forth.

X Terminals

The ultimate in intelligent terminals is a terminal that contains a CPU as powerful as the main computer, along with megabytes of memory keyboard, and a mouse. One common terminal of this type is the **X terminal,** which runs M.I.T.'s X Window System. Usually, X terminals talk to the main computer over an Ethernet.

An X terminal is a computer that runs the X software. Some products are dedicated to running only X; others are general-purpose computers that simply run X as one program among many others. Either way, an X terminal has a large bitmapped screen, usually 960 × 1200 or better resolution, in black and white, grayscale, or color, a full keyboard, and a mouse, normally with three buttons.

The program inside the X terminal that collects input from the keyboard or mouse and accepts commands from a remote computer is called the **X server.** It communicates over the network with **X clients** running on some remote host. It may seem strange to have the X server insides the terminal and the clients on the remote host, but the X server's job is to display bits, so it makes sense to be near the user. The arrangement of client and server is shown in Fig. 11.33

The screen of the X terminal contains some number of windows, each in the form of a rectangular grid of pixels. Each window usually has a title bar at the top, a scroll bar on the left, and a resizing box in the upper right-hand corner. One of the X clients is a program called a **window manager.** Its job is to control the creation, deletion, and movement of windows on the screen. To manage windows, it sends commands to the X server telling what to do. These commands include draw point, draw line, draw rectangle draw polygon, fill rectangle, fill polygon, and so on.

The job of the X server is to coordinate input from the mouse, keyboard, and X clients and update the display accordingly. It has to keep track of which window is currently selected (where the mouse pointer is), so it knows which client to send any new keyboard input to.

Terminal Software

The keyboard and display are almost independent devices, so we will treat them separately here. (They are not quite independent, since typed characters must be displayed on the screen.) In MINIX the keyboard and screen derivers are part of the same task; in other systems they may be split into distinct drivers.

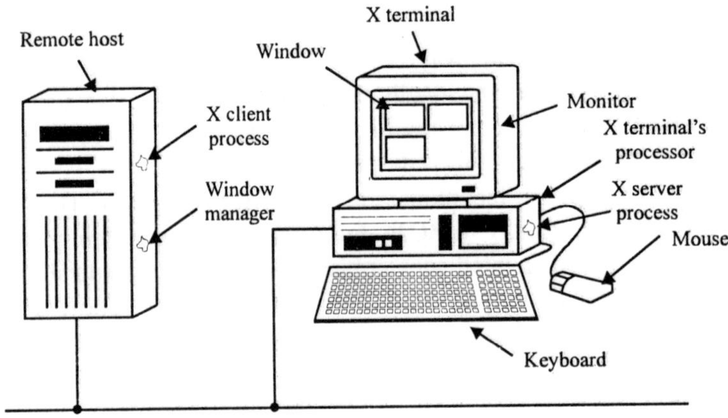

Fig. 11.34. Clients and servers in the M.I.T.X Window System.

Input Software

The basic job of the keyboard driver is to collect input from the keyboard and pass it to user programs when they read from the terminal. Two possible philosophies can be adopted for the driver. In the first one, the driver's job is just to accept input and pass it upward unmodified. A program reading from the terminal gets a raw sequence of ASCII codes. (Giving user programs the key numbers is too primitive, as well as being highly machine dependent.)

This philosophy is well suited to the needs of sophisticated screen editors such as *emacs,* which allow the user to bind an arbitrary action to any character or sequence of characters. It does, however, mean that if the user types *dste* instead of *date* and then corrects the error by typing three backspaces and *ate,* followed by a carriage return, the user program will be given all 11 ASCII codes typed.

Most programs do not want this much detail. They just want the corrected input, not the exact sequence of how it was produced. This observation leads to the second philosophy: the driver handles all the intraline editing, and just delivers correct lines to the user programs. The first philosophy is character-oriented; the second one is line-oriented. Originally they were referred to as **raw mode** and **cooked mode,** respectively. The POSIX standard uses the less-picturesque term **canonical mode** to describe line-oriented mode. On most systems canonical mode refers to a well-defined configuration. **Noncanonical mode** is equivalent to raw mode, although many details of terminal behavior can be changed. POSIX-compatible systems provide several library functions that support selecting either mode and changing many aspects of terminal configuration. In MINIX the IOCTL system call supports these functions.

The first task of the keyboard driver is to collect characters. If every keystroke causes an interrupt, the driver can acquire the character during the interrupt. If interrupts are turned into messages by the low-level software, it is possible to put the newly acquired character in the message. Alternatively, it can be put in a small buffer in memory and the message used to tell the driver that something has arrived. The latter approach is actually safer if a message can be sent only to a waiting process and there is some chance that the keyboard driver might still be busy with the previous character.

Once the driver has received the character, it must begin processing it. If the keyboard delivers key numbers rather than the character codes used by application software, then the driver must convert between the codes by using a table. Not all IBM "compatibles" use standard key numbering, so if the driver wants to support these machines, it must map different keyboards with different tables. A simple approach is to compile a table that maps between the codes provided by the keyboard and ASCII (American Standard Code for Information Interchange) codes into the keyboard driver, but this is unsatisfactory for users of languages other than English. Keyboards are arranged differently in different countries, and the ASCII character set is not adequate even for the majority of people in the Western Hemisphere, where speakers of Spanish, Portuguese, and French need accented characters and punctuation marks not used in English. To respond to the need for flexibility of keyboard layouts to provide for different languages, many operating systems provide for loadable **keymaps** or **code pages,** which make it possible to choose the mapping between keyboard codes and codes delivered to the application, either when the system is booted or later.

If the terminal is in canonical (cooked) mode, characters must be stored until an entire line has been accumulated, because the user may subsequently decide to erase part of it. Even if the terminal is in raw mode, the program may not yet have requested input, so the characters must be buffered to allow type ahead. (System designers who do not allow users to type for ahead ought to be tarred and feathered, or worse yet, be forced to use their own system.)

Two approaches to character buffering are common. In the first one, the diver contains a central pool of buffers, each buffer holding perhaps 10 characters. Associated with each terminal is a data structure, which contains, among other items, a pointer to the chain of buffers for input collected from that terminal. As more characters are typed, more buffers are acquired and hung on the chain. When the characters are passed to a user program, the buffers are removed and put back in the central pool.

The other approach is to do the buffering directly in the terminal data structure itself, with no central pool of buffers. Since it is common for users to type a command that will take a little while (say, a compilation) and then type a few lines ahead, to be safe the driver should allocate something like 200 characters per terminal. In a large-scale timesharing system with 100 terminals, allocating 20K all the time for type ahead is clearly overkill, so a central buffer pool with space for perhaps 5K is probably enough. On the other hand, a dedicated buffer per terminal makes the driver simpler (no linked list management) and is to be preferred on personal computers with only one or two terminals. Figure. 11.34, shows the difference between these two methods.

Although the keyboard and display are logically separate devices, many users have grown accustomed to seeing the characters they have just typed appear on the screen. Some (older) terminals oblige by automatically displaying (in hardware) whatever has just been typed, which is not only a nuisance when passwords are being entered but greatly limits the flexibility of sophisticated editors and other programs. Fortunately, most modern terminals display nothing when keys are typed. It is therefore up to the software tc display the input. The process is called **echoing.**

Echoing is complicated by the fact that a program may be writing to the screen while the user is typing. At the very least, the keyboard diver has to figure out where to put the new input without it being overwritten by program output.

Echoing also gets complicated when more than 80-characters are typed on a terminal with 80-character lines. Depending on the application, wrapping around to the next line may be appropriate. Some drivers just truncate lines to 80 characters by throwing away all characters beyond column 80.

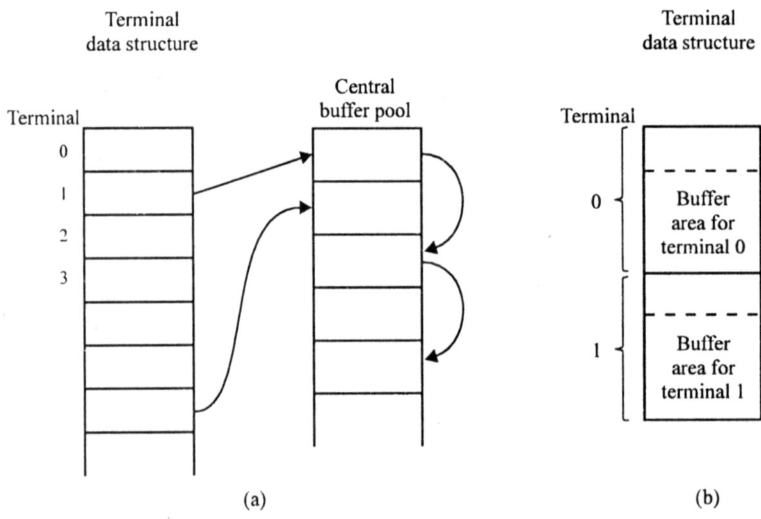

Fig. 11.35. (a) Central buffer pool. (b) Dedicated buffer for each terminal.

Another problem is tab handling. Most terminal have a tab key, but few can handle tab on output. It is up to the driver to compute where the cursor is currently located, taking into account both output from programs and output from echoing, and compute the proper number of spaces to be echoed.

Now we come to the problem of device equivalence. Logically, at the end of a line of text, one wants a carriage return, to move the cursor back to column 1, and a linefeeds, to advance to the next line. Requiring users to type both at the end of each line would not sell well (although some terminals have a key which generates both, with a 50 per cent chance of doing so in the order that the software wants them). It is up to the driver to convert whatever comes in to the standard internal format used by the operating system.

If the standard form is just to store a linefeed (the MINIX convention), then carriage returns should be turned into linefeeds. If the internal format is to store both, then the driver should generate a linefeed when it gets a carriage return and a carriage return when it gets a linefeed. No matter what the internal convention, the terminal may require both a linefeed and a carriage return to be echoed in order to get the screen updated properly. Since a large computer may well have a wide variety of different terminals connected to it, it is up to the keyboard driver to get all the different carriage return/linefeed combinations converted to the internal system standard and arrange for all echoing to be done right.

A related problem is the timing of carriage return and linefeeds. On some terminals, it may take longer to display a carriage return or linefeed than a letter or number. If the microprocessor inside the terminal actually has to copy a large block of text to achieve scrolling, then linefeeds may be slow. If a mechanical print head has to be returned to the left margin of the paper, carriage returns may be slow. In both cases it is up to the driver to insert **filler characters** (dummy null characters) into the output stream or just stop outputting long enough for the terminal to catch up. The amount of time to delay is often related to the terminal speed, for example, at 4800 bps or slower, no delays may be, but at 9600 bps or higher one filler character might be required. Terminals with hardware tabs, specially hardcopy ones, may also require a delay after a tab.

When operating in canonical mode, a number of input characters have special meanings. Figure. 11.35, shows all of the special characters required by POSIX and the additional one recognized by MINIX. the defaults are all control characters that should not conflict with text input or codes used by programs, but all except the last two can be changed using the *stty* command, if desired. Older versions of UNIX used different defaults for many of these.

Character	POSIX name	Comment
CTRL-D	EOF	End of file
	EOL	End of line (undefined)
CTRL-H	ERASE	Backspace one character
DEL	INTR	Interrupt process (SIGINT)
CTRL-U	KILL	Erase entire line being typed
CTRL-\	QUIT	Force core dump (SIGQUIT)
CTRL-Z	SUSP	Suspend (ignored by MINIX)
CTRL-Q	START	Start output
CTRL-S	STOP	Stop output
CTRL-R	REPRINT	Redisplay input (MINIX extension)
CTRL-V	LNEXT	Literal next (MINIX extension)
CTRL-O	DISCARD	Discard output (MINIX extension)
CTRL-M	CR	Carriage return (unchangeable)
CTRL-J	NL	Linefeed (unchangeable)

***Fig. 11.36.** Characters that are handled specially in canonical mode.*

The *ERASE* character allows the user to rub out the character just typed. In MINIX it is the backspace (CTRL-H). It is not added to the character queue but instead removes the previous character from the queue. It should be echoed as a sequence of three characters, backspace, space, and backspace, in order to remove the previous character from the screen. If the previous character was a tab, erasing it requires keeping track of where the cursor was prior to the tab. In most systems backspacing will only erase characters on the current line. It will not erase a carriage return and back up into the previous line.

When the user notices an error at the start of the line being typed in, it is often convenient to erase the entire line and start again. The *KILL* character (in MINIX CTRL-U) erases the entire line. MINIX makes the erased line vanish from the screen, but some systems echo it plus a carriage return and linefeed because some users like to see the old line. Consequently, how to echo *KELL* is a matter of taste. As with *ERASE* it is usually not possible to go further back than the current line. When a block of characters is killed, it may or may not be worth the trouble for the driver to return buffers to the pool, if one is used.

Sometimes the *ERASE* or *KILL* characters must be entered as ordinary data. The *LNEXT* character serves as an **escape character.** In MINIX CTRL-V is the default. As an example, older UNIX systems often used the @ sign for *KILL,* but the Internet mail system uses addresses of the form *linda@cs.washington.deu.* Someone who feels more comfortable with older conventions might redefine *KILL* as @, but the need to enter an @ sign literally to address e-mail. This can be done by typing CTRL-V @. The CTRL-V itself can be entered literally by typing CTRL-V CTRL-V. After seeing a CTRL-V, the driver sets a flag saying that the next character is exempt from special processing. The *LNEXT* character itself is not entered in the character queue.

To allow users to stop a screen image from scrolling out of view, control codes are provided to freeze the screen and restart it later. In MINIX these are *STOP,* (CTRL-S) and *START,* (CTRL-Q), respectively. They are not stored but are used to set and clear a flag in the terminal data structure. Whenever output is attempted, the flag is inspected. If it is set, no output occurs. Usually, echoing is also suppressed along with program output.

It is often necessary to kill a runway program being debugged. The *INTR* (DEL) and *QUIT* (CTRL-\) characters can be used for this purpose. In MINIX, DEL sends the SIGINT signal to all the processes started up from the terminal. Implementing DEL can be quite tricky. The hard part is getting the information from the driver to the part of the system that handles signals, which, after all, has not asked for this information. CTRL-\ is similar to DEL, except that it sends the SIGQUIT signal, which forces a core dump if not caught or ignored. When either of these key is struck, the driver should echo a carriages return and linefeed and discard all accumulated input to allow for a fresh start. The default value for *INTR* is often CTRL-C instead of DEL, since many programs use DEL interchangeably with the backspace for editing.

Another special character is *EOF* (CTRL-D), which in MINIX causes any pending read requests for the terminal to be satisfied with whatever is available in the buffer, even if the buffer is empty. Typing CTRL-D at the start of a line causes the program to get a read of 0 bytes, which is conventionally interpreted as end-of-file and causes most programs to act the same way as they would upon seeing end-of-file on an input file.

Some terminal drivers allow much fancier intraline editing than we have sketched here. They have special control characters to erase a worked, skip backward or forward characters or words, go to the beginning or end of the line being typed, and so forth. Adding all these functions to the terminal driver makes it much larger and, furthermore, is wasted when using fancy screen editors that work in raw mode anyway.

To allow programs to control terminal parameters, POSIX requires that several functions be available in the standard library, of which the most important are *tcgetattr* and *tecetattr. Tcgetattr* retrieves a copy of the structure shown in Fig.11.36, the *termiso* structure, which contains all the information needed to change special characters, set modes, and modify other characteristics of a terminal. A program can examine the current settings and modify them as desired. *Tcsetattr* then writes the structure back to the terminal task.

```
struct temios {
    tcflag_t c_iflag;        /* input modes */
    tcflag_t c_iflag;        /* output modes */
    tcflag_t c_cflag;        /* output modes */
    tcflag_t c_oflag;        /* local modes */
    speed_t c_ispeed;        /* input speed */
    speed_t c_ospeed;        /* output speed */
    cc_t c_cc[NCCS];         /* control characters */
};
```

Fig. 11.37. *The termios structure. In MINIX tc_flag_t is a short, speed_t is an int, cc_t is a char.*

POSIX does not specify whether its requirements should be implemented through library functions or system calls. MINIX provides a system call, IOCTL, called by

ioctl(file_descriptor, request, argp),

that is used to examine and modify the configurations of many I/O devices. This call is used to implement the *tcgetattr* and *tcsetattr* functions. The variable *request* specifies whether the *termios* structure is to be read or written, and in the latter case, whether the request is to take effect immediately or should be deferred until all currently queued output is complete. The variable *argp* is a pointer to a *termios* structure in the calling program. This particular choice of communication between program and driver was chosen for its UNIX compatibility, rather than for its inherent beauty.

A few notes about the termios structure are in order. The four flag words provide a great deal of flexibility. The individual bits in *c_iflag* control various ways input is handled. For instance, the *ICRNL* bit causes *CR* characters to be converted into *NL* on input. This flag is set by default in MINIX. The *c_oflag* holds bits that affect output processing. For instance, the *OPOST* bit enables output processing. It and the *ONLCR* bit, which causes *NL* characters in the output to be converted into a *CR NL* sequence, are also set by default in MINIX. The *c_cflag* is the control flag. The default settings for MINIX enable a line to receive 8-bit characters and cause a modern to hang up if a user logs out on the line. The *c_lflag* is the *local mode* flag field. One bit, *ECHO,* enables echoing (this can be turned off during a login to provide security for entering a password). Its most important bit is the *ICANON* bit, which enables canonical mode. With *ICANON* off, several possibilities exists. If all other settings are left at their defaults, a mode identical to the traditional **cbreak mode** is entered. In this mode characters are passed to the program without waiting for a full line, but the *INTR, QUIT, START,* and *STOP* characters retain their effects. All of these can be disabled by resetting bits in the flags, however, to produce the equivalent of traditional raw mode.

The various special characters that can be changed, including those which are MINIX extensions, are held in the *c_cc* array. This array also holds two parameters which are used in noncanonical mode. The quantity *MIN*, stored in *c_cc[VMIN],* specifies the minimum number of characters that must be received to satisfy a READ call. The quantity *TIME* in *c_cc[VTIME]* sets a time limit for such calls. *MIN* and *TIME* interact as shown in Fig. 11.37. A call that asks for *N* bytes is illustrated. With *TIME* = 0 and *MIN* = 1, the behaviour is similar to the traditional raw mode.

Output Software

Output is simpler than input, but drivers for RS-232 terminals are radically different from drivers for memory-mapped terminals. The method that is commonly used for RS-232 terminals is to have output buffers associated with each terminal. The buffers can come from the same pool as the input buffers, or be dedicated, as with input. When programs write to the terminal, the output is first copied to the buffers. Similarly, output from echoing is also copied to the buffers. After all the output has been copied to the buffers (or the buffers are full), the first character is output, and the driver goes to sleep. When the interrupt comes in, the next character is output, and so on.

	TIME=0	TIME>0
MIN=0	Return immediately with whatever is available, 0 to N bytes	Timer starts immediately. Return with first byte entered or with 0 bytes after timeout
MIN>0	Return with at least MIN and up to N bytes. Possible indefinite block	Interbyte timer starts after first byte. Return N bytes if received by timeout, or at least 1 byte at timeout. Possible indefinite block

Fig.11.38. *MIN and TIME determine when a call to read returns in noncanonical mode. N is the number of bytes requested.*

With memory-mapped terminals, a simpler scheme is possible. Characters to be printed are extracted one at a time from user space and put directly in the video RAM. With RS-232 terminals, each character to be output is just sent across the line to the terminal. With memory mapping, some characters require special treatment, among them, backspace, carriage return, linefeed, and the audible bell (CTRL-G). A driver for a memory-mapped terminal must keep track is software of the current position on the video RAM, so that printable characters can be put there and the current position advanced. Backspace, carriage return, and linefeed all require this position to be updated appropriately.

In particular, when a linefeed is output on the bottom line of the screen the screen must be scrolled. To see how scrolling works, look at Fig. 11.32. If the video controller always began reading the RAM at 0xB0000, the only way to scroll the screen would be to copy 24 × 80 characters (each character requiring 2 bytes) from 0xB00A0 to 0xB0000, a time-consuming proposition.

Fortunately, the hardware usually provides some help here. Most video controllers contain a register that determines where in the video RAM to begin fetching bytes for the top line on the screen. By setting this register to point to 0xB00A0 instead of 0xB0000, the line that was previously number two moves to the top, and the whole screen scrolls up one line. The only other thing the driver must do is copy whatever is needed to the new bottom line. When the video controller gets to the top of the RAM, it just wraps around and continues fetching bytes starting at the lowest address.

Another issue that the driver must deal with on a memory-mapped terminal is cursor positioning. Again, the hardware usually provides some assistance in the form of a register that tells where the cursor is to go. Finally, there is the problem of the bell. It is sounded by outputting a since or square wave to the loudspeaker, a part of the computer quite separate from the video RAM.

It is worth nothing that many of the issues faced by the terminal driver for a memory-mapped display (scrolling, bell, and so on) are also faced by the microprocessor inside an RS-232 terminal. From the viewpoint of the microprocessor, it is the main processor in a system with a memory-mapped display.

Screen editor and many other sophisticated programs need to be able to update the screen in more complex ways than just scrolling text onto the bottom of the display. To accommodate them, many terminal drivers support a variety of escape sequences. Although some terminal support idiosyncratic escape sequence sets, it is advantageous to have a standard to facilitate adapting software from one system to another. The American National Standards Institute (ANSI) has defined a set of standard escape sequences, and MINIX supports a subset of the ANSI sequences, shown in Fig. 3-36, that is adequate for may common operations. When the driver sees the character that starts the escape sequences, it sets a flag and waits until the rest of the escape sequence comes in. When everything has arrived, the driver must carry it out in software. Inserting and deleting text require moving block of characters around the video RAM. The hardware is of no help with anything except scrolling and displaying the cursor.

Escape Sequence	Meaning
ESC [*n*A	Move up *n* lines
ESC [*n*B	Move down *n* lines
ESC [*n*C	Move right *n* spaces
ESC [*n*D	Move left *n* spaces
ESC [*m; n*H	Move cursor to (*m,n*)
ESC [*s*J	Clear screen from cursor (0 to end, 1 from start, 2 all)
ESC [*s*K	Clear line from cursor (0 to end, 1 from start, 2 all)
ESC [*n*L	Insert *n* lines at cursor
ESC [*n*M	Delete *n* lines at cursor
ESC [*n*P	Delete *n* lines at cursor
ESC [*n*@	Insert *n* chars at cursor
ESC [*n*m	Enable rendition *n*(0 = normal, 4 = bold, 5 = blinking, 7 = reverse)
ESC M	Scroll the screen backward if the cursor is on the top line

Fig. 11.39. *The ANSI escape sequences accepted by the terminal driver on output. ESC denotes the ASCII escape character (0x1B), and n, m, and s are optional numeric parameters.*

Overview of the Terminal Driver in MINIX

The terminal driver is contained in four C files (six if RS-232 and pseudo terminal support are enabled) and together they far and away constitute the largest driver in MINIX. The size of the terminal driver is partly explained by the observation that the driver handles both the keyboard and the display, each of which is a complicated device in its own right, as well as two other optional types of terminals. Still, it comes as a surprise to most people to learn that terminal I/O requires thirty times as much code as the scheduler. (This felling is reinforced by looking at the numerous books on operation systems that devote thirty times as much space to scheduling as to all I/O combined.)

The terminal driver accepts seven message types:

1. Read from the terminal (from FS on behalf of a user process).
2. Write to the terminal (from FS on behalf of a user process).
3. Set terminal parameters for IOCTL (from FS on behalf of a user process).
4. I/O occurred during last clock tick (from the clock interrupt).
5. Cancel previous request (from the file system when a signal occurs).
6. Open a device.
7. Close a device.

The message for reading and writing have the same format as shown in Fig.11.20, except that no *POSITION* field is needed. With a disk, the program has to specify which block it wants to read. With a terminal, there is no choice: the program always gets the next character typed in. Terminals do not support seeks.

The POSIX functions *tcgetattr* and *tcgetattr,* used to examine and modify terminal attributes (properties), are supported by the IOCTL system call. Good programming practice is to use these functions and others in *include/termios.h* and leave it to the C library to convert library calls to IOCTL system calls. There are, however, some control operations needed by MINIX that are not provided or in POSIX, for example, loading an alternate keymap, and for these the programmer must use IOCTL explicitly.

The message sent to the driver by an IOCTL system call contains a function request code and a pointer. For the *tcesetattr* function, an IOCTL call is made with a *TCSETS, TCSETSW,* or *TCSETSF* request type, and a pointer to a *termios* structure like the one shown in Fig.11.36. All such calls replace the current set of attributes with a new set, the differences being that a *TCSETS* request takes effect immediately, a *TCSETSW* request does not take effect until all output has been transmitted, and a *TCSETSF* waits for output to finish and discards all input that has not yet been read. *Tcgetattr* is translated into an IOCTL call with a *TCGETS* request type and returns a filled in *termios* structures to the caller, so the current state of a device can be examined. IOTCL calls that do not correspond to functions defined by POSIX like the *KIOCSMAP* request used to load a new keymap, pass pointers to other kinds of structures, in this case to a *keymap_t* which is a 1536-byte structure (16-bit codes for 128 keys × 6 modifiers). Figure 11.45 summarizes how standard POSIX calls are converted into IOCTL system calls.

The terminal driver uses one main data structure, *tty_table*, which is an array of *tty* structures, one per terminal. A standard PC has only one keyboard and display, but MINIX can support up to eight virtual terminals, depending upon the amount of memory on the display adapter card. This permits the person at the console to log on multiple times, switching the display output and keyboard input from one "user" to another. With two virtual consoles, pressing ALT-F2 selects the second one and ALT-F1 returns to the first. ALT plus the arrow keys also can be used. In addition, serial lines can support two users at remote locations, connected by RS-232 cable or modem, and **pseudo**

terminals can support users connected through a network. The driver has been written to make it easy to add additional terminals. The standard configuration illustrated in the source code in this text has two virtual consoles, with serial lines and pseudo terminal disabled.

Each *tty* structure in *tty_table* keeps track of both input and output. For input, it holds a queue of all characters that have been typed but not yet read by the program, information about requests to read characters that have not yet been received, and timeout information, so input can be requested without the task blocking permanently if no character is typed. For output, it holds the parameters of write requests that are not yet finished. Other fields hold various general variables, such as the *termiso structure* discussed above, which affects many properties of both input and output. There is also a field in the *tty* structure to point to information which is needed for a particular class of devices but is not needed in the *tty_table* entry for every device. For instance, the hardware-dependent part of the console driver needs the current position on the screen and in thte video RAM, and the current attribute byte for the display, but this information is not needed to support an RS-232 line. The privates data structures for each device type are also where the buffers that receive input from the interrupt service routines are located. Slow devices, such as the keyboard, do not need buffers as large as those needed by fast devices.

Terminal Input

When a user logs in one the system console, a shell is created for him with */dev/console* as standard input, standard output, and standard error. The shell starts up the tries to read from standard input by calling the library procedure *read.* This procedure sends a message that contains the file descriptor, buffer address, and count to the file system. This message is shown as (1) in Fig.11.39. After sending the message, the shell blocks, waiting for the reply. (User processes execute only the SEND_REC primitive, which combines a SEND with a RECEIVE from the process sent to.)

The file system gets the message and locates the i-node corresponding to the specified file descriptor. This i-node is for the character special file */dev/console* and contains the major and minor device numbers for the terminal. The major device type for terminals is 4; for the console the minor device number is 0.

The file system indexes into it device map, *dmap,* to find the number of the terminal task. Then it sends a message to the terminal task, shown as (2) in Fig. 11.39. Normally, the user will not have typed anything yet, so the terminal driver will be unable to satisfy the request. It sends a reply back immediately to unblock the file system and report that no characters are available, shown as (3). The file system records the fact a process is waiting for terminal input in the console's structure in *tty_table* and then goes off to get the next request for work. The user's shell remains blocked until the requested characters arrive, of course.

When a character is finally typed on the keyboard, it causes two interrupts, one when the key is depressed and one when it is released. This rule also applies to modifier keys such as CTRL and SHIFT, which do not transmit any data by themselves but still cause two interrupts per key. The keyboard interrupt is IRQ 1, and *hwin01* in the assembly code file *mpx386.s* activates *kbd_hw_int* which in turn calls *scan_keyboard* to extract the key code from the keyboard hardware. If the code is for an ordinary character, it is put into they keyboard input queue, *ibuf,* if the interrupt was generated by a key being depressed, but it is ignored if the interrupt was generated by the release of a key. Codes for modifier keys like CTRL and SHIFT are put into the queue for both types of interrupt but can be distinguished later by a bit that is set only when a key is released. Note that at this point the codes received and stored in *ibuf* are not ASCII codes; they are simply the scan codes produced by the IBM keyboard. *Kbd_hw_int* then sets a flag, *tty_events* (part of the keyboard's section of the *tty_table*), calls *force_timeout,* and returns.

Unlike some other interrupt service routines, *kbd_hw_int* does not send a message to wake up the terminal task. The call to *force_timeout* is indicated by the dashed lines marked (4) in the figure. These are not messages. They set the *tty_timeout* variable in the address space common to the interrupt service routines. On the next clock interrupt clock *handler* finds that *tty_timeout* indicates it is time for a call to *tty_wakeup* which the sends a message (5) to the terminal task. Not that although the source code for *tty_wakeup* is in the file *tty.c,* runs in response to the clock interrupt, and thus we say the clock interrupt sends the message to the terminal task. If input is arriving rapidly, a number of character cods may be queued this way, which is why multiple call to *force_timeout* (4) are shown in the Figure 11.40.

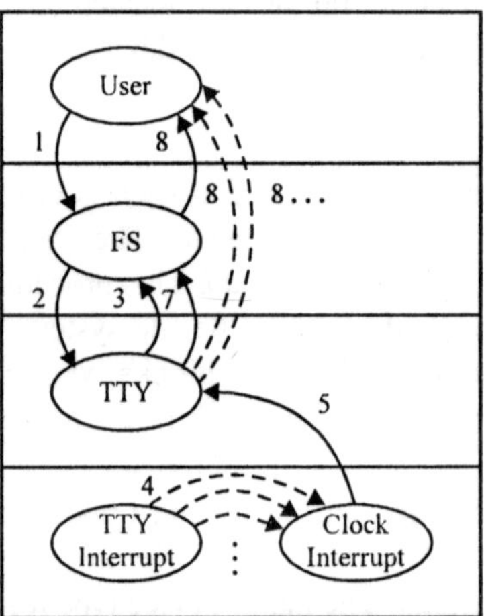

Fig. 11.40. *Read request from terminal when no characters are pending. FS is the file system. TTY is the terminal task. The interrupt handler for the terminal queues characters as they are entered, but it is the clock interrupt handler that awakens TTY.*

Upon receiving the wakeup message the terminal task inspects the *tty_events* flag for each terminal device, and, for each device which has the flag set, call *handle_events*. The *tty_events* flag can signal various kinds of activity (although input is the most likely), so *handle_events* always call the device-specific functions for both input and output. For input from the keyboard this results in a call to *kb_read,* which deeps track of keyboard cods that indicate pressing or releasing of the CTRL, SHIFT, and ALT keys and converts keyboard codes into ASCII codes. *kb_read* in turn calls in *in_process,* which processes the ASCII codes, taking into account special characters and different flags that may be set, including whether or not canonical mode is in effect. The effect is normally to add characters to the console's input queue in *tty_table,* although some codes, for instance BACKSPACE, have other effects. Normally, also, *in_process* initiates echoing of the ASCII codes to the display.

When enough characters have come in, the terminal task calls the assembly language procedure *phys_copy* to copy the data to the address requested by the shell. This operation also is not message passing and for that reason is shown by dashed lines (6) in Fig.11.39. There is more than one such line shown because there may be more than one such operation before the user's request has been completely fulfilled. When the operation is finally complete, the terminal driver sends a message to the file system telling it that the work has been done (7), and the file system reacts to this message by sending a message back to the shell to unblock it (8).

The definition of when enough characters have come in depends upon the terminal mode. In canonical mode a request is complete when a linefeed, end-of-line, or end-of-file code is received, and, in order for proper input processing to be done, a line of input cannot exceed the size of the input queue. In noncanonical mode a read can request a much larger number of characters, and *in_process* may have to transfer characters more than once before a message is returned to the file system to indicate the operation is complete.

Note that the terminal driver copies the actual characters directly from its own address space to that of the shell. It does not first go through the file system. With block I/O, data do pass through the file system to allow it to maintain a buffer cache of the most recently used blocks. If a requested block happens to be in the cache, thee request can be satisfied directly by the file system, without doing any disk I/O.

For terminal I/O, a cache makes no sense. Furthermore, a request from the file system to a disk driver can always be satisfied in at most a few hundred milliseconds, so there is no real harm in having the file system just wait. Terminal I/O may take hours to complete, or may never be complete (in canonical mode the terminal task waits for a complete line, and it may also wait a long time in noncanonical mode, depending upon the settings of *MIN* and *TIME*). Thus, it is unacceptable to have the file system block until a terminal input request is satisfied.

Later on, it may happed that the user has typed ahead, and that characters are available before they have been requested, from previous occurrences of events 4 and 5. In that case, events 1, 2, 6, 7, and 8 all happen in quick succession after the read request; 3 does not occur at all.

If the terminal task happen to be running at the time of a clock interrupt, no messages can be sent to it because it will not be waiting for one. However, in order to keep input and output flowing smoothly when the terminal task is busy, the *tty_events* flags for all terminal devices are inspected at several other times, for instance, immediately after processing and replying to a message. Thus, it is possible for characters to be added to the console queue without the aid of a wakeup message from the clock. If two or more clock interrupts occur before the terminal driver finishes what it is doing, all the characters are stored in *ibuf,* and *tty_flags* is repeatedly set. Ultimately, the terminal task gets one message; the rest are lost. But since all the characters are safely stored in the buffer, no typed input is lost. It is even possible that by the time a message is received by the terminal task the input is complete and a reply has already been sent to the user process.

The problem of what to do in a unbuffered message system (rendezvous principle) when an interrupt routine wants to send a message to a process that is busy is inherent in this kind of design. For most devices, such as disk, interrupts occur only in response to commands issued by the driver, so only one interrupt can be pending at any instant. The only devices that generate interrupts on their own are the clock and terminals (and when enabled, the network). The clock is handled by counting pending ticks, of if the clock task does not receive a message from, the clock interrupt it can compensate later. Terminals are handled by having the interrupt routine accumulate the characters in a buffer and raising a flag to indicate characters have been received. If the terminal task is running, it checks all of these flags before it goes to sleep and postpones going to sleep if there is more work it can do.

The terminal task is not awakened directly by terminal interrupts due to the excessive overhead doing so would entail. The clock sends an interrupt to the terminal task on the next tick following each terminal interrupt. At 100 words per minute a typist enters fewer than 10 characters per second. Even with a fast typist the terminal task will probably be sent an interrupt message for each character typed at the keyboard, although some of these messages may be lost. If the buffer should fill before being emptied, excess characters are discarded, but experience shows that, for the keyboard, a 32-character buffer is adequate. In the case of other input devices higher data rates are probable—rates 1000 or more times faster than those of a typist are possible from a serial port connected to a 28,800-bps mode. At that speed approximately 48 characters may be received between clock ticks by the modem, but to allow for data compression on the modem link the serial port connected to the modem must be able to handle at least twice as many.

We have some regrets that the terminal task cannot be implemented without some compromise of our general design principles, but the method we use does the job without too much additional software complexity and no loss in performance. The obvious alternative, to throw away the rendezvous principle and have the system buffer all messages sent to destinations not waiting for them, is much more complicated and also slower.

Real system designers are often faced with a trade-off between using the general case, which is elegant all the time but somewhat slow, and using simpler techniques, which are usually fast but in one or two cases require a trick to make them work properly. Experience is rally the only guide to which approach is better under given circumstances.

We will complete our overview of terminal input by summarizing the events that occur when the terminal task is first activated by a read request and when it is reactivated after receipt of keyboard input. In the first case, when a message comes in to the terminal task requesting characters from the keyboard, the main procedure, *tty_task* calls *do_read* to handle the request. *Do_read* stores the parameters of the call in the keyboard's entry in *tty_table,* in case there are insufficient characters buffered to satisfy the request.

Then it calls *in_transfer* to get any input already waiting, and the *handle_events* which in turn calls *kb_read* and then *in_transfer* once again, in order to try to milk the input stream for a few more characters. *Kb_read* calls several other procedures not shown in Fig.11.39 to accomplish its work. The result is that whatever is immediately available is copied to the user. If nothing is available, nothing is copied. If the read is completed by *in_transfer* or by *handle_events,* a message is sent to the file system when all characters heave been transferred, so the file system can unblock the caller. If the read was not completed (no characters, or not enough characters) *do_read* reports back to the file system, telling it whether it should suspend the original caller, or, if a nonblocking read was requested, cancel the read.

The right side of Fig.11.39, summarizes the events that occur when the terminal task is awakened subsequent to an interrupt from the keyboard. When a character is typed, the interrupt procedure *kb_hw_int* puts the character code received into the keyboard buffer, sets a flag to identify that the console device has experienced an event, and then arranges for a timeout to occur on the next clock tick. The clock task sends a message to the terminal task telling it something has happened. Upon receiving this message, *tty_task* checks the event flags of all terminal devices and calls *handle_event* for each devices with a raised flag. In this case of the keyboard, *handle_event* calls *kb_read* and *in_transfer,* just as was done on receipt of the original read request. The events shown on the right side of the figure may occur several times, until enough characters are received to fulfil the request accepted by *do_read* after the first message from the FS. If the FS tries to initiate a request for more characters from the same device before the first request is complete, an error is returned. Of course, each device is independent; a read request on behalf of a user at a remote terminal is processed separately from one for a user at the console.

The functions not shown in Fig.11.40 that are called by *kb_read* include *map_key,* which converts the key codes (scan codes) generated by the hardware into ASCII codes, *make_break,* which keeps track of the state of modifier keys such as the SHIFT key, and *in_process,* which handles complications such as attempts by the user to backspace over input entered by mistake, other special characters, and options available in different input modes. *In_process* also calls *echo,* so the typed characters will be displayed on the screen.

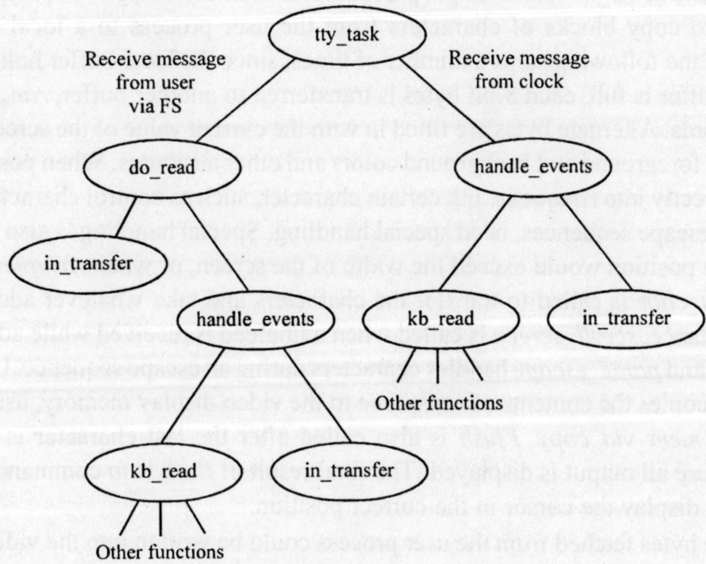

Fig. 11.41. Input handling in the terminal driver. The left branch of the tree is taken to process a request to read characters. The right branch is taken when a character-has-been-typed message is sent to the driver.

Terminal Output

In general, console output in simpler than terminal input, because the operating system is in control and does not need to be concerned with requests for output arriving at inconvenient times. Also, because the MINIX console is a memory-mapped display, output to the console is particularly simple. No interrupts are needed; the basic operation is to copy data from one memory region to another. On the other handle, all the details of managing the display, including handling escape sequences, must be handled by the driver software. As we did with keyboard input in the previous section we will trace through the steps involved in sending characters to the console display. We will assume in this example that the active display is being written; minor complications caused by virtual consoles will be discussed later.

When a process want to print something, it generally calls *printf. Printf* calls WRITE to send a message to the file system. The message contains a pointer to the characters to be printed (not the characters themselves). The file system then sends a message to the terminal deriver, which fetches them and copies them to the video RAM. Figure11.41 shows the main procedures involved in output.

When a message comes in to the terminal task requesting it to write on the screen, *do_write* is called to store the parameters in the console's *tty* struct in the *tty_table*. The *handle_events* (the same function called whenever the *tty_events* flag is found set) is called. On every call this function calls both in input and output routines for the device selected in its argument. In the case of the console display this means that any keyboard input this is waiting is processed first. If their is input waiting, characters to be echoed are added to whatever characters are already awaiting output. Then a call is make to *coms_write,* the output procedure for memory-mapped displays. This procedure uses *phys_copy* to copy blocks of characters from the user process to a local buffer, possibly repeating this and the following steps a number of times, since the local buffer holds only 64 bytes. When the local buffer is full, each 8-bit bytes is transferred to another buffer, *ranqueue.* This is an array of 16-bit words. Alternate bytes are filled in with the current value of the screen attribute byte, which determines foreground and background colors and other attributes. When possible, characters are transferred directly into *ranqueue,* but certain character, such as control characters or characters that area parts of escape sequences, need special handling. Special handling is also required when a character's screen position would exceed the width of the screen, or when *ramqueue* becomes full. In these cases *out_char* is called to transfer the characters and take whatever additional action is called for. For instance, *scroll_screen* is called when a linefeed is received while addressing the last line of the screen, and *parse_escape* handles characters during an escape sequence. Usually *out_char* calls *flush* which copies the contents of *ramqueue* to the video display memory, using the assembly language routine *mem_vid_copy. Flush* is also called after the last character is transferred into *ramqueue* to be sure all output is displayed. The final result of *flush* is to command the 6845 video controller chip to display the cursor in the correct position.

Logically, the bytes fetched from the user process could be written into the video RAM one per loop iteration. However, accumulating the characters in *ramqueue* and then copying the block with a cal to *mem_vid_copy* are more efficient in the protected memory environment of Pentium-class processors. Interestingly, this technique was introduced in early versions of MINIX that ran older processors without protected memory. The precursor of *mem_vid_copy* dealt with a timing problem—with older video displays the copy into the video memory had to be done when the screen was blanked during vertical retrace of the CRT beam to avoid generating visual garbage all over the screen. MINIX no longer provides this support for obsolete equipment as the performance penalty is too great. However, the modern version of MINIX benefits in other ways from copying *ramqueue* as a block.

The video RAM available to a console is delimited in the *console* structure by the fields *c_start* and *c_limit.* The current cursor position is stored in the *c_column* and *c_row* fields. The coordinate (0, 0) is in the upper left corner of the screen, which is where the hardware starts to fill the screen. Each video scan begins at the address given by *c_org* and continues for 80 × 25 characters (4000 bytes). In other words, the 6845 chip pulls the word at offset *c_org* from the video RAM and displays the character byte in the upper left-hand corner, using the attribute byte to control color, blinking, and so forth. Then it fetches the next word and displays the character at (1,0). This process continues until it gets to (79,0), at which time it begins the second line on the screen, at coordinate (0,1).

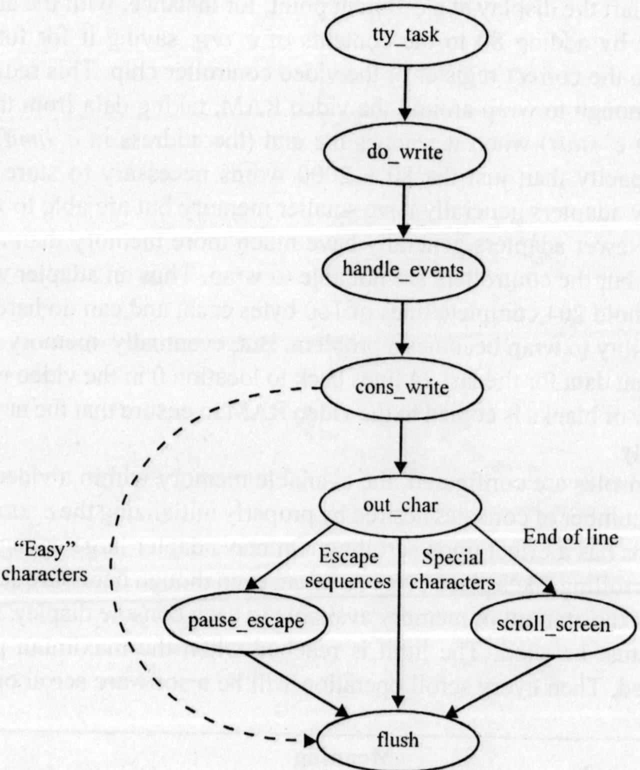

***Fig. 11.42.** Major procedures used on terminal output. The dashed line indicates characters copied directly to ramqueue by cons_write.*

When the computer is first started, the screen is cleared, output is written into the video RAM starting at location *c_start,* and *c_org* is assigned the same value as *c_start*. Thus the first line appears on the top line of the screen. When output must go to a new line, either because the first line is full or because a newline character is detected by *out_char,* output is written into the location given by *c_start* plus 80. Eventually all 25 lines are filled, and **scrolling** of the screen is required.

Some programs, editor, for example, require scrolling in the downward direction too, when the cursor is on the top line and further movement upward within the text is required.

There are two ways scrolling the screen can be managed. In **software scrolling** the character to be displayed at position (0,0) is always in the first location in video memory, word 0 relative to the position pointed to by *c_start,* and the video controller chip is commanded t display this location first by keeping the same address in *c_org.* When the screen is to be scrolled, the contents of relative location 80 in the video RAM, the beginning of the second line on the screen, is copied to relative location 0, word 81 is copied to relative location, 1, and so on. The scan sequence is unchanged, putting the data at location 0 in the memory at screen position (0,0) and the image on the screen appears to have moved up one line. The cost is that the CPU has moved 80 × 24 = 1920 words. In **hardware scrolling** the data are not moved in the memory; instead the video controller chip is instructed to start the display at a different point, for instance, with the data at word 80. The bookkepping is done by adding 80 to the contents of *c_org,* saving it for future reference, and writing this value into the correct register of the video controller chip. This requires either that the controller be smart enough to wrap around the video RAM, taking data from the beginning of the RAM (the address in *c_start*) when it reaches the end (the address in *c_limit*), or that the video RAM have more capacity than just the 80 × 2000 words necessary to store a single screen of display. Older display adapters generally have smaller memory but are able to wrap around and to hardware scrolling. Newer adapters generally have much more memory than needed to display a single screen of text, but the controllers are not able to wrap. Thus an adapter with 32768 bytes of display memory can hold 204 complete lines of 160 bytes each, and can do hardware scrolling 179 times before the inability to wrap becomes a problem. But, eventually memory copy operation will be needed to move that data for the last 24 lines back to location 0 in the video memory. Whichever method is used, a row of blanks is copied to the video RAM to ensure that the new line at the bottom of the screen is empty.

When virtual consoles are configured, the available memory within a video adapter is divided equally between the number of consoles desired by properly initializing the *c_start* and *c_limit* fields for each console. This has a effect upon scrolling. On may adapter large enough to support virtual consoles. Software scrolling takes place every so often, even though hardware scrolling is nominally in effect. The smaller the amount of memory available to each console display, the more frequently software scrolling must be sued. The limit is reached when the maximum possible number of consoles is configured. Then every scroll operation will be a software scroll operation.

Field	Meaning
c_start	Start of video memory for his console
c_limit	Limit of video memory for this console
c_column	Current column (0-79) with 0 at left
c_row	Current row (0-24) with 0 at top
c_cur	Offset into video RAM for cursor
c_org	Location in Ram pointed to by 6845 base register

Fig. 11.43 Fields of the console structure that relate to the current screen position.

The position of the cursor relative to the start of the video RAM can be derived from *c_column* and *c_row;* but it is faster to store it explicitly (*in c_cur*). When a character is to be printed, it is put into the video RAM at location *c_cur*, which is then updated, as is *c_column*. Figure 11.42 summarizes the fields of the *console* structure that affect the current position and the display origin.

The characters that affect the cursor position (e.g., linefeed, backspace) are handled by adjusting the values of *c_column, c_row,* and *c_cur.* This work is done at the end of *flush* by a call to *set_6845* which sets the registers in the video controller chip.

The terminal driver supports escape sequences to allow screen editors and other interactive programs to update the screen in a flexible way. The sequences supported are a subset of an ANSI standard and should be adequate to allows many programs written for other hardware and other operating systems to be easily ported to MINIX there are two categories of escape sequences: those that never contain a variable parameter, and those they many contain parameters. In the first category the only representative supported by MINIX is ESC M, which reverse indexed the screen, moving the cursor up one line and scrolling the screen down ward if the cursor is already on the first line. The other category can have one or two numeric parameters. Sequences in this group all begin with ESC [. The "[" is the **control sequence introducer**. A tale of escape sequences defined by the ANSI standard and recognized by MINIX was shown in Fig 11.38

Parsing escape sequences is not trivial. Valid escape sequences in MINIX can be as short as two characters, as in ESC M, or up to 8 characters long in the case of a sequence that accepts two numeric parameters that each can have a two-digit values as in ESC [20;60H, which moves the cursor to line 20, column 60. In a sequence that accepts a parameter, the parameter may be omitted, and in a sequence that accepts two parameters either or both may be omitted. When a parameter is omitted or one that is outside the valid range is used, a default is substituted. The default is the lowest valid value.

Consider the following ways one could construct a sequence to move to the upper-left corner of the screen:

- ESC [H is acceptable, because if no parameters are entered the lowest valid parameters are assumed.
- ESC [1; 1H will correctly send the cursor to row 1 and column 1 (with ANSI, the row and column numbers start at 1).
- Both ESC [1;H and ESC [; 1H have an omitted parameter, which defaults to 1 as in the first example.
- ESC [0;0H will do the same, since each parameter is less than the minimum valid value the minimum is substituted.

These examples are presented not to suggest one should deliberately use invalid parameters but to show that the code that parses such sequences is nontrivial.

MINIX implements a finite state automaton to do this parsing. The variable *c_esc_state* in the console structure normally has a value of 0. When *out_char* detects an ESC character, it changes *c_esc_state* to 1, and subsequent characters are processed by *parse_escape*. If the next character is the control sequence introducer, state 2 is entered; otherwise the sequence is considered complete, and *do_escape* is called. In state 2, as long as incoming characters are numeric, a parameter is calculated by multiplying the previous value of the parameter (initially 0) by 10 and adding the numeric value of the current character. The parameter values are kept in an array and when a semicolon is detected the processing shifts to the next cell in the array. (The array in MINIX has only two elements, but the principle is the same). When a nonnumeric character that is not a semicolon is encountered the sequence is considered complete, and again *do_escape* is called. The current character on entry to *do_escape then* is used to select exactly what action to take and how to interpret the parameters, either the defaults or those entered in the character stream.

Loadable Keymaps

The IBM PC keyboard does not generate ASCII codes directly. The keys are each identifiesd with a number, starting with the keys that are located in the upper left of the original PC keyboard—1 for the "ESC" key, 2 for the "1", and so on. Each key is assigned a number, including modifier keys like the left SHIFT and right SHIFT keys, numbers 42 and 54. When a key is pressed, MINIX receives the key number as a scan code. A scan code is also generated when a key is released, but the code generated upon release has the most significant bit set (equivalent to adding 128 to the key number). Thus a key press and a key release can be distinguished. By keeping track of which modifier keys have been pressed and not yet released, a large number of combinations are possible. For ordinary purposes, of course, two-finger combinations, such as SHIFT-A or CTRL-D, are most manageable for two-handed typists, but for special occasions three-key (or more) combinations are possible, for instance, CTRL-SHIFT-A, or the well-known CTRL-ALT-DEL combination that PC users recognize as the way to reset ad reboot the system.

The complexity of the PC keyboard allows for a great deal of flexibility in how it used. A standard keyboard has 47 ordinary character keys defined (26 alphabetic, 10 numeric, and 11 punctuation). If we are willing to use three fingered modifier key combinations, such as CTRL-ALT-SHIFT, we can support a character set of 376 (8 × 47) members. This is by no means the limit of what is possible, but for now let us assume we do not want to distinguish between the left and right-hand modifier keys, or use any of the numeric keypad or function keys. Indeed, we are not limited to using just the CTRL, ALT and SHIFT keys as modifiers; we could retire some keys from the set of ordinary keys and use them as modifies if we desired to write a driver that supported such a system.

Operating systems that use such keyboards use a **keymap** to determine what character code to pass to a program based upon the key being pressed and the modifiers in effect. The MINIX keymap logically is an array of 128 rows, representing possible scan code values (this size was chosen to accommodate Japanese keyboards; U.S. and European keyboards do not have this many keys) and 6 columns. The columns represent no modifier, the SHIFT key, the Control key, the left ALT key, the right ALT key, and a combination of either ALT key plus the SHIFT key. There are thus 720 ((128 – 6) × 6) character codes that can be generated by this scheme, given an adequate keyboard. This requires that each entry in the table be a 16-bit quantity. For U.S. keyboards the ALT and ALT2 columns are identical. ALT2 is named ALTGR on keyboards for other languages, and many of these keymaps support keys with three symbols by using its key as a modifier.

A standard keymap (determined by the line

#include keymaps/us-std.src

in *keyboard.c*) is complied into the MINIX kernel at compilation time, but an

ioctl (0, KIOCSMAP, keymap)

call can be sued t load a different map into the kernel at address *keymap*. A full keymap occupies 1536 bytes (128 × 6 ×2). Extra keymaps are stored in compressed form. A program called *genmap* is used to make a new compressed keymap. When complied, *genmap* includes the *keymap.src* code for a particular keymap, so the map is complied within *genmap*. Normally, *genmap* is executed immediately after being compiled, at which time it outputs the compressed versions to a file, and then the *genmap* binary is deleted. The command *loadkeys* reads a compressed keymap., expands it internally, and then calls IOCTL to transfer the keymap into the kernel memory. MINIX can execute *loadkeys* automatically upon starting, and the program can also be invoked by the use at any time.

Scan code	Character	Regular	SHIFT	ALT1	ALT2	ALT+SHIFT	CTRL
00	none	0	0	0	0	0	0
01	ESC	C('[')	C('[')	CA('[')	CA('[')	CA('[')	CA('[')
02	'1'	'1'	'!'	A('1')	A('1')	A('!')	C('A')
13	'='	'='	'+'	A('=')	A('=')	A('+')	C('@')
16	'q'	L('q')	'Q'	A('q')	A('q')	A('Q')	C('Q')
28	CR/LF	C('M')	C('M')	CA('M')	CA('M')	CA('M')	C('J')
29	CTRL	CTRL	CTRL	CTRL	CTRL	CTRL	CTRL
59	F!	F1	SF1	AF1	AF1	ASF1	CF1
127	???	0	0	0	0	0	0

Fig. 11.44. A few entries from a keymap source file.

The source code for a keymap defines a large initialized array, and in the interest of saving space a keymap file is not printed with the source code. Figure 11.43 shows in tabular form the contents of a few lines of *src/kernel/keymaps/usstd.src* which illustrate several aspects of keymaps. There is no key on the IBM-PC keyboard that generates a scan code of 0. The entry for code 1, the ESC key, shows that the value returned is unchanged when the SHIFT key or CTRL key are pressed, but that a different code is returned when an ALT key is pressed simultaneously with the ESC key. The values compiled into the various columns are determined by macros defined in *include/minix/keymap.h:*

```
#define C(c)     ((c) & 0×1F)      /* Map to control code */
#define A(c)     ((c) 1 0×80)      /* Set eight bit (ALT) */
#define CA(c)    A(C(c))           /* CTRL-ALT */
#define L(c)     ((c) 1 HASCAPS)   /* Add "Caps Lock has effect" attribute */
```

The first three of these macros manipulate bits in the code for the quoted character to produce the necessary code to be returned to the application. The last one sets the HASCAPS bit in the high byte of the 16-byte values. This is a flag that indicates that the state of the capslock variable has to be checked and the code possibly modified before being returned. In the figure, the entries for scan codes 2, 13 and 16 show how typical numeric, punctuation, and alphabetic keys are handled. For code 28 a special feature is seen—normally the ENTER key produces a CRC (0×0D) code, represented here as C('M'). Because the newline character in UNIX files is the LF (0×0A) code, and it is sometimes necessary to enter this directly, this keyboard map provides for a CTRL-ENTER combination, which produces this code, C('J').

Scan code 29 is one of the modifier codes and must be recognized no matter what other key is pressed, so the CTRL value is returned regardless of any other key that may be pressed. The function keys do not return ordinary ASCII values, and the row for scan code 59 shows symbolically the values (defined in *include/minix/keymap.h*) that are returned for the F1 key in combination with other modifiers. These values are F1: 0×0110, SF1: 0×1010, AF1 0×0810, ASF1: 0×0C10, and CFI: 0×0210. The last entry shown in the figure, for scan code 127, is typical of many entires near the end of the array. For many keyboards, certainly most of those used in Europe and the Americas, there are not enough keys to generate all the possible codes, and these entire in the table are filled with zeroes.

Loadable Fonts

Early PCs had the patterns for generating characters on a video screen stored only in ROM, but the displays used on modern systems provide RAM on the video display adapters into which custom character generator patterns can be loaded. This is supported by MINIX with a

ioctl(0, TIOCSFON, font)

IOCTL operation MINIX supports an 80 lines × 25 rows video mode, and font files contain 4096 bytes. Each byte represents a line of 8 pixels that are illuminated if the bit value is 1, and 16 such lines are needed to map each character. However the video display adapter uses 32 bytes to map each character, to provide higher resolution in modes not currently supported by MINIXA. The *loadfont* command is provided to convert these files into the 8192-byte *font* structure referenced by the IOCTL call and to use that call to load the font. As with the keymaps, a font can be loaded at startup time, or at any time during normal operation. However, every video adapter has a standard font built into its ROM that is available by default. There is no need to compile a font into MINIX itself, and the only font support necessary in the kernel is the code to carry out the *TIOCSFON* IOCTL operation.

Implementation of the Device-Independent Terminal Driver

In this section we will begin to look at the source code of the terminal driver in detail. We saw when we studied the block devices that multiple tasks supporting several different devices could share a common base of software. The case with the terminal devices is similar, but with the difference that there is one terminal task that supports several different kinds of terminal device. Here we will start with the device-independent code. In later sections we will look at the device-dependent code for the keyboard and the memory-mapped console display.

Terminal Task Data Structure

The file *tty.h* contains definitions used by the C files which implement the terminal drivers. Most of the variables declared in this file are identified by the prefix *tty_*. There is also one such variable declared in *glo.h* as *EXTERN*. This-is *tty_timeout,* which is used by both the clock and terminal interrupt handlers.

Within *tty.h,* the definitions of the *O_NOCTTY* and *O_NONBLOCK* flags (which are optional arguments to the OPEN call) are duplicates of definitions in *include/fcntl.h* but they are repeated here so as not to require including another file. The *devfun_t* and *devfunarg_t* types are used to define pointers to functions, in order to provide for indirect calls using a mechanism similar to what we saw in the code for the main loop of the disk drivers.

The most important definition in *tty.h* is the *tty* structure. There is one such structure for each terminal device (the console display and keyboard together count as a single terminal). The first variable in the *tty* structure, *tty_events,* is the flag that is set when an interrupt causes a change that requires that the terminal task to attend to the device. When this flag is raised, the global variable *tty_timeout* is also manipulated to tell the clock interrupt handler to awaken the terminal task on the next clock tick.

The rest of the *tty* structure is organized to group together variables that deal with input, output, status, and information about incomplete operations. In the input section, *tty_inhead* and *tty_intail* define the queue where receive characters are buffered. *Try_incount* counts the number of characters in this queue, and *tty_eotct* counts lines or characters, as explained below. All device-specific calls are done indirectly, with the exception of the routines that initialize the terminals, which are called to set up the pointers used for the indirect calls. The *tty_devread* and *tty_icancel* fields hold pointers to device-specific code to perform the read and input cancel operations. *Tty_min* is used in comparisons with *tty_eotct.* When the latter becomes equal to the former, a read operation is complete. During canonical input, *tty_min* is set to 1 and *tty_eotct* counts lines entered. During noncanonical input, *tty_eotct* counts characters and *tty_min* is set from the *MIN* field of the *termios* structure. The comparison of the two variables thus tells when a line is ready or when the minimum character count is reached, depending upon the mode.

Try_time holds the timer value that determines when the terminal task should be awakened by the clock interrupt handler, and *tty_timenext* is a pointer used to chain the active *tty_time* fields together in a linked list. The list is sorted whenever a timer is set, so the clock interrupt handler only has to look at the first entry. MINIX can support many remote terminals, of which only a few may have timers set at any time. The list of active timers makes the job of the clock handler easier than it would be if it had to check each entry in *tty_table.*

Since queueing of output is handled by the device-specific code, the output section of *tty* declares no variables and consists entirely of pointers to device-specific functions that write, echo, send a break signal, and cancel output, in the status section the flags *tty_reprint*, *tty_escaped,* and *tty_inhibited* indicate that the last character seen has a special meaning; for instance, when a CTRL-V (LNEXT) character is seen, *tty_escaped* is set to 1 to indicate that any special meaning of the next character is to be ignored.

The next part of the structure holds data about *DEV_READ DEV_WRITE, and DEV_IOCTL* operations in progress. There are two processes involved in each of these operations. The server managing the system call (normally FS) is identified in *tty_incaller*. The server calls the *tty* task on behalf of another process that needs to do an I/O operation, ad this client is identifies in *tty_inproc*. As described in Fig 11.39 during a READ characters are transferred directly from the terminal task to a buffer within the memory space of the original caller. *Try_inproc* and *tty_in_vir* locate this buffer. The next two variables, *tty_inleft* and *tty_incum*, count the characters still needed and those already transferred. Similar sets of variables are needed for a WRITE system call. For IOCTL there may be an immediate transfer of data between the requesting process and the task, so a virtual address is needed, but there is no need for variables to mark the progress of an operation. An IOCTL request may be postponed, for instance, until current output is complete, but when the time is right the request is carried out in a single operation. Finally the *tty* structure includes some variables that fall into no other category, including pointers to the functions to handle the DEV_IOCTL and DEV_CLOSE operations at the device level, a POSIX-style *termios* structure, and a winsize structure that provides support for window-oriented screen displays. The last part of the structure provides storage for the input queue itself in the array *tty_inuf*. Note that this is an array of u16_t, not of 8-bit char characters. Although applications and devices use 8-bit codes for characters, the C language requires the input function *getchar* to work with a larger data type so it can return a symbolic *EOF* value in addition to all 256 possible byte values.

The *tty_tables*, an array of *tty* structures, is declared using the *EXTERN* macro. There is one element offer each terminal enabled by the *NR_CONS, NR_RS_LINES, and NR_PTYS* definitions in *include/minix/Config.h*. For the configuration discussed in this book, two console are enable, but MINIX may be recompiled to add up to 2 serial lines, and up to 64 pseudo terminals.

There is one other *EXTERN* definition in *tty.h*. *Tty_timelist* is a pointer used by the timer to hold the head of the linked list of *tty_time* fields. The *tty.h* header file is included in many files and storage for *tty_table* and *tty_timelist* is allocated during compilation of *table.c,* in the same way as the *EXTERN* variables that are defined in the *glo.h* header file.

At the end of *tty.h* two macros, *buflen* and *bufend* are defined. These are used frequently in the terminal take code, which does much copying of data into and out of buffers.

The Device-Independent Terminal Driver

The main terminal task and the device-independent supporting functions are all in *tty.c*. Since the task supports many different devices, the minor device numbers must be used to distinguish which device is being supported on a particular call. Following, this there are a number of macro definitions. If a device is not initialized, the pointers to that device's device-specific functions will contain zeroes put there by the C compiler. This makes it possible to define the *tty_active* macro which returns *FALSE* if a null pointer is found. Of course, the initialization code for a device cannot be accessed indirectly if part of its job is to initialize the pointers that make indirect access possible. These are conditional macro definitions tc equate initialization calls for RS-232 or pseudo terminal devices to calls to a null function when these devices are not configured. *Do_pty* may be similarly disables in this section. This makes it possibled to omit the code for these devices entirely if it is not needed.

Since there are so many configurable parameters for each terminal, and there may be quite a few terminals on a networked system, a *termios_defaults* structure is declared and initialized with default values (all of which are defined in *include/termios.h*). This structure is copied into the *tty_table* entry for a terminal whenever it is necessary to initialize or reinitialize it. Figure 11.44 shows the default values for the various flags. On the following line the *winsize_defaults* structure is similarly declared. It is left to be initialized to all zeros by the C compiler. This is the proper default action, it means "window size is unknown, use*/etc/termcap*."

Field	Default values
c_iflag	BRKINT ICRNL IXON IXANY
c_oflag	OPOST ONLCR
c_cflag	CREAD CS8 HUPCL
c_lflag	ISIG IEXTEN ICANON ECHO ECHOE

Fig. 11.45. Default termios flag values.

The entry point for terminal task is *tty_task.* Before entering the main loop a, call is made to *tty_init* for each configured terminal and then the MINIX startup message is displayed.

Although the source code shows a call to *printf,* when this code is compiled the macro that convents calls to the *pirntf* library routine into calls to *printk* is in effect. *Printk* uses a routine called *putk* within the console driver, so the FS is not involved. This message goes only to the primary console display and cannot be redirected.

The main loop is in principle, like the main loop of any task—it receives a message, execute a switch on the message type to call the appropriate function, and then generates a return message. However, there are some complications. First, much work is done by low-level interrupt routines, especially in handling terminal input. In the previous section we saw that individual characters from the keyboard are accepted and buffered without sending a message to the terminal task for each character. Thus, before attempting to receive a message, the main loop always sweeps thorough the entire *tty_table,* inspecting each terminal's *tp->tty_events* flag and calling *handle_events* as necessary, to take care to unfinished business. Only when there is nothing demanding immediate attention is a call made to receive. If the message received is from the hardware a continue statement short-circuits the loop, and the check for events is repeated.

Second, this task services several devices. If a received message is from a hardware interrupt, the device or devices that need service are identified by checking the *tp->tty_events* flags. If the interrupt is not a hardware interrupt the *TTY_LINE* field in the message is used to determine which device should respond to the message. The minor device number is decoded by a series of comparisons, by means of which *tp* is pointed to the correct entry in the *tty_table.* If the device is a pseudo terminal *do_pty (in pty.c)* is called and the main loop is restarted. In this case *do_pty* generates the reply message. Of course, if pseudo terminals are not enabled, the call to *do_pty* uses the dummy macro defied earlier. One would hope that attempts to access nonexistent devices would not occur, but it is always easier to add another check than to verify that there are no errors elsewhere in the system. In case the device does not exist or is not configured, a reply message with an *ENXIO* error message is generated and, again, control returns to the top of the loop.

The rest of the task resembles what we have seen in the main loop of other tasks, a switch on the message type. The appropriate function for the type of request, *do_read, do_write,* and so on, it called. In each case the called function generates the reply message, rather than pass the information needed to construct the message back to the main loop. A reply message is generated at the end of the main loop only if a valid message type was not received, in which case an *EINVAL* error message is sent. Because reply messages are sent from many different places within the terminal task a common routine *tty_reply,* is called to handle the details of constructing reply messages.

If the message received by *tty_task* is a valid message type, not the result of an interrupt, and does not come from a pseudo terminal, the switch at the end of the main loop will dispatch to one of the functions *do_read, do_write, do_ioctl, do_open, do_close*, or *do_cancel*. The arguments to each of these calls are *tp*, a pointer to a *tty* structure, and the address of the message. Before looking at each of them, we will mention a few general considerations. Since *tty_task* may service multiple terminal devices, these functions must return quickly so the main loop can continue. However, *do_read, do_write,* and *do_ioctl* may not be able to complete immediately all the requested work. In order to allow FS to service other calls, an immediate reply is required. If the request cannot be completed immediately, the *SUSPEND* code is returned in the status field of the reply message. This corresponds to the message marked (3) in Fig 11.39 and suspends the process that initiated the call, while unblocking the FS. Message corresponding to (7) and (8) in the figure will be sent later when the operation can be completed. If the request can be fully satisfied, or an error occurs, either the count of bytes transferred or the error code is returned in the status field of the return message to the FS. In this case a message will be sent immediately from the FS back to the process that made the original call, to wake it up.

Reading from a terminal is fundamentally different from reading from a disk device. The disk driver issues a command to the disk hardware and eventually data will be returned, barring a mechanical or electrical failure. The computer can display a prompt upon the screen, but there is no way for it to force a person sitting at the keyboard to start typing. For that matter, there is no guarantee that anybody will be sitting there at all. In order to make the speedy return that is required, *do_read* starts by storing information that will enable the request to be completed later, when and if input arrives. There are a few error checks to be made first. It is an error if the device is still expecting input to fulfil a previous request, or if the parameters in the message are invalid. If these tests are passed, information about the request is copied into the proper fields in the device's *tp->tty_table* entry. The last step, setting *tp->tty_inleft* to the number of characters requested, is important. This variable is used to determine when the read request is satisfied. In canonical mode *tp->tty_inleft* is decremented by one for each character returned, until an end of line is received, at which point it is suddenly reduced to zero. In noncanonical mode it is handled differently, but in any case it is reset to zero whenever the call is satisfied, whether by a timeout or by receiving at least the minimum number of bytes request. When *tp->tty_inleft* reaches zero, a reply message is sent. As we will see, reply messages can be generated in several places. It is sometimes necessary to check whether a reading process still expects a reply; a nonzero value of *tp->tty_inleft* serves as a flag for that purpose.

In canonical mode a terminal device waits for input until either the number of characters asked for in the call has been received, or the end of a line or the end of the file is reached. The *ICANON* bit in the *termios* structure is tested to see if canonical mode is in effect for the terminal. If it is not set, the *termios MIN* and *TIME* values are checks to determine what action to take.

In Fig. 11.37 we saw how *MIN* and *TIME* interact to provide different ways a read call can behave. TIME is tested. A value of zero corresponds to the left-hand column in Fig. 11.37, and in this case no further tests are needed at this point. If *TIME* is nonzero then *MIN* is tested. If it is zero, *settimer* is called on to start the timer that will terminate the *DEV_READ* request after a delay, even if no bytes have been received. *Tp->tty_min* is set to 1 here, so the call will terminate immediately if one or more bytes are received before the timeout. At this point no check for possible input has yet been made, so more than one character may already by waiting to satisfy the request. In that case, as many characters as are ready, up to the number specified in the READ call, will be returned as soon as the input is found. If both *TIME* and *MIN* are nonzero, the timer has a different meaning. The timer is used as an inter-character timer in this case. It is started only after the first character is received and is restarted after each successive character. *Tp->tty_eotect* counts characters in noncanonical mode, and if it is zero at, no characters have been received yet and the inter-byte timer is inhibited. *Lock* and *unlock* are used to protect both of these calls to *settimer* to prevent clock interrupts when *settimer* is running.

In any case, *in_transfer* is called to transfer any bytes already in the input queue directly to the reading process. Next there is call to *handle_events*, which may put more data into the input queue and which calls *in_transfer* again. This apparent duplication of calls requires some explanation. Although the discussion so far has been in terms of keyboard input, *do_read* is in the device-independent part of the code and also services input from remote terminals connected by serial lines. It is possible that previous input has filled the RS-232 input buffer to the point where input has been inhibited. The first call to *in_transfer* does not start the flow again, but the call to *handle_events* can have this effect. The fact that it then caused a second call to *in_transfer* is just a bonus. The important thing is to be sure the remote terminal is allowed to send again. Either of these calls may result in satisfaction of the request and sending of the reply message to the FS. *Tp->tty_inleft* is used as a flag to see if the reply has been sent: if it is still nonzero, *do_read* generates and sends the reply message itself. If the original request specifies a nonblocking read, the FS is told to pass an *EAGAIN* error code back to original caller. If the call is an ordinary blocking read, the FS receives a *SUSPEND* code, unblocking it but telling it to leave the original caller blocked. In this case the terminal's *tp->tty_inrepcode* field is set to *REVIVE*. When and if the *READ* is later satisfied, this code will be palaced in the reply message to the FS to indicate that the original caller was put to sleep and needs to be revived.

Do_write is similar to *do_read*, but simpler, because there are fewer options to be concerned about in handling a WRITE system call. Checks similar to those made by *do_read* are made to see that a previous write is not still in progress and that the message parameters are valid, and then the parameters of the request are copied into the *tty* structure. *Handle_events* is then called, and *tp->tty_outleft* is checked to see if the work was done. If so, a reply message already has been set by *handle_events* and there is nothing left to do. If not, a reply message is generated, with the message parameters depending upon whether or not the original WRITE call was called in nonblocking mode.

The next function, *do_ioctl* is a long one, but not difficult to understand. The body of *do_ioctl* is two switch statements. The first determines the size of the parameter pointed to by the pointer in the request message. If the size is not zero, the parameter's validity is tested. The contents cannot be tested here, but what can be tested is whether a structure of the required size beginning at the specified address fits within the segment it is specified to be in. The rest of the function is another switch on the type of *IOCTL* operation requested. Unfortunately, supporting the *POSIX*-required operations with the *IOCTL* call meant that names for *IOCTL* operations had to be invented that suggest, but do not duplicate, names required by *POSIX*. Figure 11.45 shows the relationship between the *POSIX* request names and the names used by the *MINIX IOCTL* call. A *TCGETS* operation services a tcgetattr call by the user and simply return a copy of the terminal device's *tp->tty_termios* structure. The next four request types share code. The *TCSETSW*, *TCSETSF*, and *TCSETS* request types correspond to use calls to the POSIX-defined function tcsetattr, and all have the basic action of copying a new *termios* structure into a terminal's *tty* structure. The copying is done immediately for *TCSETS* calls and may be done from *TCSETSW* and *TCSETSF* calls if output is complete, by a *phys_copy* call to get the data for the user, followed by a call to *setattr*. If *tcsetattr* was called with a modifier requesting postponement of the action until completion of current output, the parameters for the request are placed in the terminal's tty structure for later processing if the test of *tp->tty_outleft* reveals output is not complete. *Tcdrain* suspends a program until output is complete and is translated into an *IOCTL* call of type *TCDRAIN*. If output is already complete. It has nothing more to do. If not, it also must leave information in the *tty* structure.

POSIX function	POSIX operation	IOCTL type	IOCTL parameter
tcdrain	(none)	TCDRAIN	(none)
tcflow	TCOOFF	TCFLOW	int-TCOOFF
tcflow	TCOON	TCFLOW	int=TCOON
tcflow	TCIOFF	TCFLOW	int=TCIOFF
tcflow	TCION	TCFLOW	int=TCION
Ttcflush	TCIFLUSH	TCFLSH	int=TCIFLUSH
tcflush	TCOFLUSH	TCFLSH	int=TCOFLUSH
tcflush	TCIOFLUSH	TCFLSH	int=TCIOFLUSH
tcgetattr	(none)	TCGETS	termios
tcsetattr	TCSANOW	TCSETS	termios
tcsetattr	TCSADRAIN	TCSETSW	termios
tcsetattr	TCSAFLUSH	TCSETSF	termios
tcsendbreak	(none)	TCSBRK	int=duration

Fig. 11.46. POSIX calls and IOCTL operations.

The POSIX *tcflush* function discards unread input and/or unsent output data, according to its argument, and the *IOCTL* translation is straightforward, consisting of a call to the *tty_icancel* function that services all terminals, and/or the device-specific function pointed to by *to->tty_ocancel*. *Tcflow* is similarly translated in a straightforward way into an IOCTL call. To suspend restart output, it sets a *TRUE* or *FALSE* value into *tp->tty_inhibited* and then sets the *tp->tty_events* flag. To suspend or restart input, it sends the appropriate *STOP* (normally CTRL-S) or *START* (CTRL-Q) code to the remote terminal, using the device-specific echo routine pointed to by *tp->tty_echo*.

Most of the rest of the operations handled by *do_ioctl* are handled on one line of code, by calling an appropriate function. In the cases of the *KIOCSMAP* (load keymap) and *TIOCSFON* (load font) operations, a test is made to be sure the device really is a console, since these operations do not apply to other terminals. If virtual terminals are in use the same keymap and font apply to all consoles, the hardware does not permit any easy way of doing otherwise. The windows size operations copy a *winsize* structure between the user process and the terminal task. Note, however, the comment under the code for the *TIOCSWINSZ* operation. When a process changes its window size, the kernel expected to send a *SIGWINCH* signal to the process group under some versions of UNIX. The signal is not required by the POSIX standard. But, anyone thinking of using these structures should consider adding code here to initiate this signal.

The last two cases in *do_ioctl* support the POSIX required *tcgetpgrp* and *tcsetpgrp* functions. There is no action associated with these cases, and they always return an error. There is nothing wrong with this. These functions support **job control**, the ability to suspend and restart a process from the keyboard. Job control is not required by POSIX and is not supported by MINIX. However, POSIX requires these functions, even when job control is not supported, to ensure portability of programs.

Do_open has a simple basic action to perform —it increments the variable *tp->tty_openct* for the device so it can be verified that it is open. However, there are some tests to be done first. POSIX specifies that for ordinary terminals the first process to open a terminal is the **session leader**, and when a session leader dies, access to the terminal is revoked from other processed in its group. Daemons need to be able to write error messages, and if their error output is not redirected to a file, it should go to a display that cannot be closed. For this purpose a device called/dev/log exists in MNIX. Physically it is the same device *as/dev/console,* but it is addressed by a separate minor device number and is treated differently. It is a write-only device, and thus *do_open* returns and *EACCESS* error if an attempt is made to open it for reading. The other test done by *do_open* is to test the *O_NOCTTY* flag. If it is not set and the device is not/dev/log, the terminal becomes the controlling terminal for a process group. This is done by putting the process number of the caller into the *tp->tty_pgrp* field of the *tty_table* entry. Following this, the *tp->tty_openct* variable is incremented and the reply message is sent.

A terminal device may be opened more than once, and the next function, *do_close*, has nothing to do except decrement *tp->tty_openct.* The test foils an attempt to close the device if it happens to be */dev/log*. If this operation is the last close, input is cancelled by calling *tp->tty_icancel.* Device-specific routines pointed to by *tp->tty_ocancel* and *tp->tty_close* are also called. Then various fields in the *tty* structure for the device are set back to their default values and the reply message is sent.

The last message type handler is *do_cancel*. This is invoked when a signal is received for a process that is blocked trying to read or write. There are three states that must be checked:

1. The process may have been reading when killed.
2. The process may have been writing when killed.
3. The process may have been suspended by *tcdrain* until its output was complete.

A test is made for each case, and the general tp->*tty_icancel,* or the device-specific routine pointed to by *tp->tty_ocancel*, is called as necessary. In the last case the only action required is to rest the flag tp->*tty_ioreg*, to indicate the IOCTL operation is now complete. Finally, the *tp->tty_events* flag is set and a reply message is sent.

Terminal Driver Support Code

Now that we have looked at the top-level functions called in the main loop of *tty_task*, it is time to look at the code that supports them. We will start with *handle-events*. As mentioned earlier, on each pass through the main loop of the terminal task, the *tp->tty_events* flag for each terminal device is checked and *handel_events* is called if it shows that attention is required for a particular terminal. *Do_read* and *do_write* also call *handel_events*. This routine must work fast. It resets the *tp->tty_events* flag and then calls device-specific routines to read and write, using the pointers to the functions tp->*tty_devread* and tp->*tty_devwrite.* These are called unconditionally, because there is no way to test whether a read or a write caused the raising of the flag—a design choice was made here, that checking two flags for each device would be more expensive than making two calls each time a device was active. Also, most of the time a character received from a terminal must be echoed, so both calls will be necessary. As noted in the discussion of the handling of *tcsetattr* calls by *do_ioctl*, POSIX may postpone control operations on devices until current output is complete, so immediately after calling the device-specific *tty_devwrite* function is a good time take care of *ioctl* operations.

Since the *tp->tty_events* flag is raised by interrupts, and characters may arrive in a rapid stream from a fast device, there is a chance that by the time the calls to the device-specific read and write routines and *dev_ioctl* are completed, another interrupt will have raised the flag again. A high priority is placed on getting input moved along from the buffer where the interrupt routine places it initially. Thus *handle_events* repeats the calls to the device-specific routines as long as the *tp->tty_events* flag is found raised at the end of the loop. When the flow of input stops (it also could be output, but input is more likely to make such repeated demands), *in_transfer* is called to transfer characters from the input queue to the buffer within the process that called for a read. operation. *In_transfer itself* send a reply message if the transfer completes the request, either by transferring the maximum number of characters requested or by reaching the end of a lien (in canonical mode). If it does so, tp->*tty_left* will be zero upon the return to *handle_events.* Here a further test is made and a reply message is sent if the number of character transferred has reached the minimum number requested. Testing *tp->_inleft* prevents sending a duplicate message.

Next we will look at *in_transfer*, which is responsible for moving data from the input queue in the task's memory space to the buffer of the user process that requested the input. However, a straightforward block copy is not possible. The input queue is a circular buffer and characters have to be checked to see that the end of the file has not been reached, or, if canonical mode is in effect, that the transfer only continues up through the end of a line. Also, the input queue is a queue of 16-bit quantities, but the recipient's buffer is an array of 8-bit characters. Thus an intermediate local buffer is used. Characters are checked one by one as they are placed in the local buffer, and when it fills up or when the input queue has been emptied, *phys_copy* is called to move the contents of the local buffer to the receiving process' buffer.

Three variables in the *tty* structure, tp->*tty_inleft, tp->tty_eotct,* and tp->*tty_min,* are used to decide whether *in_transfer* has any work to do, and the first two of these contor its main loop. As mentioned earlier, *tp->tty_inleft* is set initially to the number of characters requested by a READ call. Normally, it is decremented by one whenever a character is transferred but it may be abruptly decreased to zero when a condition signalling the end of input is reached. Whenever it becomes zero, a reply message to the reader is generated, so it also serves as a flag to indicate whether or not a message has been sent. Thus in the test on finding that *tp->tty_inleft* is already zero is a sufficient reason to about execution of *in_transfer* without sending a reply.

In the next part of the test, *tp->tty_eotect* and tp->*tty_min* are compared. In canonical mode both of these variables refer to complete lines of input, and in noncanonical mode they refer to characters. *Tp–>tty_eotct* is incremented whenever a "line break" or a byte is placed in the input queue and is decremented by *in_transfer* whenever a line or byte is remove form the queue. Thus it counts the number of lines or bytes that have been received by the terminal task but not yet passed on to a reader. *Tp->tty_min* indicates the minimum number of lines (in canonical mode) or characters (in noncanonical mode) that must be transferred to complete a read request. Its value so always 1 in canonical mode and may be any value from 0 up to *MAX_INPUT* (225 in MINIX) in noncanonical mode. The second half of the test causes *in_transfer* to return immediately in canonical mode if a full line has not yet been received. The transfer is not done until a line is complete so the queue contents can be modified if, for instance, an ERASE or KILL character is subsequently typed in by the user before the ENTER key is pressed. In noncanonical mode an immediate return occurs if the minimum number of characters is not yet available.

A few lines later, *tp->tty_inleft* and tp->*eotect* are used to control the main loop of *in_transfer.* In canonical mode the transfer continues until there is no longer a complete line left in the queue. In noncanonical mode *tp->tty_eotct* is a count of pending characters. *Tp->tty_min* controls whether the loop is entered but is not used in determining when to stop. Once the loop is entered, either all available characters or the number of characters requested in the original call will be transferred, whichever is smaller.

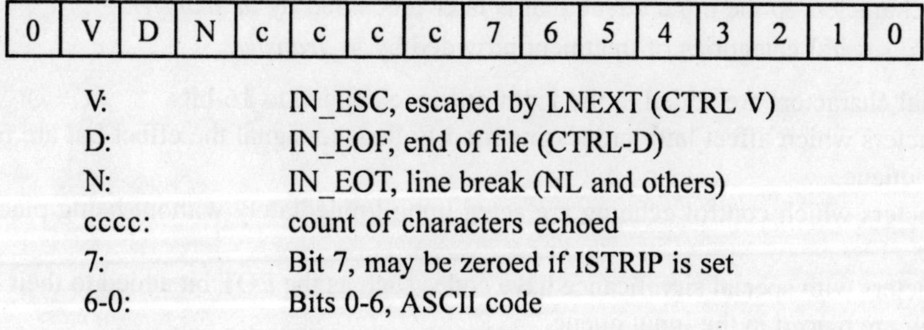

***Fig. 11.47.** The fields in a character code as it is placed into the input queue.*

Characters are 16-bit quantities in the input queue. The actual character code to be transferred to the use process is in the low 8 bits. Fig 11.47 shows how the high bits are used. Three are used to flag whether the character is being escaped (by CTRL-V), whether it signifies end-of-file, or whether it represents one several codes that signify a line is complete. Four bits are used for a count to show how much screen space is used when the character is echoed. The test checks whether the *IN_EOF* bit (*D* in the figure) is set. This is tested at the top of the inner loop because an end-of-file (CTRL-D) is not itself transferred, a reader, nor is it counted in the character count. As each character is transferred, a mark is applied to zero the upper 8 bits, and only the ASCII value in the low 8 bits is transferred into the local buffer.

There is more than one way to signal the end of input, but the device-specific input routine is expected to determine whether a character received is a linefeed, CTRL-D, or other such character and to mark each such character. *In_transfer* only needs to test for its mark, the IN_EOT bit. If this is detected, *tp->tty_eotect* is decremented. In noncanonical mode every character is counted this way as it is put into the input queue, and every character is also marked with the IN_EOT bit at that time, so *tp->tty_eotct* counts characters not yet removed from the queue. The only difference in the operation of the main loop of *in_ransfer* in the two different modes is found. Here *tp->tty_inleft* is zeroed in response to finding a character marked as a line break, but only if canonical mode is in effect. Thus when control returns to the top of the loop, the loop terminates properly after a line break in canonical mode, but in noncanonical line breaks are ignored.

When the loop terminates there is usually a partially full local buffer to be transferred. Then a reply message is sent if *tp->tty_inleft* has reached zero. This is always the case in canonical mode, but if noncanonical mode is in effect and the number of characters transferred is less than the full request, the reply is not sent. This may be puzzling if you have a good enough memory for details to member that where we have seen calls to *in-transfer* (in *do_read* and *handle_events*), the code following the call to *in_transfer* sends, a reply message if in_transfer returns having transferred more than the amount specified in *tp->tty_min,* which will cettainly be the case here. The reason why a reply is not made unconditionally from *in_transfer* will be seen when we discuss the next function, which calls *in_transfer* under a different set of circumstances.

That next function is *in_proecess*. It is called from the device-specific software to handle the common processing that must be done on all input. Its parameters are a pointer to the *tty* structure for the source device, a pointer to the array of 8-bit characters to be processed, and a count. The count is returned to the caller. *In_process* is a long function, but its actions are not complicate. It adds 16-bit characters to the input queue that is later processed by *in_transfer*.

There are several categories of treatment provided by *in_transfer.*

- Normal characters are added to the input queue, extended to 16-bits.
- Characters which affect later processing modify flags to signal the effect but are not places in the queue.
- Characters which control echoing are acted upon immediately without being placed in the queue.
- Characters with special significance have codes such as the EOT bit added to their high byte as they are placed in the input queue.

Let us look first at a completely normal situation, an ordinary character, such as "x" (ASCII code 0×78), typed in the middle of a short line, with no escape sequence in effect, on a terminal that is set up with the standard MINIX default properties. As received from the input device this character occupies bits 0 through 7 in Fig. 11.46. It would have its most significant bit, bit 7, reset to zero if the *ISTRIP* bit were set, but the default in MINIX is not to strip the bit, allowing full 8-bit codes to be entered. This would not affect our "x" anyway. The MINIX default is to allow extended processing of input, so the test of the *IEXTEN* bit in *tp->tty_termios.c_1flag* passes, but the succeeding tests fail under the conditions we postulate: no character escape is in effect, this input is not itself the character escape character, and this input is not the *REPRINT* character.

Tests on the next several lines find that the input character is not the special *POSIX*–VDISABLE character, nor is it a *CR* or an *NL*. Finally, a positive result: canonical mode is in effect, this is the normal default. However our "x" is not the ERASE character, nor is it any of the *KILL*, *EOF*

(CTRL-D), *NL*, or *EOL* characters. Here it is found that the *IXON* bit is set, by default, allowing use of the *STOP* (CTRL-S) and *START* (CTRL-Q) characters, but in the ensuing tests for these no match is found. It is found that the *ISIG* bit, enabling the use of the *INTR* and QUIT characters, is set by default, but again no match is found.

In fact, the first interesting thing that might happen to an ordinary character occurs, where a test is made to see if the input queue is already full. If this were the case, the character would be discarded at this point, since canonical mode is in effect, and the user would not see it echoed on the screen. (The continue statement discards the character, since it causes the outer loop to restart). However, since we postulate completely normal conditions for this illustration, let us assume the buffer is no full yet. The next test, to see if special noncanonical node processing is needed. Here *echo* is called to display the character to the user, since the *ECHO* bit in *tp->tty_termios.c_1flag* is set by default.

Finally, the character is disposed of by being put into the input queue. At this time *tp->tty_incount* is incremented, but since this is an ordinary character, not marked by the *EOT* bit, *tp->tty_eotect* is not changed.

The last line in the loop calls *in_transfer* if the character just transferred into the queue fills it. However, under the ordinary conditions we postulate for this example, *in_transfer* would do nothing, even if called, since assuming the queue has been serviced normally and previous input was accepted when the previous line of input was complete) *tp->tty_eotct* is zero, *tp->tty_min* is one, and the test at the start of *in_transfer* causes an immediate return.

Having passed through *in_process* with an ordinary character under ordinary conditions, let us now go back to the star of *in_process* and look at what happens in less ordinary circumstances. First, we will look at the character escape, which allows a character which ordinarily has a special effect to be passed on to the user process. If a character escape is in effect, the *tp->tty_escaped* flag is set, and when this is detected the flag is reset immediately and the *IN_ESC* bit, bit V, is added to the current character. This causes special processing when the character is echoed—escaped control characters are displayed as "^R" plus the character to make them visible. The *In_ESC* bit also prevents the character from being recognized by tests for special characters. The next few lines process the escape character itself, the *LNEXT* character (CTRL-V by default). When the *LNEXT* code is detected the *tp->tty_escaped* flag is set, and *rawecho* is called twice to output a followed by a backspace. This reminds the user at the keyboard that an escape is in effect, and when the following character is echoed, it overwrite the "^". The *LNEXT* character is an example of one that affect later characters (in this case, only the very next character). It is not placed in the queue, and the loop restarts after the two calls to rawecho. The order of these two tests is important, making it possible to enter the *LNEXT* character itself twice in a row, in order to pass the second copy on to a process.

The next special character processed by *in_process* is the REPRINT character (CTRL-R). When it is found a call to *reprint* ensues, causing the current echoed output to be redisplayed. The *REPRINT* itself is then discarded with no effect upon the input queue.

Going into detail in the handling of every special character would be tedious, and the source code of *in_process* is straightforward. We will mention just a few more points. One is that the use of special bits in the high byte of the 16-bit value placed in the input queue makes it easy to identify a class of characters that have similar effects. Thus, *EOT* (CTRL-D), *LF*, and the alternate *EOL* character (undefined by default) are all marked by the EOT bit, bit D, making later recognition easy. Finally, we will justify the peculiar behavior of *in_transfer* noted earlier. A reply is not generated each time it terminates, although in the calls to *in_transfer* we have seen previously, it seemed that a reply would always be generated upon return. Recall that the call to *in_transfer* made by *in_process* when the input queue is full has no effect when canonical mode is in effect. But if noncanonical processing is desired, every character is marked with the *EOT* bit, and thus every character is counted by *tp->tty_eotect*. In turn, this causes entry into the main loop of *in_transfer* when it is called because of a full input queue in noncanonical mode. On such occasions no message should be sent at the termination of *in_transfer*, because there are likely to be more characters read after retiring to *in_process*. Indeed, although in canonical mode input to a single READ is limited by the size of the input queue (255 characters in MINIX), in noncanonical mode a READ call must be able to deliver the POSIX-required *_POSIX_SSIZE_MAX* number of characters. Its value in MINIX is 32767.

The next few functions in *tty.c* support character input. Echo treats a few characters in a special way, but most just get displayed on the output side of the same device being used for input. Output from a process may be going to a device at the same time input is being echoed, which makes things messy if the user at the keyboard tries to backspace. To deal with this, the *tp->tty_reprint* flag is always set to *TRUE* by the device-specific output routines when normal output is produced, so the function called to handle a backspace can tell that mixed output has been produced. Since *echo* also users the device-output routines, the current value of *tp->tty_reprint* is preserved while echoing, using the local variable, *rp*. However, if a new line of input has just begun, *rp* is set to *FALSE* instead of taking on the old value, thus assuring that t*p->tty_repring* will be reset when echo terminates.

ch = ecno(tp, ch)

The value returned by *echo* contains the number of spaces used on the screen for the echo display, which may be up to eight if the character is a *TAB*. This count is placed in the *cccc* field. Ordinary characters occupy one space on the screen, but if a control, character (other than *TAB*, *NL*, or *CR* or A *DEL* (0×7F) is echoed, it is displayed as a "^R" plus a printable ASCII character and occupies two positions on the screen. On the other hand an *NL* or *CR* occupies zero spaces. The actual echoing must be done by a device-specific routine, of course and whenever a character must be passed to the device, an indirect call is made using *tp->tty_echo,* as, for instance.

The next function, *rawecho*, is used to bypass the special handling done by echo. It checks to see if the *ECHO* flag is set, and if it is, sends the character along to the device-specific *tp->tty_echo* routine without any special processing. A local variable *rp* is used here to prevent *rawecho's* own call to the output routine from changing the value of *tp->tty_reprint*.

When a backspace is found by *in_process*, the next function, *backover* is called. It manipulates the input queue to remove the previous head of the queue if backing up is possible—if the queue is empty or if the last character is a line break, then backing up is no possible. Here the *tp->tty_reprint* flag mentioned in the discussions of *echo* and *rawecho* is tested. If it is TRUE, then *reprint* is called to put a clean copy of the output line on the screen. Then the *len* field of the last character displayed is consulted to find out how many characters have to be deleted on the display, and for each character a sequence of backspace-space-backspace characters is sent through *rawecho* to remove the unwanted character from the screen.

Reprint is the next function. In addition to being called by backover, it may be invoked by the user pressing the *REPRINT* key (CTRL-R). The loop searches backward through the input queue for the least line break. If it is found in the last position filled, there is nothing to do and *reprint* returns. Otherwise, it echos the CTRL-R, which appears on the display as the two character sequence "^R", and then moves to the next line and redisplays the queue from the last line break to the end.

Now we have arrived at *out_process*. Like in *in_process*, it is called by device-specific output routines, but it is called by the RS-232 and pseudo terminal device-specific output routines, but not by the console routine. *Out_process* works upon a circular buffer of bytes but does not remove them from the buffer. The only change it makes to the array is to insert a *CR* character ahead of an *NL* character in the buffer if the *OPOST* (enable output processing) and *ONLCR* (map NL to CR-NL) bits in *tp->tty_termios.oflag* are set. Both bits are set by default in MINIX. Its job is to keep the *tp->tty_position* variable in the device's *tty* structure up to data. Tabs and backspaces complicate life.

The next routine is *dev_ioctl*. It supports *do_ioctl* in carrying out the *tcdrain* function and tcsetattr function when it is called with either the *TCSADRAIN* or *TCSAFLUSH* options. In these cases, *do_ioctl* cannot complete the action immediately if output is incomplete, so information about the request is stored in the parts of the *tty* structure reserved for delayed IOCTL operations. Whenever *handle_events* runs, a it checks the *tp->tty_ioreq* field after calling the device-specific output routine and calls *dev_ioctl* if an operation is pending. *Dev_ioctl* tests *tp->tty_outleft* to see if output is complete, and if so, carries out the same actions that *do_ioctl* would have carried out immediately if there had been no dealy. To service *tcdrain*, the only action is to reset the *tp->tty_ioreq* field and send the reply message to the FS, telling it to wake up the process that made the original call. The *TCSAFLUSH* variant of *tcsetattr* calls *tty_icancel* to cancel input. For both variants of *tcsetattr*, the *termios* structure whose address was passed in the original call to IOCTL is copied to the device's *tp->tty_termios* structure. *Setattr* is then called, followed, as with *tcdrain*, by sending a reply message to wake up the blocked original caller.

Setattr is the next procedure. As we have seen, it is called by *do_ioctl* or *dev_ioctl* to change the attributes of a terminal device, and by *do_close* to reset the attributes back to the default settings. *Setattr* is always called after copying a new *termios* structure into a device's *tty* structure, because merely copying the parameters is not enough. If the device being controlled is now in noncanonical mode, the first action is to mark all characters currently in the input queue with the *IN_EOT* bit, as would have been done when these characters were originally entered in the queue if noncanonical mode had been in effect then. It easier just to go ahead and do this than to test whether the characters already have the bit set. There is no way to know which attributes have just been changed and which still retain their old values.

The next action is to check the *MIN* and *TIME* values. In canonical mode tp->*tty_min* is always 1; that is set. In noncanonical mode the combination of the two values allows for four different modes of operation, *tp->tty_min* is first set up with the value passed in *tp->tty_trmiso.cc*[*VMIN*], which is then modified if it is zero and *tp->tty_termios.cc*[*VTIME*] is not zero.

Finally, *setattr* makes sure output is not stopped if XON/XOFF control is disabled, sends a *SIGHUP* signal if the output speed is set to zero, and makes an indirect call to the device-specific routine pointed to by to->*tty_ioctl* to do what can only be done at the device level.

The next function, *tty_reply* has been mentioned many times in the preceding discussion. Its action is entirely straightforward, constructing a message and sending it. If for some reason the reply fails, a panic ensues. The following functions are equally simple. *Sigchar* asks MM to send a signal. If the *NOFLASH* flag is not set, queued input is removed—the count of characters or lines received is zeroed and the pointers to the tail and head of the queue are equated. This is the default action. When a *SIGHUP* signal is to be caught, *NOFLSH* can be set, to allow input and output to resume after catching the signal. *Tty_icancel* unconditionally discards pending input in the way described for *sigchar*, and in addition calls the device-specific function pointed to by tp->*tty_icancel,* to cancel input that may exist in the device itself or be buffered in the low-level code.

Try_init called once for each device when *tty_task* first starts. It sets up defaults. Initially a pointer to *tty_devnop*, a dummy function that does nothing, is set into the *tp->_tty_icancel, tp->tty_ocancel, tp->tty_ioctl,* and *tp->tty_close* variables. *Try_init* then calls a device-specific initialization functions for the appropriate category of terminal (console, serial line, or pseudo terminal). These set up the real pointers to indirectly called device-specific functions. Recall that if there are no devices at all configured in a particular category, a macro that returns immediately is created, so no part of the code for a nonconfigured device need be compiled. The call to *scr_init* initialized the console driver and also calls the initialization routine for the keyboard.

Tty_wakeup, although short, is extremely important in the functioning of the terminal task. Whenever the clock interrupt handler runs, that is to say, for every tick of the clock, the global variable *tty_timeout*, is checked to see if it contains a value less than the present time. If so *tty_wakeup* is called. *Tty_timeout* is set to zero by the interrupt service routines for terminal drivers, so wakeup is forced to run at the next clock tick after any terminal device interrupt. *Tty_timeout* is also altered by *settimer* when a terminal device is servicing a READ call in noncanonical mode and needs to set a timeout, as we will see shortly. When *tty_wakeup* runs, it first disables the next wakeup by assigning *TIME_NEVER*, a value very far in the future, to *tty_timeout*. Then it scans the linked list of timer values, which is stored with the earliest scheduled wakeups first, until it comes to one that is latert than the current time. This is the next wakeup, and it is then put into tty_timeout. .Tty_wakeup also sets tp->*tty_min* for that device to 0, which ensures that the next read will succeed even if no bytes have been received, sent the *tp->tty_events* flag for the device to ensure it gets attention when the terminal task runs next, and removes the device from the timer list. Finally, it calls *interrupt* to send the wakeup messages to the task. As mentioned in the discussion of the clock task, *tty_wakeup* is logically part of the clock interrupt service code, since it is called only from there.

The next function, *settimer*, sets timers for determining when to return from a READ call in noncanonical mode. It is called with parameters of *tp*, a pointer to a *tty* structure, and *on*, an integer which represents *TRUE* or *FALSE*. First the linked list to *tty* structures pointed to be *timelist* is scanned, searching for an existing entry that matched the *tp* parameter. If one is found, it is removed from the list. If *settimer* is called to unset a timer, this is all it must do. If is called to set a timer, the *tp->tty_time* element in the *tty* structure of the device is set to the current time plus the increment in tenths of a second specified in the *TIME* value in the device's *termios* structure. Then the entry is put into the list, which is maintained in sorted order. Finally, the timeout just entered on the list is compared with the value in the global *tty_timeout*, and the latter is replaced if the new timeout is due sooner.

Finally, the last definition in *tty.c* is *tty_devnop*, a "no-operation" function to be indirectly addressed where a advice does not require a service. We have seen *tty_devnop* used in *tty_init* as the default value entered into various function pointers before calling the initialization routine for a device.

Implementation of the Keyboard Driver

Now we turn to the device-dependent code that supports the MINIX console, which consists of a IBM PC keyboard and a memory-mapped display. The physical devices that support these are entirely separate: on a standard desktop system the display used an adapter card (of which there are at least a half-dozen basic types) plugged into the backplane, while the keyboard is supported by circuitry built into the parentboard which interfaces with an 8-bit single-chip computer inside the keyboard unit. The two subdevices require entirely separate software support, which is found in the files *keyboard.c* and *console.c*.

The operating system sees the keyboard console as parts of the same device, /dev/console. If there is enough memory available on the display adapter, **virtual console** support may be compiled, and in addition to */dev/console* there may be additional logical devices, */dev/ttyc*1, */dev/ttyc*2, and so on. Output from only one goes to the display at any given time, and there is only one keyboard to use for input to whichever console is active. Logically the keyboard is subservient to the console, but this is manifested in only two relatively minor ways. First, *tty_table* contains a *tty* structure for the console, and where separate fields are provided for input and output, for instance, the *tty_devread* and *tty_devwrite* fields, pointers to functions in *keyboard.c* and *console.c* are filled in at startup time. However, there is only one *tty_priv* field, and this points to the console's data structures only. Second, before entering its main loop, *tty_task* calls each logical device once to initialize it. The routine called for */dev/console* is in *console.c*, and the initialization code for the keyboard is called from there. The implied hierarchy could just as well have been reversed, however. We have always looked at input before output in dealing with I/O devices and we will continue that pattern, discussing *keyboard.c* in this section and leaving the discussion of *console.c* for the following section.

Keyboard.c begins, like most source files we have seen, with several #include statements. One of these is unusual, however. The file *keymaps/us-std.src* is not an ordinary header; it is a C source file that results in compilation of the default keymap within keyboard as an initialized array. The keymap source file is not included in the listings at the end of the book because of its size. Following the #includes are macros to define various constants. The first group are used in low-level interaction with the keyboard controller. Many of these are I/O port addresses or bit combination that have meaning in these interactions. The next group includes symbolic names for special keys. The macro *kb_addr* always returns a pointer to the first element of the *kb_lines* array, since the IBM hardware supports only one keyboard. On the next line the size of the keyboard input buffer is symbolically defined as *KB_IN_BYTES*, with a value of 32. The next 11 variables are used to hold various states that must be remembered to properly interpret a key press. They are use in different ways. For instance, the value of the *capslock* flag is toggled between *TRUE* and *FLASE* each time the Caps Lock key is pressed. The *shift* flag is set to *TRUE* when the Shift key is pressed and to *FALSE* when the Shift key is released. The *esc* variable is set when a scan code escape is received. It is always reset upon receipt of the following character.

The *kb_s* structure is used to keep track of scan codes as they are entered. Within this structure the codes are held in a circular buffer, in the array *ibuf,* of size *KB_IN_BYTES*. An array *kb_lines*[*NR_CONS*] of these structures is declared, one per console, but in fact only the first one is used, since the *kbaddr* macro is always used to determine the address of the current *kb_s*. However, we usually refer to variables within *kb_lines*[0] using a pointer to the structure, for example, kb->*ihead,* for consistency with the way we treat other devices and to make the references in the text consistent with those in the source code listing a small amount of memory is wasted because of the unused array elements, for course. However, if someone manufactures a PC with hardware support for multiple keyboards, MINIX is ready; only a modification of the *kbaddr* macro is required.

Map_key0 is defined as a macro. It returns the ASCII code that corresponds to a scan code, ignoring modifiers. This is equivalent to the first column (unshifted) in the keymap array. Its big brother is *map_key* which pertiorms the complete mapping of a scan code to an ASCII code, including accounting for (multiple) modifier keys that are depressed at the same time as ordinary keys.

The keyboard interrupt service routine is *kbd_hw_int,* called whenever a key is pressed or released. It calls *scan_keyboard* to get the scan code from the keyboard controller chip. The most significant bit of the scan code is set when a key release causes the interrupt, and in this case the key is ignored unless it is one of the modifier keys. If the interrupt is caused by a press of any key, or the release of a modifier key, the raw scan code is placed in the circular buffer if there is space the *tp->tty_events* flag for the current console is raised and then *force-timeout* is called to make sure the *clock task* will start the terminal task on the next clock tick. Figure 11.47 shows scan codes in the buffer for a short line of input that contains two upper case character, each preceded by the scan code for depression of a shift key and followed by the code for that release of the shift key.

42	35	170	18	38	38	24	57	54	17	182	24	19	38	32	28
L+	h	L-	e	l	l	o	SP	R+	w	R-	o	r	l	d	CR

Fig. 11.48. Scan codes in the input buffer, with corresponding key presses below, for a line of text entered at the keyboard. L+, L-, R+ and R-represent, respectively, pressing and releasing the left and right Shift Keys. The code for a key release is 128 more than the code for a press of the same key.

When the clock interrupt occurs, the terminal task itself runs, and upon finding the *tp->tty_events* flag for the console device set, it calls *kb_read* the device-specific routine, using the pointer in the tp->*tty_devread* field of the console's *tty* structure. *Kb_read* takes scan codes from the keyboard's circular buffer and places ASCII codes in its local buffer, which is large enough to hold the escape sequences that must be generated in response to some scan codes from the numeric keypad. Then it calls *in_process* in the hardware-independent code to put the character into the input queue *lock* and *unlock* are used to protect the decrement of kb->*icount* from a possible keyboard interrupt arriving at the same time. The call to *make_break* returns the ASCII code as an integer. Special keys, such as keypad and function keys, have values greater than 0×FF at this point. Codes in the range from *HOME* to *INSRT* (0 × 101 to 0×10C, defined in *include/minix/keymap.h*) result from pressing the numeric keypad, and are converted into 3-character escape sequences shows in Fig. 11.18 using the *numpad_map* array. The sequences are then passed to *in_process.* Higher codes are not passed on to *in_process*, but a check is made for the codes for ALT-LEFT-ARROW, ALT-RIGHT-ARROW, or ALT-F1 through ALT-F12, and if one of these is found, *select_console* is called to switch virtual consoles.

Key	Scan code	"ASCII"	Escape sequence
Home	71	0×101	ESC [H
Up Arrow	72	0×103	ESC [A
Pg Up	73	0×107	ESC [V
–	74	0×10A	ESC [S
Left Arrow	75	0×105	ESC [D
5	76	0×109	ESC [G
Right Arrow	77	0×106	ESC [C
+	78	0×10B	ESC [T
End	79	0×102	ESC [Y
Down Arrow	80	0×104	ESC [B
Pg Dn	81	0×108	ESC [U
Ins	82	0×10C	ESC [@

Fig. 11.49. *Escape codes generated by the numeric keypad. When scan codes for ordinary keys are translated into ASCII codes the special keys are assigned "pseudo ASCII" codes with values greater than 0×FF.*

Make_break converts scan codes into ASCII and then updates the variables that keep track of the state of modifier keys. First, however, it checks for the magic CTRL-ALT-DEL combination that PC uses all know as the way to force a reboot under MS-DSO. An orderly shutdown is desirable, however, so rather than try to start the PC BIOS routines, a *SIGABRT* signal is sent to *init*, the parent process of all other processes. *Init* is expected to catch this signal and interpret it as a command to begin an orderly process of shutting done, prior to causing a return to the boot monitor, from which a full restart of the system or a reboot of MINIX can be commanded. For course, it is not realistic to expect this to work every time. Most uses understand the dangers of an abrupt shutdown and do not press CTRL-ALT-DEL until something is really going wrong and normal control of the system has become impossible. At this point it is likely that the system may be so disrupted that an orderly sending of a signal to another process may be impossible. This is why there is a static variable *CAD_count* in *make_break*. Most system crashes have the interrupt system still functioning, so keyboard input scan still be received and the clock task can keep the terminal task running. Here MINIX takes advantage of the expected behavior of computer users, who are likely to bang on the keys repeatedly when something does not seem to work correctly. If the attempt to send the *SIGABRT* to *init* fails and the user presses CTRL-ALT-DEL twice more, a call to *wreboot* is made directly, causing a return to the monitor without going through the call to *init*.

The main part of *make_break* is not hard to follow. The variable make records whether the scan code was generated by a key press or a key release, and then the call to *map_key* returns the ASCII code to *ch*. Next is a switch on *ch*. Let us consider two cases, an ordinary key and a special key. For an ordinary key, none of the cases match, and nothing should happen in the default case either since ordinary keys codes are supposed to be accepted only on the make (press) phase of a key press and release. If somehow an ordinary key code is accepted at key release, a value of –1 is substituted here, and this is ignored by the caller, *kb_read*. A special key, for example *CTRL*, is identified at the appropriate place in the switch, in this case. The corresponding variable, in this case control, records the state of *make*, and –1 is substituted for the character code to be returned (and ignored). The handling of the ALT, CALOCK, NLOCK, and SLOCK keys is more complicate, but for all of these special keys the effect is similar: a variable records either the current state (for keys that are only effective while pressed) or toggles the previous state (for the lock keys).

There is one more case to consider, that of the *EXTKEY* code and the *esc* variable. This is not to be confused with the ESC key on the keyboard, which returns the ASCII code 0×1B. There is no way to generate the *EXTKEY* code along by pressing any key or combination of keys; it is the PC keyboard's **extended key prefix**, the first byte of a 2-byte scan code that signifies that a key that was not part of the original PC's complement of keys but that has the same scan code, has been pressed. In many cases software treats the two keys identically. For instance this is almost always the case for the normal "/" key and the gray "/" key on the numeric keyboard. In other cases, one would like to distinguish between such keys. For instance, many keyboard layouts for languages other than English treat the left and right ALT keys differently, to support keys that must generate three different character codes. Both ALT keys generate the same scan code (56), but the *EXTKEY* code precedes this when the right-hand ALT is pressed. When the *EXTKEY* code is returned, the *esc* flag is set. In its case, *make_break* returns from within the switch, thus by passing the last step before a normal return, which sets *esc* to zero in every other case. This has the effect of making the *esc* effective only for the very next code received. If you are familiar with the intricacies of the PC keyboard as it is ordinarily used, this will be both familiar and yet a little strange, because the PC BIOS does not allow one to read the scan code for an ALT key and returns a different value for the extended code than does MINIX.

Set_leds turns on and off the lights that indicate whether the Num Lock, Caps Lock, or Scroll Lock keys on a PC keyboard have been pressed. A control byte, *LED_CODE*, is written to an output port to instruct the keyboard that the next byte written to that port is for control of the lights, and the status of the three lights is encoded in 3 bits of that next byte. The next two functions support this operation. *Kb_wait* is called to determine that the keyboard is ready to receive a command sequence, and *kb_ack* is called to verify that the command has been acknowledged. Both of these commands use busy waiting, continually reading until a desired code is seen. This is not a recommended technique for handling most I/O operations, but turning lights on and off on the keyboard is not gong to be done very often and doing it inefficiently does not waste much time. Note also that both *kb_wait* and *kb_ack* could fail, and one can determine form the return code if this happens. But setting the light on the keyboard is no important enough to merit checking the value returned by either call, and *set_leds* just proceeds blindly.

Since the keyboard is part of the console, its initialization routine, *kb_init* is caller from *scr_init* console, not directly from *tty_init* in *tty.c*. If virtual consoles are enabled, (i.e., *NR_CONS* in *include/minix/config.h* is greater than 1) *kb_init* is called once for each logical console. After the first time the only part of *kb_init* that is essential for additional consoles is setting the address of *kb_read* into *tp->tty_devread,* but no harm so done by repeating the rest of the function. The rest of *kb_init* initializes some variables, sets the lights on the keyboard, and scans the keyboards to be sure no leftover keystroke is read. When all is ready, it calls *put_irq_handler* and then *enable_irq*, so *kbd_hw_int* will be executed whenever a key is pressed or released.

The next three functions are all rather simple. *Kbd_loadmap* is almost trivial. It is called by *do_ioctl* in *tty.c* to do the copying of a keymap from user space to overwrite the default keymap compiled by the inclusion of a keymap source file at the start of *keyboard.c.*

Func_key is called from *kb_read* to see if a special key meant for local processing has been pressed. Figure 11.49 summarizes these keys and their effects. The code called is found in several files. The *F1* and *F2* codes activate code in *dum.c*, which we will discuss in the next section. The *F3* code activates *toggle_scroll,* which is in *console.c*, also to be discussed in the next section. The *CF7*, *CF8*, and *CF9* codes cause calls to *sigchar*, in *tty.c.* When networking is added to MINIX, an additional case, to detect the *F5* code, is added to display Ethernet statistics. A large number of other scan codes are available that could be used to trigger other debugging messages or special events from the console.

Scan_ keyboard works at the hardware interface level, by reading and writing bytes from I/O ports. The keyboard controller is informed that a character has been read by the sequence which reads a byte, writes it again with the most significant bit set to 1, and then rewrites it with the same bit rest to 0. This prevents the same data from being read on a subsequent read. There is no status checking in reading the keyboard, but there should be no problems in any case, since *scan_keyboard* is only called in response to an interrupt, with the exception of the call from *kb_init* to clear out any garbage.

Key	Purpose
F1	Display process table
F2	Display details fo process memory use
F3	Toggle between hardware and software scrolling
F5	Show Ethernet statistics (id network support compiled)
CF7	Send SIGQUIT, same effect as CTRL-\
CF8	Send SIGINT, same effect as DEL
CF9	Send SIGKILL, same effect as CTRL-U

Fig. 11.50. The function keys detected by func_key().

The last function in *keyboard.c* is *wreboot*. If invoked as a result of a system panic, it provides an opportunity for the user to use the function keys to display debugging information. The keyboard is read repeatedly until an ESC is typed. Certainly no one can claim that a more efficient technique is needed after a crash, while awaiting a command to reboot. Within the loop, *func_key* is called to provide a possibility of obtaining information that might help analyze the cause of a crash. We will not discuss further details of the return to the monitor. The details, are very hardware-specific and do not have a lot to do with the operating system.

Implementation of the Display Driver

The IBM PC display may be configured as several virtual terminals, if sufficient memory is available. We will examine the console's device-dependent code in this section. We will also look at the debug dump routines that use low-level services of the keyboard and display. These provide support for limited interaction with the user at the console, even when other parts of the MINIX system are not functioning and can provide useful information even following a near-total system crash.

Hardware-specific support for console output to the PC memory-mapped screen is in *console.c*. In a sense this structure is an extension of the *tty* structure defined in *tty.c.* At initialization the *tp->tty_priv* field of a console's *tty* structure is assigned a pointer to its own console structure. The first item in the *console* structure is a pointer back to the corresponding *tty* structure. The components of a console structure are what one would expect for a video display: variables to record the row and column of the cursor location, the memory addresses of the start and limit of memory used for the display, the memory address pointed to by the controller chip's base pointer, and the current address of the cursor. Other variables are used for managing escape sequences. Since characters are initially received as 8-bit bytes-and must be combined with attribute bytes and transferred as 16-bit words to video memory, a block to be transferred is built up in *c_ramqueue*, an array big enough to hold an entire 80-columnn row of 16-bit character attribute pairs. Each virtual console needs one *console* structure, and the storage is allocated in the array *cons_table*. As we did with the *tty* and *kb_s* structures, we will usually refer to the elements of a *console* structure using a pointer, for example, cons->_*tty.*

The function whose address is stored in each console's *tp->tty_devwrite* entry is *cons_write*. It is called from only one place, *handle_events* in *tty.c*. Most of the other functions in console.c exist to support this function. When it is called for the first time after a client process makes a WRTIE call, the data to be output are in the client's buffer, which can be found using the *tp->tty_ouproc* and *tp*->ot_*vir*fields in the *tty* structure. The *tp->tty_outleft* field tells how many characters are to be transferred, and the tp->*tty_outcum* field is initially zero, indicating none have yet have been transferred. This is the usual situation upon entry to *cons_write*, because normally, once called, it transfers all the data requested in the original call. However, if the user wants to slow the process in order to review the data on the screen, he may enter a *STOP* (CTRL-S) character at the keyboard, resulting in raising of the *tp->tty_inhibited flag. Cons_write* returns immediately when this flag is raised, even though the WRITE has not been completed. In such a case *handle-events* will continue to call *cons_write*, and when *tp->tty_inhbited* finally reset, by the user entering a *START* (CTRL-Q) character, *cons_write* continues with the interrupted transfer.

Cons_write's sole argument is a pointer to the particular console's *tty* structure, so the first thing that must be done is to initialize *cons*, the pointer to this console's *console* structure. Then, because *handle-events* calls *cosn_write* whenever it runs, the first action is a test to see if three really is work to be done. A quick return is made if not. This loop very similar in structure to the main loop of *in_transfer* in *tty.c.* A local buffer that can hold 64 characters is filled by calling *phys_copy* to get the data from the clients; buffer, the pointer to the source and the counts are update, and then each character in the local buffer in transferred to the cons->*c_ramqueue* array, along with an attribute byte, for later transfer to the screen by flush.. *Out_char* can be called to do this for each character, but is predictable that none of the special services of *out_char* will be needed if the character is a visible caracter, an escape sequence is not in progress, the screen width has not been exceeded, and cons->*c_ramqueue* is not full. If the full service of *out_char* is not needed, the character is placed directly into *cons_>c_ramqueue,* along with the attribute byte (retrieved from *cons->c_attr*), and *cons->c_rwords* (the index into the queue), *cons->*c_*column* (which keeps track of the column on the screen), and *tbuf*, the pointer into the buffer, are all incremented. This direct palcement of characters into *cons->c_ramqueue* corresponds to the dashed line. If needed; *out_char* is called. It does all of the bookkeeping, and additionally calls *flush*, which does the final transfer to screen memory, when necessary. The transfer from the user buffer to the local buffer to the queue is repeated as long as *tp->tty_outlef* indicates there are still characters to be transferred and the flag *tp->tty_inhibited* has not been raised. When the transfer stops, whether because the WRITE operation is complete or because *tp->tty_inhibited* has been raised, *flush* is called again to transfer the last characters in the queue to screen memory. If the operation is complete (tested by seeing if *tp->tty_outleft* is zero), a reply message is sent by calling *tty-reply.*

In addition to calls to *cons_write* from *handle_events*, characters to be displayed are also sent to the console by *echo* and *rawecho* in the hardware-independent part of the terminal task. If the console is the current output device, calls via the *tp->tty_echo* pointer are directed to the next function, *counts_echo. Cons_echo* does all of its work by calling *out_char* and then flush. Input from the keyboard arrives character by character and the person doing the typing wants to see the echo with no perceptible delay, so putting characters into the output queue would be unsatisfactory.

Now we arrive at *out_char*. It does a test to see if an escape sequence is in progress, calling *parse_escape* and then returning immediately if so. Otherwise, a switch is entered to check for special cases: null, backspace, the able character, and so on. The handling of most of these is easy to follow. The linefeed and the tab are the most complicated, since they involve complicated changes to the position of the cursor on the screen and may require scrolling as well. The last test is for the *ESC* code. If it is found, the *cons->_esc_state* flag is set and future calls to *out_char* are diverted to *parse_escape* until the sequence is complete. At the end, the default is taken for printable characters. If the screen width has been exceeded, the screen may need to be scrolled, and *flush* is called. Before a character is placed in the output queue a test is made to see that there queue is not full, and *flush* is called if it is. Putting character into the queue requires the same bookkeeping we saw earlier in *cons_write.*

The next function is *scroll_screen. Scroll_screen* handles both scrolling up, the normal situation that must be dealt with whenever the bottom line on the screen is full, and scrolling down, which occurs when cursor positioning commands attempt to move the cursor beyond the top line of the screen. For each direction of scroll there are three possible methods. These are required to support different kinds of video cards.

We will look at the scrolling up case. To begin, *chars* is assigned the size of the screen minus one line. Softscrolling is accomplished by a single call to *vid_vid_copy* to move *chars* characters lower in memory, the size of the, move being the number of characters in a line. *Vid_vid_copy* can wrap, that is, if asked to move a block of memory that overflows the upper end of the block assigned to the video display, it fetches the overflow portion from the low end of the memory block and moves it to an address higher than the part that is moved lower, treating the entire block as a circular array. The simplicity of the call hides a fairly slow operation. Even though *vid_vid_copy* is an assembly language routine defined in *klib386.s*, this call requires the CPU to move 3840 bytes, which is a large job even in assembly language.

The softscroll method is never the default; the operator is supposed to select it only if hardware scrolling does not work or is not desired for some reason. One such reason might be a desire to use the *screendump* command to save the screen memory in a file. When hardware scrolling is in effect, *screendump* is likely to give unexpected results, because the start of the screen memory is likely not to coincide with the start of the visible display.

The *wrap* variable is taste as the first part of a compound test. *Wrap* is true for order displays that can support hardware scrolling, and if the test fails, simple hardware scrolling occurs, where the origin pointer used by the video controller chip, *cons->c_org,* if updates to point to the first character to be displayed at the upper-left corner of the display. If *wrap* is *FALSE,* the compound test continue with a test of whether the block to be moved up in the scroll operation overflows the bounds of the memory block designated for this console. If this is so, *vid_vid_copy* is called again to make a wrapped move of the block to the start of the console's allocated memory, and the origin pointer is updated. If three is no overlap, control passes to the simple hardware scrolling method always used by older video controllers. This consists of adjusting *cons->c_org* and then putting the new origin in the correct register of the controller chip. The call to do this is done later, as is a call to blank the bottom line on the screen.

The code for scrolling down is very similar to that for scrolling up. Finally, *mem_vid_copy* is called to blank out the line at the bottom (or top) addressed by *new_line*. Then set_6845 is called to write the new origin from *cons->c_org* into the appropriate registers, and *flush* makes sure all changes become visible on the screen.

We have mentioned *flush* several times. It transfers the characters in the queue to the video memory using *mem_vid_copy,* updates some variables, and then makes sure the row and column numbers are reasonable, adjusting them if, for instance, an escape sequence has tried to move the cursor to a negative column position. Finally a calculation of where the cursor ought to be is made and is compared with *cons->c_cur.* If they do not agree, and if the video memory that is currently being handled belongs to the current virtual console, a call to *set_6845* is made to set the correct value in the controller's cursor register.

Figure 11.49 shows how escape sequence handling can be represented as a finite state machine. This is implemented by *parse_escape* which is called at the start of *out_char* is *cons->c_esc_state* is nonzero. An ESC itself is detected by *out_char* and makes *cons->c_esc_state* equal to 1. When the next character is received, parse_escape prepares for further processing by putting a'\0' in *cons->c_esc_intro,* a pointer to the start of the arry of paramenters, *cons->c_esc_parmv*[0] into *cons-c_esc_parmp*, and zeroes into the parameter array itself. Then the first character following the ESC is examined—valid values are either "[" or "M". In the first case the "[" is copied to *cons->c_esc_intro* and the state advanced to 2. In the second case, *do_escape* is called to carry out the action, and three escape state is reset to zero. If the first character after the ESC is not one of the valid ones. It is ignored and succeeding characters are once again displayed normally.

When an ESC [sequence has been seen, the next character entered is processed by the escape state 2 code. There are three possibilities at this point. If the character is a numeric character, its value is extracted and added to 10 times the existing value in the position currently pointed to by *cons->c_esc_parmp,* initially *cons->c_esc_parmv*[0] (which was initialized to zero). The escape state does not change. This makes it possible to enter a series of decimal digits and accumulate a large numeric parameter, although the maximum value currently recognized by MINIX is 80, used by the sequence than moves the cursor to an arbitrary position. If the character is a semicolon, the pointer to the parameter string is advanced, so succeeding numeric values can be accumulated in the second parameter. If *MAX_ESC_PARMS* were to be change to allocate a larger array for the parameters, this code would not have to be altered to accumulate additional numeric values after entry of additional parameters. Finally, if the character is neither a numeric digit nor a semicolon, *do_escape* is called.

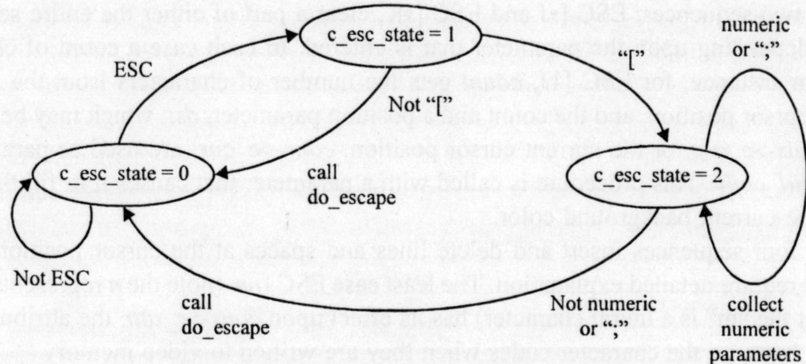

Fig. 11.51. Finite state machine for processing escape sequences.

Do_escap is one of the longer functions in the MINIX system source code, even though MINIX's complement of recognized escape sequences is relatively modest. For all its length, however, the code should be easy to follow. After an initial call to *flush* to make sure the video display is fully updated, there is a simple if choice, depending upon whether the character immediately following the ESC character was a special control sequence introducer or not. If not, there is only one valid action, moving the cursor up one line of the sequence was ESC M. Note that the test for the "M" is done within a switch with a default action, as a validity check and in anticipation of addition of other sequences that do not use the ESC [format. The action is typical of many escape sequences: the *cons->c_row* variable is inspected to determine if scrolling is required. If the cursor is already on row 0, a *SCROLL_DOWN* call is made to *scroll_scree*; otherwise the cursor is moved up one line. The latter is accomplished just by decrementing *cons->c_row* and then calling *flush*. If a control sequence introducer is found, the code following the else is taken. A test is made for "[". The only control sequence introducer currently recognized by MINIX. If the sequence is valid, the first parameter found in the escape sequence, or zero if no numeric parameter was entered, is assigned to *value*. If the sequence is invalid, nothing happens except that the large switch that ensues is skipped and the escape state is reset to zero before returning from *do_escape*. In the more interesting case that the sequence is valid, the switch is entered. We will not discuss all the cases; we will just note several that are representative of the type of actions governed by escape sequences.

The first five sequences are generated, with no numeric arguments, by the four "arrow" keys and the Home key on the IBM PC keyboard. The first two, ESC [A and ESC [B, are similar to ESC M, except they can accept a numeric parameter and move up and down by more than one line, and they do not scroll the screen if the parameter specifies a move that exceeds the bounds of the screen. In such cases, *flush* catches requests to move out of bounds and limits the move to the last row or the first row, as appropriate. The next two sequences, ESC [C and ESC [D, which move the cursor right and left, are similarly limited by *flush*. When generated by the "arrow" keys there is no number argument, and thus the default movement of one line or column occurs.

The next sequence, ESC [H, can take two numeric parameters, for instance, ESC [20;60H. The parameters specify an absolute position rather than one relative to the current position and are converted from 1-based numbers to 0-based numbers for proper interpretation. The Home key generates the default (no parameters) sequence which moves the cursor to position (1 ,1).

The next two sequences, ESC [*s*J and ESC [*s*K, clear a part of either the entire screen or the current line, depending upon the parameter that is entered. In each case a count of characters is calculated. For instance, for ESC [1J, *count* gets the number of characters from the start of the screen to the cursor position, and the count and a position parameter, *dst*, which may be the start of the screen, *cons->c_org,* or the current cursor position, *cons->c_cur*, are used as parameters to a call to *mem_vid_copy*. This procedure is called with a parameter that causes it to fill the specified region with the current background color.

The next four sequences insert and delete lines and spaces at the cursor position, and their actions do not require detailed explanation. The least case ESC [*nm* (note the *n* represents a numeric parameter, but the "m" is a literal character) has its effect upon *cons->c_attr,* the attribute byte that is interleaved between the character codes when they are written to video memory.

The next function, *set_6845*, used whenever it is necessary to update the video controller chip. The 6845 has internal 16-bit registers that are programmed 8 bits at a time, and writing a single register requires four I/O port write operations. *Lock* and *unlock* calls are used to disable interrupts, which can cause problems if allowed to disrupt the sequence. Some of the registers of the 6845 video controller chip are shown in 11.52.

Register	Function
10 – 11	Cursor size
12 – 13	Start address for drawing screen
14 – 15	Cursor position

Fig. 11.52. Some of the 6845's registers.

The beep function is called when a CTRL-G character must be output. It takes advantage of the built in support provided by the PC for making sounds by sending a square wave to the speaker. The sound is initiated by more of the kind of magic manipulation of I/O ports that only assembly language programmars can love, again with some concern that a critical part of the process should be protected from interrupt. The more interesting part of the code is the use of the clock task's capability to set an alarm, which can be used to initiate a function. The next routine, *stop_beep*, is the one whose address is put into the message to the clock task. It stops beep after the designated time has elapsed and also resets the *beeping* flag which is used to prevent superfluous calls to the beep routine from having any effect.

Scr_init is called by *tty_init NR_CONS* times. Each time its argument is a pointer to a *tty* structure, one element of the *tty_table*. It is to be used as the index into the *cons_table* array, is calculated, tested for validity, and, if valid, used to initialize *cons*, the pointer to the current console table entry. At this point the *cons->c-tty* field can be initialized with the point to the main *tty* structure for the device, and in turn, *tp->tty_priv* can be pointed to this device's *console_t* structure. Next, *kb_init* is called to initialize the keyboard, and then the pointers to device specific routines are set up, *tp->tty_devwrite* pointing to *cons_write* and *tp->tty_echo* pointing to *cons_echo*. The I/O address of the base register of the CRT controller is fetched and the address and size of the video memory are determined and the *wrap* flag (used to determine how to scroll) is set according to the class of video controller in use.

Next comes the initialization of virtual consoles. Each time *sct_init* is called, the argument is a different value of *tp*, and thus a different *line* and *cons* are used to provide each virtual console with its own share of the available video memory. Each screen is then blanked, ready to start, and finally console 0 is selected to be the first active one.

The remaining routines in *console.c* are short and smile and we will review them quickly. Put has been mentioned earlier. It prints a character on behalf of any code linked into the kernel image that needs the service, without going through the FS. *Toggle_scroll* does what its name says, it toggles the flag that determines whether hardware or software scrolling is used. It also display's a message at the current cursor position to identify the selected mode. *Cons_stop* reinitializes the console to the state that the boot monitors expects, prior to a shutdown or reboot. *Cons_org0* is used only when a change of scrolling mode is forced by the F3 key, or when preparing to shut down. *Select_console* selects a virtual console. It is called with the new index and calls set_6845 twice to get the video controller to display the proper part of the video memory.

The last two routines are highly hardware-specific. *Con_loadfont* loads a font into a graphics adapter, in support of the IOTCL *TIOCSFON* operation. It calls *ga_program* to do a series of magical writes to an I/O port that cause the video adapter's font memory, which is normally not addressable by the CPU, to be visible. Then *phys_copy* is called to copy the font data to this area of memory, and another magic sequence is invoked to return the graphics adapter to its normal mode of operation

Debugging Dumps

The final group of procedures we will discuss in the terminal task were originally intended only for temporary use when debugging MINIX. They can be removed when this assistance is no longer needed, but many users, fined them useful and leave them in place. They are particularly helpful when modifying MINIX.

As we have seen, *func_key* is called at the start of *kb_read* to detect scan codes used for control and debugging. The dump routines called when the F1 and F2 keys are detected are in *dmp.c*. The first, *P_dum* displays basic process information for all processes, including some information on memory use, when the F1 key is pressed. The second, *map_dump* provides more detailed information on memory use in response to F2. *Proc_name* supports *P_dum* by looking up process names.

Since this code is completely contained within the kernel binary itself and does not run as a user process to task, it frequently continues to function correctly, even after a major system crash. Of course, these routines are accessible only from the console. The information provided by the dump routines cannot be redirected to a file or to any other device, so hardcopy or use over a network connection are not options.

We suggest that the first step in trying to add any improvement to MINIX might very well be to extend the dumping routines to provide more information on the aspect of the system you wish to improve.

12

Distributed Computing

Pipelining

Pipelining is a performance enhancement technique that enables several machine language instructions to be in various stages of execution at once (Be89). Multi-stage pipelines are much like assembly lines in automobile factories. Each station in the instruction pipeline performs a different operation on an instruction, then the instruction moves on to the next station; all stations operate in parallel. Pipelines enable many instructions, each in different phases of execution, to be in progress at once. These phases typically include instruction fetch, operand fetch, instruction decode, and instruction execution. Early computers executed a single machine language instruction at a time, start to finish. Today's pipelined systems begin working on the next instruction, and often the next several, while the current instruction is executing.

Vector Processing

There is much confusion in the literature between the terms pipelining and *vector processing*. Vector processing specifically requires vectors instructions in the machine language. Vector processing requires pipelined hardware, but not vice versa. A vector instruction indicates the operation to be performed, and specifies the list of operands (called a *vector*) on which it is to operate. When a vector instruction is executed, the elements of the vector are fed into the appropriate pipeline one at a time, delayed by the time it takes to complete one stage of the pipeline. Compilers "vectorize" programs to run efficiently on vector processors.

The Cray-1 vector processor has 13 pipelines that can operate in parallel; these are dedicated to operations such as floating addition, floating multiplication, reciprocal approximation, fixed addition, and so on.

Array Processors

Array processors are SIMD machines; they perform the same instruction simultaneously on all elements of an array. The reader familiar with electronic spreadsheets undoubtedly sees an immediate application for array processors. Array processors are not useful for general-purpose computing environments characterized by the need to perform independent tasks in parallel. One of the earliest array processors was the ILLIAC IV, developed at the University of Illinois. The MPP (Massive

Parallel Processor) is an SIMD machine that has 16, 384 processors. It can perform a total of more than 6 billion 8-bit operations per second. It was designed for NASA by Goodyear Aerospace to perform image processing tasks. This level of parallelism has been surpassed by the 65,536-processor Connection Machine (CM), an array processor built by Thinking Machines Corp. A detailed case study on the CM appears at the end of this chapter.

Data Flow Computers

In sequential processors, control of what to do next resides in the program counter which, after the completion of one instruction, normally points to the next instruction to be performed.

Data flow computers can perform many operations in parallel. These machines are said to be *data driven* because they perform each instruction (potentially simultaneously if enough processors are available) for which the needed data is available. Data flow machines have not been implemented commercially, data flow techniques are already being incorporated in compilers that prepare programs for optimal execution on various kinds of parallel architectures.

An example of how a data flow computer might outperform a sequential computer is shown in Fig.12.1, in which a series of assignment statements is evaluated for both a parallel data flow architecture and a sequential architecture.

On a sequential processor, seven separate evaluation steps must be executed sequentially; three of these involve the slower operations of multiplication and division. On a parallel data flow processor, only four evaluation steps need to be performed; only two of these involve multiplication and division.

Multiprocessors

One appeal of multiprocessing systems is that if a processor fails, the remaining processors can normally continue operating. A failing processor must somehow inform the other processors to take over; functioning processors must be able to detect a processor that has failed. The operating system must note that a particular processor has failed and is no longer available for allocation.

Instead of talking about multiprocessing in today's sense, i.e., two (or perhaps a few more) processors, we now commonly talk about *massive parallelism*. The theoretical question of interest is: "Given the availability of massive parallelism, what is the minimum time required to execute a particular algorithm?"

By utilizing many CPUs, systems may realize many goals. Increased computing power is made possible by combining the processing power of several processors. With decreasing hardware costs, it has become common to connect a large number of microprocessors to form a multiprocessor; in this way, large-scale computer power can be achieved without the use of costly ultrahigh-speed processors.

Fault Tolerance

One of the most important capabilities of multiprocessors operating systems is their ability to withstand equipment failures in individual processors and to continue operation; this ability is referred to as *fault tolerance*.

Fault tolerant systems can continue operating even when portions of the system fail. This kind of operation is especially important in so-called *mission critical systems* such as those for which Ada has become the language of choice. Ethical systems design considerations are increasing the interest in building highly-reliable systems. Fault-tolerant designs are especially important in systems in which it may not be possible for humans to intervene and repair the problem, such as in deep-space probes, aircraft, and the file. It is also appropriate for systems in which the consequences of failure are so huge, and in which these consequences could happen so quickly that humans could not intervene quickly enough.

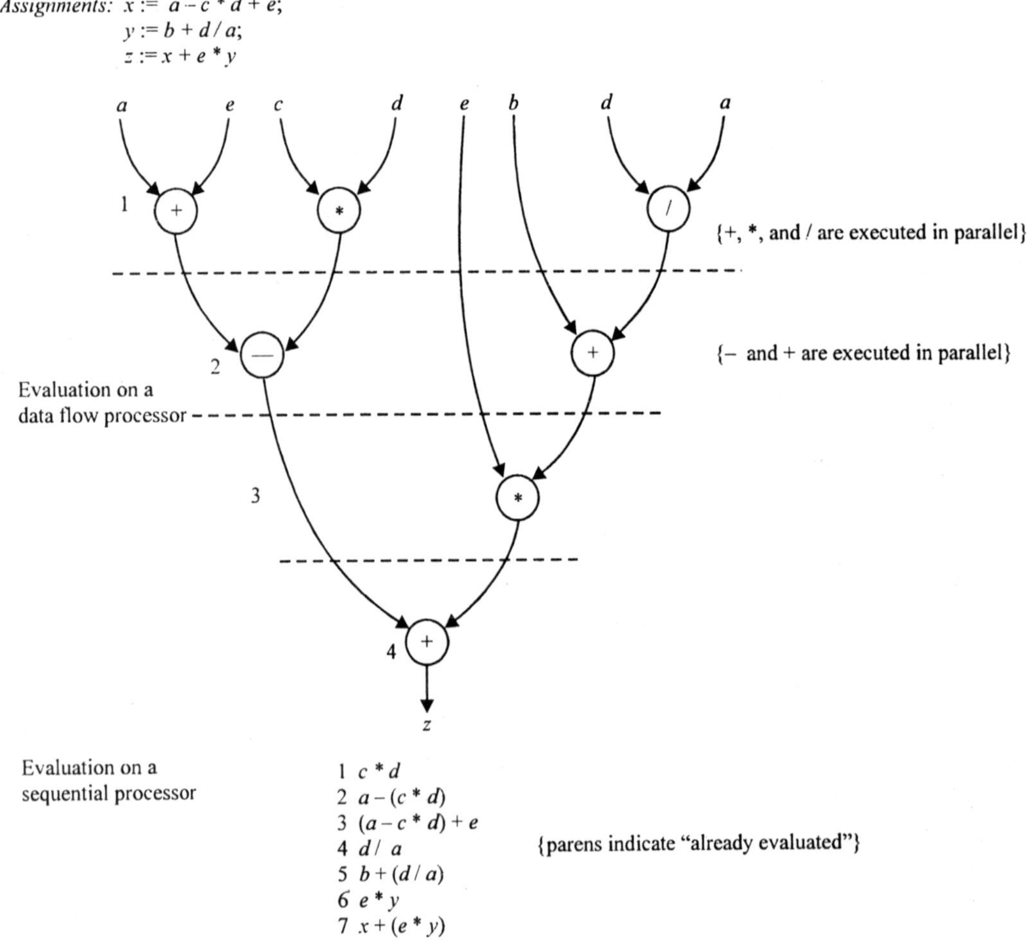

Fig. 12.1. Evaluation of assignment statements on a data flow computer.

Many techniques are commonly used to facilitate fault tolerance. These include

- Critical data for the system and the various processes should be maintained in multiple copies. These should reside in separate storage banks so that failures in individual components will not completely destroy the data.
- The operating system must be designed so that it can run the maximal configuration of hardware effectively, but it, must also be able to run subsets of the hardware effectively in case of failures.
- Hardware error detection and correction capabilities should be implemented so that extensive validation is performed without interfering with the efficient operation of the system.
- Idle processor capacity should be utilized to attempt to detect potential failures before they occur.

Computational Complexity Issues

Researchers in the field of computational complexity have been showing intense interest in the study of parallel algorithms. Parallel architectures can only speed the solution of problems if effective parallel algorithms can be found to replace existing sequential algorithms.

The availability of parallel processors has no effect on whatever or not a problem is *solvable* in the theoretical sense; it merely enables the result of a solvable problem to be computed in less time. This benefit is certainly not to be ignored, however, because it still enables us to attack larger classes of solvable problems more efficiently. It is not unusual for researchers in the field of parallel supercomputing to say that they want to perform computations in an hour that currently take a month.

There are very large classes of interesting problems which to be solved effectively on a parallel processors would require such massive parallelism that it would never be feasible to build an appropriate computer system to handle these problems. If, for example, the computational complexity of a problem demands 2^n processors cycles to solve a problem of "size *n*," then a problem of only size 100 would require more computing time than the suspected age to the universe! No matter what degree of massive parallelism we might eventually be able to realize, we can trivially extend the size of such problems to demand vast increases in computing power.

NP-complete problems ("nondeterministic polynomial") are characterized by having a best-known algorithm whose computation time is an exponential function of the "size" of the problem. Parallel processors are of little use in solving such problems efficiently in the general case; these problems are said to be *intractable*. The class of algorithms whose computation time is a polynomial function of the problem size (and for which parallel algorithms can be found) can benefit more directly by the application of massive parallelism, these problems are said to be *tractable*.

Garey and Johnson discuss many important problems known to be NP complete. Rosenkrantz and Stearns offer a number of suggestions for attacking such problems: choose problems of small size, solve only special cases, solve for the limited cases that occur in practice, and in the case of optimization problems—seek fast running solutions that may be only "near optimal." Their final suggestion is to "work on some other problem."

Detecting Parallelism

The detection of parallelism—by the programmer, the language translator (Pa86) (Bu88), the hardware, or the operating system, is a complex problem of intense interest to researchers today. Regardless of how parallelism is detected, multiprocessors may exploit it by executing th parallel portions of computations simultaneously.

Explicit parallelism is indicated by a programmer using a concurrency construct such as cobegin/coend as follows.

```
cobegin
    statement-1;
    statement-2;
    ...
    statement-n
coend
```

In a multiprocessing system designed to exploit this concurrency, separate processors might be used to execute each of the statements.

Explicit indication of parallelism is time consuming, and the programmer may erroneously indicate that certain operations can be performed in parallel when they cannot. The programmer is likely to code explicit parallelism only for the more obvious situations. Modifying a program with explicit parallelism could introduce subtle bugs.

The real hope is the automatic detection of *implicit parallelism*, i.e., parallelism intrinsic to the algorithm. Detection mechanisms may be included in compilers, operating systems, and computer hardware to exploit implicit parallelism. Two common techniques used by compilers for exploiting implicit parallelism are *loop distribution* and *tree height reduction.*

Loop Distribution

The statements within a loop body are such that parallel execution may be possible. Consider the following

```
for i = 1 to 4 do
    a(i) = b(i) + c(i)
```

which adds the corresponding elements of arrays b and c and places the sums in array a. This loop causes a sequential processor to perform the four iterations of the loop in sequence. These iterations are independent of one another and may be performed concurrently by four processors in a multiprocessors system. A compiler could convert the preceding **for** loop into the parallel execution structure

```
cobegin
    a (1) = b (1) + c (1);
    a (2) = b (2) + c (2);
    a (3) = b (3) + c (3);
    a (4) = b (4) + c (4)
coend
```

which is a technique called *loop distribution.*

Tree Height Reduction

Compilers may detect implicit parallelism in algebraic expressions and produce object code for multiprocessors, indicating that certain operations may be performed simultaneously. A compiler uses rules of operator precedence to assign a unique sequential ordering to the operations in an algebraic expression. The compiler may then proceed to generate the appropriate machine code.

Often, the uniqueness and the sequential ordering is not necessary. For example, since addition and multiplication are both commutative operations, a compiler generating code to multiply p by q may generate either $p * q$ or $q * p$; the result of the computations will be identical. Similarly, adding p to q may be accomplished by either $p + q$ or $q + p$. Taking advantage of commutativity, associativity, and distributivity, compliers may rearrange expressions so that they are more amenable to parallel computation.

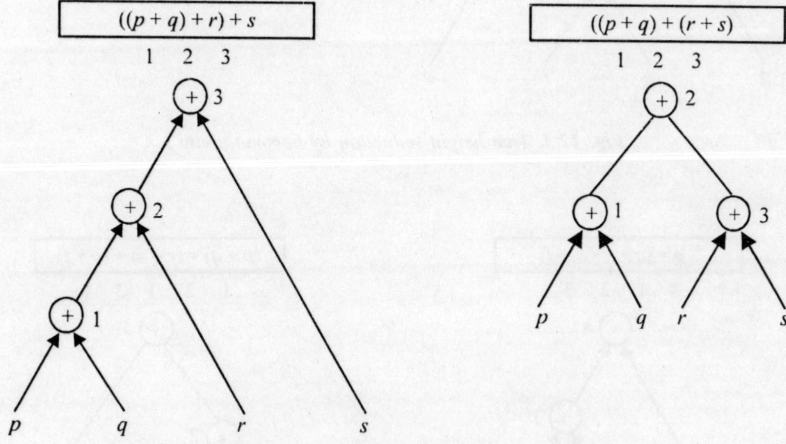

Fig. 12.2. Tree height reduction by associativity.

Figure 12.2 illustrates how an algebraic expression would be translated by a conventional compiler and how it might be manipulated by a compiler designed to locate implicit parallelism. The diagram at the left of the figure shows a tree structure indicating how a conventional compiler might generate code to perform the indicated operations. The numbers 1, 2, and 3, are used to indicate the order in which the various operations would be performed. By taking advantage of the associative property of addition, it is possible to manipulate the expression

$$[(p + q) + r] + s$$

to yield the expression

$$(p + q) + (r + s)$$

which is more amenable to parallel execution. The first expression requires three levels in the tree structure. The second expression only requires two, so it may be executed faster on a multiprocessor.

Figure 12.2 illustrates how the commutative property of addition may be used to convert a sequential computation involving three levels in the tree structure to a parallel computation involving only two levels. Figure 12.4 show how the distributive property of multiplication across addition may be used to reduce the depth of the associated tree structure from four to three.

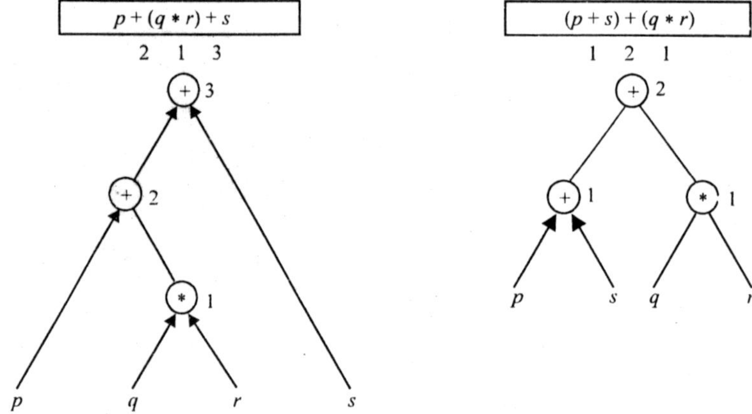

Fig. 12.3. Tree height reduction by commutativity.

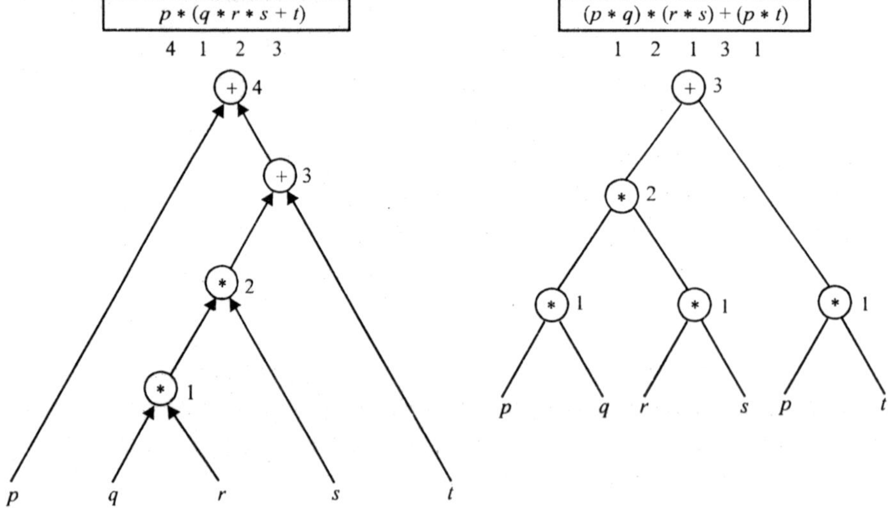

Fig. 12.4. Tree height reduction by distributivity.

The "Never Wait" Rule

The *never wait rule* states that it is better to give a processor a task that may or may not be used eventually than it is to let the processor sit idle. The point is that if the task is eventually needed, it will be possible to perform computations faster. Consider the following example

```
a := c * c;
if a = 9 then d := 10;
e := d * f
```

Based on the result of the first statement, the second statement may alter the value of *d*, or it may leave *d* as if. If *d* is left as is, then the third statement could have been performed in parallel with the first statement. If *d* is altered, then the third statement needs to use this new value. The strategy of "never wait" is to perform the third statement in parallel with the first statement. If *d* changes, then the third statement will have to be re-executed. If *d* does not change, then the third statement has already been performed, so the computation may complete faster.

Processor Interconnection Schemes

One of the key problems in the design of multiprocessor systems is determining the means of connecting the multiple processors and input/output processors to the storage units. Several popular schemes have evolved. We are concerned in the next several sections only with true multiprocessors, which have two or more processors of comparable capabilities, share access to common storage, share access to input/output channels, control units, and devices, and are controlled by one operating system.

Shared Bus

The *shared bus* multiprocessor organization, shown in Fig. 12.5 uses a single communication path between all the processors, the storage units, and the I/O processors. In this simple scheme, the bus is essentially a *passive* unit, i.e., transfer operations between the functional units are controlled by the *bus interfaces* of the units themselves. The Ethernet local area networking scheme uses a shared bus.

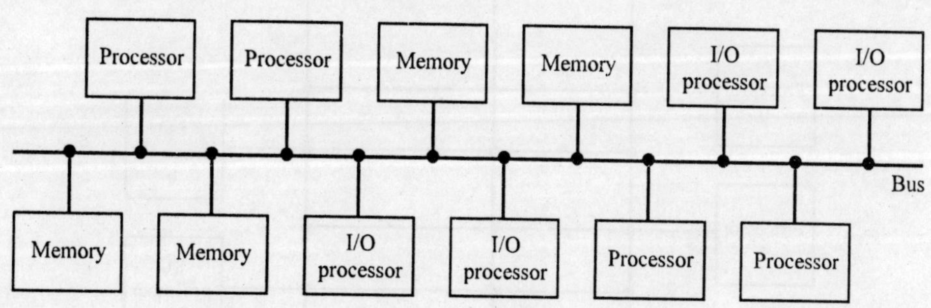

Fig. 12.5. Shared bus multiprocessor organization.

The processors or I/O processors wishing to transfer data must check the availability of the bus and the availability of the destination unit, and initiate the actual data transfer. The receiving units must be able to recognize which messages on the bus are addressed to them, and they must interpret and acknowledge the control signals received from the sending unit.

The shared bus organization makes it easy to add new units by simply attaching them directly to the bus. For communication to occur, each unit must know what other units are on the bus; this is generally handled in software.

The most serious disadvantages of this organizational scheme come from the single communication path. The bus can handle only one transmission at a time. The entire system fails if the bus fails (i.e., a *catastrophic failure*). The transmission rate of the system is constrained by the transmission rate of the bus. *Contention* for the use of the bus in a busy system can cause serious performance degradation.

These limitations constraint the use of the shared bus to smaller multiprocessing systems. Some designers have used multiple-bus schemes to improve throughput and reliability.

Crossbar-Switch Matrix

Increasing the number of buses in a shared bus-system to the number of storage units creates a multiprocessor organization called the *crossbar-switch matrix*, in which three is a separate path to every storage unit. With this scheme, references to two different storage units may occur simultaneously—one reference cannot block the other. A crossbar-switch matrix system can support simultaneous transmissions for all storage units; thus the crossbar switch is the best performing interconnection scheme.

The hardware required to build a crossbar switch can become complex. For example, the switch must be capable of resolving conflicts for the same storage unit. Although the switch is complex, the interfaces at the functional units are simpler than with the shared bus organization. The cost of the switch increases as the product of the number of functional units and the number of memory units, so it is not a viable structure for massive parallel processors.

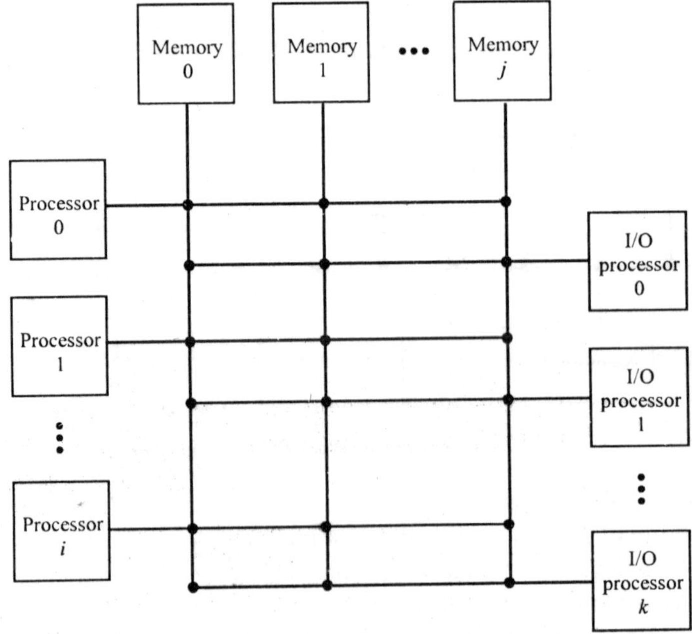

Fig. 12.6. Crossbar-switch matrix multiprocessor organization.

The Hypercube

The *hypercube interconnection network* provides a means of connecting very large numbers of processors in a relatively economical manner. A two-dimensional hypercube is simply square; a three-dimensional hypercube is formed by connecting the corresponding elements of two, two-dimensional hypercubes. A four-dimensional hypercube is formed by connecting the corresponding elements of two, three-dimensional hypercubes, and so on. The Connection Machine uses a 16-dimensional hypercube connection scheme to interconnect 65,536 processors. Another hypercube machine that has been offered as a commercial product is Intel's iPSC system.

Multistage Networks

The primary disadvantage of the crossbar-switch matrix scheme is its exceptionally high cost when a large number of nodes need to be interconnected. Consider the problem of flying between small cities. Instead of having flights between every possible pair of airports, airlines tend to use "hubs." The major traffic between large cities involves only a single "leg" of travel. The traffic between remote locations may require many legs; *multistage networks* use this kind of connection scheme. The case study on the BBN Butterfly multiprocessor presents a detailed explanation of operation of the Butterfly switch, a multistage interconnection scheme.

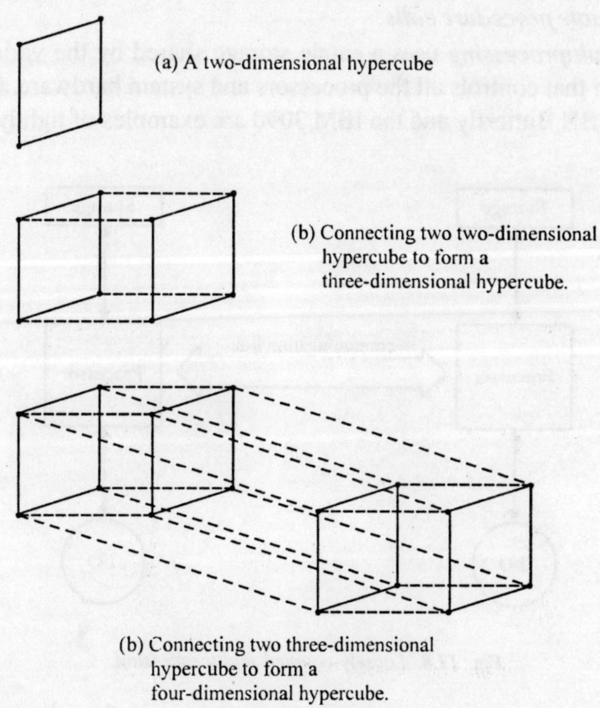

Fig. 12.7. Hypercube interconnection networks.

The multistage network is a "compromise" scheme. It enables any unit to connect with any other unit, but greatly reduces the complexity of the interconnection scheme to make it feasible to connect large number of processors. The term multistage comes from the fact that each message must pass through multiple switching elements to reach its destination. The delays encountered as a message transverses multiple legs make this a slower scheme than crossbar switching, but the number of switching elements in much smaller, especially when connecting large numbers of processors. The scheme provides a unique path through the network, but connection may develop at the various switching elements involved in multiple paths. Some multistage networks buffer colliding messages at the switching elements until the elements clear and the messages can proceed; this increases the cost of the switching network. Other systems accept and process only one message at the switch and back out all other colliding messages to be retransmitted after a random delay.

Loosely-Coupled Vs. Tightly-Coupled Systems

Loosely-coupled multiprocessing involves connecting two or more independent computer systems via a communication link. Each system has its own operating system and storage. The systems can function independently and can communicate when necessary. The separate systems can access each other's files across the communication link, and in some cases, the systems can switch task to lightly-loaded processors to achieve load balancing. Communication between processors is by *message passing* or *remote procedure calls*.

Tightly-coupled multiprocessing uses a single storage shared by the various processors and a single operating system that controls all the processors and system hardware. Communication is by *shared memory*. The BBN Butterfly and the IBM 3090 are examples of tightly-coupled systems.

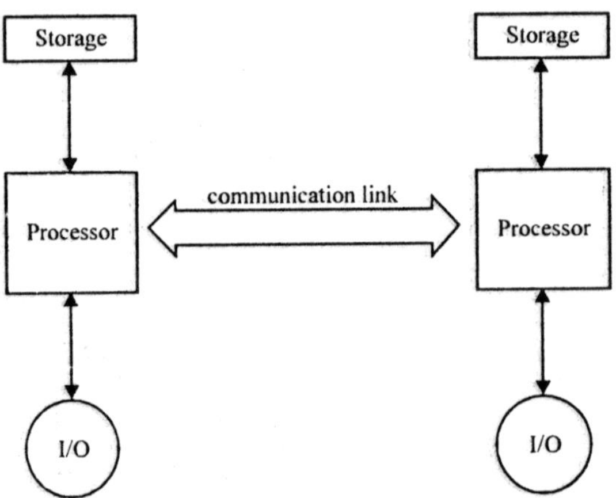

Fig. 12.8. Loosely-coupled multiprocessing.

A key concern in tightly-coupled systems is *contention* over shared memory. Various studies indicate that balancing the architecture and distributing the load across the system minimizes contention. A hardware approach called a *combining switch* handles multiple references to a single location in a manner requiring only a single access to the memory location; this technique is discussed in the next section.

Fetch-And-Add

We discussed the *testandset* instruction and showed how it can be used to implement mutual exclusion primitives. In a uniprocessor system, clearly only one processor can be attempting testandset at a time. If a lock variable is available to be captured, then the next process to run (and execute testandset) will ordinarily capture the lock. In multiprocessing systems the problem is more complex, because many processors could be executing testandset simultaneously, so the system needs to be able to arbitrate these requests.

Testandset has another weakness, namely that each of the pending operation requires a separate memory access; these are performed sequentially because only one access to a memory location may normally occur at a time. Worse yet, only one processor actually captures the lock and all the others fail; this can result in the considerable waste associated with busy waiting.

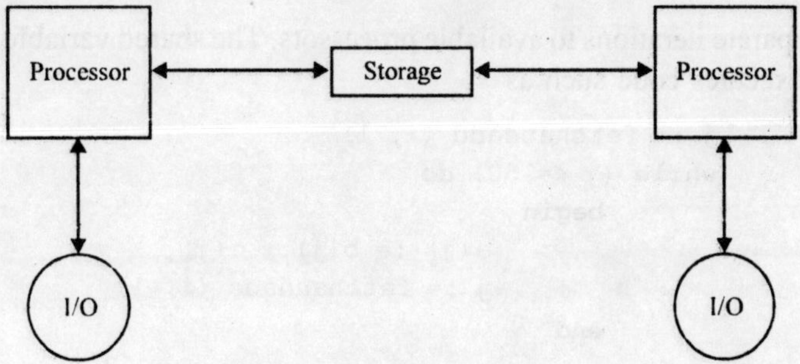

Fig. 12.9. Tightly-coupled multiprocessing.

Memory contention can certainly occur in uniprocessor systems as I/O and processing occur in parallel. But this is minor compared to the potential for collisions in multiprocessors, and especially in massive parallel processors. Such collisions can quickly saturate various kinds of interconnection networks, causing serious performance problems.

To deal with this problem, the designers of NYU's *Ultracomputer* developed the *fetch-and-add instruction*. The indivisible (or "atomic") instruction

```
fetchandadd (s, i)
```

increments shared variable *s* by *i* and returns the original value of *s*. When a several processors simultaneously execute this instruction on *s*, the switching elements in the interconnection network performs an operation called *combining*; it adds the increment values of all the colliding fetchandadd instructions to form a sum, *I*, and then performs only the single instruction

```
fetchandadd (s, I)
```

on shared variables *s*. This memory location is thus accessed only once to get the value of *s*. The switching network then returns the *unique* value s, $s + i_1$, $s + i_2$, ... to the various processes referencing *s*. This is a way of serializing the requests.

Suppose a multiprocessing system assigns any available processor from its pool of identical processors to the ready process at the head of the ready list. Maintaining such a ready list as a shared queue structure is made more efficient by fetchandadd (than with testandset); several processors attempting to place processes in the list collide and the fetchandadd sequentializes the accesses.

A particular elegant use of fetchandadd occurs when assigning separate iterations of a loop to different processors to be executed in parallel.

In sequential Pascal, we might write a statement such as

```
for i   := 1 to 50 do
        a(i) := b(i) + c(i)
```

All 50 iterations of the loop can be executed in parallel because the assignments are independent of one another. So, the above loop can be replaced by a parallel versions such as

```
forall I := 1 to 50 do
        a(i) := b(i) + c(i)
```

which assigns the separate iterations to available processors. The shared variable, *I*, is initially set to 1. Each processor executes code such as

```
j := fetchandadd (i, 1)
while (j <= 50) do
        begin
                a(j) := b(j) + c(j)
                j := fetchandadd (i, 1)
        end
```

The beauty of this code is that it is not sensitive to the number of available processors. Available processors get as much work as they can handle. If 50 processors can work on the expression at once, then as each does the fetchandadd (i, 1) it will receive a unique number from 1 to 50, designating the array element it is supposed to work with. If fewer than 50 processors are available, the while/do loops running on the available processors will keep requesting more work until all 50 elements of array *a* have been calculated.

Clearly, the fetchandadd combining mechanism is expensive to build. The point is that it delivers high-performance parallel computing. Eventually may make it economical to incorporate combining switches into machines for commercial use.

Multiprocessor Operating System Organizations

The ability to exploit parallelism in the hardware and in the programs is central to multiprocessing system. Adding more processors, as well as the complex connections to storage and I/O processors, adds considerably to the cost of the hardware.

A major difference between multiprocessor and uniprocessor operating systems is certainly the organization and structure of the operating system with regard to the multiple processors. The basic operating systems organizations for multiprocessors are master/slave, separate executive for each processor, and symmetric (or anonymous) treatment of all processors.

Master/Slave

In *master/slave multiprocessor organization* one processor is designated as the *master* and the others are the *slaves*. The master performs input/output and computation. The slaves can run compute-bound jobs effectively, but I/O-bound jobs running on the slaves cause frequent calls for services only the master can perform. From a reliability standpoint, if a slave fails, some computing capability is lost, but the system can still function. If the master fails, the system cannot perform I/O.

Thus the largest problem with master/slave multiprocessing is the *asymmetry* of the hardware.

Only the *master* may execute the operating system. A slave processor can execute only user programs. When a process executing on a slave requires the attention of the operating system, it generates an interrupt and waits for the master to handle the interrupt. Interestingly, the operating system does not have to be reentrant, since it can be used by only one processor at a time, and in behalf of only one user at a time.

Separate Executives

In the *separate executives* organization, each processor has its own operating system, and responds to interrupts from users running on that processor. A process assigned to run on a particular processor runs to completion on that processor. Some tables contain information global to the entire system (for example, the list of processors known to the system); access to these tables must be controlled with mutual exclusion techniques.

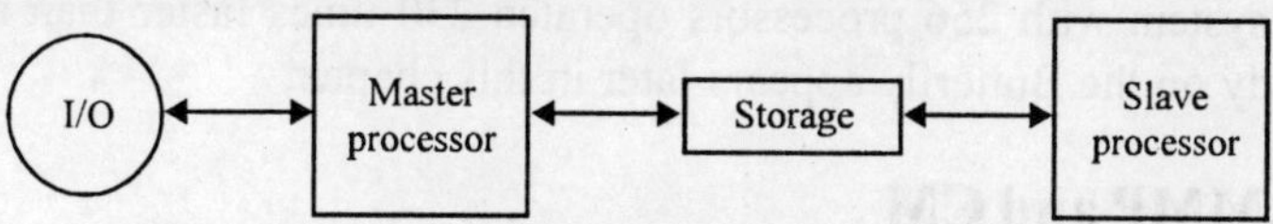

Fig. 12.10. Master/slave multiprocessing.

The separate executives organization is more reliable than the master/slave organization; the failure of a single processor is unlikely to cause catastrophic system failure.

Each processor control its own dedicated resources, such as files and I/O devices. I/O interrupts return directly to the processors that initiate them. Reconfiguring the I/O devices on the system may involve switching the devices to different processors with different operating system.

There is minimal contention over operating system data because the data are distributed among the individual operating systems for their own use. The processors do not cooperate on the execution of an individual process. Some of the processors may remain idle while one processor executes a lengthy process.

Symmetrical Organization

Symmetrical multiprocessing is the most complex organization to implement, and the most powerful. All processors are identical. The operating system manages a pool of identical processors, any one of which may be used to control any I/O device or to reference any storage unit.

Because many processors may be executing the operating system at once, re-entrant code and mutual exclusion are necessary. Because of the symmetry, it is possible to balance the work load more precisely than with the other organizations.

Conflict resolution hardware and software are important. Conflicts between processors attempting to access the same storage at the same time are ordinarily resolved by hardware. Conflicts in accessing system-wide data are ordinarily resolved by software.

Symmetrical multiprocessing systems are generally the most reliable—a failure in one processor causes the operating system to remove that processor from its pool of available processors and to note the difficulty. The system may continue to function at reduced levels (i.e., *graceful degradation*) while repairs are made.

A process running on a symmetric multiprocessor may be run at different times by any of the equivalent processors. The operating system *floats* from one processor to the next. The processor currently responsible for system data and system functions is called the *executive processor*. Only one processor at a time may be executive—this prevents conflicts over global system information.

Contention problems can become severe, especially because several processors may be in the supervisor at once. Careful design of system data structures is essential to prevent excessive *lockouts*. A technique that minimizes contention is to divide the system data structures into separate and independent entities that may be locked individually.

Even in completely symmetrical multiprocessing systems, the addition of new processors does not cause system throughput to increase by the rated capacity of the new processor. There are many reasons for this, including additional operating system overhead, increased contention for system, resources, and hardware delays in switching and routing transmissions between an increased number of components. A number of performance studies have been attempted. In one experiment, an early Butterfly system with 256 processors operated 230 times faster than a single processor system. A case study on the Butterfly appears later in this chapter.

Case Study: C.MMP and CM

Researchers at Carnegie-Mellon University have developed several significant multiprocessor systems. These include C.mmp and Cm. C.mmp was a 16-processors tightly-coupled system consisting of PDP-11/40 minicomputers. The processors shared 16 storage modules through a crossbar-switch matrix. Accesses from any processor to any storage module had the same cost because of the symmetry of the connection scheme. Sixteen storage references could occur concurrently.

Cm is a lossely-coupled system consisting of 50 LSI-II microprocessors. It is constructed from processor-storage pairs called *computer modules*. Each of these is referred to as a Cm. Cm's are grouped into five *clusters*. Clusters are connected by *interclusters buses*; communication between clusters is by *message passing*. The cost of a storage reference depends on whether it is directed to a module's local storage to the storage of another module in the same cluster, or to the storage of a module in another cluster. These three different types of storage references have a cost ratio of 1:3:12. Thus, optimal performance depends on ensuring that most storage references in an application are directed to the local storage of the modules making those references. These kinds of performance issues are important in loosely-coupled systems. Two operating systems developed for the Cm system are StarOS and Medusa.

Schwan and Jones describe processor and memory scheduling heuristics for Cm, and they introduce the notion of high-level language constructs called *resources directives* that enable programmers to supply useful information to the resource allocation mechanisms. For example, resources directives may specify proximity values for objects to ensure that they are optimally placed in the same Cm, in the same cluster, or in different clusters (the default action leaves the placement decision to the operating system). Some people would argue that requiring users to issue such machine-dependent directives is contrary to conventional wisdom, which has the operating system performing dynamic resource allocation. But in supercomputing environments the single most important goal is processing performance; users of such sophisticated systems are often willing to assume much greater responsibilities to realize this goal.

Both C.mmp and Cm have been used to solve a large number of problems exhibiting a high degree of inherent parallelism. In many cases, nearly linear improvements in performance (over the uniprocessor approach) have been achieved. A *linear improvement* means that with *n* processors the job will execute *n* times faster. The results of these efforts have demonstrated the importance of large-scale multiprocessing as a means of greatly reducing the execution times of highly-parallel algorithms.

Case Study: The Butterfly

Permission credit: This case study was condensed and adapted with permission from documentation supplied to the author by BBM Advanced Computer Inc. of Cambridge, Massachusetts. The author is grateful to Deborah Fanton of BBN Advanced Computers Inc. for facilitating the preparation and review of these materials.

The *Butterfly* is a multiprocessor system developed by BBN Advanced Computers Inc. of Cambridge, Massachusetts. The multistage processor interconnection mechanism, called the *Butterfly switch*, enables up to 128 processors to be connected and to execute a total of over 300 MIPS.

Groups of processors called *clusters* may be dedicated to specific applications; this is especially significant in real-time applications. A cluster may run one of two operating systems—the pSOS real-time operating system developed by Software Concepts, Inc., or the Mach 1000 system developed at Carnegie Mellon University and extended by BBN; Mach 1000 is based on UNIX operating systems.

The Butterfly is an MIMD multiprocessor in which each processor may execute independently on private data or shared data; processors can access one another's data using symmetric shared global memory. Applications programmers need not specify which tasks are to execute on which processors, although they may do so if they wish.

Each identical processor card contains a complete computer system, including a Motorola 68020 microprocessor, a 68882 floating point coprocessor, a 68851 pagedmemory management unit, a Butterfly switch interface, and on-board memory.

Users may add processor cards to add computing power. The Butterfly uses the *X* Window System developed at MIT. It communicates over distributed computing networks using Ethernet with TCP/IP protocols. The virtual address space can be as large as four gigabytes.

The Mach 1000 operating system extends Berkeley's UNIX 4.3 BSD operating system to a multiprocessing, shared-memory environment. Mach 1000 performs *dynamic load balancing* among processors so that available processor capacity is utilized.

Jobs may run independently of one another, or they may communicate asynchronously. Processors may share some or all of the system memory. Primary memory can be as large as 512 megabytes. Access to a remote memory on another processor is performed almost as fast as access to a processor's local memory.

The Butterfly is a *homogeneous multiprocessor*—all processor cards are identical and any processor may perform any task. This simplifies programming because the programmer need not be concerned with assigning tasks to specific processors, nor with how many processors there are. This also facilitates *scaling* and *fault tolerance;* programs need not be recorded to run on larger or smaller configurations, and programs can run on available processors even in the presence of failed processors.

Each processor card delivers 2.5 MIPS. The *processor node controller* (PNC) on each card provides multiprocessing capabilities not available in the 68020. The PNC sends messages to other processors over the Butterfly switch and receives messages from the switch. The PNC provides various indivisible atomic operations to application programs. For example, *atomicadd* enables one processor to read and increment a memory location while preventing other processors from accessing the location simultaneously. Atomic operations are used to implement mutual exclusion constructs in the operating system.

The Butterfly Switch

The butterfly switch uses *packet switching* techniques like those used in computer networks to effect interprocessor communication, handle remote memory access, and interface with the PNCs.

Data operations on the MC68020 trigger the switch. A data request issue by a processor causes the local MMU (memory management unit) to convert the virtual address of the data to a physical address. References to local memory may occur directly. References to remote memory cause the local PNC to form a *message packet* consisting of the *destination address* and the *data request*; the message is then passed between switching elements in the Butterfly switch to the destination where it is processed.

Figure 12.11 shows a 16-input/16-output Butterfly switch module. Each of the eight boxes in the figure is a custom VLSI chip containing a 4-input/4-output crossbar switch. By combining eight of these chips in two banks of four switches each, we implement a multistage network with only 16 internal paths. Each switching phase has a 125-nanosecond delay, so messages arrive more slowly than if travelling over point-to-point connections, but this is acceptable considering the greatly reduced cost of the switching network.

To see how the Butterfly switch works, let us follow a message from the processor at switch input node 5 to the processor at switch output node 14 (= 1110 binary). The PNC creates a message packet with the destination switch output node address and the data to be transmitted, and passes this to the first switching chip. This chip strips off the two low-order bits (10) of the destination switch output node address, and uses these bits to direct the message to the switch's output port 2. The appropriate switch chip in the second column now receives the message packet and strips off the remaining two address bits to select this chip's output port 3. At this point the proper circuit path has been established and the data transmission proceeds until an end-of-data indication is reached.

The switch makes all references to memory appear to be logically equivalent; the programmer does not differentiate between local references and remote references. A read from a remote memory location causes the PNC to send a request for the data to the appropriate processor card. The remote PNC receives the message, reads the contents from the specified location, and returns a reply message to the source processor card.

All the switching is in the hardware and is completely transparent to the application programmer. The Butterfly switch is tightly coupled; this eliminates the need for buffering messages within the switch as is often necessary in loosely-coupled designs. Data can be transferred between pairs of processors at a net rate of approximately 24 Mbits/second. Many such transfers may be in progress at once, yielding a maximum 4-gigabits-per-second transfer rate.

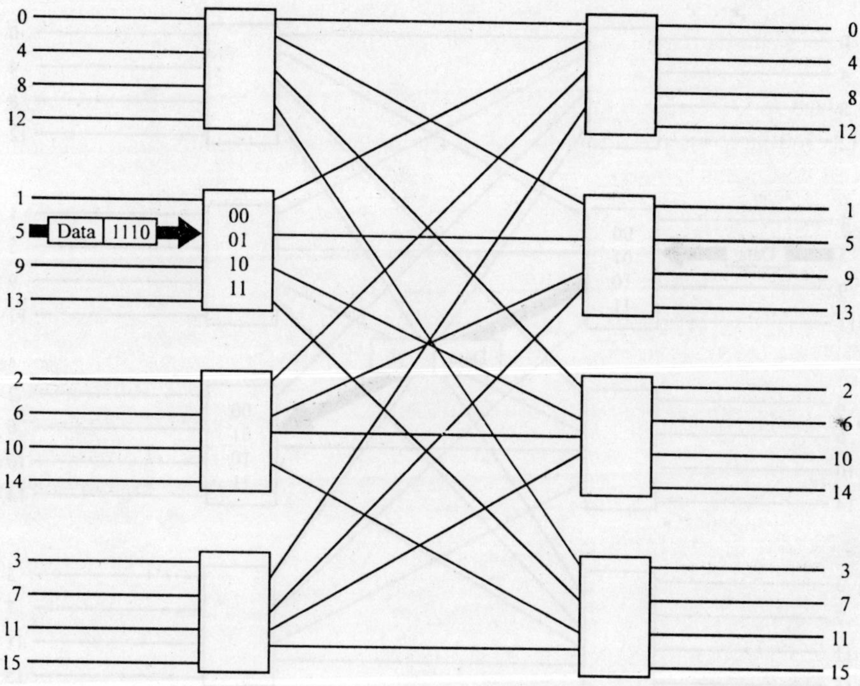

Fig. 12.11. First step through the Butterfly switch.

Contention can become a problem in shared-memory systems, especially as separate processors attempt to access the same memory locations. The Butterfly has several features that reduce contention. Each of the switching elements in the Butterfly switch has four independent output ports, so arriving messages are likely to exit simultaneously at different ports. The Butterfly switch is *nonblocking*; all but one of the messages that collide at the same output ports are returned to their sources to free the switch paths. The PNC waits for a short random period and transmits again over an alternate path. A blocking system would allow waiting messages to back up in the switch until they could be serviced; this could cause congestion in the switch and consequent performance degradation.

To maximize parallelism and minimize contention, the Butterfly can distribute data across its various local memories. A *scattering routine* is provided in the Butterfly's library of operating system routines.

The Butterfly may be expanded by adding more processor cards and switching elements; this does not require additional programming. This kind of modular expansion differs from that on bus-based multiprocessors where the bus may become saturated and require the addition of other buses and appropriate software for coordinating the separate buses.

Most Butterfly systems incorporate extra switching nodes to allow two separate paths between every pair of processor card. This allows messages "backed off" from the switch to be transmitted almost instantaneously.

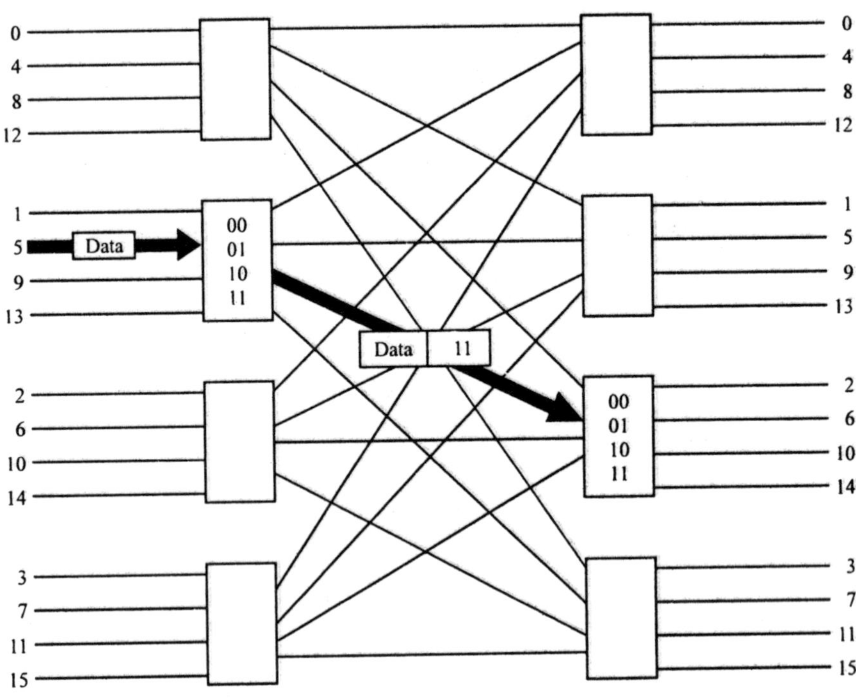

Fig. 12.12. Second step through the Butterfly Switch.

The Mach 1000 Operating System

Mach provides various means for accessing specific processors and for interprocessor communication. Mach uses its own virtual memory subsystem. Memory region have *inheritance* and *protection* attributes. Inheritance provides shared memory between related processes.

The Mach kernel uses various *objects*. *Per process address maps* are objects that define a process's virtual address space. *Virtual memory objects* define the backing store for a group pf pages, keep track of where the pages are, and identify the paging routines. *Shared memory maps* are objects that enable separate per-process address maps to share the same virtual memory object. *Resident page tables* are objects that maintain the status of physical pages (free, active, or inactive).

Pages to be swapped are placed in the *disk buffer cache* where they remain until they must be written. Thus, page-outs generally only result in high-speed processor-card-to-processor-card copying; Mach spreads the disk buffer cache across the memories in all the processor cards. With a large buffer cache, it is likely that a needed page will be in the buffer cache and will be accessible at very high speed compared with the time required for to a disk access.

A user may create a new process on a specific processor with the *fork-and-bind ()* system call. Potions of virtual memory may be allocated to a specific processor with the *vm-allocate-and-bind ()* call; this call is helpful in establishing shared memory to support interprocess communication. Mach 1000 currently executes single-threaded tasks.

Mach 1000 enables processors to be grouped in *clusters*. The *public cluster* contains processors that any user can access. The *free cluster* contains idle processors. *Private clusters* are owned by their creators.

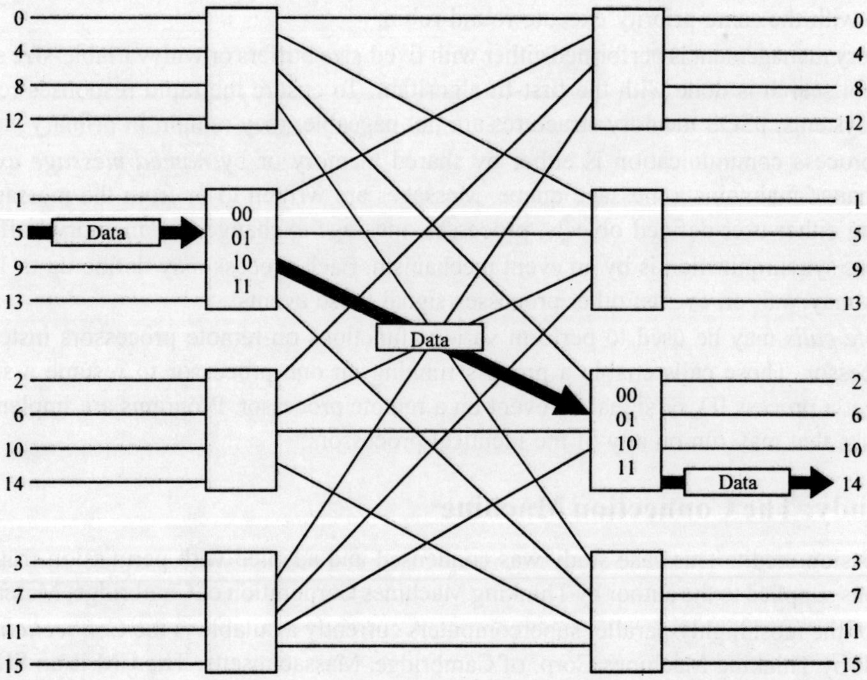

Fig. 12.13. Third step through the Butterfly switch.

Mach's virtual memory scheme has a *copy-on-write* capability (Fi89). Normally, only a single copy of data being read by several tasks exits. Only when a process attempts to modify that data does the process get its own copy. This simple scheme saves considerable time and memory.

To simply shared-memory parallel programming, Mach 1000 supports the Uniform System run-time applications library. This optional set of system calls frees the programmer from explicitly managing memory resources and processor resources.

The memory management system tries to keep all memory modules busy; in doing so, it spreads the work around to avoid contention over one or a few memory modules. Processor management tries to keep all the processors busy. Each processor can be given its own set of frequently-referenced data. Variables can be shared among processors so changes are immediately apparent to all processors.

Processors may also be schedules just once at the beginning of the run time. Static processor scheduling assign specific tasks to specific processors; dynamic load balancing distributes the work to keep all the processors busy and achieve maximum processing throughput. Both methods have their uses for specific applications.

The pSOS Real-Time Operating System

The pSOS operating system is a fast, predictable-response operating system for supporting real-time applications (BN88). Processes may be scheduled with 255 priority levels. Processes may be designated as nonpreemptible. Processes may be either running, ready, blocked, or suspended. Processes with the same priority execute round-robin.

Memory management is performed either with fixed-size buffers or with variable-size segments; the segment search is done with the first-fit algorithm. To ensure the rapid responses required in real-time systems, pSOS memory structures are not pageable; they remain in primary storage.

Interprocess communication is either by shared memory or by *named message exchanges*. Each exchange maintains a message queue. Messages are written to or from the message queue. Objects are either user-defined objects, processes, message exchanges, or memory buffers.

Process synchronization is by an event mechanism. Each process may define up to 15 events. A process may wait on events; other processes signal those events.

Remote calls may be used to perform various functions on remote processors instead of the local processor. Those calls enable a process running on one processor to resume a suspended process, get a process ID, or signal an event on a remote processor. Programs are implemented as sets of tasks that may run on any of the identical processors.

Case Study: The Connection Machine

Permission credit: This case study was condensed and adapted with permission from various publications supplied to the author by Thinking Machines Corporation of Cambridge, Massachusetts.

One of the most highly-parallel supercomputers currently available is the *Connection Machine* (CM) built by Thinking Machines Corp. of Cambridge, Massachusetts. The CM is an SIMD array processor; it has up to 64K (65,536) processors and can execute several billion instructions per second. No other machine today has attempted such massive parallelism. The CM was designed by Daniel Hillis and is based on work he did while a graduate student at MIT working with Marvin Minsky, one of the founders of the field of artificial intelligence.

It is simply too tedious to program each of tens of thousands of processors separately. Therefore, programmers attempt to take advantage of *data-level parallelism* i.e., applications in which it is possible to perform the same operations simultaneously on perhaps thousands of separate data items. Such applications include database retrieval, text searching, and image processing. The parallelism is achieved automatically by cooperation between the CM and its compilers.

The CM processors are controlled by as many as four front-end computers. Each of the processors has a relatively small local memory. Interprocess or communication uses a packet switching approach.

The CM is programmed in parallel extensions of Fortran, C, and Lisp. A 10-gigabyte mass storage is connected via a high-bandwidth I/O channel. The high-resolution (1280 × 1024) color display can be refreshed at 1-gigabit per second; this is sufficiently fast for real-time animation.

Each processor has an arithmetic-logic unit (ALU), 64K bits of bit-addressable memory, four 1-bit flag registers, an optional floating point accelerator, a router interface, a connection grid interface, and an I/O interface. The processors communicate by data parallel message passing; every processor can send or fetch data to or from the local memory of another processor simultaneously. The largest CM-2 can have 512 megabytes of memory.

The Connection Machine has two built-in processor interconnection schemes namely a *broadcast network*, which ties every processor to a central computer, and a *16-dimensional hypercube*, which connects all the processors together so that no message from one processor need pass through more than 16 connections to reach any destination processor.

Data Parallel Computation

A front-end system such as a VAX, a Sun, or a Symbolics system controls interaction with the CM. Users work on the front-end system; the front passes appropriate work to the CM and receives responses.

With data parallel computing the CM assigns a separate processor to every data element. Processors process information in their own local memories and they can communicate with one another.

The front-end machine stores and executes the program. The CM stores the data objects. The front end issues commands to the CM to operate in parallel on data objects. The front end can also operate on data in the CM memory. Instructions are broadcast to the CM processors by the front end; these instructions are then executed simultaneously by all the processors.

The CM uses *ANSI Fortran 8x* which includes various array-processing extensions. The CM assembly language is called *Paris*; the various high-level language compilers translate source code to Paris.

The processors can communicate with memory at a total rate of 300 gigabytes per second. At capacity, the CM-2 can perform 32-bit additions at 2500 MIPS; with its floating point accelerator option it can perform 3500 megaflops using single precision, or 2500 megalops using double precision.

The *router* allows any processor to reference any memory location in any of the local memories, thus providing the view of a very large shared memory. The router typically performs 32-bit data accesses at 80 million to 250 million per second.

Instead of simply using a two-dimensional grid, CM-2 enables grids such as 256 × 256, 1024 × 64, 8 × 8192, 64 × 32 × 32, 16 × 16 × 16 × 16, and 8 × 8 × 4 × 8 × 8 × 4 to be formed dynamically. This makes it convenient to configure the Connection Machine to the parallel structures appropriate for different kinds of problems.

The front end sends Paris instructions to the CM-2. The CM-2 appears as an extension to the front end. Paris includes options such as integer arithmetic, floating point arithmetic, interprocessor communication, vector summation, matrix multiplication, and sorting. Paris instructions are processed by a sequencer, which breaks down the instructions into more fundamental operations. The sequencer then broadcasts operations to the processors.

The CM routes the separate elements of each data structure to separate processors so that each element of data structure can be processed simultaneously. A scalar involved in an operation that yields a parallel data structure (such as multiplying every element of an array by a constant) is broadcast to all the processors.

Parallel data can be involved in an operation that yields a scalar result such as summing the elements of an array. Such as operation would be performed on the CM by organizing the elements into a *balanced binary tree*.

Connection Machine Fortran

The Connection Machines uses ANSI standard Fortran 77 extended to include *ANSI Fortran 8x*. The 8x features treat arrays as *parallel data structures*, thus enabling the separate processors of the Connection Machine to operate on each element of an array simultaneously. Fortran 8x is an evolving standard so some of the features described here may change. Some Fortran 8x features implemented on the CM include

- vector-valued subscript
- the *FORALL* statement (which can assign values to all the elements of an array simultaneously)
- various intrinsic functions such as *DIAGONAL, REPLICATE, RANK, PROJECT, FIRSTLOC*, and LASTLOC.

The Current version of Fortran runs under the Ultrix operating system on a DEC VAX front ends with a VAXBI bus connected to a Connection Machine.

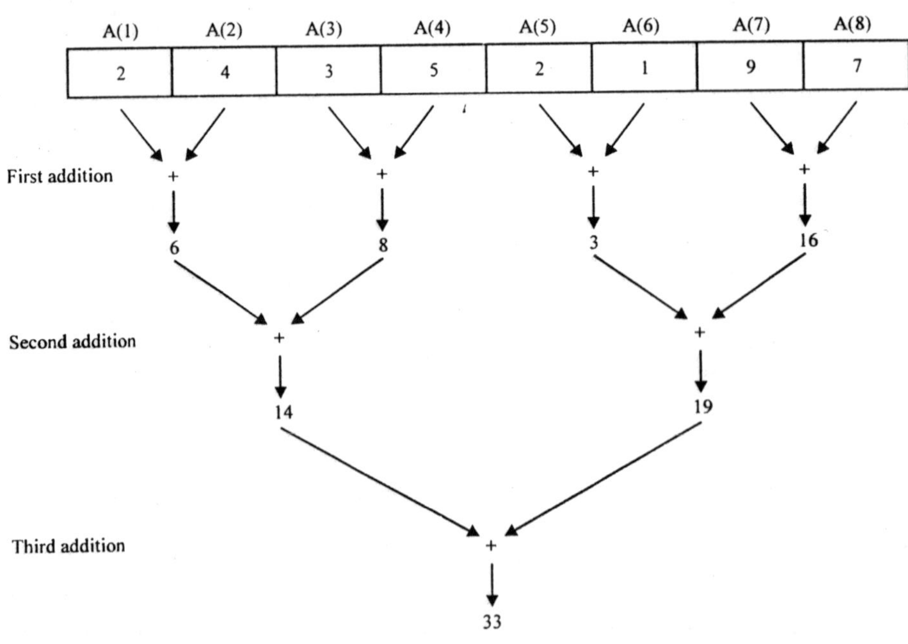

Fig. 12.14. Summing the elements of an array in parallel with the Connection Machine.

Let us consider some of the array processing features of Fortran 8x. The statement

```
A = B + C
```

works equally well for scalars, vectors, matrices, and *n*-dimensional arrays; it adds all the elements of *C* to the corresponding elements of *B* and stores the results in the corresponding elements of *A*.

Array elements are placed in the CM, one per processor. The communications grid of the CM is a natural environment for array processing; the grid can mirror the structures of various types of arrays. *Context flags* are set to highlight all the elements of an array to be processed; the CM then processes only those elements simultaneously.

Fortran 8x includes the *array reduction operations* of *SUM, PRODUCT, MAXVAL, MINVAL, ANY,* and *ALL*. It also provides operations such as a vector dot product (*DOTPRODUCT*) and matrix multiplication (*MATMUL*).

Given matrix *M* with 30 rows and 56 columns, the call

```
SUM (M, DIM = 1)
```

Produces a 56-element vector of the column sums; the call

```
MAXVAL (M, DIM = 2)
```

Produces a 30-element vector of the maximum values stored in each of the rows.

Reduction operations may be modified by a *mask argument*. The mask is simply a boolean vector specifying which subset of the elements of an array is to be processed; the CM processes only those elements.

Fortran 8x includes various operations that treat entire arrays as individual objects. These includes *MERGE*, which merges two arrays under the control of a mask, *SPREAD* which replicates an array along a new dimension, *TRANSPOSE* which transposes a two-dimensional matrix, *CSHIFT* which circular shifts an array, and *EOSHIFT* which does an end-off array shift.

The *WHERE* statement uses a boolean mask array to select the elements of an array to be processed. The statement

```
WHERE (A .GE. 0) A = SQRT (A)
```

causes each element of *A* that is greater than or equal to zero to be replaced by its square root; negative elements remain as is. All selected elements of the array are processed simultaneously.

The statement

```
WHERE (B .NE. 0)
      C = A / B
ELSEWHERE
      C = INFINITY
END WHERE
```

divides only the nonzero elements of *B* into the corresponding elements of *A* and stores the results in the corresponding elements of *C*; for those elements of *B* that are equal to zero, the corresponding elements of *C* are set to *INFINITY*. Again, all appropriate elements of the arrays are processed simultaneously.

The *FORALL* statement enables the use of indices (and additionally a mask, if desired) to specify the array elements to be processed. The statement

```
FORALL (I - 1:N, J = 1:N) H(I,J) = 1.0 / REAL (I + J - 1)
```

sets all elements of rows *1* to *N* and columns *1* to *N* to the indicated expression; the value of the expression in this statement is sensitive to both the row subscript and the column subscript of each particular element.

The statement

```
FORALL (I = 1:N, J = 1:N, I .GT. J) H(I,J) = 0.0
```

uses a mask expression to zero every element of the array below the diagonal.

Interprocessor Communication in Fortran 8x

Fortran 8x enables the specification of *array sections*. These are portions of arrays that may be used anywhere entire arrays are used. If A is a 10 × 10 matrix, then the upper left quadrant of *A* is specified by *A(1:5, 1:5)*, which is a 5 × 5 array. The upper-right quadrant of *A* is specified by *A*(1:5, 6:10), also a 5 × 5 array. Then statement

```
A (1:5, 1:5) = A (1:5, 6:10)
```

copies the array section consisting of the upper-right quadrant of *A* to the array section consisting of the upper-left quadrant of *A*. The statement

```
A (1:3, 1:4) = A (1:10:4, 1:10:3)
```

replaces the 3 × 4 array section at the top lefty portion of *A* with the array 3 × 4 section consisting of these selected elements

```
A(1,1)    A(1,4)    A(1,7)    A(1,10)
A(5,1)    A(5,4)    A(5,7)    A(5,10)
A(9,1)    A(9,4)    A(9,7)    A(9,10)
```

Fortran 8x enables the use of vector-valued subscripts to effect interprocessor communication. A *subscript vector* is used to select elements from a *source vector*; these elements may then be assigned to a *destination vector*. Remembering that individual elements are stored at different processors, this provides a straightforward means of interprocessor communication. For example, to transmit values from the processors storing array *V* to the processors storing array *B*, we might use a series of statement such as

```
S = [1,2,2,3,3,3,2,2,1,7,1,1,3,3,3,2]
V = [15,20,25,30,35,40,45]
B = V(S)
```

After these statements are executed on the Connection Machine, the elements of *B* will be

```
[15,20,20,25,25,25,20,20,15,45,15,15,25,25,25,20]
```

Fortran 77 certainly has the ability to perform the types of operations we have discussed in this section, but these operations are performed on individual scalars sequentially; Fortran 8x running on the Connection Machine operates on every element of an array simultaneously, offering a huge increase in performance.

Data Parallel Programming: The Sieve of Eratosthenes

The sample Fortran 8x program finds all prime numbers less than 100,000 by the method of the Sieve of Eratosthenes. The *PRIME* array is a 99999-element boolean array, each element of which is initially set to *.FALSE.* Elements are set to *.TRUE.* as their subscripts are determined to be prime. *CANDIDATE* is a 99999-element boolean array with each element initially set to *.TRUE.* with the exception of *CANDIDATE (1)*. Elements are set to *.FALSE.* as it is determined that their subscripts are not prime. Statement 20 returns the subscript of the first *.TRUE.* element in *CANDIDATE*, initially 2, so this element of the *PRIME* array is set to *.TRUE.* The *FORALL* statement now sets every elements whose subscript is a multiple of 2 to *.FLASE.* because these subscripts cannot be primes. The *IF* statement tests if there are any remaining candidates to be checked. If not, the subroutine returns the *PRIME* array. If candidates remain, the program proceeds to statement 20, where it gets the subscript of the next candidate, identifies this number as a prime, removes all multiples of this number from candidacy, and so on.

```
      SUBROUTINE FINDPRIMES (PRIME)
      PARAMETER (N = 99999)
      LOGICAL PRIME(N), CANDIDATE(N)
      PRIME= .FALSE.
      CANDIDATE = .TRUE.
      CANDIDATE(1) = .FALSE.
   20 NEXTPRIME = MINLOC([1,N], CANDIDATE)
      PRIME(NEXTPRIME) = .TRUE.
      FORALL (I = 1:N, MOD(I, NEXTPRIME) .EQ. 0)
          CANDIDATE(I) = .FALSE.
      IF (ANY(CANDIDATE)) GO TO 20
      RETURN
      END
```

Fig. 12.15. ***Finding prime numbers using the Sieve of Eratosthenes with Fortran 8x on the Connection Machine.***

Let us consider how the massive parallelism of the Connection Machine speeds the execution of this algorithm. Each of the parallel operations requires two "cycles" of the machine (because the arrays are larger than the number of processors in the machine). Each array is initialized in parallel, the smallest candidate is located with a parallel search, the multiples of *NEXTPRIME* are eliminated in parallel, and the test if any candidates remain is performed in parallel. Each of these operations on a sequential machine requires execution time proportional to the size of the array. On the Connection Machine the execution time flattens to a single "cycle" for arrays smaller than 64K; for arrays larger than 64K execution time is proportional to the number of elements divided by 64K (and rounded up to the next higher integer).

Summary

A multiprocessing system employs several processors. Few programs written today exploit concurrency. The real hope in this area is for hardware, compilers, and operating system to detect parallelism automatically.

Two common techniques used to exploit implicit parallelism are loop distribution and tree height reduction. In loop distribution, iterations that may be performed independently of one another are separated into concurrently executable units. Tree height reduction applies the commutative, associative, and distributive properties of arithmetic to rearrange algebraic expressions to make them amenable to concurrent execution. The never wait rule states that it is better to give a processor a task that may or may not be used eventually than to let processor sit idle.

The most common processor interconnection schemes are the shared bus, the crossbar switch matrix, the hypercube, and the general multistage network. The shared bus uses a single communication path between all the functional units. Its disadvantages are that the entire system fails if bus fails, the transmissions rate of the system is constrained by the transmission rate of the bus, and contention for the bus can cause performance degradation.

In the crossbar-switch matrix there is a separate path to every storage unit. This allows transmission to and from all possible pairs of storage units simultaneously. The main disadvantage of this organization is the complexity of the crossbar switch.

Loosely-coupled multiprocessing involves connecting two or more independent computer systems via a communication link. Tightly-coupled multiprocessing uses a single storage shared by all the processors.

The basic operating system organizations for multiprocessors are master/slave, separate executives, and symmetric treatment of all processors. Master/slave is the easiest to implement. Only the master may execute the operating system. The operating system does not have to be reentrant, and mutual exclusion for system data is greatly simplified. A failure to the master causes catastrophic system failure.

In the separate executives organization each processor has its own operating system and controls it own resources. A process runs to completion on the processor to which it is assigned.

Symmetrical multiprocessing is the most complex organization to implement and the most powerful. The operating system manages a pool of identical processors. A failure of a single processor causes the operating system to remove the processor from the pool of processors, but the system continues to function. A process may be run at different times by different processors. Contention can become a problem because several processors may be in the supervisor state at once.

Several multiprocessor system were discussed, including C.mmp, Cm*, the Butterfly. And the Connection Machine.

Parallel computation is growing in importance and is certain to be a major influence on the evaluation of operating systems.

13

File and Database Systems

Introduction

A *file* is a named collection of data. It normally resides on a secondary storage device such as disk or tape. It may be manipulated as a unit by operations such as

- *Open*—Prepare a file to be referenced.
- *Close*—Prevent further reference to a file until it is reopened.
- *Create*—Build a new file.
- *Destroy*—Remove a file.
- *Copy*—Create another version of the file with a new name.
- *Rename*—Change the name of a file.
- *List*—Print or display the contents of a file.

Individual data items within the file may be manipulated by operations like

- *Read*—input a data item to a process from a file.
- *Write*—Output a data items from a process to a file.
- *Update*—Modify an existing data item in a file.
- *Insert*—Add a new data item to a file.
- *Delete*—Remove a data item from a file.

Files may be characterized by

- *Volatility*—This refers to the frequency with which additions and deletions are made to a file.
- *Activity*—This refers to the percentage of a file's records accessed during a given period of time.
- *Size*—This refers to the amount of information stored in the file.

The File System

An important component of an operating system is the *file system* (Go86). File systems generally contain

- *Access methods*—These are concerned with the manner in which data stored in files is accessed.
- *File management*—This is concerned with providing the mechanisms for files to be stored, referenced, shared, and secured.
- *Auxiliary storage management*—This is concerned with allocating space for files on secondary storage devices.
- *File integrity mechanism*—These are concerned with guaranteeing that the information in a file is uncorrupted. When file integrity is assured, whatever information is supposed to be in a file is there, information not supposed to be in a file is kept out of the file.

The file system is primarily concerned with managing secondary storage space, particularly disk storage. For the purposes of this discussion, let us assume an environment of a large-scale timesharing system supporting approximately 100 active terminals accessible to a user community of several thousand users. Each of these users may have several *accounts* on the computer which they use to distinguish work performed, perhaps for various *projects*. Each of these accounts may have files. Some files might be small, such as a letter to be sent in an electronic mail system. Other files may be large, such as a master list of parts in an inventory control application.

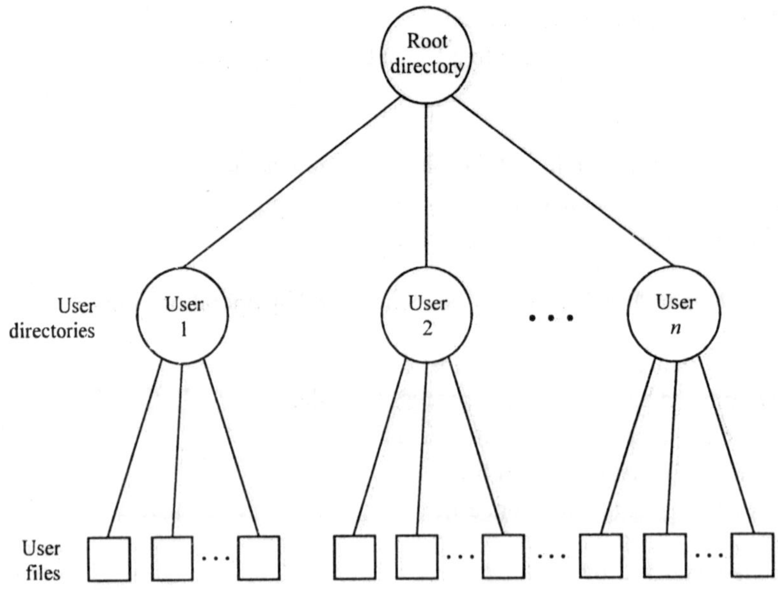

Fig. 13.1. Two-level hierarchical file system.

On large-scale timesharing systems and distributed processing systems, it is common for user accounts to contain between 10 and 100 files. Thus with a user community of several thousand users, a system's disks might easily contain 50,000 to 100,000 or more separate files. These files need to be accessed quickly to keep response times small.

A file system for this type of environment may be organized as follows. A *root* is used to indicate where on disk the *root directory* begins. The root directory points to the various *user directories*. A user directory contains an entry for each of a user's files; each entry points to where the corresponding file is stored on disk.

File names need only be unique within a given user directory. The system name of a file, however, must be unique within the file system. In *hierarchically structured file systems*, the system name of a file is usually formed as the *pathname* from the root directory to the file. For example, in a two-level file system with users SMITH, JONES, and DOE, and in which JONES has files PAYROLL and INVOICES, the *pathname* for file PAYROLL might be formed as JONES:PAYROLL. Specific file system structures are considered in depth in the case studies.

File System Functions

Some of the functions normally attributed to file system follows:

(1) Users should be able to create, modify, and delete files.

(2) Users should be able to share each other's files in a carefully controlled manner in order to build upon each other's work.

(3) The mechanism for sharing files should provide various types of controlled access such as *read access*, *write access*, *execute access* or various combinations of these.

(4) Users should be able to structure their files in a manner most appropriate for each application.

(5) Users should be able to order the transfer of information between files.

(6) *Backup* and *recovery* capabilities must be provided to prevent either accidental loss or malicious destruction of information.

(7) Users should be able to refer to their files by *symbolic names* rather than having to use *physical device names* (i.e., *device independence*).

(8) In sensitive environments in which information must be kept secure and private, such as in electronic funds transfer systems, criminal records systems, medical records systems, etc., the file system may also provide *encryption* and *decryption* capabilities. This makes information useful only to its intended audience (i.e., to those who possess the *decryption keys*).

(9) Most important, the file system should provide a user-friendly interface. It should give users a *logical view* of their data and the functions to be performed upon it rather than a *physical view*. The user should not have to be concerned with the particular devices on which data is stored, the form the data takes on those devices, or the physical means of transferring data to and from those devices.

The Data Hierarchy

Bits are grouped together in *bit patterns* represent virtually all data items of interest in computer systems. There are 2^n possible bit patterns for a string of n bits.

The next level up in the data hierarchy is comprised of *bytes* or *characters*, which are fixed length patterns of bits. Most computers systems today use 8-bit bytes, and thus can have 2^8 or 256 possible characters represented in their *character sets*.

The usefulness of the eight-bit byte may be short-lived because there is tremendous pressure to expand computer character sets to accommodate international character sets. Also, the surge in computer use due to the personal computing phenomenon has caused a proliferation of special-purpose applications that demand on broader variety of characters.

The two most popular character sets in use today are *ASCII (American Standard Code for Information Interchange)* and *EBCDIC (Extended Binary Coded Decimal Interchange Code)*. ASCII is particularly popular in personal computers and in data communication systems. EBCDIC is popular for representing data internally in mainframe computer systems, particularly those of IBM. Both representations are so widely used that many systems contain mechanisms to use both codes and convert between them.

A *field* is a group of characters. A *record* is a group of fields. A students record may contain, for example, separate fields for identification number, name, address, telephone number, cumulative grade point average, major field of study, expected date of graduation etc. A *record key* is a control field that uniquely identifies the record. In a payroll application, for example, the record key might be the employee's social security number.

Blocking and Buffering

A *physical record* or *block* is the unit of information actually read from or written to a device. A *logical record* is a collection of data treated as a unit from the user's standpoint. When each physical record contains exactly one logical record, the file is said to consist of *unblocked records*. When each physical record may contain several logical records, the file is said to consist of *blocked records*. In a file with *fixed-length records*, all records are the same length; the blocksize is ordinarily an integral multiple of the record size. In a file with *variable-length records*, records may vary in size up to the blocksize. Figure 13.2 shows some common record formats.

Buffering allows computation to proceed in parallel with input/output. Spaces are provided in primary storage to hold several physical blocks of a file at once—each of these spaces is called a *buffer.* The most common scheme is called *double buffering* and it operates as follows (for output). There are two buffers. Initially, records generated by a running process are deposited in the first buffer until it is full. The transfer of the block in the first buffer to secondary storage is then initiated. While this transfer is in progress, the process continues generating records that are deposited in the second buffer. When the second buffer is full, and when the transfer from the first buffer is complete, transfer from the second buffer is initiated. The process continues generating records that are now deposited in the first buffer. This alteration between the buffers allows input/output to occur in parallel with a process's computations.

File Organization

File organization refers to the manner in which the records of a file are arranged on secondary storage. The most popular file organization schemes in use today follow.

- *Sequential*—Records are placed in physical order. The "next" record is the one that physically follows the previous record. This organization is natural for files stored on magnetic tape, an inherently sequential medium. Disk files may also be sequentially organized, but for various reasons, records in a sequential disk file are not necessarily stored continguously.
- *Direct*—Records are directly (randomly) accessed by their physical addresses on a direct access storage device (DASD). The application user places the records on the DASD in any

order appropriate for a particular application. Direct files require that the application user be familiar with the detailed physical organization of the DASDs upon which the files are stored. Hashing techniques (En88) are often useful in locating data in direct access files.

- *Indexed sequential*—Records are arranged in logical sequence to a key contained in each record. The system maintains an index containing the physical addresses of certain principal records. Indexed sequential records may be accessed sequentially in key order, or they may be accessed directly, by a search through the system-created index. Indexed sequential files are normally stored on disk.
- *Partitioned*—This is essentially a file of sequential subfiles. Each sequential subfile is called a *member*. The starting address of each member is stored in the file's *directory*. Partitioned files are often used to store program libraries or macro libraries.

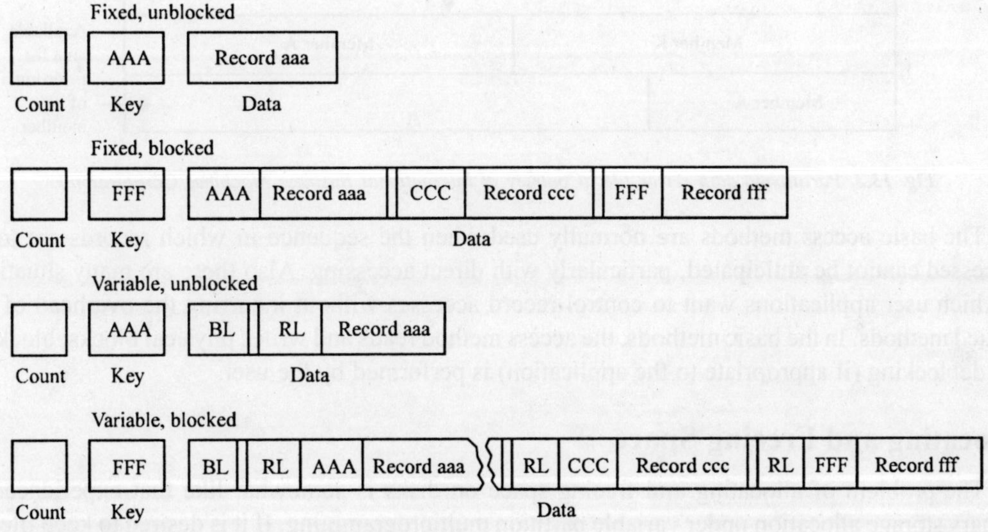

Fig. 13.2. *Record formats. BL is nlock length. RL is record length. Count contains various control information such as cylinder number, head number, record number length of data position record, and error control bytes. (Courtsey of International Business Machines Corporation.)*

The term *volume* is used to refer to the recording medium for each particular auxiliary storage device. The volume used on a tape drive is a reel of magnetic tape; the volume used on a disk drive is a disk.

Queued and Basic Access Methods

Large operating systems generally provide many *access methods*. These are sometimes grouped into two categories, namely *queued access methods* and *basic access method.* The queued methods provide more powerful capabilities than the basic methods.

Queued access methods are used when the sequence in which records are to be processed can be anticipated, such as in sequential and indexed sequential accessing. The queued methods perform *anticipatory buffering* and scheduling of I/O operations. They try to have the next record available for processing as soon as the previous record has been processed. More than one record at a time is maintained in primary storage; this allows processing and I/O operations to be overlapped. The queued access methods also perform automatic blocking and deblocking so the user need do not be concerned with these chores.

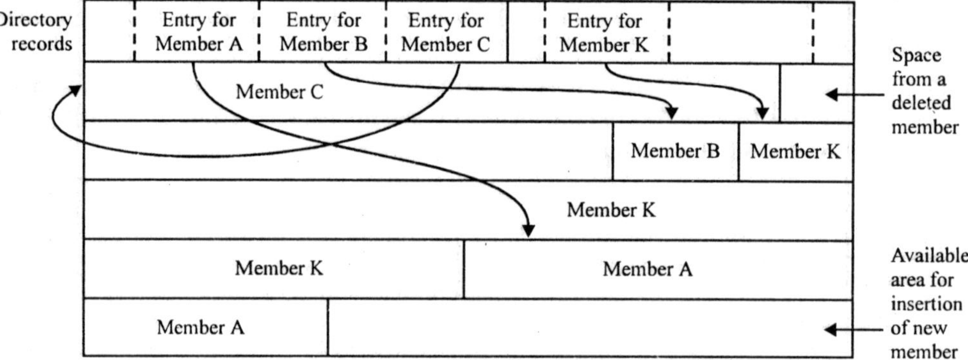

Fig. 13.3. Partitioned data set or file. (Coutrsey of International Business Machines Corporation.)

The basic access methods are normally used when the sequence in which records are to be processed cannot be anticipated, particularly with direct accessing. Also there are many situations in which user applications want to control record accesses without incurring the overhead of the queued methods. In the basic methods, the access method reads and writes physical blocks; blocking and deblocking (if appropriate to the application) is performed by the user.

Allocating and Freeing Space

The problem of allocating and freeing space on disks is somewhat like that experienced is primary storage allocation under variable partition multiprogramming. If it is desired to keep files in adjacent areas of the disk, then such areas need to be collected. But as files are allocated and freed it is common for the space on disk to become increasingly *fragmented.* Thus any further allocation causes files to be spread throughout widely dispread blocks, and this can cause performance problems.

One technique for alleviating this problem is to perform periodic *compaction* or *garbage collection.* Files may be reorganized to occupy adjacent areas of the disk, and free areas may be collected into a single block or a group of large blocks. This garbage collection is often done during the off-hours when the system can be shut down; some systems perform compaction dynamically while in operation. A system may choose to reorganize the files of users not currently logged in, or it may reorganize files that have not been referenced for a long time.

It may not be useful to perform garbage collection on certain systems, particularly those in which a single disk contains the files of hundreds of users. Each time a user process issues an I/O request, that process loses the processor to another process; this process may in turn issue an I/O, causing a seek to a distant track on that disk. So even if successive references to data on a file are to adjacent areas on the disk, long seeks may still be necessary as the system switches between processes.

Designing a file system requires knowledge of the user community, including the number of users, the average number and size of files per user, the average duration of user sessions, the nature of applications to be run on the system, and the like. These factors must be carefully considered to determine the most appropriate file organizations and directory structures.

In paged systems, the smallest amount of information transferred between secondary and primary storage is a page, so it makes sense to allocate secondary storage in blocks of the page size or a multiple of the page size. Locality tells us that once a process has referred to a data item on a page it is likely to references additional data items on that page; it is also likely to reference data items on pages contiguous to that page in the user's virtual address space. Therefore it is desirable to store the logically contiguous pages of a user's virtual storage as physically contiguous pages on secondary storage, especially when several pages are stored per physical block.

Contiguous Allocation

In *contiguous allocation*, files are assigned to contiguous areas of secondary storage. A user specific in advance the size of the area needed to hold a file to be created. If the desired amount of contiguous space is not available, the file cannot be created.

One advantage of contiguous allocation is that successive logical records are normally physically adjacent to one another. This speeds access compared to systems in which successive logical records are dispersed throughout the disk.

The file directories in contiguous allocation systems are relatively straightforward to implement. For each file it is necessary merely to retain the address of the start of the file and the file's length.

Contiguous allocation does have certain disadvantages. As files are deleted, the space they occupied on secondary storage is reclaimed. This space becomes available for allocation of new files, but these new files must fit in the available holes. Thus contiguous allocation schemes exhibits the same types of fragmentation problems inherent in variable partition multiprogramming systems—adjacent secondary storage holes must be coalesced, and periodic compaction may need to be performed to reclaim storage areas large enough to hold new files.

Noncontiguous Allocation

Because files do tend to grow or shrink over time, and because users rarely know in advance how large their files will be, contiguous storage allocation systems have generally been replaced by more dynamic noncontiguous storage allocation systems. Several noncontiguous storage allocation schemes are popular.

Sector-Oriented Linked Allocation

The disk is viewed as consisting of individual *sectors*. Files consist of many sectors which may be dispersed throughout the disk. Sectors belonging to a common file contain pointers to one another, forming a linked list. A *free space list* contains entries for all free sectors on the disk. When a file needs to grow, the process requests more sectors from the free space list. Files that shrink return sectors to the free space list. There is no need for compaction.

Noncontiguous allocation solves some of the problems inherent in contiguous allocation schemes, but it has its own drawbacks. Because the records of a file may be dispersed throughout the disk, retrieval of logically contiguous records can involve lengthy seeks. There is execution time overhead in maintaining the linked list structure. Pointers in the list structure reduce the amount of space available for file data.

Block Allocation

One scheme used to manage secondary storage more efficiently and reduce execution time overhead is called *block allocation.* This is a mixture of both contiguous allocation and noncontiguous allocation methods.

In this scheme, instead of allocating individual sectors, blocks of contiguous sectors (sometimes called *extent*) are allocated. The system tries to allocate new blocks to a file by choosing free blocks as close as possible to existing blocks of the file. Each access to the file involves determining the appropriate block and then the appropriate sector within the block.

There are several common ways of implementing block-allocation systems. These include *block chaining, index block chaining,* and *block-oriented file mapping.*

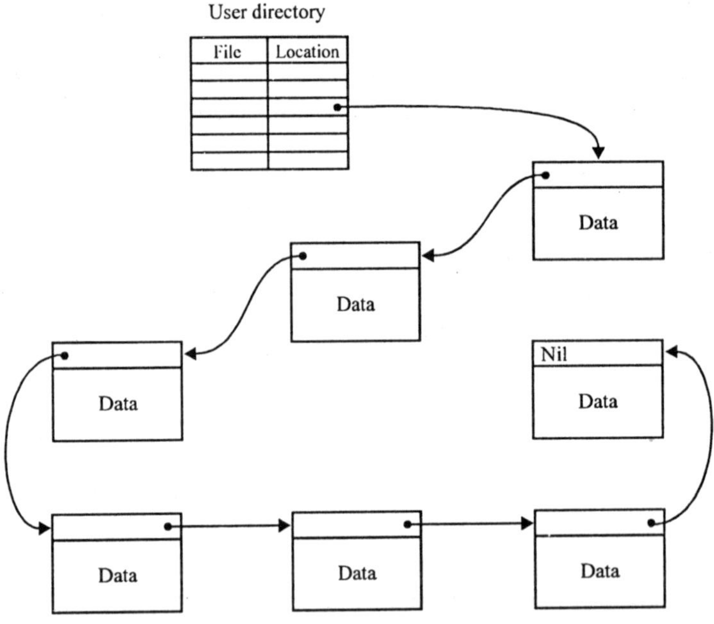

Fig. 13.4. Block chaining.

In *block chaining,* entries in the user directory point to the first block of each file. The fixed-length blocks comprising a file each contain two portions: a data block, and a pointer to the next block. The smallest unit of allocation is a fixed-sized block that ordinarily consists of many sectors. It is common to make the block size one full track on a disk. Locating a particular record requires searching the block chain until the appropriate block is found, and then searching that block until the appropriate record is found. The chain must be searched from the beginning, and if the blocks are dispersed throughout the disk (which is normal), the search process can be slow as block-to-block seeks occur. Insertion and deletion are straightforward, however. They are done by modifying the printer in the previous block. Some systems use doubly-linked lists to facilitate searching; the blocks are threaded both forward and backward so that a search may proceed in either direction.

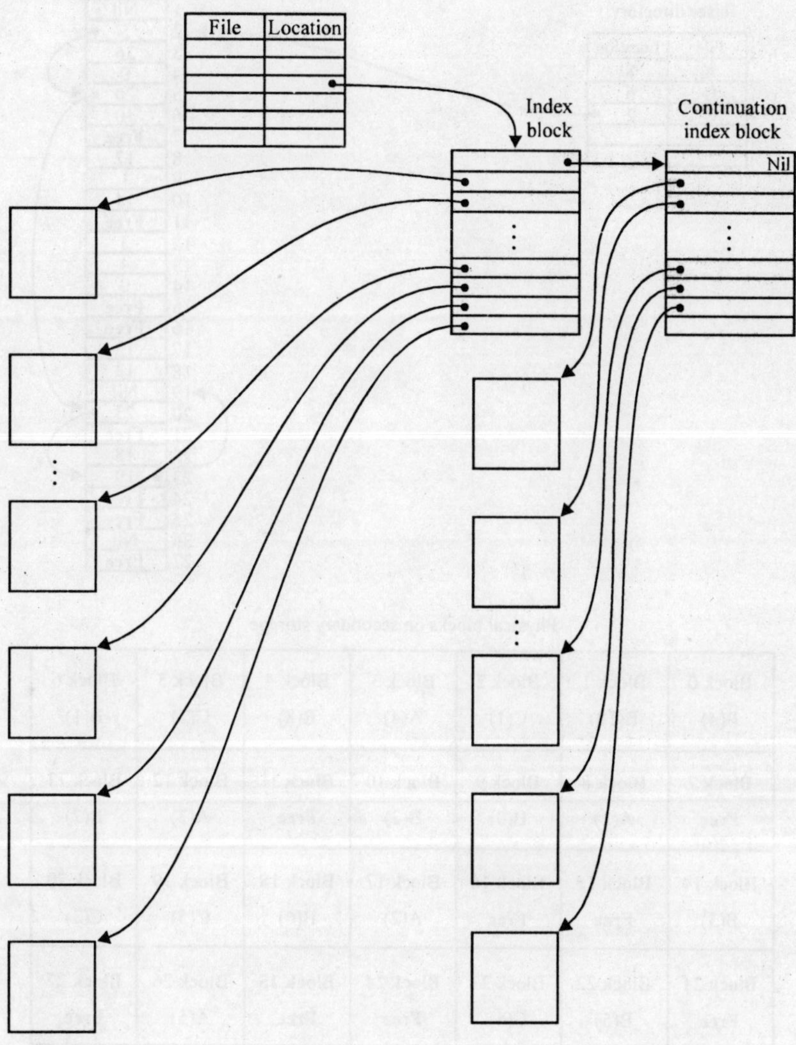

Fig. 13.5. Index block chaining.

With *index block chaining*, the pointers are placed into separate index blocks. Each index block contains a fixed number of items. Each entry contains a record identifier and a pointer to that record. If more than one index block is needed to describe a file, then a series of index blocks is chained together. The big advantage of index block chaining over simple block chaining is that

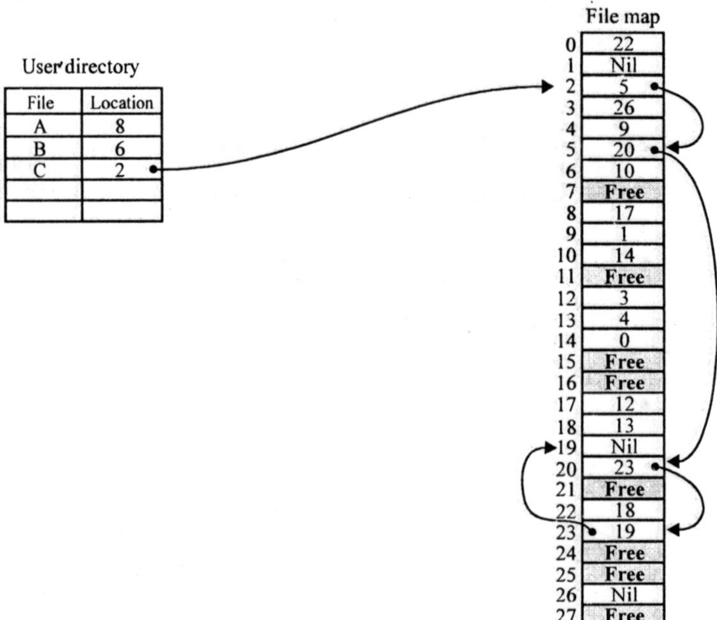

Physical blocks on secondary storage

Block 0 B(4)	Block 1 B(10)	Block 2 C(1)	Block 3 A(4)	Block 4 B(8)	Block 5 C(2)	Block 6 B(1)
Block 7 Free	Block 8 A(1)	Block 9 B(9)	Block 10 B(2)	**Block 11 Free**	Block 12 A(3)	Block 13 B(7)
Block 14 B(3)	**Block 15 Free**	**Block 16 Free**	Block 17 A(2)	Block 18 B(6)	Block 19 C(5)	Block 20 C(3)
Block 21 Free	Block 22 B(5)	Block 23 C(4)	**Block 24 Free**	**Block 25 Free**	Block 26 A(5)	**Block 27 Free**

Fig. 13.6. *Block-oriented file mapping.*

searching may take place in the index blocks themselves. The index blocks may be kept close together in secondary storage to minimize seeking. On some systems in which rapid searching is needed, the index blocks can be maintained in primary storage. Once the appropriate record is located via the index blocks, the data block containing that record is read into primary storage. The disadvantage of this scheme is that insertions can require the complete reconstruction of the index blocks, so some systems leave a certain portion of the index blocks empty to provide for future insertions.

In *block-oriented file mapping*, instead of using pointers, the system uses block numbers. Normally, these are easily converted to actual block addresses because of the geometry of the disk. A file map contains one entry for each block on the disk. Entries in the user directory point to the first entry in the file map for each file. Each entry in the file map contains the block number of the next block in that file. Thus all the blocks in a file may be located by following the entries in the file map.

The entry in the file map that corresponds to the last entry of a particular file is set to some sentinel value like "Nil" to indicate that the last block of a file has been reached. Some of the entries in the file map are set to "Free" to indicate that the block is available for allocation. The system may either search the file map linearly to locate a free block, or a free block list can be maintained. The file map can be modified to include record identifiers so that searching can be confined to the map for the most part. An advantage of this scheme is that the physical adjacencies on the disk are reflected in the file map. When a new block is to be assigned, it is relatively easy to locate a free storage block with good proximity to the other blocks of the file. Insertions and deletions are straightforward in this scheme.

File Descriptor

A *file descriptor* or *file control block* is a control block containing information the system needs to manage a file. It is a highly system-dependent structure. A typical file descriptor might include

- symbolic file name
- location of file in secondary storage
- file organization (sequential, indexed sequential, etc.)
- device type
- access control data
- type (data file, object program, C source program, etc.)
- disposition (permanent vs. temporary)
- creation data and time
- destroy data
- date and time last modified
- access activity counts (number of reads, for example)

Ordinarily, file descriptors are maintained on secondary storage. They are brought to primary storage when a file is opened. The file descriptor is controlled by the operating system—the user may not reference it directly.

Access Control Matrix

One way to control access to files is to create a two-dimensional *access control matrix* listing all the users and all the files in the system. The entry Aij is 1 if user is allowed access to file j; otherwise

Aij = 0. In an installation with a large number of users and a large number of files, this matrix would be very large—and very sparse. Allowing one user access to another user's files is the exception rather than the rule. To make such a matrix concept useful, it would be necessary to use codes to indicate various kinds of access such as readonly, writeonly, executeonly, readwrite, etc.

Access Control by User Classes

An access control matrix can become so large as to be impractical to maintain. A technique that requires considerably less space is to control access to various *user classes*. A common classification scheme is

- *Owner*—Normally, this is the user who created the file.
- *Specified user*—The owner specifies that another individual may use the file.
- *Group or project*—Users are often members of a group working on a particular project. In this case the various members of the group may all be granted access to each other's project-related files.
- *Public*—Most systems allow a file to be designated as public so that it may be accessed by any member of the system's user community. Public access normally allows users to read or execute a file, but not to write it.

User \ File	1	2	3	4	5	6	7	8	9	10
1	1	1	0	0	0	0	0	0	0	0
2	0	0	1	0	1	0	0	0	0	0
3	0	1	0	1	0	1	0	0	0	0
4	1	0	0	0	0	0	0	0	0	0
5	1	1	1	1	1	1	1	1	1	1
6	0	0	0	0	0	1	1	0	0	0
7	1	0	0	0	0	0	0	0	0	1
8	1	0	0	0	0	0	0	0	0	0
9	1	1	1	1	0	0	0	0	1	1
10	1	1	0	0	1	1	0	0	0	1

Fig. 13.7. Access control matrix.

Backup and Recovery

Disk do crash, lightning does strike, power surges do occur, fires and floods happen, theft is more common than most companies are willing to admit, and vandalism (even terrorism) cannot be ignored. The point is that destruction of information, either accidental or intentional, does occur.

Physical safeguards can be used to prevent unauthorized access to the computer room, to filter power surges, and to turn on sprinklers in case of fire. But a simple disk head crash, in which the read-write head comes in contact with the surface of the disk and scratches it, can still destroy data.

The most common technique used to ensure the continued availability of data is to do *periodic backups*, i.e., to make one or more copies of the system's files regularly and put them in a safe place. Even periodic backups may not be sufficient, however, because all updates to a file since the last backup may be lost.

Another techniques is to *log all transactions* to a file by copying them to another disk. This *redundancy* can be costly, but in case of failure, all of the lost work may be reconstructed (assuming of course that the *logging disk* is not also destroyed).

There is no way to guarantee absolute security of files. Designers must provide reasonable backup facilities that do not degrade the performance of the system, and whose costs are within the economics of the installation. In situations in which the integrity of the data must be guaranteed with high reliability, the designers may have no choice but to use an expensive and time-consuming backup procedure. In the worst case, users would have to reconstruct all their transactions since the last backup.

The periodic backup scheme has several weaknesses.

- The system may need to be shut down during the backup operation.
- File systems can be enormous; complete backups could require a great deal of time.
- When a failure occurs, recovery from the last backup can be time-consuming. When recovery is complete, the data is only current through the time of the backup. Any transactions since that time are lost.

A benefit of periodic backups is that the file system can be reorganized to allow the various blocks of user files scattered throughout the disks to be placed contiguously. This usually results in much faster access to user files when the system is restarted.

Periodic backup of the entire file system is not sufficient in systems in which recovery needs to occur quickly and be up to the minute. A more appropriate technique is called *incremental backup*. During a terminal session, all updates files are marked. When a user logs out, a list of these files can be passed to a system process which then backs up all modified files.

Incremental backup is not of much use to the user in the midst of a lengthy terminal session when a system crash occurs. A better technique is to search the file directories even while a user is logged in and backup modified files more frequently.

All the techniques discussed so far suffer from the fact that there may be significant activity between the time of the last backup and the time at which a failure occurs. In systems in which even the slightest loss of activity is unacceptable, a *transaction logging* approach may be appropriate. Here, every transaction is immediately backed up as it is occurs. This intense level of backup is somewhat easier to do in interactive systems in which activity is limited by relatively slow human response times. Even systems supporting hundreds of on-line interactive users can easily log every line typed at the terminals, so presumable such systems could be backed up to be quite current. But interactive commands could initiate substantial processing; substantial reconstruction time might still be required to perform necessary recovery procedures.

File Servers

One approach to handling nonlocal file references in a computer network is to route all such request to a *file server*, i.e., a computer system dedicated to resolving intercomputer file references.

This approach centralizes control of these references, but the file server could easily become a *bottleneck*, because all *client* computers send all requests to the server. A better approach is to let the separate computers communicate directly with one another; this is the approach taken by Sun's *Network File System (NFS)*.

Distributed File Systems

Through the 1970s, file systems generally stored and managed the files of a single computer system. On multiuser timesharing systems the file of all users were under the control of a centralized file system. Today, the trend is toward *distributed file systems* in computer networks. A real complication is that such networks are increasingly being used to connect a wide variety of computer systems, and these often have different operating systems and file systems.

A distributed files system enables users to perform operations on remote files in a computer network in much the same manner as on local files. NFS provides distributed files system capabilities for networks of heterogeneous computer systems; currently, more than 100 different computer systems from micros to supercomputers support NFS.

CD-ROMS, Worms, and Magneto-Laser Disks

The emergence of CD-ROM (for "compact disk readonly memory") laser-optical technology, and more recently read/write optical disks, has made it possible to store the equivalent of thousands of floppy disks on a single CD-ROM disk. The incorporation of this technology into recent computer systems, such as Steve Jobs' NeXT machine, indicates that optical disk technology is likely to become widely used over the next several years. The 256-megabyte capacity of its rewritable magneto-optical disks enables NeXT to supply vast amounts of information including software, system documentation, and even reference books (the works of Shakespeare, a thesaurus, a book of quotations, and a dictionary) on a single disk with substantial space left for user programs and data.

Managing such vast amounts of data requires unique file system techniques CD-ROMs are based on the designs used in the music industry. Seeking takes longer than with moving-head magnetic disk technology. But once reading begins, huge volumes of data can be accessed sequentially without noticeable interruption; this is similar to listening to music on a compact disk.

CD-ROMs contain fixed information, so the indexing and placement of this information can be optimized for last, smooth access when the disk is created.

Data is stored on CD-ROM by sector number in one continuous spiral, rather than is concentric tracks as with magnetic disks. The disk constantly adjusts its speed to read the data at a constant linear velocity. Magnetic disks generally locate and transfer information faster, but CD-ROMs have much greater capacity and they "play back" information in a smoother fashion. Helgerson and Martens discuss various indexing methods and retrieval schemes for accessing CD-ROM data.

Gait discusses the development of a file system for write-once optical disks (these are sometimes called WORM disks for "write-once-read-many"). WORM disks differ from CD-ROMs in that they can be written by the user's computer system. The file system for a WORM disk differs from that for rewritable disks in several ways. Because information cannot be deleted, the disk always contains the complete file history. The file system must provide fast access to the most recent copy of file. The file system must be able to locate all previous copies of a file as well, but this is considered to be archival information, so access can be slower. Although distant seeks on an optical disk can be much slower than on magnetic disks, local seeks are much faster. So the file system needs to cluster information that is likely to be referenced together, or performance could be poor.

Database Systems

The availability of inexpensive massive direct access secondary storage has caused a tremendous amount of research and development activity in the area of database systems. A database is an integrated collected of data which is centrally controlled; a *database system* involves the data itself, the hardware on which the data resides, the software (called a *database management system* or DBMS) that controls the storing and retrieval of data, and the users themselves.

Advantages of Database Systems

Date lists several important advantages of database systems.

- Redundancy can be reduced.
- Inconsistency can be avoided.
- The data can be shared.
- Standards can be enforced
- Security restrictions can be applied.
- Integrity can be maintained.
- Conflicting requirements can be balanced.

In conventional nondatabase systems, each distinct application maintains its own files, often with considerable redundancy and a variety of physical formats. In database systems redundancy is reduced by integrating separate files.

Sharing is one of the most important benefits of database systems. Existing applications can reference the same data; new applications can reference existing data.

Centralized control makes it possible to enforce standards rigidly. This becomes particularly important in computer networks in which *data migration* between systems occurs.

Security is an intriguing issue in database system. The data may actually be more at risk because it is collected and retained in a central location rather than being dispersed throughout physically separate files in many locations. To counter this, database systems must be designed with elaborate controls.

Data Independence

One of the most important aspects of database systems is *data independence*, i.e., applications need not be concerned with how the data is physically stored or accessed. An application is said to be *data-dependent* if the storage structure and accessing strategy cannot be changed without affecting the application significantly.

Data independence makes it convenient for various applications to have different views of the same data. From the system's standpoint, data independence makes it possible for the storage structure and accessing strategy to be modified in response to the installation's changing requirements, but without the need to modify functioning applications.

Database Languages

Users access a database via statements in some form of *database language*. Applications programs may use a conventional procedure-oriented, high-level language like COBOL, PL/I, or Pascal; a terminal user may use a specially designed *query language* that makes it convenient to express requests (usually in simple English) in the context of a particular application.

Such languages are referred to as *host languages*. Each host language ordinarily includes a *data sublanguage (DSL)* concerned with the specifics of database objects and operations. Each data sublanguage generally is a combination of two languages, namely a *data definition language (DDL)* that provides facilities for defining *database objects*, and a *data manipulation language (DML)* that provides features for specifying the processing to be performed on database objects.

Distributed Database

A *distributed database* is a database that is spread throughout the computer systems of a network. Ordinarily in such systems each data item is stored at the location in which it is most frequently used, but it remains accessible to other network users.

Distributed systems provide the control and economies of local processing with the advantages of information accessibility over a geographically dispersed organization. They can be costly to implement and operate, however, and they can suffer from increased vulnerability to security violations.

Database Models

Three different database models have achieved widespread popularity: (1) *hierarchical database*, (2) *network database*, and (3) *relational database*.

Hierarchical Database

Much of the value of the database approach comes from the fact that relationships between data items may be indicated explicitly. In the hierarchical model, data items are related in a parent/child relationship; each parent may have many children but each child may have only one parent. Hierarchical organization makes it difficult to express relationships in which children relate to more than one parent. This inflexibility has led many designers to choose another model. But when the data relationships are indeed hierarchical, the database is easy to implement, modify, and search.

Network Database

The network model is more flexible than the hierarchical model. It allows children to relate to many parents, and allows very general interdependencies to be expressed. A disadvantage to the network approach is that some network structures begin to take on a "rat's nest" appearance with pointers going off in all directions. Such a structure can be difficult to comprehend, modify, or reconstruct in case of failure. The network structure is useful in stable environments in which the complex interdependencies of the data need to be expressed to make the database useful. In more dynamic environments in which considerable growth in the database is expected, or in which new features and relationships are likely to be added, the network approach is best avoided.

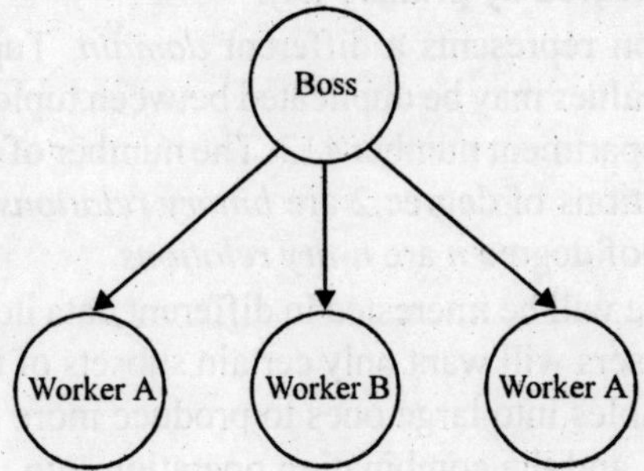

Fig. 13.8. Hierarchical database organization.

Relational Database

The relational model developed by Codd offers many advantages over the hierarchical and network models. The relational model is a logical structure rather than a physical one; the principles of relational database management can be considered without concerning oneself with the physical implementation of the data structures.

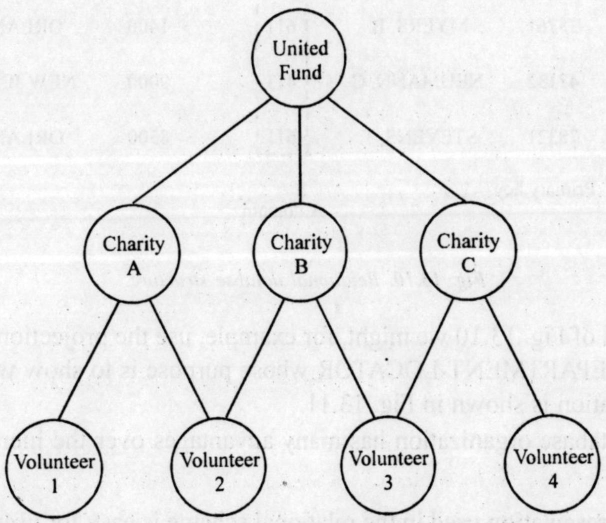

Fig. 13.9. A possible network database organization. Note that some people do volunteer work for more than one charity.

A relational database is composed of *relations*. Figure 13.10 illustrates a sample relation that might be used in a personnel system. The name of the relation is EMPLOYEE and its primary purpose is to demonstrate the relationships of various attributes of each employee with that employee. Any particular row of the relation is called a *tuple*. This relation consists of six tuples. The first field in each tuple, the employee number, is used as the *primary key* for referencing data in the relation. The tuples of the relation are ordered by primary key.

Each column of the relation represents a different *domain*. Tuples must be unique within a relation, but particular domain values may be duplicated between tuples. For example, three different tuples in the example contain department number 413. The number of domains in a relation indicates the *degree of the relation*. Relations of degree 2 are *binary relations*, relations of degree three are *ternary relations*, and relations of degree *n* are *n-ary relations*.

Different users of a database will be interested in different data items and different relationships between the data items. Some users will want only certain subsets of the table columns. Other users will wish to combine smaller tables into large ones to produce more complex relations. Codd calls the subset operation *projection*, and the combination operation *join*.

Relation: EMPLOYEE

	Number	Name	Department	Salary	Location
	23603	JONES, A.	413	1100	NEW JERSEY
	24568	KERWIN, R.	413	2000	NEW JERSEY
A tuple	34589	LARSON, P.	642	1800	LOS ANGELES
	35761	MYERS, B.	611	1400	ORLANDO
	47132	NEUMANN, C	413	9000	NEW JERSEY
	78321	STEVENS, T.	611	8500	ORLANDO
	Primary key		A domain		

Fig. 13.10. *Relational databse structure.*

Using the relation of Fig. 13.10 we might, for example, use the projection operation to create a new relation called DEPARTMENT-LOCATOR whose purpose is to show where departments are located. This new relation is shown in Fig. 13.11.

The relational database organization has many advantages over the hierarchical and network schemes.

- The tabular representation used in the relational scheme is easy for users to comprehend and easy to implement in the physical database system.
- It is relatively easy to convert virtually any other type of database structure into the relational scheme. Thus the scheme may be viewed as a universal form of representation.
- The projection and join operations are easy to implement and make the creation of new relations needed for particular applications easy to do.

- Access control to sensitive data is straightforward to implement. The sensitive data is merely placed in separate relations, and access to these relations is controlled by some sort of authority or access scheme.
- Searches can be faster than in schemes requiring following a string of pointers.
- Relational structures are easier to modify than hierarchical or network structures. In environments where flexibility is important, this becomes critical.
- The clarity and visibility of the database improves with the relational structure. It is much easier to search tabular data than it is to unwind possibly arbitrarily complex interconnections of data elements in a pointer mechanism.

Relation: DEPARTMENT-LOCATOR

Department	Location
413	NEW JERSEY
611	ORLANDO
642	LOS ANGELES

Fig. 13.11. A relation formed by projection.

Stonebraker discusses various operating system services that support database management system, namely buffer pool management, the file system, scheduling process management, interprocess communication, consistency control, and paged virtual memory. He observes that because most of the these features are not specifically optimized to DBMS environments, DBMS designers have tended to bypass operating system services in favour of supplying their own. He concludes that efficient, minimal operating systems are the most desirable for supporting the kinds of database management systems that do supply their own optimized services.

Database systems are being routinely incorporated into operating systems to provide users with far more powerful capabilities than are available in conventional file systems. This enables a more synergistic relationship between the operating system and the database management system than is possible when the DBMS is supplied separately.

Summary

A file is a named collection of data that normally resides on secondary storage. Entire files may be manipulated by operations like open, close, create, destroy, copy, rename, and list. Individual data items (normally records) may be manipulated by operations like read, write, update, insert, and delete.

The file system manages files. It provides sharing, privacy, accessing of information, backup, recovery, device independence, and encryption/decryption capabilities.

Data is structured in increasingly complex entities including bits, bytes, fields, records, files, and databases.

Records may be unblocked (one logical record per physical block) or blocked (several logical records per physical block). Blocking minimizes the number of physical transfers involving auxiliary storage during file processing. Buffering allows input/output operations to proceed in parallel with the operation of the processor.

The most popular file organization schemes are sequential, indexed sequential, direct and partitioned. Accessing of files is accomplished by operating systems functions called access methods. Queued access methods are used with sequentially organized files; they perform anticipatory buffering and scheduling of I/O, and they provide automatic blocking and deblocking. The basic access methods provide only physical block reading and writing.

In contiguous allocation, a file is allocated to a single area of secondary storage; in noncontiguous allocation the file may be dispersed throughout several areas of secondary storage. Contiguous allocation facilitates rapid access but suffers from serious fragmentation problems. Noncontiguous allocation is more flexible, but accessing can involve frequent seeks. Block allocation offers the flexibility of noncontiguous allocation with the fast access of contiguous allocation (at least with successive access to records in the same block). Block-oriented file mapping reflects the physical adjacencies on disk in the file map.

The file descriptor contains information the system needs to manage a file. The user may not reference file descriptors directly; file descriptors are controlled by the file system.

Controlling access to files can be handled by an access control matrix indicating which users have what types of access to which files. Access control is more commonly handled with user classes where, for example, access may be granted to "owner," "specified user," "group member," or "member of the general public."

Backup and recovery are important functions of any file system. The most common technique is periodic backups of the entire file system. With incremental dumping, the files modified by a user during a terminal session are backed up when that user logs out. Transaction logging copies every line typed by the user to a log file; recovery would involve literally reapplying all transactions logged since the last major periodic backup.

A database is an integrated collection of data which is centrally controlled. Many contemprorary computer systems now provide database capabilities in both their hardware and operating systems. This gives the user far more powerful data manipulation capabilities than those ordinarily provided in conventional file systems.

Data independence allows an application to be changed and new applications to be developed without having to modify the data storage structure and accessing strategy. A distributed database is one that is spread throughout the computer systems of a network.

The most popular database organizations are hierarchical, network, and relational. In the hierarchical approach, data is organized according to parent/child relationships; each child has only one parent but each parent may have many children. A hierarchical database is easy to search and maintain, but it limits the user's flexibility in defining complex data interdependencies.

The network approach allows very general interdependencies to be expressed conveniently. But the resulting structures can be difficult to comprehend, modify, or reconstruct in case of failure.

The relational database approach offers many advantages over the hierarchical and network schemes. The tabular representation is easier to comprehend and implement. Databases organized according to the other schemes may easily be converted to relational organization. Convenient operations like projection and join make it easy to create new relations. Sensitive data may be secured by placing it in separate relations. Searching is generally much faster than it is within the other schemes, modification is more straightforward, and the clarity and visibility of the database is greatly improved.

14

Operating System Security

Introduction

Computing is becoming increasingly accessible. The number of computer installations is increasing dramatically. Timesharing systems and remote access systems introduced the vulnerability of data communications as a key security issue. That vulnerability today is becoming far more serious with the proliferation of computer networking.

Another trend has been to assign computers more of the responsibilities of managing our personal and business activities. Computers are routinely handling the most sensitive correspondence. Electronic funds transfer systems pass our money around in bit streams. Air traffic control systems do much of the work previously handled by human air traffic controllers. Microprocessors have been incorporated into a huge variety of devices to provide intelligent control. Computer-controlled artificial body implant devices like pacemakers are in wide use. Intensive care units in hospitals are heavily computerized.

It is important to implement security measures to ensure the uninterrupted and uncorrupted functioning of these systems. This chapter discusses the issues of operating systems security. Hardware protection and security are equally important; these issues are treated elsewhere in the text.

The operating system normally represents only a small portion of the total base of software that runs on a particular system. But the operating system controls access to a system's resources; the other software normally requests access to those resources through the operating system. So software security considerations tend to be focused on making the operating system secure, although applications software can also present security risks.

Operating systems security is only a small part of the total problem of computer security, but it is becoming an increasingly important part. A well-designed security approach must address the total picture; operating systems security means little if anyone can walk off with the computer system!

There are several reasons why computer security is receiving so much attention today. Personal computers have brought computer savvy to the general public (Mu84a). Millions of people have taken computer courses in universities, read computer books, purchased personal computers, or used computer systems at work. Today, those who would commit fraud are often faced with penetrating a computer system's defenses to achieve their goals.

Millions of computer systems have been tied together via communication networks, most commonly through the worldwide telephone system. Where in the past, simple physical security might have been sufficient to guard a computer from outside attack, now sophisticated controls must be placed on login attempts from remote terminals, and on other network communications.

We have mentioned the notion of user-friendly systems many times in this text; if computer usage is to be brought to the general public effectively, then systems must be made more accessible and easier to use. But user friendliness often implies increased vulnerability.

A security program begins with identifying the potential threats. Threats may be from malicious or nonmalicious sources. The best one can hope to do is to identifying the vast majority of potential threats; there will always be some that cannot be anticipated.

Sharing and protection are contradictory goals. Programs may be completely isolated from one another by executing them on separate, nonnetworked computers, but this precludes sharing. Programs running on the same computer may be allowed to share resources extensively, but this reduces the amount of protection possible.

Some people might argue that complex systems deter penetration attempts, and that simple systems are more vulnerable because they are easier to understand. In fact, it is easier to verify the security of simple systems; complex systems often leave many security "holes."

The level of security appropriate for a particular system depends on the value of the resources being secured. Information in a banking system may have great financial value. Information in a medical system may have life-or-death value. Frivolous breaches of security are not to be ignored; the information obtained may be of little value to the intruders but it could be a major embarrassment to a system administrator.

Security Requirements

Security requirement for a given system what it means for that system to be secure. These requirements serve as the basis for determining if the implemented system is secure; without a precise set of security requirement it makes little sense to ask if the system is secure. Similarly, if the requirements are weakly stated (even if the system does meet the requirements), it does not say much about the true security of the system.

Formulation of security requirements has been of primary concern to the United States Government and the Armed Forces. Each of the following deals with security requirements:

- *DOD Directive 5200.28*—Specifies how classified information is to be handled in data processing systems.
- *Computer Security Technology Reference Manual*—Specifies how to evaluate the security of Air Force computer systems.
- *The Privacy Act of 1974*—Requires federal agencies to ensure the integrity and security of information about individual, particularly in the context of the government's extensive use of computers.

A Total Approach to Security

Because a total approach to computer security is essential, we also discuss some of the areas of computer security other than operating systems security. *External security* is concerned with securing the computer facility from intruders and from disasters such as fire and floods. Once a user is allowed physical access to a computer facility, the user's identification must be established by the operating system before access is allowed to the programs and data stored on the system; this might be called *user interface security*. *Internal security* deals with the various controls built into the hardware and the operating system to ensure the reliable and uncorrupted operation of the computer system and the integrity of programs and data.

External Security

External security consists of *physical security* and *operational security*. Physical security includes *protection against disasters* and *protection against intruders*. *Detection mechanisms* are important to physical security; smoke detectors and heat sensors can provide early warning in case of fire; motion detectors can determine if an intruders has entered a computing facility.

Protection against disasters can be expensive to implement and is often treated to lightly. The need for such protection depends on the consequences of loss. Most organizations simply cannot afford the expense of a thorough disaster protection scheme. The major physical security efforts are directed toward keeping out intruders. For this purpose installations use various types of physical identification systems such as identification cards with signatures and/or pictures. Fingerprint and voiceprint systems are also popular.

Operational Security

Operational security consists of the various policies and procedures implemented by the management of the computer installation. *Authorization* determines what access is allowed to what entities.

Classification parcels the problem into subproblems; the data in the system and the users are divided into classes to which various access rights are granted. This is much like the military classification scheme in which only sensitive documents might be classified as top secret, and only those persons who have been given top secret security clearances may access that information.

Personnel selection and assignment is critical. Can employee be trusted? One common approach here is *division of responsibilities*; people are given distinct sets of responsibilities, which they perform without having to know everything about a system. Thus individuals cannot see the total picture. In order to compromise a system, cooperation among many employees might be necessary; this greatly reduces the likelihood of security violations. In large computer installations, for example, only computer operators are allowed access to the computer systems; only programmers are allowed to write programs. Operators should not know how to program and programmers should not be familiar with the details of operating the computer system. Similarly, inputs to production systems should be controlled by a separate group, and outputs should be checked and verified by yet a different group.

Checks and balances should be built into the system to aid in detection of security breaches. Operational personnel should be aware of the nature of these controls; this reduces the likelihood that the controls could be by-passed. But they should be made aware of the fact that elaborate controls are built into the system; this awareness is often sufficient to deter people from attempting a security violation.

It is impossible to design effective security measures without first attempting to enumerate and understand potential security threats. This can require careful and perceptive analysis. What are the available countermeasures? What degree of security is desired?

Surveillance

Surveillance deals with monitoring and auditing the system, authenticating users. Some highly sophisticated user authentication systems are in use. These systems can be by-passed, but substantial knowledge and effort is normally required on the part of the penetrator. An interesting problem inherent in such systems is the possibility of rejecting legitimate users; a voiceprint system might reject a legitimate user who has a cold; a fingerprint system might reject a legitimate user with a cut or a burn.

Threat Monitoring

One way to minimize security risks is to have the operating system control sensitive operations rather than to give control directly to a user. If a user wishes to access a critical file, for example, some systems might allow the user to access the file directly. The user would be in control and the operating system would not be able to monitor activity against the file as it occurs. A more secure technique is called *threat monitoring*.

With threat monitoring in place, users may not access resources directly. Only operating systems routines called *surveillance programs* may do so. The user wishing access to a resource requests such access from the operating system. The operating system either grants or denies the access; then a surveillance program actually performs the access to the file and passes the results to the user program. Threat monitoring is an ongoing activity—penetration attempts are detected as they occur and the system administrator is informed immediately.

Amplification

Sometimes it is necessary to give a surveillance program greater access right (than users are allowed) so that it may effectively execute user requests. Thus to compute the average income of all taxpayers in a town, the surveillance program would need access to the individual records of each taxpayer. This is called *amplification*. Clever users might still be able to infer information about individuals by making several different requests and examining the overlap in the results. Surveillance programs can be designed to detect such attempts and notify a system administrator.

Password Protection

Three classes of items of authentication by which a person's identity may be established are

- *Something about the person*—This includes fingerprints, voiceprint, photographs and signatures.
- *Something possessed by the person*—This includes badges, identification cards and keys.
- *Something known by the person*—This includes passwords, lock combinations, and mother-in-law's maiden name.

The most common authentication scheme is simple *password protection*. The user chooses a codeword, commits it to memory, and then types it to gain admission to a computer system. Most systems suppress the printing or displaying of the password as it is entered.

Password protection has many weaknesses. Users tend to choose password, that are easy to remember, such as the name of a friend or relative. Someone who knows the user might try to log in several times using the names of people this person knows; this might result in a security breach by use of *repeated trials*. Some early systems used short passwords; these systems were easily compromised by simple attempting all possible passwords. Most systems today use longer passwords to thwart such penetration attempts. Using long password is not necessarily wise either; if passwords are difficult to remember, then users will be more inclined to make a note of them; this of course makes it easier for someone to obtain a password.

Penetration of an operating system's defenses need not necessarily result in a significant security compromise. For example, suppose someone manages to gain access to a system's master list of passwords. Ordinarily, this would mean that the penetrator would be able to access any information on the system. To make passwords useless to a penetrator, encryption can be used. Processing the passwords is then of little use unless the person also possesses the decryption key. Users are encouraged to change their passwords often; even if an intruder obtains a password, it may be changed before any real damage can be done.

A simple defense against repeated trials is to limit the number of login attempts that may be initiated in any period of time from a single terminal of workstation (or from a single account). Certainly, people make typing errors when attempting to log in. But it is unreasonable for someone who knows the correct password to require tens, hundreds, or thousands of tries. Therefore, a system might allow three or four tries and then disconnect that terminal automatically for several minutes. After a waiting period the terminal may be reconnected If another series of futile login attempts occurs, the operating system might issue a warning at the terminal that the police are being called or that an alarm is about to go off.

Auditing

Auditing is normally performed in manual systems "after the fact." Auditors are called in periodically to examine an organization's recent transactions and to determine if fraudulent activity has occurred. Auditing in computer systems can involve immediate computer processing to audit transactions that have just occurred.

An *audit log* is a permanent record of important events that occur in the computer system. It is produced automatically each time such an event occurs, and is stored in a protected area of the system; if the system is compromised, the audit log should remain intact. The audit log is an important detection mechanism. Even if the system's defenses can be penetrated, people may be discouraged from trying to do so if they fear detection after the fact.

Access Controls

The key to internal security is to control access to stored data. *Access rights* define what access various *subjects* have to various *objects*. Objects are information-holding entities. They may be physical objects that correspond to disks, tapes, processors, or storage words; or they may be *abstract objects* that correspond to data structures or processes.

Objects are protected against subjects. Authorizations within a computer system are granted to subjects. Subjects may be users, processes, programs, or other entities.

The most common access rights are read access, write access, and execute access. A straightforward way of implementing these is to use an access control matrix. The various subjects are listed in the rows and the various objects to which they require access are listed in the columns. Each slot in the matrix contains the access rights a subject has to an object. An access control matrix must be one of the most closely guarded entities in an operating system.

Security Kernels

It is much easier to make a system secure if security is designed into the system from the beginning rather than retrofitted. Security measures should be implemented throughout a computer system. If one hopes to develop a highly secure system, it is imperative to make the kernel of the operating system secure.

Many *security kernels* have been developed. The most critical security measures are implemented in the kernel, which is intentionally kept as small as possible. This makes it more reasonable to examine the kernel carefully for flaws and to demonstrate its correctness formally.

The security of an operating system depends especially on securing those functions that perform access control, logging, and monitoring, and that manage real storage, virtual storage, and the file system. These functions ordinarily occupy a large portion of operating system code, making it difficult to keep the kernel small. It appears that new approaches to operating system design will be necessary to reduce the size of security kernels to the point that truly secure systems can be built.

Hardware Security

As hardware costs decline, it is becoming increasingly desirable to incorporate operating systems functions into hardware. These functions are then more secure than when they are accessible as easily modified software instructions. Functions incorporated into hardware can run much faster than in software; various monitoring functions may be performed more frequently.

Fault-Tolerant Systems

One of the reasons for designing highly secure computer systems is to ensure their continued reliability and availability. A *fault-tolerant computer system* is one that continue to operate even after some of its components fail. For transaction processing systems, fault tolerance is becoming an increasingly important criterion. An airline stands to lose considerable revenues if its reservations system fails; if a bank's system fails, even briefly the confidence of its customers could be shaken. Building fault-tolerant distributed systems.

One key to fault tolerance is *redundancy*. If a component fails, an equivalent component picks up the slack. Some systems use a pooled approach, in which identical resources function in parallel. Other systems activate redundant resources only upon a failure.

Microprocessor architectures have been evolving into more fail-safe designs in recent years. Many of them now use dual bus structures for communication. Multiprocessing is important in any fault-tolerant system. Some features for fault tolerance are:

- Incorporation of fail-safe mechanisms into the hardware rather than the software
- Use of *transparent multiprocessing*; this allows performance upgrades without software modifications
- Use of multiple input/output subsystems
- Incorporation of major portions of the operating system in hardware
- Incorporation of fault detection mechanisms in the hardware and software

Fault-tolerant systems provide for *graceful degradation*; a fault-tolerant system with failed components provides services, but at reduced levels. Fault-tolerant systems are designed so that a failed component can be taken off-line, repaired, and placed back on-line all while the system provides uninterrupted services.

Capabilities and Object-Oriented Systems

In this section we consider the notions of capabilities and object-oriented systems. These are receiving great interest today as means of achieving more secure computer systems. Capabilities were first proposed in the classic paper by Dennis and Van Horn. Considerable interest has been shown in capabilities-based distributed systems.

An *access right* allows some *subject* to access some *object* in a prescribed manner. Subjects are users of computer systems or entities that act on behalf of users or the system. Objects are resources within the system. Subjects may be such things as jobs, processes and procedures. Objects may be files, programs, semaphore, directories, terminals, channels, controllers, devices, disk tracks, primary storage block, etc. Subjects are also considered to be objects of the system so one subject can have right to access another. Subjects are active entities; objects are passive. Systems must be able to create new types of subject and objects as they evolve.

A *capability* is a token; the possession of a capability by a subject confers access rights for an object. It is like a ticket the bearer may use to gain access to a sporting event. Capabilities are not ordinarily modified, but they can be reproduced. A *protection domain* defines the access rights that a subject has to the various objects of the system. It is the set of capabilities belonging to a subject.

A capability is a protected name for an object in the system. The name is unique across the entire system. For a subject to access a particular object, it must possess a capability for doing so. Included in a capability is a statement of the particular access rights that the capability allows its possessor to have to the named object. Capability creation is a function of carefully guarded operating system routines. Normally, capabilities may not be modified except to reduce the rights. A subject that possesses a capability may perform certain operations including copying it or passing it as a parameter.

Upon creation of an object, a capability for that object is created. This new capability immediately includes all access right to the new object. The subject that creates the capability may pass copies of the capability to other subjects. A subject receiving a capability may use it (to perform the indicated access to the object), or may create more copies to pass to other subjects. When one subject passes a capability to another, it may reduce the stated access rights. Thus as a capability is propagated through the system, its access rights can either remain the same or decrease; they cannot increase.

In a segmentation system, two-dimensional addresses $v = (s, d)$ are used; s is the segment name, and d is the displacement of the desired address within the segment. An instruction references a storage location within a segment and a capability for the segment. All references to the segment are checked against the stated access rights in the capability. A typical capability would contain an object identifier (or a pointer to the object), the type of the object, and the access rights the possessor of the capability has to the object.

Users must be prevented from creating arbitrary capabilities. This can be accomplished by placing capabilities in special *capability segments* users cannot access. Another approach is to add a *tag bit* to each primary storage location. This bit, inaccessible to the user, is set on if the location contains a capability; if the bit is on, the hardware restricts the manipulation of the location's contents to appropriate system routines.

The identifier in a capability may be implemented as a pointer to the desired object, or it may be a unique code. Pointers make it easier to reach the object, but they must be updated if the object is moved. With the unique code approach, it is not necessary to update the capabilities. The unique code approach does require, however, that on every access to the object, its address must be determined. A hashing mechanism can be implemented efficiently; associative (or cache) storage can be used to reduce the overhead of repeated references to the same object.

Movement and Storage of Capabilities

Controlling the copying and movement of capabilities is a different problem. Systems generally do not allow direct manipulation of capabilities by users; instead capability manipulation is performed by the operating system on behalf of users.

Keeping track of capabilities is an important task of the operating system. It is complicated by the fact that the number of capabilities in a multiuser system can be large. The operating system must guard the capabilities as well as guarantee rapid access to them. This is often handled by a directory structure that controls all the capabilities in a system.

Revocation of Capabilities

It is sometimes necessary to revoke capabilities passed to another subject. If a directory system handles all capabilities, this can be relatively straightforward. But without such central control, revoking a capability can be difficult; the capability could have been copied many times.

In an emergency situation, one could copy an object and destroy the original thereby disabling the questionable capability. But this would affect other subjects with capabilities to that object.

Sometimes it is desirable to revoke the capability of a particular subject and also that of any other subject that received the capability from the given subject.

One technique for *selective revocation of capabilities* is to make all capabilities created from and object's primary capability point to the object indirectly through that primary capability. Then a particular capability may be revoked without affecting either the holders of the primary capability or any of the copies.

Capabilities to I/O devices may need to be interpreted differently depending on the type of the device; a capability for a tape drive object, for example, might allow rewind, while a capability for a printer would not.

Case Study: The Object-Oriented Architecture of the IBM System/38

In the IBM System/38, operating systems functions are provided by the Control Program Facility (CPF). The System/38 incorporates a high-level machine architecture that provides many resource management and supervisory functions generally found in software in previous systems.

The architecture provides an object-oriented, uniformly addressable, very large storage. All objects in the system are storage resident. All the system's storage is addressable by a single device-independent addressing mechanism that performs dynamic integrity and authorization checking.

The System/38 provides high-level machine instructions that manipulate objects. The *create* instruction builds a new object according to the attributes in a template.

Some attributes of an object are its name, its owner, and its existence (i.e., whether or not it can be implicitly destroyed). *Generic operations* apply to all objects; *unique operations* apply only to a specific object type.

All System/38 machine objects are *encapsulated*—the internal structure of an object produced by the create instruction is known only to the machine. Figure 14.1 summarizes the object manipulated by the machine instructions of the System/38.

Object	Explanation
Access group	Allows other objects to be grouped for more efficient transfer between primary and secondary storage
Context	Contains the name, type, and subtype of other objects to establish addressability
Controller description	Represent an I/O controller for a cluster of I/O devices
Cursor	Provides addressability into a data space
Data space	Stores data space records of one particular format
Data space index	Establishes the logical ordering of records stored in a data space
Index	Stores and orders data
Logical and description	Represents a physical I/O device
Network description	Represents one of the system's physical network ports
Process control space	Contains process execution
Program	Selects and orders machine instructions
Queue	For communication between processes, and between devices and processes
Space	Stores pointer and scalars
User profile	Identifies a valid user of the machine

Fig. 14.1. *System/38 objects.*

CPF provides users with an object-oriented interface. All data in the system is stored in object form and manipulated by object-oriented commands. Generic functions handle authorization, moving, renaming, dumping, locking, saving, and restoring objects. Specific functions dictate how an object can be used.

When an object is created, CPF places the object's name into a machine object called *context*. Contexts are seen by users as libraries or catalogs of objects.

CPF uses machine objects as building blocks to construct objects for users. For example, to create a user-oriented object called a database file, CPF combines a data space, a data space index, a cursor, and a space. The user actually sees only a single object, namely the database file. A higher-level object constructed from machine objects and other objects is called a *composite object*.

Each object consists of a functional portion and an associated space. The functions portion might be a program. The associated space is a region of bytes the machine user may manipulate directly. A *space object* has no functional part; it provides storage for buffer pointers, control blocks, and various other data items.

An *unresolved system pointer* specifies the name of an object but not its location. Once the object is referenced and found, its location is filled in; the system pointer is then *resolved*. Objects are located by searching contexts.

Security is rigidly enforced; every reference to an object is examined to be certain that the user has the right to access the object in the desired manner, if not, the reference is disallowed and a record is made of the attempted security violation.

The System/38 incorporates implicit synchronization into the object access mechanism to prevent simultaneous accesses. When one process is writing an object and another attempts to read it, the accesses are automatically serialized. When simultaneous reads are attempted, however, they are both allowed to proceed.

Users may perform synchronization explicitly with locks. Record-level locks may be used in database references; this greatly reduces the contention that would occur if the entire database were locked.

With CPF, one user is designated as *security administrator*. This user has access to all objects in the system. IBM supplies a standard set of user profiles with CPF; the profile for the security administrator includes all-objects authority and the authority to create new user profiles and modify existing profiles.

Cryptography

Cryptography was once of interest almost exclusively to the military and the diplomatic communities. Today it is particularly important in computing systems. Eavesdropping is becoming easier. Huge volumes of business are handled over the telephone. Computer networking is growing rapidly. Use of electronic mail and electronic funds transfer (EFT) is increasing.

The National Institute of Standards and Technology (NIST) (formerly the National Bureau of Standards) has adopted the *Data Encryption Standard (DES)* for transmission of sensitive federal information.

Cryptography is the use of data transformations to make the data incomprehensible to all except its intended users. The *privacy problem* is concerned with preventing the unauthorized extraction of information from a communication channel. The *authentication problem* is concerned with preventing one's opponents from modifying a transmission or inserting false data into a transmission. The *problem of dispute* is concerned with providing the receiver of a message with legal proof of the sender's identity, i.e., the electronic equivalent of a written signature.

A Cryptographic Privacy System

In a cryptographic privacy system, the *sender* wishes to transmit a certain unenciphered message (called a *plaintext*) to a legitimate *receiver*; the transmission is to occur over an *insecure channel* assumed to be monitored or tapped by an *eavesdropper* (Ri84).

The sender passes the plaintext to an encryption unit that transforms the plaintext into *ciphertext* or *cryptogram*; the ciphertext is not discernible to the eavesdropper. The ciphertext is then transmitted over the insecure channel. At the receiving end, the ciphertext passes through a decryption unit to regenerate the plaintext.

Cryptanalysis

Cryptanalysis is the process of attempting to regenerate plaintext from ciphertext but without knowledge of the decryption key; this is the normal task of the eavesdropper. If the eavesdropper, or *cryptanalyst*, cannot determine the plaintext from the ciphertext (without the key), then the cryptographic system is *secure*.

Public Key Systems

A cryptographic system is only as secure as its key. Key distribution must be handled over highly secure channels; this can be time-consuming, and sometimes such secures channels are simply not available.

Public key systems circumvent the key distribution problem (De83a). In conventional cryptographic systems, enciphering and deciphering are intimately related. Someone who processes the single key to encipher messages can also decipher them. In public key systems, the enciphering and deciphering functions are separated; the enciphering key cannot be used to decipher a message. These systems use an enciphering key, *E*, and a deciphering key, *D*, in a manner in which it is not computationally feasible (within a "reasonable" time) to determine *D* from *E*.

Thus *E* may be made public without compromising the security of *D*. This simplifies the problem of key distribution. Every user generates an enciphering key and a deciphering key. The enciphering key is made public; the deciphering key is kept secret. Thus anyone can send an encrypted messages to a particular user (because the enciphering key is public), but only that user can decipher the message (because the deciphering key is private). *E* is called a *public key* and *D* is called a *private key*.

Digital Signatures

. We have grown to accept the use of handwritten signatures as legal proof that a person agrees to the terms of a contract as stated on a sheet of paper, or that a person has authorized a transfer of funds as indicated on a check. But the use of written signatures involves the physical transmission of a paper document; this is not practical if electronic communication is to become more widely used in business.

A written signature can be produced by one person only (although forgeries certainly occur), but it can be recognized by many people as belonging uniquely to its author. A *digital signature*, then, to be accepted as a replacement for a written signature would have to be easily authenticated by anyone, but producible only by its author.

Public key cryptosystems offer a means of implementing digital signatures. The sender uses the private key to create a signed message. The receiver uses the sender's public key to encipher the message.

The receiver saves the signed message for use in resolving disputes. If the sender later denies that the message was sent, the receiver can present the signed message to a court of law where the judge then uses the sender's public key to check that the enciphered message corresponds to a meaningful plaintext message with the sender's name, the proper time sent, etc. Only the sender could have generated the message (assuming that the private key had not been compromised), and therefore the receiver's claim could be upheld in court.

This technique has one significant disadvantage: it allows an eavesdropper who possesses the sender's public key to determine the message. The defect is easy to correct: The sender can add a second level of encryption to the already encrypted messages by using the receiver's public key; the receivers private key is then used to recover the signed encrypted message and the sender's public key is used to recover the original plaintext.

The DES and RSA Schemes

Two schemes that the reader interested in cryptography might want to explore further are the Data Encryption Standard (DES) and the Rivest, Shamir, and Adleman (RSA) scheme. DES is a *symmetric encryption scheme*—the same key is used for both encryption and decryption. RSA is an *asymmetric encryption scheme*—different key are used for encryption and decryption.

Applications

Cryptography is particularly useful in timesharing systems and computer networks. Passwords should be stored in encrypted form so that even if the operating system is penetrated, the password list will be of no use. This is the most common application of cryptography in today's computer systems.

Cryptography may also be used to protect all stored data in a computer system. But the encryption/decryption overhead could be so large as to make this prohibitive. The advent of special hardware for this purpose may eventually make this practice feasible. File encryption would solve one serious problem with shared systems: every system has at least one person designated as having unrestricted access to all system files, so users are reluctant to store sensitive information. File encryption would enable users to trust even their most sensitive information to computers. Encrypted backups needs not be guarded as heavily as unencrypted ones.

In *link encryption* the network assumes the responsibility for encryption/decryption at each node; the data is transmitted between nodes in encrypted form, decrypted at each node to determine where to pass it next, and then reencrypted.

In *end-to-end encryption* a message is encrypted at its source and decrypted only at its destination. The message is thus protected throughout its transmission even if security at one of the nodes has been compromised. In a store-and-forward packet switching network with end-to-end encryption, the destination address associated with a packet cannot be encrypted; it must be readable at each node for routing purposes.

Password logins can also be protected with encryption. A *challenges and response procedure* can be helpful here. The user transmits a login request "in clear" (i.e., not encrypted). The system, to authenticate the user, sends a *challenge* string to the user in clear. The challenge string should be one that is guaranteed not to repeat; the date and time carried to millionths of a second would be appropriate. The user's terminal encrypts this challenge using a key supplied by the user (and known to the system) and transmits the result to the system. The system authenticates the user by comparing the response with an internal encrypted version of the challenge. Then all future transmissions during this session are encrypted with the user's key. Because the key is never transmitted, an eavesdropper would have to cryptanalyze the transmissions to understand them or to impersonate the valid user.

Operating System Penetration

A favourite pastime of many people, especially university students, is to call in to a timesharing system or a computer network, penetrate its defenses, and then happily publicize their success. The people who do this often intend no harm; rather they simply wish to show that the systems can be broken into. Such people are often called *hackers*. Instructors have found their student grade files modified, and system administrators have been horrified to discover master lists of all user passwords posted on public bulletin boards! Operating systems students thoroughly enjoy the explanations of complex successful security penetration attempts. At one major university (legend has it) the instructor in the operating system course guaranteed a grade of "A" to any student who could penetrate the university's operating system; a disproportionately large number of "A" grades were awarded that semester!

In some systems, the ultimate penetration consists simply of flipping the machine state bit from problem state to supervise state. Once this is accomplished, the penetrator may execute privileged instruction to gain access to virtually any data protected by the operating system.

Penetration studies are designed to determine if a system's defenses against attacks by nonprivileged users are adequate. Their goal is to expose design deficiencies so that they may be corrected.

I/O control is a favourite area for penetration attempts. I/O code is often complex; various types of errors and omissions are often exposed upon detailed analysis. Because I/O channels have access to primary storage, they could modify critical system information. An I/O channel can be forced into an infinite loop, thus denying I/O capability to the system; this could be devastating in systems that must operate reliably.

One goal of penetration tests is to estimate the *penetration work factor*, an indication of how much effort and resources must be expended by a potential penetrator to obtain unauthorized access to system resources. A key goal of security mechanisms is to make this factor large; actual penetration studies may reveal that it is not as large as the system's designers intended it to be.

Generic System Functional Flaws

Several flaws have been found to be common to many computing systems. These include

- *Authentication*—On many systems, users cannot determine if the hardware and software are what they are supposed to be. This makes it easy for a penetrator to replace a program without the user's knowledge. A user might obligingly type a password into a counterfeit login program, for example.

- *Encryption*—The master list of passwords should be stored in encrypted form (Gt78). It is often is not.
- *Implementation*—A well-thought-out design for a security mechanism may be improperly implemented.
- *Implicit trust*—A common problem; one routine assumes that another is functioning properly when, in fact, it should be carefully examining parameters supplied by the other.
- *Implied sharing*—The system may inadvertently deposit critical system information in a user's address space.
- *Interprocess communication*—The penetrator may use a send/receive mechanism to test various possibilities. For example, the penetrator may request a system resource and supply a password; the return information may indicate "password correct", confirming the penetrator's guessed password.
- *Legality checking*—The system may not be performing sufficient validation of user parameters.
- *Line disconnect*—In timesharing and networking, when the line is lost (for any reason) the operating system should immediately logout the user or place the user in a state such that reauthorization is necessary for the user to regain control. Some systems let a process "float" after a line disconnect. A penetrator may be able to gain control of the process and use whatever resources the process may access.
- *Operator carelessness*—A penetrator may trick an operator into mounting a counterfeit operating system disk.
- *Parameter passing by reference vs. by value*—It is safer to pass parameter directly in registers than it is to have the registers point to the locations containing the parameters. Passing by reference can lead to a situation in which the parameters are still in the user's address space after legality checking occurs; the user could thus supply legitimate parameters, have them checked, and then modify them just before the system uses them.
- *Passwords*—Passwords are often easy to guess or to obtain by repeated trials.
- *Penetrator entrapment*—Systems should contain *entrapment mechanisms* to lure the unskilled penetrator. This is a good first line of detection. Most systems have inadequate entrapment mechanisms.
- *Privilege*—In some systems, too many programs are given too much privilege. This is contrary to the principle of least privilege.
- *Program confinement*—A program borrowed from another user can act as a Trojan Horse; it might steal or alter the borrower's files.
- *Prohibition*—Often users are warned not to use certain features because the results may be "indeterminate," but indeed these features remain accessible to the users.
- *Residue*—Often the penetrator may find a list of passwords by simply looking in a wastebasket. Residues are sometimes left in storage after a system routine runs. Sensitive information should always be overwritten or destroyed before the media it occupies (storage, paper, etc.) is released or discarded. Paper shredders are popular for this purpose.
- *Shielding*—A current in a wire generates a magnetic field around the wire; penetrators may actually tap a transmission line or computer system without making physical contact. Electrical shielding may be used to prevent such "invisible instructions."

- *Threshold values*—These are designed to discourage repeated login attempts, for example. After a certain number of invalid login attempts, that user (or the terminal at which the logins are being attempted) should be locked out and the system administrator should be notified. Many systems lack this feature.

Generic Operating System Attacks

Certain penetration methodologies have been used effectively on many systems.

- *Asynchronism*—With multiple processes progressing asynchronously it is possible for one process to modify parameters that another has tested for validity but not as yet used; thus one process can pass bad values to another even if the second perform extensive checking.
- *Browsing*—A user searches the computer system attempting to locate privileged information.
- *Between lines*—A special terminal is used to tap into a communication line held by an inactive logged-in user.
- *Clandestine code*—A patch is made under the guise of correcting a bug in the operating system; the code contains *trapdoors*, which allow subsequent unauthorized reentry to the system.
- *Denial of access*—A user writes a program to crash the system, set the system into an infinite loop, or monopolize the system's resources. The intent here is to deny access or service to legitimate users.
- *Interacting synchronized processes*—Processes use the system's synchronization primitives to share and pass information to one another.
- *Line disconnect*—The penetrator attempts to gain access to a user's job after a line disconnect, but before the system acknowledges the disconnect.
- *Masquerade*—The penetrator assumes the identity of a legitimate user after having obtained the proper identification through clandestine means.
- *"NAK" attack*—Many systems allow a user to interrupt a running process (such as by pressing the "negative acknowledge" key on a terminal), perform another operation, and then resume the interrupted process. In some cases the penetrator can "catch" the system in an unprotected state and easily seize control.
- *Operator spoof*—A clever penetrator can often fool a computer operator into performing an action that compromises system security.
- *Piggyback*—The penetrator uses a special terminal to tap a communication line. The penetrator intercepts messages between the user and the processor, and either modifies the messages or replaces them entirely.
- *Trojan Horse*—The penetrator places code in the system to allow subsequent unauthorized access. The Trojan Horse may be left in the system permanently, or it may erase all traces of itself after a penetration.
- *Unexpected parameters*—The penetrator supplies unexpected values in a supervisor call to take advantage of a weakness in the system's legality checking mechanisms.

Case Study: Penetrating an Operating System

A graduate-level computer science class at the University of Michigan in Ann Arbor successfully penetrated the Michigan Terminal System (MTS) operating system. The study was concerned only with software security. The goals were for an authorized and knowledgeable but nonprivileged user to gain access to files (to which this user did not have access), and to cause the system to crash.

Team members were regular users of MTS. They were given access to internal system documentation. They performed a comprehensive analysis of the system and produced a report listing all suspected flaws. They employed the flaw hypothesis methodology developed by System Development Corporation. This involves

- *Flaw hypothesis generation*—The team examines well-known system weaknesses, and uses its collective knowledge about the system to list suspected flaws.
- *Flaw hypothesis confirmation*—Tests are run to determine if the suspected flaws are in fact real flaws.
- *Flaw generalization*—The confirmed flaws are carefully studied to determine if they imply other flaws or general design weaknesses. If they do, these cause this cycle to begin again with flaw hypothesis generation.

The team discovered a flaw in some of the system subroutines. The parameter checking mechanisms were weak; they would allow a user to cause arbitrary bit sequences to be stored into the *system segment* that contains much of the system's control information about a task. The flaws made it possible for a user to modify the system's accounting information, and to change the user's privilege level. The MTS protection system's information, also stored in the system segment, could be altered to completely disable the protection mechanisms. The user could switch the system from user mode to system mode and execute privileged supervisor calls. One of these could disable hardware storage protection, allowing the user to modify shared storage segments. The MTS supervisor core resided in such shared segments, and so the user could switch the machine to supervisor state and freely access arbitrary portions of the supervisor and any other software for that matter. Voila! A total penetration.

Another type of flaw exposed was that portions of the system could be forced to store their critical information in user-accessible segments. The students were able to obtain free computer time in an interesting way: they forced a job into abnormal termination in such a manner that the system's accounting routines were bypassed. A careful examination of user-accessible shared storage revealed that some highly sensitive information (like password) was being stored in these areas. The team was also able to crash the system; they discovered that a certain instruction sequence forced the supervisor into an infinite loop.

The control relationships within the operating system security mechanisms were found to depend on one another's correct operation. Once one mechanism was compromised, the group found it relatively easy to compromise other security mechanism even at highly privilege levels.

UNIX Operating System Security

UNIX systems are designed to be friendly and accessible, and to encourage interaction between people via the computer system. This makes these systems more difficult to secure. UNIX systems are intended to be open systems; their specifications are made widely available. The source code is available. Many of the problems referred to in the section are not unique to UNIX systems.

The UNIX systems password file is stored in encrypted form. When a user enters a password, a one-way transformation is applied to form the encrypted version and a comparison is made. A decryption transformation is not known. Thus, even the system administrator cannot help users who have lost their passwords (except to change passwords to new values). UNIX systems use *salt* when encryption passwords. The salt is a two-character string randomly selected via a function of the time and the process ID. Twelve bits of the salt then modify the encryption algorithm. Thus, users who choose the same password (by coincidence or intentionally) will have different encrypted passwords. Some installations modify the password program to prevent users from choosing bad passwords.

With the UNIX systems *setuid* feature, a program may be built in such a way that when a user executes the program, the user's individual ID or group ID or both are changed to that of the program's owner only while the program executes. This powerful feature has also generated security flaws, particularly when the resulting ID is that of the "superuser" (who has access to all files in a UNIX system). For example, if a regular user is able to execute a shell belonging to the superuser, and for which the *setuid* bit has been set, then the regular user essentially becomes the superuser. Clearly, *setuid* should be carefully employed. Users, including the superuser, should periodically examine their directories to confirm the presence of *setuid* files and detect any that should not be *setuid.*

A relatively simple means of compromising security in UNIX systems (and other operating systems as well) is to install a program that prints out the login prompt, copies what the user then types, fakes an invalid login, hangs up the phone, and lets the user try again. The user has unwittingly given away his or her password! One defense against this is that if you are confident you typed the password correctly the first time, you should log on to a different terminal and choose a new password immediately.

UNIX systems include the *crypt* command, which allows a user to enter a key and cleartext; ciphertext is output. The transformation can be reversed trivially with the same key. One problem with this is that users tend to use the same key repeatedly; once the key is discovered, all other files encrypted with this key can be read. Users sometimes forget to delete their cleartext files after producing encrypted versions. This makes discovering the key much easier.

Too many people are often given superuser *(su)* privileges. All *su* activity should be logged; this command lets any user who types a correct password of another user assume that user's identity, possibly even becoming the superuser.

A popular Trojan Horse technique is to install a fake *su* program, which obtains the user's password, mails it to the penetrator, and then restores the regular *su* program (Fa86). Never allow others to have write permissions on your files, especially on your directories; if you do, you're inviting someone to install a Trojan Horse.

UNIX systems contain a feature called *password aging* in which the administrator determines how long passwords are good for; when a password expires, the user receives a message and is asked to enter a new password. This has several problems:

1. Users often supply easy-to-crack passwords.
2. The system often prevents a user from resetting to the old (or any other) password for a week, so the user cannot strengthen a weak password.

3. Users can indeed switch back and forth between only two passwords once a week.
4. Since the expiration is coded in the password file, some one can easily print a list of abandoned accounts and go to work on corrupting them without fear of immediate reprisal.

Logging unsuccessful login attempts often gets passwords because people sometimes accidentally type their password when they mean to type their login id.

One obvious feature with an unanticipated consequence is that of disabling accounts after a small number of unsuccessful login attempts. This is a defense against the intruder who tries all possible passwords. But an intruder who has penetrated the system can then turn it around in his favour and use it to disable the account or accounts of those such as the system administrator who might attempt to detect the intrusion.

The perpetrator who temporarily gains superuser privileges can install a trapdoor program with undocumented features. For example, someone with access to source code could rewrite the login program to accept a particular login name and automatically let this user become the superuser without even typing a password.

It is possible for individual users to "grab" the system, thus preventing other users from gaining access. A user could accomplish this by spawning dozens of concurrent processes each of which opens dozens of files, thus filling all the slots in the file table. Installations can guard against this by setting reasonable limits, but this in turn could hinder legitimate users who in fact need the additional resources.

Worms and Viruses

For the first few decades of modern computing, the industry experienced many computer crimes and penetrations, but few of these could be labelled "spectacular." In November of 1988, however, a spectacular intrusion did occur when a *worm* program crawled its way through thousands of computers in the U.S. government sponsored Internet. The worm exploited weaknesses in various UNIX utility programs. Fortunately these weaknesses were not apparent in every computer on the Internet, or the damage would have been far greater.

This worm was supposedly innocuous in the sense that it did not seek to destroy files or perform other serious damage. But it did use substantial computer time on each of the infected systems, bringing many of these computers "to their knees." Programs that to designed to do damage are often called *viruses*. *Worm* programs were originally designed to travel between computers in a distributed system to do useful work, but this was certainly not the case with Internet worm.

The incident immediately captured the world's attention. Indeed, two of the more important areas of interest in operating systems today—UNIX systems and computer networks—were highlighted as being easy targets for a monumental breach of security.

UNIX systems have developed a reputation for not being particularly secure (Fa86a) certainly the Internet incident corroborates this. But few, if any, operating systems are known for their impressive security (the reader might try to name a few super secure operating systems at this point).

Networks by nature are designed to increase the accessibility of information, and this certainly increases security problems. Encryption is absolutely essential as a first defense against eavesdropper, but it is insufficient by itself to guard against all possible security breaches. *Spoofers*, for example, tap network traffic and retransmit certain types of packets to force the network to perform operations the spoofers want. Even if the captured that packets are encrypted, the spoofer can still retransmit them, observe the network behaviour and conceivably infer what really is in the packets.

The Department of Defense publishes guidelines for security operating systems. Its so-called "orange book" lists various classifications defining increasingly secure systems. Some of these treat all information at the same level of security, and so are appropriate only for user communities in which each user has the same security clearance. Several of these computer security classifications treat information at distinct levels, thus enabling users with different security classifications (such as confidential, secret, and top secret) to share the same system.

To have highly secure systems we must have tight control over the software in these systems. We must have a way of ensuring that the software we are using is in fact the software that has been certified to be secure. This is a nontrivial problem given that software is normally changing and evolving to meet the developing needs of organizations. Configuration management systems can be used to maintain software and log all modifications (but are still troubled with the notion of who maintains the configuration management system).

Government UNIX systems procurements are big business, and the government resource highly secure systems. This has fostered significant activity in developing increasing secure UNIX systems that meet government specifications. Thus, the open systems phenomenon of which UNIX systems are such a critical part, has actually fostered an increase in the research and development of secure computer systems. Is the phrase "secure systems" an oxymoron? Perhaps not.

Viruses and worms differ in at least one primary way from most of the other kinds of programs that cause security problems: they can propagate copies of themselves among the programs and data of a computer system, and among the computer systems in a network. Thus, after a virus has been cleared from one user or system, the copies of the virus can be reading through other systems, perhaps reinfecting the original targets.

Viruses can infect in subtle ways, or their presence can be blatant. The virus that destroy files, monopolizes system resources, or displays expletives is certainly making its presence felt in a dramatic way. But the more insidious virus is the one that infects and can no easily detectable traces of its existence. A favourite technique is to let the virus lie permanent and be triggered by an event such as the system clock reaching a certain value possibly years later than the infection), or the login of a particular user (such as the boss regulated of employee). One of the all-time favourite virus triggering events is the arrival of Friday the 13th.

How Worms and Viruses Work

There are many types of viruses, and yes, they are called *strains*. *Boot infectors* try to get into boot sectors on disks. Each time the system is booted (i.e., the operating system loaded and initiated), the virus is activated. The virus stays in control by inserting itself in a "stream" of activity; for example, it can catch interrupts and traps. One of these tells the system that a new disk has been inserted and must be initialized—the virus takes advantage such an opportunity to copy itself to the boot sector of the new disk. Other strains of rules infect system files and applications programs.

Viruses spread by contact (at this point the reader should already be reflecting on how computer viruses are similar to the viruses that afflict humans). This contact may come by string disks, or it may come through network connectivity. A virus infects either by completely replacing a code segment, or by binding itself to a code segment. This fact can detection because the size of the infected code segment is likely to be larger than the original.

The spread of viruses can be halted or slowed by using programs that prevent and recover from viruses.

Some observations about viruses that help us detect them are that they infected program (not data), that these infections change the infected programs, and that they themselves must eventually be executed.

There are several types of programs that fight viruses. These either prevent information detect infections, or identify and recover from particular strains of viruses.

Prevention programs operate as watchdogs monitoring all system activity and a data. *Any attempt to access or modify a program is a possible warning of a virus*. Viruses can be designed, however, that work around such detection mechanisms, that require much greater knowledge of system internals.

Infections can be detected by looking for "muddy footprints." How can one detect if a program has been modified? A detection program can simply run a hash total of its instructions in the program and compare it to hash total supplied with the supposedly nonmodifiable program. Any program that has been modified would produce different total. Such a mechanism could be thwarted, of course, by modifying the proper copy of the original hash total; but, again, this would require far more familiarity with system internals.

Various kinds of "sweeper programs" locate and remove specific strains of virus. Once the system knows what to look for, it is generally easy to find a virus. Unfortunately given the myriad of virus strains in existence, and given the rapid evolution of infection the sweeper programs are often created too late in the virus's evolution to be effective.

A number of safety techniques are apparent. First, users must establish a point of. For many, this will be software supplied directly by responsible vendors in original packing. This places a significant burden on software developers to certify not only to their programs perform the desired functions according to specifications, but also that is programs are virus free. The potential for litigation is so serious here that major software vendors are devoting substantial resources to the development and implementation of virus-free certification procedures. The user who borrows copies of software, or who public domain software obtained from electronic bulletin boards, is inviting trouble for telltale signs of infection are excess disk-seeking activity, "soggy" performance, a reduced amounts of available primary memory and disk space.

Case Study: The Internet Worm

The text went to press shortly after what was probably the all-time greatest penetration of computer network, an effort that has been labelled the *Internet worm*. The penetration is thousands of computers on the U.S. Government-sponsored Internet occurred on November 1988. Over the next several weeks, hundreds of articles appeared in major application describing the worm program itself, speculating on the author's identity and estimating the damage that was done, and describing the phenomenal response of industry to rid the Internet of the worm program. One of the most detailed accounts and it was prepared by Eugene Spafford of the Department of Computer Sciences at the University. The reader is urged to obtain and study this remarkable paper; markable both for its incisive analysis and the fact that it was published within weeks or the worm incident occurred.

The worm program exploited only a few weaknesses in certain of the UNIX systems in Internet (patches to eliminate these flaws were designed and distributed within hours or the worm was detected). After the worm penetrated a system, it "looked around" to detect other systems to penetrate over the network. As it crawled from system to system, it repeatedly infected some systems; some of these had so many active copies of the worm competing for execution time that the systems could no longer function.

User may have accounts on several machines in the Internet. If the worm compromised a user's account on one machine, it would then try compromising that user's accounts on remote machines.

The worm also took advantage of a weakness in *sendmail*, a program for transmitting mail between systems in a network. Sendmail has a debugging option, which, when on, variables commands, rather than data, to be transmitted. The debug option should have been detected it had been inadvertently left on in many of the systems on the Internet.

Passwords are stored in UNIX systems in encrypted form in a public file. Even though there is no reverse transformation known to read the file, a program can generate test towards, apply the forward encryption algorithm, and compare these encrypted test passwords with the encrypted password in the file. With good guesses, the worm was usually able to determine many users' passwords. It did this by two different methods. First was to try certain popular passwords (which the worm had in a table). The second was various transformations on information the worm was able to determine about each one, some of these transformations were as simple as spelling certain user facts backwards.

Once the worm was discovered, it was easy to stop. It did not destroy files, but it did monopolize resources and thus bring down many systems. The Internet researchers who analyzed the binary code concluded that the worm was not a particularly well-written program, and that it did not take advantage of some of the more subtle known UNIX systems security flaws.

As this text went to press, a suspect had been identified, but prosecution had not begun. The scope of the penetration was enormous. Some estimates of lost people time and computer time go as high as $100,000,000. The incident has become legendary. Some people view the worm invasion as a heinous criminal act; others feel that the perpetrator(s) may have done the computer industry—and society as a whole—a great service by attention on how careless the industry has been in constructing systems that proved to compromise.

Perhaps incidents like this, and the ensuing publicity and public concern, which are the development of legislation and penalties strict enough top deter future penetration attempts. The incident will surely intensify the research and development of operating systems that are much harder to penetrate. Will there ever be a system that is virtually impossible to break? Probably not. Does this mean we should not build complex system? We simply may not have that choice. Our best hope should be to do a much better attempting to construct more secure systems. One has to believe that the Internet incident will not be the last large-scale network penetration we will see. But it may more research in the important areas of operating systems security than any other incident in the history of computing.

Summary

As computing continues to become more accessible, security problems increase. The communications and networking greatly increase the vulnerability of computer-based systems. User-friendliness also implies increased vulnerability.

Sharing and protection are conflicting goals. It is easier to verify the security of systems rather than complex systems. Security requirements for a given system define what means for that system to be secure.

A total approach to computer security is essential. External security deals with protecting the computer system from intruders and disasters. User interface security that concerned with establishing a user's identity before that user is allowed to access a system. Internal security deals with ensuring the reliable and uncorrupted operation of the computer system and the integrity of programs and data.

Authorization determines what access is allowed to what entities. Division of responsibilities gives people distinct subsets of the responsibilities; no one employee deals with large portion of the operation of the system, so a security compromise would have to involve several employees.

Surveillance deals with monitoring and auditing the system, and authenticating users. In threat monitoring, the operating system controls sensitive operations rather than give control directly to the users. Surveillance programs perform the sensitive operations. Which surveillance programs must have greater access than user programs in order to service and requests, this is called amplification.

The most common authentication scheme in use today is simple password protection. Short passwords can often be determined by repeated trials. Encryption of the master list of passwords helps keep passwords secure even if a system is penetrated. Passwords should be changed frequently.

An audit log is a permanent record of events that occur in a computer system; it is heavily protected. The audit log act as a deterrent to those who would attempt a security violation.

Access rights define what access various subjects have to various objects. Objects are protected against subjects. The most critical security measures are implemented in a security kernel. A fault-tolerant computer system is one that continues to operate even after one or more components fail. Fault tolerance is facilitated by incorporation of fail-safe mechanisms into hardware, use of transparent multiprocessing, use of multiple input/output subsystems, incorporation of much of the operating system into hardware, and incorporation of fault detection mechanisms into hardware.

Capabilities-based object-oriented systems are being investigated today as a means of achieving secure computing systems. A protection domain defines the access rights that a subject has to the various objects of a system. Small protection domains are important for enforcing the principle of least privilege. For a subject to access a particular object, it must possess a capability to do so. The lost object problem is concerned with what happens when the last capability to an object is deleted. Revoking capabilities can be difficult; a capability could have been copied many times.

The IBM System/38 provides an object-oriented capabilities-based environment. It provides high-level machine instructions that directly manipulate objects. System/38 machine objects are encapsulated; their internal structure is known only to the machine. All object names are placed in cataloglike objects called contexts. A summary of System/38 machine objects was presented in the chapter.

System/38 implements capabilities through system pointers. Security is rigidly enforced; every reference to an object is examined to be sure the user has the right to access the object in the desired manner.

Cryptography is important to the security of today's computing systems. The National Bureau of Standards had adopted the Data Encryption Standard (DES) for the transmission of sensitive federal information. Some interesting issues in cryptography are the privacy problem, the authentication problem, and the problem of dispute.

A sender encrypts plaintext to create ciphertext, which is transmitted to a receiver over in insecure channel monitored by an eavesdropper. The receiver decrypts the ciphertext to reconstruct the original plaintext. Cryptanalysis is the process of attempting to regenerate a plaintext from a ciphertext, but without knowledge of the decryption key.

In public key systems the enciphering and deciphering functions are separated; each requires a different key. One key is made public; the other is kept private. When a message is encrypted with a user's public key, only that user can decipher the message. Using public key systems, it is possible to implement digital signatures that guarantee the authenticity of the sender of a message.

Two of the most significant cryptography schemes are the Data Encryption Standard (DES) and the Rivest, Shamir, and Adleman scheme. DES is a symmetric scheme, in which a single key is used for encryption and decryption; RSA is an asymmetric scheme, in which different keys are used for these purposes.

The most common use of encryption in today's operating systems is to protect a system's master list of passwords. Encryption is also used to protect data stored in files, and to protect data being transmitted over networks.

Encrypted backup tapes and disks need not be guarded as heavily as unencrypted ones. Link encryption is concerned with encryption/decryption at each node of a computer network. With end-to-end encryption, messages are encrypted only at their source and decrypted only at their destination. A challenge and response procedure can enable its system to authenticate a user during login without the need for transmitting a key.

An operating system's defenses should be able to withstand a penetration attempt by a nonprivileged user; making an operating system absolutely impenetrable is an impossible task. The best one can hope to do is to make the system highly resistant to penetration. Penetration studies attempt to estimate a system's penetration work factor, that is, how much effort and resources must be expanded to penetrate the system.

Numerous generic system functional flaws that enable successful penetrations were enumerated in the chapter. The chapter also presented an enumeration of generic operating system attacks. The operating system designer must be aware of the techniques used by system penetrators if the designer is to attempt to produce a secure system.

The chapter concluded with a discussion of a penetration study performed at the University of Michigan. The Michigan Terminal System (MTS) was successfully penetrated in several ways by a team of students with access to system documentation and source listings, but who could only access the system as conventional nonprivileged users. The students used the flaw hypothesis methodology developed by System Development Corporation; suspected flaws were enumerated, confirmed, and then generalized to expose other flaws and design weaknesses. The key flaw that enabled a total penetration was a defect in the parameter checking mechanisms. After parameters were verified, the user was able to change them before the operating system actually used them.

15

Distributed Operating Systems: Algorithms

A *distributed operating system* governs the operation of a distributed computer system and provides a virtual-machine system abstraction to its users. The key objective of a distributed operating system is *transparency*. Ideally, component and resource distribution should be hidden from users and application programs unless they explicitly demand otherwise. That is, the network becomes "invisible," analogous to the way that virtual memory hides the secondary storage.

Computer network environment and operating systems usually support intersite communication and supply protocols for bulk data exchanges, such as file transfer, but do not support transparent access to distributed resources. A key difference between a network and a distributed operating system is manifested in the degree of user's awareness of the physical resource distribution. A network operating system may provide remote operations and remote file access, but the user is almost invariably required to be aware that the resource being operated on is remote. As an example, naming of a remote file usually requires that a site or location prefix be added to the remote pathname, such as *siteID: pathname*. Similarly, remote operations, such as *login*, usually have special names, such as *rlogin*, that differentiate them from the functionally equivalent local operations. A distributed operating system, on the other hand, provides a virtual-machine abstraction of the system and offers a unified interface for resource access and manipulation regardless of its location. Network and distributed operating systems have a common hardware base; the differences between them lie almost exclusively in software. This chapter introduces the fundamental concepts of networking and algorithms for distributed processing.

Rationale for Distributed Systems

Why Distributed

The evolution of computer communication technology led to the implementation of a major computer network called ARPANET in the late sixties. It was funded by the defense Advanced Research Projects Agency (DARPA) of the U. S. Department of Defense. ARPANET connected a number of universities and research sites dispersed across a vast geographic area. It provided a large-scale operational experience and stimulated a lot of early research on computer networks. Ever since, researchers and practitioners alike have labored at realizing the promise of distributed processing. Its major potential benefits include:

- Resource sharing and load balancing
- Communication and information sharing
- Incremental growth
- Reliability, availability, fault tolerance
- Performance

Resource sharing is one of the major potential advantages of distributed systems. Temporary surpluses and shortages of resources such as processing power, storage capacity, and information from databases may be balanced to improve cost-effectiveness and performance of a distributed system.

On a greater scale, a distributed system effectively merges a number of previously autonomous user populations, such as several different time-sharing systems and/or LANs, into a larger union. The resulting enlarged pool of commonly accessible resources introduces the benefits of economy of scale. It effectively enlarges the base of service providers and its potential customers, and provides the communication network as a medium for access and exchange of resources and services. For example, smaller departments that occasionally need the services of a supercomputer but cannot justify the purchase of one may be able to lease time on a remote supercomputer and access it via the network. Similarly, an institution that own an underutilized supercomputer may offer its services via the network. Given the combined processing and storage power of a federation of computer systems connected to a given network, ample opportunities for resource sharing and load balancing present themselves.

Communication and information sharing are forms of resource sharing. In our classification they are presented as a separate category in order to emphasize their special importance. One of the major surprise experiences largely unforeseen by system designers was that communication and electronic mail became so popular that they represented a very significant portion of the traffic on early computer networks such as ARPANET. The user's need and desire to communicate and share information was also one of the discoveries resulting from the use of time-sharing systems. Personal computers, which were initially heralded as providing the ultimate freedom and self-sufficiency, are increasingly abandoning isolation and being connected via networks in order to enable their users to communicate and share information.

Distributed systems generally serve much larger, possibly geographically dispersed, user communities and thus represent an attractive opportunity for communication and information sharing. Electronic mail has a number of appealing characteristics, such as fast delivery and the possibility of instant reply, as well as a store-and-forward capability that allows interested parties to converse at their convenience. Unlike the telephone, electronic mail gives time for reflection and thus has a potential for more effective communication. It can involve entire work groups; broadcast or forward specific messages to all interested parties; be received by remote log-ins, even by parties that are on leave; and promptly each to changes of user residence. Other interesting forms of information sharing that are gaining popularity in distributed systems include access to online databases and bulletin boards.

Due to the economy of scale, the point of cost-effectiveness for connecting to information databases, such as large depositories of technical abstracts and indexed references, is much more easily reached in a distributed system than in a time-sharing system. Bulletin boards and electronic forms are a relatively novel form of teleconferencing and topical information exchange. User benefits include the possibility of focusing only on the specific areas of interest and the ability to offer or solicit peer opinions on any given topic therein. Expert opinions and instant reactions to new technologies and other developments may be pooled and amended to from a body of knowledge within a time frame that is vastly superior to other forms of information acquisition, dissemination, and retrieval.

Incremental growth may be accomplished in a distributed system by gradually augmenting the equipment as the needs of applications and user requirements change. Moreover, distribution allows selective upgrades by making it possible to add resources of a particular type as necessary to remove a specific system bottleneck. Likewise, software changes that do not disrupt existing applications, such as addition of new function, are possible in distributed systems implemented using the client/server model.

Centralized systems are much less flexible. They can support hardware and software upgrades only until the limit of the existing equipment is reached. Subsequent growth to accommodate expanding user and application needs is possible only by means of costly equipment replacement and retirement of the old hardware and possibly software. It is rarely possible to improve the processing capacity in a centralized system by a factional amount, say, 10%, without costly equipment replacement.

Reliability, availability, and ***fault tolerance*** are quite different issues, but their common thread is that they have significant potential advantages in distributed systems over the centralized environment. Increased reliability comes from duplication of equipment and the possibility of storing replicated data at different locations. This may be accomplished in a graduated manner by configuring incremental excess capacity or partially replicating the important data. Availability may be improved by having multiple copies of resources to draw upon in case of overloading or failures. This also leads to fault tolerance and graceful degradation rather than the complete loss of service as in case of individual component failures. Disaster protection can be improved greatly in distributed systems by placing multiple copies of data in geographically dispersed locations.

Performance improvements come mostly from the potential for parallel operation when multiple nodes cooperate on solving a single problem. Response time, a measure of performance, may be improved in a distributed system by virtue of the ability to place frequently used data close to their users.

Other potential advantages of distributed systems include reduced costs, greater capacity than a single processor can deliver, and better ability to parallel real-world organizational structure due to local control of local data.

Major drawbacks of distributed processing are:

- Reduced ability to pool memory and processor resources among distinct nodes
- Increased dependence on network performance and reliability
- Security weaknesses
- More complex system administration and maintenance

What is Distributed

Distribution basically spans three dimensions:

- Hardware
- Control
- Data

System resources generally fall into one of the two categories (1) physical resources, such a processors and devices, and (2) logical resources, such as files and processes. Distributed algorithms and processing often involve multiple processes that execute on different nodes. These processes need to communicate in order to cooperate, and to synchronize in order to maintain system integrity while they access shared resources. Control includes resource management and coordination of activities that take place on individual nodes. Distribution of resources does not necessarily imply distribution of control. Control over any particular class of resources may be centralized or distributed.

Centralized control requires delegation of an arbiter node that manages a set of system resources. All requests for accessing any member of that particular set must be sent to the control node for authorization. The central arbiter thus has complete information about the state of the resources under its jurisdiction and of pending requests for their use. Problems of centralized resource control include a single point of failure, traffic congestion at the control node, and delays in obtaining permits. As discussed later, the single-point failure problem may be alleviated by implementing algorithms for election of the successor node, at the cost of added complexity, logging of outstanding requests, and potentially long transition delays.

Hierarchical and decentralized forms of control can eliminate most of these problems. However, they require the use of distributed control algorithms and protocols that must be known to and obeyed by all participating nodes. Several such algorithms are discussed later in this chapter.

Distribution of data may be achieved by partitioning, replication, or both. In some applications judicious partitioning of data can contribute to performance and availability by placing frequently used items close to their points of processing. When the ratio of queries to updates is high, replication of data at multiple sites can contribute to performance, availability, and fault tolerance. A high update/query ratio is quite common in directions, name databases, and some applications. In general, the flexibility to partition and/or replicate arbitrary subsets of data is an important benefit of distributed processing.

Computer Networks

This section contain a brief introduction to some of the basic concepts of computer networking, such as types, topology, and communication protocols.

Autonomous machines that execute application programs and constitute the computational resource of a distributed system are usually called *hosts*. They are connected for purposes of communication by means of *a communication network* or subnetwork. Depending on the physical distance spanned by their communication subnetworks, computer networks are usually classified as

- Wide-area networks (WANs)
- Local-area networks (LANs)

While no specific delimiting distance is defined, it is reasonable to think of a local-area network within the confines of a single building or a small campus. Wide-area network, on the other hand, may connect hosts that are many miles apart, including even intercontinental distances. Mostly for technological reasons, WANs tend to have comparatively *low bandwidth* and *high communication delays*. LANs, on the other hand, are often characterized by *high bandwidth* and *low communication delays*. These fundamental differences have a significant impact on the design choices and selection of the distributed algorithms whose characteristics may make them more suitable for one type of the network than the other.

Wide-Area Networks

Figure 15.1 illustrates a typical architecture of a wide-area network. As indicated, the communication subnet itself consists of a number of communication processors connected by physical communication lines. Dedicated communication processors act as switching elements between two or more communication lines (also called transmission lines, trunks, circuits, or channels). After the original ARPANET implementation, the communication processors are often called *interface message processors*, or IMPs for short.

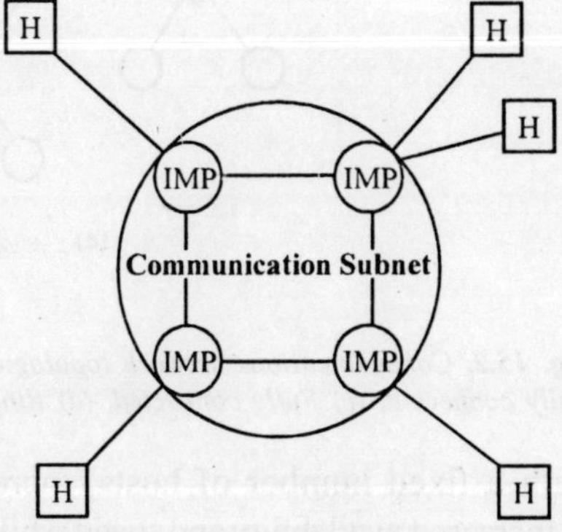

Fig. 15.1. Architecture of a wide-area network.

A host processor wishing to communicate with another host typically presents its request to the designated IMP. Usually each host is availed the services of a specific IMP, although a single IMP may serve several hosts. The IMP-to-IMP communication channels may be of one of the two broad types:

- Point to point
- Broadcast

Point-to-point links are dedicated physical lines used to connect a specific pair of IMPs. The actual number and topology of these links are determined by taking into consideration factors such as *cost*, *communication delays*, and *reliability*. Common topologies of physical circuits that connect different IMPs are illustrated in Figure15.2 they are:

- Star
- Partially connected

- Fully connected
- Ring
- Hierarchical or tree-structured network

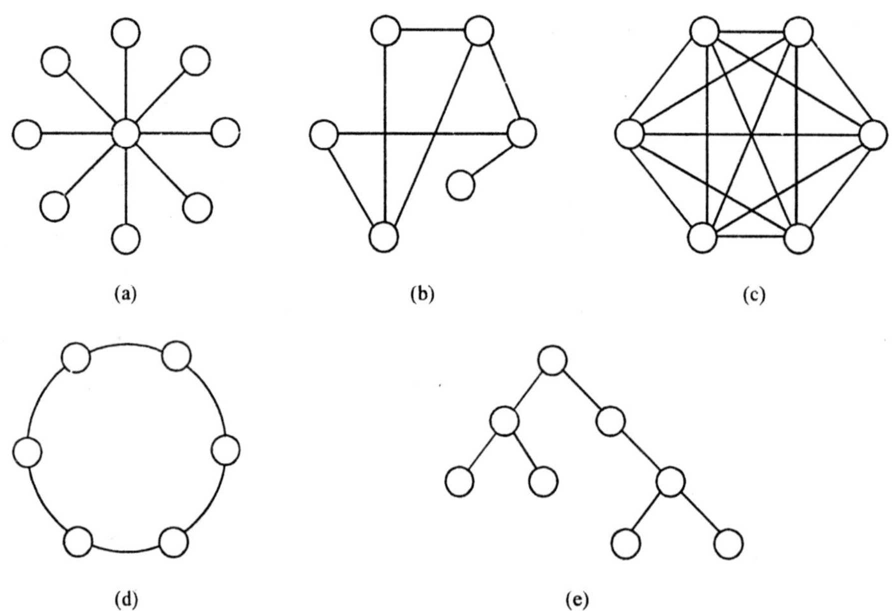

Fig. 15.2. Communications network topologies:
(a) Star, (b) Partially connected, (c) Fully connected, (d) Ring, (e) Hierarchical

In general, in a system with a fixed number of hosts, increasing the number of physical communication circuits results in increased availability and speed while reducing delays. Unfortunately, it also increased the cost of the system. The star configuration routes all communication through a single central point, which may be a node or a switch. The star has a fixed, two-hop host-to-host communication delay but suffers from the single point of failure. Fully connected systems are fast and reliable but expensive since the number of links grows as the square of the number of hosts. Partially connected and mesh networks have direct links between some but not all nodes. Lowering the number of physical connections reduces costs. On the negative side, it requires routing of messages exchanged between hosts that are not directly connected, and it increases the danger of *network partitioning*, where a single link failure can break up the communication subnet into two or more disjoint subsets unable to communicate with each other.

Single-link ring networks are low in cost but have variable and potentially long delays, especially when a host wants to communicate with its immediate neighbour in the direction opposite the ring flow. Rings are generally sensitive to link failures, especially in naïve implementations, where each node must act as an active repeater for all traffic.

Regardless of the topology of direct IMP-to-IMP connections, network software typically allows any host to logically communicate directly with any other. As a result, IMPs that need to deliver messages to IMPs to which they are not directly connected, must go through intermediate IMPs. This possibility requires the communication subnet to provide *routing* of messages between IMPs that are not directly connected. Often-used routing strategies include:

- Fixed routing
- Virtual circuit
- Dynamic routing

In *fixed routing*, the routed between all specific sender-receiver pairs are determined once, before or during the system startup, and they remain fixed thereafter. This scheme is obviously simple to implement, but it is inflexible and unable to adapt to communication load variations and IMP failures.

The *virtual circuit* approach establishes and fixed a path between two end nodes for the duration of an individual communication session. The path may be shared with other processes that require the same physical connection, but when such sharing does occur it is transparent to processes. Communication over virtual circuits is as if a private physical link is assigned to a pair of communicating processes.

Dynamic routing establishes end-to-end paths on the fly, typically on a per-message basis. Its ultimate flexibility allows the originating IMP to provide only a partial routing specification, which is finalized by intermediate IMPs visited by the message on its journey towards the destination. With dynamic routing, consecutive messages between two hosts may take different routes in response to individual channel and IMP loading and availability. This scheme imposes the heaviest computational burden on the IMPs and must be able to cope with out-of-order message delivery, which can confuse some distributed algorithms.

Another issue in communication subnetwork design is the *connection strategy*. The question here is for how long a communication link should be dedicated to a given sender-receiver pair. The common approaches to this problem include:

- Circuit switching
- Message switching
- Packet switching

Circuit switching is patterned after the phone system. It works by establishing and maintaining a dedicated physical end-to-end circuit between the communication hosts during the entire communication session.

In *message switching*, a temporary physical link is established between the sender and the receiver for the duration of a single message transfer. Physical links are allocated to users for short periods of time and rapidly switched around in order to increase the physical-line utilization.

Packet switching attempts to further increase line utilization, system throughput, and some aspects of IMP buffer management by dividing longer messages into fixed-size chunks called *packets*. Different packets may then be sent via different routes and reassembled at the destination for delivery to the recipient.

In general, choosing among these schemes includes considerations such as setup time, per-message overhead, message communication delays, system throughput, and utilization of the communication circuits. Circuit switching requires setup time but has lower per-message overhead and shorter delays. Message and packet switching require less setup time and provide potentially higher utilization factors. On the negative side, they tend to have higher overhead since addresses and possibly sequencing information must be included in each message or packet. They also tend to complicate IMP software by adding requirements for services such as buffer allocation, packet formation and reassembly, and more involved error handling and recovery procedures.

Local-Area Networks

As indicated earlier, local-area networks (LANs) are characterized by highbandwidth, low-delay communication links. They often rely on a relatively highspeed common access communication medium to carry the message traffic. LAN communication speeds range from the order of several Mbps (megabits per second) to the order of a Gbps (gigabits per second) with special cabling or optical fibers. These speeds approximate transfer rates of other high-speed peripherals, such as disks. As a result of potentially very fast access to resources anywhere on the network, LANs present a great challenge as well as opportunity for designers regarding placement of peripherals and services in the system.

The LAN communication medium itself is passive in the sense that it provides none of the processing power, routing, or storage functions found in the store-and-forward communication subnets. In-LANs, communication functions and processing are provided by the nodes (host machines), either directly or by their integral dedicated communication processors.

The passive communication medium and the absence of en route processing result in potentially high reliability of local-area network communication subsystems. The network topology is usually a bus or a ring. A star topology may be found in special-purpose systems and in some early designs.

In *ring-based systems*, messages circulate around the ring. They are then recognized and copied by their addresses. Depending on the acknowledgment scheme in use, either the destination or the source node may be charged with removing the consumed message from the ring. The ring topology appears to be very vulnerable to node and link outages, as any single failure apparently breaks the ring and thus halts further traffic. Commercial ring implementations avoid this problem by using relays to attach nodes to the ring. The relay is designed so that it must be actively powered in order to allow traffic to flow through its attached node. When faults are detected or the node is not powered, the relay closes and bypasses the failed node. This and other similar techniques provide ring continuity in the presence of node malfunctions, enabling uninterrupted communication between unaffected nodes.

For increased availability and optional throughput improvement, the logical ring may be implemented in the from of two physical rings. The dual-ring arrangement also provides many possibilities for optimization and reduction of delays by enabling the two rings to be active simultaneously to carry the traffic in opposite directions.

Since a ring logically connects all nodes to the communication channel, some strategy must be devised to control *access* to the medium and to prevent collisions that garble transmissions. Circulating tokens are commonly used for access control in ring networks. A *token*, also called a circulating permit, is a special message that circulates around the ring. In a simple but common protocol, each node wishing to transmit a message on the ring must wait until it receives the token. After communicating its message, the node sends the token down the ring to enable subsequent transmissions by other nodes. This scheme results in predictable message transmission delays of at most nT, where n is the number of nodes in the ring and T is the message transmission time.The official token-ring standard, IEEE 802.05, evolved from a commercial product offering of the IBM corporation.

In a typical bus topology, a commonly accessible passive conduit carries the message traffic. All nodes tap the bus, listen to all the traffic, and extract the messages addressed to them. Taps themselves are usually passive and do not physically break the bus. As a result, bus-oriented LANs are reliable and able to sustain communication between healthy parties in the presence of multiple node failures.

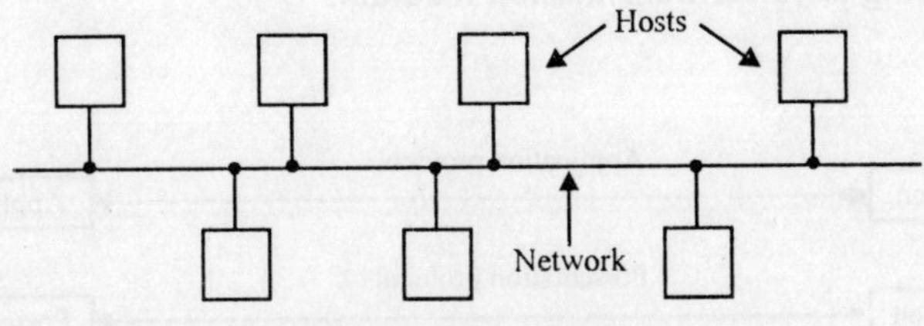

Fig. 15.3. Bus topology.

The broadcast nature of bus-based LANs necessitates some form of access control. A popular one is the so-called *carrier sense multiple access* (CSMA) protocol, which is usually implemented by hardware. In this scheme, all nodes refrain from sending if they sense a line carrier frequency indicating that a transmission is in progress. When the line is free (no carrier), nodes are free to transmit at will. Since it takes some time for a carrier of the new transmission to propagate through the cable and taps, there is a possibility of *collision* when two or more nodes overlap their transmissions. Collisions result in garbled transmissions that must be repeated without interference. They can be detected by having each actively transmitting node compare the bits is sends to the ones that it receives from the network. Consistent discrepancies indicate a collision. The communication scheme described here is called *carrier sense multiple access with collision detection*, or CSMA/CD. The IEEE standard for a CSMA/CD type of LAN is designated as 802.3. It is based on a commercial offering called Ethernet that was initially conceived by the Xerox Corporation.

Collision detection is only a part of the job needed to ensure eventual error-free transmission. A simple strategy where each affected node backs out and retransmits upon detecting a collision can easily cause repeated collisions by replaying the same sequence of events over and over again. A more effective way to deal with the problem is to have the affected nodes retransmit after a variable random delay, and to increase the backout time in case of repeated collisions. Due to collisions and their resolution, the performance of CSMA/CD networks such as Ethernet tends to deteriorate with increasing load. As a rough rule of thumb, CSMA/CD networks should not be expected to carry sustained traffic generated at rates much higher than half their normal bandwidth. In general, CSMA/CD LANs have unpredictable and theoretically unbounded delays.

Communication Protocols and the OSI Model

Computer communication and networking software is generally very complex. In order to be manageable, networking software is usually designed and implemented in a layered fashion. Each layer provides to the upper layers a set of services that may be invoked through a well-defined interface.

An influential layered network-architecture model that incorporates ideas and experiences from many earlier designs was proposed by the International Standards Organization (ISO) it is called the *open systems interconnection reference model* or ISO OSI for short. The OSI model has seven layers. It is depicted in Figure 15.4. Brief descriptions of the layers bottom-up fashion follow.

Physical Layer

The physical layer is in charge of communicating raw streams of bits over the communication channel. It is mostly concerned with the communication circuits and their physical and procedural interface to the underlying physical transmission medium.

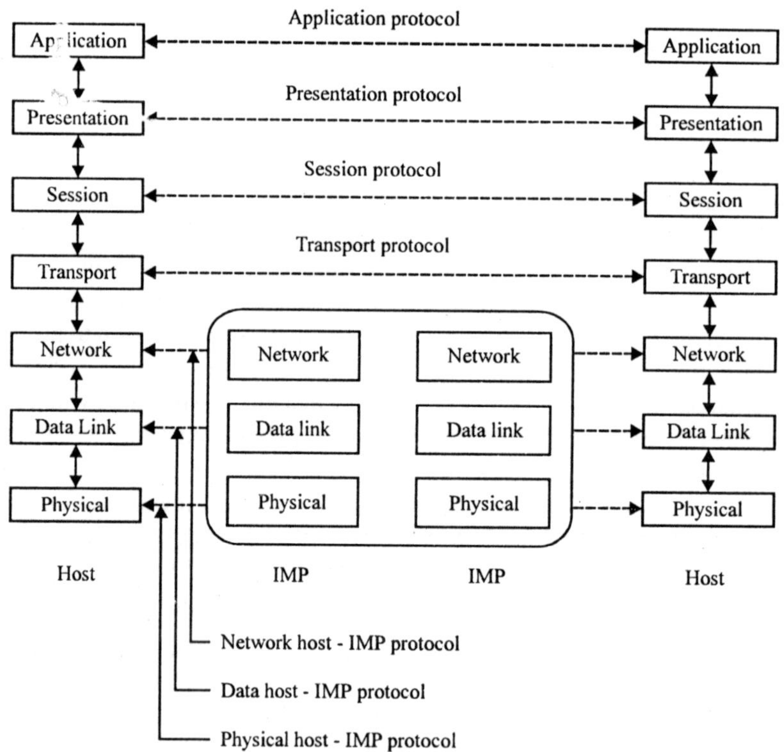

Fig. 15.4. ISO OSI protocol architecture.

Data Link Layer

The data link layer takes the raw bit-stream transmission facility and enhances it to provide apparent error-free communication lines between computers that are directly connected. Due to differences in the communication subnet implementations discussed earlier, in store-and-forward networks the data-link layer operates on IMP-IMP and host-IMP connections, and in LANs it handles host-host communications.

Error-free line abstraction is provided by breaking bit streams into frames and by adding extra bits for error detection. The data link layer also processes the acknowledgment frames sent back by the receiver. Garbled and lost acknowledgments can result in the generation of duplicate frames. The data link layer is charged with solving the problems related to damaged, lost, and duplicate messages. It is also charged with flow control, a mechanism designed to prevent flooding of nodes that can result from, among other reasons, speed discrepancies between senders and receivers.

Network Layer

The network layer controls the operation of the communication subnet. Its primary functions are packet routing, accounting, and congestion control. Internetworking considerations and problems resulting from the merging of heterogeneous networks are also entrusted to the network layer. These can include conversions between different addressing schemes and packet sizes.

In many broadcast networks and in LANs, the network layer is either thin or nonexistent, as there is little for it to do.

Transport Layer

The transport layer's task is to provide network-independent message transport between pairs of network endpoints, or ports. As Figure 15.4 indicates, the transport layer is the first to provide true source-to destination connection. In the lower layers, communication is between a machine and its immediate neighbours, and not necessarily between the source and destination hosts engaged in a conversation.

The transport layer accepts data from the session layer, splits it into smaller units such as packets if necessary, and ensures that all pieces are assembled properly at the receiving end. The actual transporting of the pieces is performed by the network layer.

The transport layer supports two modes of communication:

- Virtual circuit
- Datagram

A *virtual circuit* is modelled after the phone system. It is a logical communication channel established between two hosts for the purposes of a conversation. A virtual circuit reliably delivers messages in the order they were sent. The mode of communication that uses virtual circuits is called *connection oriented* service because it requires the interested parties to explicitly establish a communication link in order to exchange messages.

A *datagram* is regarded as an unreliable message delivery mechanism, because receipt of messages is not acknowledged. Datagram service is modelled after the postal service, where individual messages are sent independently and without prior handshaking. True to this analogy, messages sent as datagrams may be lost or received out of order. Datagram service has less overhead than the virtual circuit, and it is generally faster because it does not require the link setup. Datagrams are popular in local-area networks, whose reliability is often good enough to reduce concerns about message loss.

Session Layer

The session layer allows processes residing on different hosts to communicate with each other. The layer establishes interprocess *sessions* that provide ordinary data transport and some enhanced services such as remote log-in and file transfer.

The session layer is also charged with providing synchronization and token management to support interprocess interactions via the virtual circuits that it establishes.

Presentation Layer

Instead of just moving data between the end parties, the presentation layer performs certain common functions that may require knowledge of the syntax and semantics of the information transmitted. A typical example is encoding of the data in some standard, machine-independent way. This encoding allows conversions of data formats, such as byte ordering and floating-point representation, to allow communication between heterogeneous machines. In addition, the presentation layer provides optional encryption and data compression. The required decoding is performed by the presentation layer at the receiving end.

Application Layer

The application layer provides a variety of commonly needed protocols to the application processes running on separate computers on behalf of user tasks. The protocols may include electronic mail, remote job entry, and file transfer that bridges possible differences in naming and representation between the end users. The application layer also provides an abstraction of a terminal called the *network virtual terminal*. This allows application providers to write code, say, a screen editor, for a single terminal type—the virtual terminal—and rely on the application layer to map the relevant commands into control sequences appropriate for the specific local terminal type or types.

Algorithms for Distributed Processing

In a distributed system, cooperating processes may reside on different nodes. Like their single-site counterparts, distributed cooperating processes rely on interprocess synchronization and communication mechanisms to collectively and coherently accomplish a common mission. Interprocess communication and synchronization in distributed systems is considerably more complicated than in centralized systems. These complexities are largely due to the differences between distributed and centralized systems which include:

- Absence of shared, commonly accessible memory
- Internode communication delays that can exceed intranode communication delays by orders of magnitude
- Global system state is not observable by component machines due to communication delays, component failures, and absence of shared memory
- .A much richer set of failure modes and the desire to continue at least degraded operation in the presence of partial failures.

As a first approximation, a common approach when venturing into the unfamiliar is to adapt the well-known existing algorithms to the new environment. In the case of distributed systems, such a possibility is available by exercising centralized control over some or all system resources. In this approach, exclusive control over a set of resources is delegated to a single controller. All other nodes wishing to access those resources must first obtain permission from the controller in charge. The controller thus has complete information that enables it to use the more or less unchanged centralized resource control and management algorithms. However, centralized control in distributed systems suffers from two major drawbacks: (1) It is vulnerable to failures of the control node. (2) Traffic congestion tends to develop at control nodes. The failure problem may be alleviated by incorporating the algorithms for election of the successor node and for recovery of the control information.

The Environment and Common Assumptions

The two basic components of distributed control algorithms are (1) processes and (2) communication paths. A number of distributed algorithms rely on the request/reply protocol, where a process sends a message to a group of other processes and then collects and analyzes their replies. Since the specific order in which replies are received is generally unpredictable, processes communicating in a distributed system should be equipped to cope with parallelism and run-time nondeterminism. A communicating process should be able to wait on any of a set of events, process whichever happens first, and not lose track of the events that occur during the processing. For example, the Ada SELECT mechanism provides a nondeterministic run-time control structure that meets this requirement. Otherwise, such a facility may have to be simulated by means of a multitude of processes interlinked via a complex set of control structures and interprocess synchronization mechanisms.

Communicating processes are often the clients of higher-level communication protocols that provide for logical peer-to-peer communication, broadcasting, and multicasting regardless of the architecture of the underlying communication network. However implicit or explicit assumptions and use of certain facilities, such as broadcast, make performance of some algorithms sensitive to the communication subnet topology.

Common assumptions about the *logical* behaviour of communication links in distributed algorithms include:

- Messages exchanged by a pair of communicating processes are received in the order in which they were sent. This implies the absence of message reordering in end-to-end transit and is sometimes referred to as the *pipelining property*.
- Every message is delivered to its destination error-free in finite time (this also implies that there are no lost messages). There is no duplication of messages.
- The network is logically fully connected in the sense that each site can communicate directly with every other site.

These properties are rarely inherent in the communication networks, so they need to be provided by the higher-level communication protocols. For simplicity of exposition, in this section we assume that there are N distinct nodes in the system, with exactly one active process of interest per node. Under the stated assumptions, the terms *nodes* and *processes* can be used interchangeably. In actually, however, processes and not nodes are the only active agents that can send and receive messages.

Desirable properties of algorithms with distributed control include:

- All nodes should have an equal amount of information.
- Each node should make decisions solely on the basis of local information. The algorithm must ensure that different nodes make consistent and coherent decisions.
- All nodes expend approximately equal effort in reaching the decision (equal effort rule).
- Failure of a node should not result in the breakdown of the algorithm by affecting the ability of other nodes to make their decisions and to access the available resources.

Functional role partitioning among the various participating processes in different algorithms ranges from various degrees of symmetry to full asymmetry. *Symmetry* refers to the code (text) and run-time behaviour of processes that execute on different nodes and that, as a collection, constitute an implementation of a given algorithm. For example, total symmetry implies that all processes are cloned and behave identically at run-time. Other flavors are strong symmetry and textual summery, where the code of each of the processes is identical but their run-time behaviour may differ as a function of the type of received message. In asymmetrical approaches, each process has different code and behaviour. An example of the asymmetrical approach is the client/server model. In general, increased symmetry tends to increase resilience to failures; increased specialization tends to reduce it.

Communication and processing overhead affect performance and implementation costs of a distributed algorithm. A frequently used measure of overhead is the *number of internode* messages required by the algorithm. The cost of exchanging a message includes

1. Communication cost and delay incurred in the physical transfer between the two endpoints
2. The computational component, that is, message formation, buffering, and protocol processing at both ends.

Broadcasts are usually counted as $n - 1$ messages in a system with n nodes. This should only be regarded as a first approximation, given that the communication cost of a broadcast can vary depending on the topology of the communication subnetwork. The computational cost of a broadcast, however, is fairly constant and much less sensitive to topological variations.

Other measures of the complexity and cost of distributed algorithms include storage overhead, the degree of system concurrency (parallelism) that they permit, and the duration of blackouts in resource availability that may course in the course of internode negotiations.

Time and Ordering of Events

The notion of time is implicit in many single-site centralized algorithms. These algorithms are often specified in terms of a sequence of events whose relative order of occurrence is either known or discernible in relation to the single common time base (system clock).

Ordering of events in distributed systems is considerably more complex due to the practical near impossibility of maintaining synchrony among the physical clocks in spatially dispersed nodes. Lamport (1978) devised a method for ordering events in a distributed system without using synchronized physical clocks. His approach assumes that the system is composed of a collection of processes, and that each process consists of a sequence of events with a priori total ordering. This is realistic given the sequential nature of individual process execution.

While allowing considerable freedom of choice of granularity of events within a single process, it is explicitly assume that sending and receiving of messages each constitutes a distinct event. The *happened-before* relationship, denoted by $\rightarrow$, is precisely defined as follows:

1. If a and b are events in the same process, and a comes before b, then $a \rightarrow b$.
2. If a represents the sending of a message by one process and b the receipt of the same message by another process, then $a \rightarrow b$.
3. The relation is transitive. That is, if $a \rightarrow b$ and $b \rightarrow c$, then $a \rightarrow c$. Two distinct events are said to be *concurrent* if no ordering exists between them. That is, if neither a happened before b nor b happened before a, then a and b are concurrent.

Logical clocks provide a way to implement the happened-before relationship is a distributed system without reliance on synchronized physical clocks. In this abstraction, it is convenient to think of a logical clock as a way to assign a number to an event. In a system with logical clocks, the happened-before relationship should follow the usual notion of time. That is, if an event a occurs before another event b, the logical clocks should behave in such a way that $C(a)$, the time (clock count) assigned to a, should be earlier (a smaller number) than the time assigned to b. This condition may be stated more formally as follows:

Clocks condition: For any events a and b: if $a \rightarrow b$, then $C(a) < C(b)$.

From the definition of the $\rightarrow$ relationship, it follows that the clock condition is satisfied if the following two conditions hold:

C1. If a and b are events in process P_i, and a comes before b, then $C_i(a) < C_i(b)$.

C2. If a is the event of sending a message m by process P_i and b is the receipt of that message by process P_j, then $C_i(a) < C_j(b)$.

Conditions C1 and C2 can be satisfied by implementing the logical clocks so that the following conditions hold:

- Process P_i increments its logical clock C_i between any two successive events.
- Messages are *time-stamped* by the sending process in the following way. If event a is the sending of message m by process P_i, then the message m contains the time stamp $T_m = C_i(a)$.
- The receiving process adjusts its logical clock upon receipt of a message as follows. Upon receipt of a message m, process P_j sets C_j to $\max(C_j + 1, T_m)$.

The partial ordering of events provided by the happened-before relationship, $\rightarrow$, may be extended to total ordering by introducing an arbitrary total ordering, $\angle$, of the processes to break the ties. The resulting total ordering of processes in a distributed system, denoted by $\Rightarrow$, is defined as follows: If a is an event in process P_i and b is an event in process P_j, then a $\Rightarrow$b if and only if

(a) $C_i(a) \angle C_j(b)$ or

(b) $C_i(a) = C_j(b)$ and $P_i \angle P_j$.

A simple way to implement the relation $\angle$ is to assign a unique number to each process and to define $P_i \angle P_j$ if $i < j$.

Mutual Exclusion in Distributed Systems

This class of distributed algorithms is based on the notion of a circulating permit message, also called a token. Problems resulting from the loss of a token are also discussed. The remainder of this section introduces algorithms for mutual exclusion that use messages solely for interprocess communication and not for synchronization. Conceptually, these algorithms are an outgrowth of semaphore-based solutions to mutual exclusion.

For simplicity and without loss of generality, assume that a distributed system consists of N nodes, and that there is exactly one process at each node that may wish to enter a critical section. In this expositional simplification, the terms *processes* and *nodes* may be used interchangeably. The problem of mutual exclusion in a distributed system is to guarantee that at most one process may be in the critical section at any given point in time.

- Different requests must be granted in the order in which they are made.

The distributed-control requirement precludes the use of a single control node. The distributed environment rules out the use of semaphores and similar mechanisms that depend on globally accessible shared memory. The requirement that the requests must be granted in the order in which they are made is quite strong, and it implies that every request to access the critical section will be granted in finite time, provided that every process granted exclusive access to the critical section eventually releases it. This requirement is not trivial, and it is not automatically satisfied by a centralized scheduler that grants requests in the order in which it received them. To see this, consider a system with two user processes, P_1 and P_2, and a scheduling process P_0. Suppose P_1 sends a request to P_0 and then sends a message to P_2. Upon receiving the latter message, P_2 sends a request to P_0. If P_2's request reaches P_0 before P_1's request does (this is possible, because the pipelining property holds for each individual link but provides no guarantees between different links), P_0 may grant P_2's request first and thus violate the stated requirement.

With the time-stamping mechanism outlined previously, it is relatively straightforward to extend the strategy of the classical centralized solution to the distributed case. Basically, the requesting process announces its intention to enter the critical section by sending a (time-stamped) request to every other node in the system. This communication is used to construct distributed replicas of the time-stamp-ordered requests at all interested nodes. The requests are then granted in the order in which they were made. Upon exiting the critical section, the process that owns the resource sends a release message to all other nodes so that they may update their respective request queues.

Lamport's Algorithm

Assuming the presence of the pipelining property and eventual delivery of all messages, the solution requires time-stamping of all messages, and it also assumes that each process maintain a request queue, initially empty, that contains *request* messages ordered by the relation $\Rightarrow$. The algorithm is defined by the following five rules.

1. (Initiator: i) When process P_i desires to acquire exclusive ownership of the resource, it sends the time-stamped message request T_i, i), where $T_i = C_i$, to every other process and records the request in its own queue.
2. (Other processes: $j, j \neq i$) When process P_j receives the request (T_i, i) message, it places the request on its own queue and sends a time-stamped replay (T_j, j) to process P_i.

3. Process P_i is allowed to access the resource when the following two conditions are satisfied:
   (a) P_i's request message at the front of the queue, and
   (b) P_i has received a message from every other process with a time stamp latte than (T_i, i).
4. Process P_i releases the resource by removing the request from its own queue and by sending a time-stamped release message to every other process.
5. Upon receipt of P_i's release message, process P_j removes P_i's request from its request queue.

Correctness of the algorithm follows from rule 3, which guarantees that the initiating process P_i learns about all potentially conflicting requests that precede it. Given that message cannot be received out of order (the pipelining property assumption) and that the relation $\Rightarrow$ provides a total ordering of events in the system and in the per-process request queues, rule 3a permits only one process to access the resource at a time.

The solution is deadlock-free due to the time-stamp ordering of requests, which precludes formation of the wait-for loops. Granting of requests in the order in which they are made prevents process starvation and lockouts.

The communication cost of the algorithm is $3(N-1)$ messages: $(N-1)$ request messages, $(N-1)$ reply messages, and $(N-1)$ release messages. Given that request and release notifications are effectively broadcasts, the algorithm clearly performs better in a broadcast-type network such as the bus.

Ricart and Agrawala's Algorithm

Ricart and Agrawala's algorithm is a more efficient version of Lamport's algorithm. It is based on identical communication assumptions and on the total ordering of events as provided by the $\Rightarrow$ relation.

1. (Initiator: *i*) When process P_i requests the resource, it sends the time-stamped message request (T_i, i), where $T_i = C_i$, to every other process and records the request in its own queue.
2. (Other processes: $j, j \neq i$) When process P_j receives the request message, it acts as follows:
   (a) If P_j is not currently requesting the resource, it return a time-stamped reply.
   (b) If P_j is currently requesting the resource, and the time-stamp of its request (T_j, j) precedes (T_i, i), process P_i's request is retained; otherwise, a time-stamped reply message is returned.
3. Process P_i is allowed to access the resource when the following two conditions are satisfied:
   (a) P_i's request message is at the front of the queue.
   (b) P_i has received a message from every other process with a time-stamp latter that (T_i, i).
4. When process P_i releases the resource, it sends a reply message for each pending request message.

The algorithm offers the same basic guarantees as Lamport's algorithm, but it is more efficient in that it requires at most $2(N-1)$ messages to service a request.

As implied by phrased such as "upon receiving replies from *all* other nodes," both algorithms require each initiating node to somehow know or find out the identities of all potentially competing processes in the system. This makes both solutions sensitive to node and link failures, and requires some mechanism for updating and reconnecting of failed nodes upon recovery.

Transactions

As discussed earlier, a distributed operation system may distribute and replicate some of its data structures to increase availability and fault tolerance. For example, multiple copies of the name-service database may be maintained at different sites to share the load and provide faster local service to clients at different localities.

Management and concurrency control of partially distributed data structures is quite complex, Distribution of data may require a process to visit several sites in order to perform a complicated update. Updates of redundant data must preserve *mutual consistency* of all copies. *Mutual consistency* means that all copies must converge to the same consistent state and that they would become identical should the update activity cease.

Techniques for decentralized management of data were originally developed within the framework of distributed data base systems. These systems introduced the notions of transactions and atomic operations, which are useful for data management, concurrency control, and server implementation in distributed operating systems.

A *transaction* is a sequence of operations on one or more objects that transforms a (current) consistent state of the database into a new consistent state. In other words, a transaction is a unit of consistency. In operational terms, a transaction is a sequence of database operations bracketed by the **transaction begin** and **transaction end** keywords. Temporary inconsistent values that may occur during the execution of a transaction are hidden by making the affected database entities inaccessible to other clients.

For performance reasons, transactions are often executed concurrently. The task of concurrency control is to schedule execution of transactions in a way that preserves consistency of the database. An important goal is to do so in a manner that allows as much parallelism as possible, especially between transactions whose data sets do not overlap. Increased parallelism may be achieved by scheduling execution of transactions so that some of their steps are interleaved. A schedule is called *consistent.* If it gives each transaction a consistent views of the database entities of interest. A sufficient condition for schedule consistency is to make it equivalent to some serial ordering of transactions. The resulting schedule is said to be *serializable* or *linearizable.*

An operation of a file or a database entity is *atomic* if its only possible outcomes are:

1. If the operation terminates successfully, all of its effects are made permanent.
2. If the operation fails, the state of the file or database remains unchanged.

An atomic transaction has the all-or-nothing property: it either runs to completion and transforms the database to a new consistent state, or it fails and has no effect whatsoever. Atomicity is usually implemented by making all database updates of an ongoing transaction tentative pending its successful completion. In case a transaction fails, its tentative updates are discarded, which effectively rolls the database back to a previous consistent state. The concept of atomicity is central to fault tolerance and recovery in distributed systems.

Distributed Concurrency Control and Deadlocks

In a distributed system, a single transaction can span files residing at several different sites. Resource acquisition by multiple concurrent transactions originating at different sites can lead to deadlocks.

Necessary conditions for a deadlock are the same in centralized and in distributed systems. They are: (1) mutual exclusion, (2) hold-and-wait, (3) no preemption, and (4) circular waiting. The added dimension in distributed systems is that the chain of waiting processes or transactions can span several different sites.

Techniques for dealing with deadlocks include deadlock prevention, deadlock avoidance, and deadlock detection and recovery. Deadlocks can be prevented by ordering and honoring requests according to their time stamps. The mechanics of Lamport's solution to mutual exclusion provides an indication of how to order waiting processes or transactions according to their time stamps in a decentralized system.

Several decentralized algorithms for concurrency control that avoid deadlocks have been devised for use in distributed systems. They typically rely on time stamps for ordering transaction and make decisions solely on the basis of locally available information.

In this section we describe two such protocols, called wait-die and wound-wait due to Rosenkrantz et al. Both protocols are essentially database concurrency control algorithms that avoid deadlocks. The assumed environment is a distributed system with partially redundant data. Executing transactions travel among the data sites as necessary to access the data that they operate on. Each transaction is time-stamped at its creation by the originating site. Each site maintains a lock queue for each of its publicly available resources. Lock queues are ordered according to the time stamps of participating transactions. A transaction at the head of a queue owns the resource. In case of conflicts, a node where lock requests collide applies locally one of two rules:

- *Wait-die*:. If the requestor is older (has an earlier time stamp), than the transaction that owns the desired lock—the requestor—waits, otherwise, the requestor dies.
- *Wound-wait*: If the requestor is older than the owner of the lock, the requestor wounds the owner. Otherwise, the requestor waits.

Dying means that the affected process or transactions is aborted. For transactions aborting implies the undoing of all partial effects and the releasing of all locks acquired by the transaction thus far. The aborted transaction is usually restarted at a later time. *Wounding* means that an older transaction instructs the younger, conflicting one to die—that is, to abort, undo its partial effects, and release the locks.

In the wait-die scheme, an older transaction is permitted to wait. This is safe because circular waiting chains cannot be formed, since a younger transaction never waits for an older one. Therefore, the younger transaction eventually, terminates (either completes or aborts) and releases its locks, thus allowing the older waiting transaction to proceed.

In the wound-wait scheme, an older transaction does not wait for younger ones. After wounding, the transaction has to wait for the wound to take effect and for the younger transaction to die and release the lock.

Both algorithms are conceptually simple and decentralized in the sense that they make decisions solely on the basis of local information. Neither requires preclaiming of resources or maintenance and processing of resource-allocation matrices described in relation to centralized deadlock avoidance. The drawback, however, is that transactions are aborted in case of *conflicts* as opposed to deadlocks. This is unfortunate because a conflict is a necessary but not a sufficient condition for a deadlock. Thus, transactions may be aborted unnecessarily. Moreover, in the wait-die algorithm a single transaction can be restarted several times due to conflicts with the same older transaction, especially when the older transaction is a long-lasting one. Restarting of a transaction is usually costly in a distributed system, because it involves wasting the work done to date, undoing a transaction's partial effects, and rolling back to an earlier consistent state. Due to distribution of data, this process may span several sites and require expensive intersite messages.

Some of these problems may be ameliorated by using a hybrid of the wait-die and wound-wait algorithms coupled with a global allocation graph that captures the can-wait-for relationships among transactions and thus reduces the number of unnecessary restarts. Some research studies indicate that these algorithms are best suited for systems where the probability of conflicts is low.

In general, deadlock detection is performed by detecting cycles in the wait-for graph. In a distributed system with no shared memory, a site can perform deadlock detection by communicating with its peers and constructing a global wait-for graph. This activity may be initiated when a process or a transaction fails to complete within a reasonable time frame. Figure 15.5 illustrates one method of decentralized deadlock detection in a distributed system.

Figure 15.5 depicts a system with three sites and seven resource-acquiring agents (processes or transactions) that form a wait-for graph. The figure represents the system from the point of view of an ideal observer, a knowledge that is not directly available to any given site. After failure of agent 1 to complete in some expected time, site 1 may initiate the deadlock detection process. One way of detecting cycles in the global wait-for graph is to send probe messages along the wait-for route. If the probe eventually returns to its originator, the cycle is detected. In a distributed deadlock detection algorithm due to Chandy et al, the probe is a triplet (i, j, k) denoting that it belongs to a deadlock detection for process P_i and being sent by the home site of P_j to the home site of P_k.

In the situation depicted in Figure 15.5 site 1 acting on behalf of agent 1 would send the first probe (1, 2, 3) it site 2, due to a wait-for dependency between agent 2 in site 1 and agent 3 in site 2. Site 2 sends two probes on its outgoing wait-for arcs, (1, 5, 7) and (1, 4, 6). Site 3 sends the probe (1, 6, 1) which returns to site 1 and the cycle is detected.

There are a number of algorithms for deadlock detection in distributed systems. Many of them rely on some variation on the construction of the global wait-for graph and the detection of cycles in it. The common problems include costly and lengthy intersite communication and the possibility of "detection" of false deadlocks. *False deadlocks* are reported when, due to delays in intersite communication, a cycle is constructed on the basis of some transient, time-varying wait-for dependencies that existed at various sites at different points in the past. True deadlocks occur and persist only as a consequence of cycles formed at the same point in time. The inability of any node to assess the global state of a distributed system at a given point in time without freezing it and thus impairing performance makes it difficult to dispense with false deadlocks.

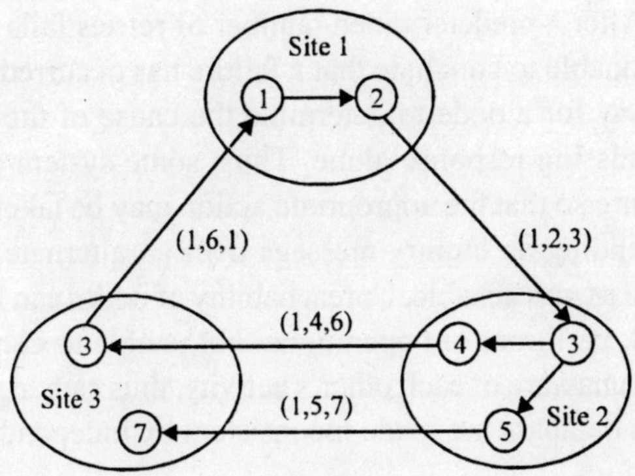

Fig. 15.5. Decentralized deadlock detection.

Coping with Failures

One of the major potential benefits of distributed processing is resilience to failures and increased system availability. Mere distribution of hardware and data does not automatically yield an inherently more reliable system. In fact, due to its dependence on multiple nodes and communication links, a distributed system may be less reliable than a single-site centralized system. However, the distributed architecture provides a better foundation for increasing availability and resilience to failures by incorporating a multitude of service providers and exploiting partial redundancy. The promise of distributed system can only be realized when the proper hardware foundation is augmented with fault tolerance mechanisms and data redundancy provided and managed by the systems software. This section discusses some common types of failures in distributed systems and presents several algorithms for dealing with the resulting problems.

Failures in Distributed Systems

Common failures in distributed systems include:

- Communication-link failures
- Node failures
- Lost messages

In order to function properly, the rest of the system must (1) *detect* failures; (2) *determine the cause*, such as identifying the type of failure and the failed component; (3) *reconfigure* the system so that it can continue to operate; and (4) recover when the failed component is repaired.

The use of time-outs is a common technique for detecting missing responses or acknowledgements. However, the choice of a specific time-out value presents some practical problems. Too long a time-out results in slow detection of missing messages. On the other hand, too short a time-out may trigger false alarms by declaring as missing messages that are just delayed. Moreover, short time-outs require the communication subsystem to deal with duplicate messages sent in response to hurriedly requested replays.

Given the possibility of lost messages, it is common to go through a few retries before declaring a failure to communicate. After a predetermined number of retries fails to be acknowledged within the time-out limit, it is reasonable to conclude that a failure has occurred. In general, in a distributed system there is no direct way for a node to determine the cause of the failure, such as a link or a node, on the basis of the missing response alone. Thus, some system component must engage in detection of the type of failure so that the appropriate action may be taken, for example, link failures may be distinguished by sending an inquiry message over an alternate path. If no other paths are available, the node is marked as unreachable. Unreachability of nodes can lead to *network partitioning*, where two or more network partitions are operational but unable to communicate with each other. Such partitions may also be unaware of each other's activity, thus causing serious recovery problems when redundant copies of a database are made inconsistent by independent, uncoordinated updates occurring in separate partitions.

Failure of a node can result in simple stoppage, called *fail-stop*, or in erratic malfunctioning behaviour. The latter is much more difficult to deal with, as the malfunctioning node may continue to exchange messages but may violate the protocol and thus confuse other nodes, withhold answers intermittently, or disseminate corrupt or forged messages.

Reconfiguration in the case of link failures consists of choosing an alternate path and updating the corresponding routing information by all affected nodes. Moreover, in systems where logical rings or some other fixed node-spanning order is maintained, reconfiguration includes bypassing the failed links and nodes so as to maintain the expected logical relationship among the remaining, reachable nodes.

Recovery from link failures consists of relatively simple updating of the routing information. Node recovery is more complex since it requires updating of state information and possibly replaying of missed messages by some of the active nodes, in addition to updating of system topological maps. In some systems, a recovering node slowly brings itself up to date by querying other nodes for state information. In such cases, the recovered node may passively observe the traffic in the system for a while before regaining the status of a voting participant.

Election of a Successor

Asymmetric algorithms and algorithms with centralized control assign unique roles to some nodes whose failures can result in the breakdown of the algorithm. One way to make such algorithms robust is to devise mechanisms for election of a successor to resume the special control function in the event of critical node failures. Additional provisions are also needed to enable the successor, once elected, to somehow reconstruct the state information held by its predecessor. In this section we focus only on the first part of the problem, the distributed election of a successor.

Due to the rich variety of failure nodes and possible outages, the distributed run-time election of a successor is generally more effective and reliable than its static counterpart based on a complication of anticipated scenarios. Many distributed election algorithms require that nodes be numbered in some way that reflects their priority in becoming a successor. Following a critical node failure, the algorithm basically consists of finding the extremum, that is, the highest priority active node.

The algorithm assumes that all nodes in the system are connected via a logical unidirectional ring. The nodes are numbered from 1 to N, and each node knows its own number. Any node can start the election when it detects failure of the control node. The node marks itself as a participant and communicates the election message together with its number to the next node down the ring, say, its left neighbour. Each recipient of the election message becomes a participant, compares the received number to its own, and sends the greater of the two numbers to its neighbour. The overhead is reduced by this selective extinction of messages as soon as the bids that they carry become recognized as unwinnable. The election is completed when a participating node receives its own identifier. That node becomes the elected new coordinator and, if necessary, transmits its identity to other nodes.

The steps of the algorithms are:

1. When node i detects failure of the current coordinator, it marks itself as a participant and sends the election message to its closest neighbour in the direction of the ring flow: send (election, i).
2. When node j receives an election messages, say, (election, k), it acts as follows:
   (a) If $k > j$, node j marks itself as a participant and relays the election message, that is, send (election, k).
   (b) If $k < j$ and the node is not marked as a participant, it sends the election message with its own number, send (election, j).
   (c) If $k = j$, node j is elected, and it sends the message send (elected, j).
3. (Other nodes) Upon receiving the (elected, j) message, node l unmarks itself as a participant, records the identity of the new coordinator, and, if $j \neq l$, relays the message, send (elected, j).

In step 2b, if the node is already a participant, it simply extinguished the received message because its own bidding message, which has a higher priority number, is already on the ring.

Informally, the correctness of the algorithm follows from the observation that the unidirectional nature of the ring ensures that the message with the highest number must make a complete circuit and be seen by all other nodes. Upon reaching its participating originator, the message must have the highest active number in the system, for it would be extinguished otherwise. The unique node numbering ensures that election is unambiguous regardless of which node initiated the election.

In terms of performance, the fastest election occurs when all nodes initiate election at the same time, thus completing in an amount of time proportional to one round around the ring, or $(n-1)$ internode delays. The worst case in terms of timing is when the left neighbour of the *max* numbered active node is the sole initiator of the election. In that case, two circles around the ring, yielding a $2(n-1)$ message-propagation delay, is incurred for election: one round for the election message to reach the *max* node, and the other to circulate its modified message uncontested.

The number of messages varies accordingly between $O(n)$ in the best case to $O(n^2)$ in the worst case, with the average case being $O(n \log n)$, as demonstrated by the algorithm's authors. Other authors have subsequently devised more efficient successor election algorithms that limit the worst case of the number of messages to $O(n \log n)$.

Regeneration of a Lost Token

Given that messages are a primary form of interprocess communication in distributed systems, it is natural to use them for interprocess synchronization as well. A minor modification customary in distributed systems is to consider messages as being exchanged between endpoints, such as processes, directly. This is easily accomplished by regarding mailboxes as being owned exclusively by the sending or the receiving process, as appropriate.

A distributed message-based solution to the mutual-exclusion problem is provided by creating a special type of message, called token, that acts as a permit to access the resource. This message is circulated among the nodes wishing to access the shared resource in a mutually exclusive manner. Circulating of the access permit may be performed in a specific order by arranging the sites in a logical ring. Naturally, this is most efficient in systems with the physical ring communication topology. The method is often referred to as the *circulating permit*, where each node wishing to access the shared resource follows the same protocol:

receive(*token*); {from the ring neighbour $P\ (i-1) \bmod n$}
use_resource; {critical section}
send(*token*);

This simple algorithm breaks down when the token is lost. A number of algorithms for token regeneration deal with this problem. Many of them depend on time-outs and require all process identities to be known to all nodes. In this section we present an algorithm due to Misra (1983) that requires no knowledge of delays or process identities.

The algorithm assumes that nodes in the system form a logical ring. It uses two independently circulating token, each of which serves to detect the possible loss of the other. When a process sees the same token twice without having seen the other and without the two tokens having met, a loss is detected, and the missing token is generated. The algorithm requires the detecting token to complete a full circle without getting lost itself. When this is a concern, the algorithm may be generalized to any number of tokens, and it will work as long as one of them survives long enough to generate another.

Let us call the two tokens *ping* and *pong*. The value of each token, *nping* and *npong*, respectively, counts the number of times the two tokens have met. For convenience, the values of the two tokens have opposite signs. Initially, token values are set as follows:

$$nping = 1,\ npong = -1$$

The two token circulate around the ring in opposite directions. Whenever they meet at a node, the value of *nping* is incremented by 1 and the value of *npong* is decremented by 1. Numeric values of the two tokens are thus related by the invariant

$$npong + nping = 0$$

whose preservation indicates the presence of both tokens in the system. Otherwise, a token is lost and must be regenerated. The algorithm assumes that each process P_i maintains a variable n_i that records the number associated with the last token that the process has seen. Initially, n_i is set to 0. The algorithm operates as follows:

1. When the two tokens meet at a node, it sets their associated values as follows:

   nping = *nping* + 1
   npong = *npong*–1;

2. When a node *i* receives the token (*ping, nping*), it acts as follows:

   (a) If $n_i \neq nping$, the node set $n_i = nping$ and relays the token. Otherwise,

   (b) If $n_i = nping$, the pong token is lost and needs to be regenerated. The node sets

   nping = *nping* + 1;

   npong = – *nping*;

   and sends the token along: send (*ping*, *nping* and send (*pong, npong*).

When node *i* receives the messages (*pong, npong*), it acts as in step 2, just reversing the roles of *ping* and *pong*.

Reaching Agreement

An implicit and fundamental assumption in such algorithms is that all nodes receive the broadcast correctly. *Reliable broadcast* implies that all processes operating reliably receive identical copies of the originally issued message. In effect, all reliable processes reach the same agreement regarding the contents of a given broadcast. Implementation of reliable broadcasts and reaching of agreement are very difficult to accomplish in the presence of failures. This section presents some results and algorithms for reaching consensus in distributed systems.

Communication failures can corrupt messages. Faulty processes can withhold, alter, or fail to relay messages to other nodes on multihop links. The initiating process itself may be faulty and communicate different values to different recipients of the same broadcast. Consequently, some nodes may not receive the broadcast, and others may receive a distortion of a forgery. In a system where failures are possible, there is no guarantee that all nodes will have the same perception of the item being broadcast.

- Several divisions of the Byzantine army, each commanded by its own general, surround an enemy city. Divisions are dispersed, so their generals communicate by messengers. The generals must reach an agreement on the common plan of action. However, some generals are traitors trying to prevent loyal generals from reaching an agreement. The agreement is crucial since attack by only some of the divisions would result in defeat. The problem is to devise an algorithm that guarantees that all loyal generals decide upon and execute the same plan of action regardless of what the traitors say or do.

Assuming a network of *n* nodes that can communicate only via messages over bidirectional channels, the problem is to ensure that whenever a node issues an item of information, all other nodes receive that item unchanged. In other words, all nodes have the same perception of the item. This translates into the following two conditions, which must hold whenever a node dispatches an item of information to others:

C1. All processes that operate reliably receive the same item.

C2. If the issuing process is operating reliably, then every process operating reliably receives the same item.

If the issuing process operates reliably, condition C2 follows from C1. However, the issuer need not be reliable, and the recipient cannot tell the difference on the basis of the received message. The difficulty of the problem lies in the types of faults that can occur and the absence of knowledge concerning processes that have failed. Loss of messages is fairly easy to detect by means of acknowledgements and time-outs. However, no amount of direct message exchange is adequate to get two processes to agree on their respective states.

To see why this is true, consider two processes P_i and P_j, each of which maintains a private copy of a logically global variable v. With no shared memory, the two processes exchange a series of messages and acknowledgements to establish that v has the same value, say s, at both ends. Suppose that a minimal sequence of messages exists so that after their delivery the two processes agree. Let k be the last message sent by P_i to P_j. Since P_i has no way of knowing whether message k will be delivered (it can get lost), process P_i can only assume that s is a common values. Given this lack of certainty, message k may be removed from the sequence without affecting the decision process. Therefore, the sequence is not minimal, and our claim is proved by contradiction. Two processes residing on separate nodes of a distributed system without shared memory can never be sure that they have the same perception of a given common item.

It is convenient to present the agreement problem by thinking in term of values. That is, the issuing node sends a value v, and other nodes confer to make sure that all reliable ones perceive the same value v despite possible failures and alterations by unreliable nodes. In general, algorithms for reaching consensus operate by exchanging series of messages in synchronized stages. Stages are synchronized to detect missing messages. When a process does not receive an expected message at a given stage of message exchanges, it is free to assume a default values v_{def}. In the first round, the issuer sends the message containing the value to all other processes. If the issuer is operating reliably, it sends v to all other processes. Some processes or even the issuer may be unreliable, so nothing can be concluded from the first round of messages. The second round ensure, in which each recipient relays the received value to all processes other than the original issuer (who either is reliable and knows the values, or is faulty and so its perception is irrelevant anyway).The relayed messages are signed by each forwarding process, so they take the form "I, the undersigned P_i certify that P_0 has sent me this message and it has the value v." Of course, unreliable processes may make false claims.

Second, no solution with fewer than $3m+1$ reliable processes can cope with m unreliable ones. As an illustration, consider a system with three processes, P_0, P_1, and P_2. For simplicity, let there be only two possible values in messages, v and z. Assume that P_0 is an initiator and that it sends the value v to both P_1 and P_2. Assume that P_2 is faulty and that it relays a modified value z to P_1 in the second round of exchanges. Now consider another scenario in which P_0 is faulty, so that it sends two different values, v and z to processes P_1 and P_2, respectively. In the second round, process P_2 relays the received values, z, to process P_1. Hence, based on the messages it receives, the two scenarios look identical to process P_1. Discrepant values alert P_1 that something is wrong, but it cannot distinguish which of the other two nodes is faulty.

Process P_1 has to make a choice, so it adopts the value received from the initiator, which is v. By similar reasoning in the second scenario, process P_2 receives discrepant messages, z from P_0 and v from P_1. Process P_2 must make a choice, so it adopts the value sent by the initiator, which is z. In the scenario presented, the two reliable processes P_1 and P_2 adopt different values in response to the same broadcast, thus violating condition C1. Increasing the number of stages of message exchanges serves no useful purpose, as the same amount of information is communicated over and over again.

When reliable processes have a $3m+1$ majority over the m faulty ones, the agreement can be reached by having each node adopt the value received in the majority of messages. This may be accomplished by means of the function *majority* with the property that if a majority of the values v_i equal v, then *majority* $(v_1,\ldots\ldots v_{n-1})$ equals v.

The algorithm *OM* (m) solves the Byzantine Generals problem under the assumption of no communication failures, that is all messages sent are received correctly. The algorithm does allows for arbitrary types of process faults, including intermittent stoppage and forging of message. In the Byzantine metaphor, messengers are reliable, but up to m of the generals are not. A traitor can forge the message while relaying it and use the (unsuspecting) messenger to deliver it. Messengers themselves do not alter messages. The algorithm is defined recursively for a system with n nodes, numbered $(0,\ldots, n-1)$, as follows.

Algorithm $OM(0)$:

1. The initiating process sends the initiator's local value to every other node.
2. Each recipient uses the value it receives from the initiator, or assumes v_{def} if it receives no value.

Algorithm $OM(m)$, $m > 0$:

3. The initiating process sends the initiator's local value to every other process.
4. For each i, let v_i be the value that process i receives from the initiator (or else v_{def} if i receives no values). Process i acts as the initiator in algorithm $OM(m-1)$ to send the value v_i to each of the $n-2$ other noninitiator nodes.
5. For each i, and each $j \neq i$, let v_j be the value that process i received from process j in step 2 [using algorithm $OM(m-1)$, or else v_{def} if it received no such value]. Process i uses the value majority$(v_1,\ldots.v_{n-1})$.

Figure 15.6 illustrates working of the algorithm for case $n = 4$, $m = 1$.

Figure 15.6 a shows two stages of message exchange assuming that process P_2 is faulty. As indicated, in the first stage the initiator, process P_0, sends its value, v to all other processes. In the second stage, noninitiator processes relay the received message to each other. Process P_2, which is faulty, sends a forged value x to process P_1 and no message to P_3. With one faulty process, two rounds of message exchanges are sufficient for other processes to reach an agreement. As a result of the assumed message exchange, each process received the following messages:

P_1: (v, x, v)

P_2: (v, v, v)

P_3: (v, v_{def}, v)

Process P_3 receives no value from P_2, so it assumes v_{def}. The two noninitiator processes that are not faulty each apply the majority function to their respective received values. Each process obtains the value v, and consensus is reached. All operational processes perceive the same value

In the second case—part (b) of Figure 15.6 process P_0, which is the initiator, is assumed to be faulty. As shown, P_0 sends three different values to the remaining processes. In the second stage, each of them faithfully relays the receives value to its peers. After two rounds of exchanges, each reliable process received all three different values: (x, y, z). Depending on the definition of the function majority, each reliable process arrives at the same value, and agreement is reached. For example, function majority may evaluate *to* v_{def} when all values are different, or it may compute their median value. Either way, as long as all processes apply the same definition of majority, they will reach agreement on the basis of the messages received.

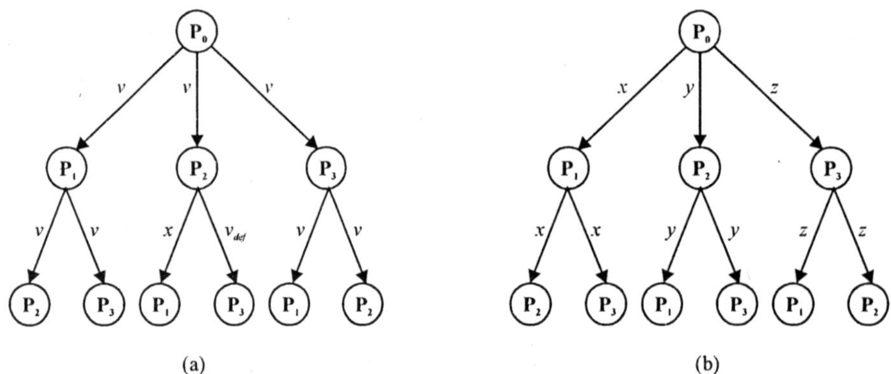

Fig. 15.6. Operation of algorithm OM: (a) Process P_2 faulty, (b) Process P_0 faulty.

The recursive algorithm $OM(m)$ invokes $n-1$ separate executions of the algorithm $OM(m-1)$, each of which invokes $n-2$ executions of $OM(m-2)$, and so on. Overall, the presented algorithm generates $O(n^{m+1})$ messages with n nodes and m stages of message exchange. A receiver can distinguish all these different messages if each sender i prefixes its number i to the value v_i that it sends in step 2.

The cost and complexity of the algorithm result largely from having to deal with faulty processes that can alter messages that they retransmit. Considerable simplifications are possible by assuming that in-transit modifications to the original message can be detected by the receiver. This may be accomplished by using digital signatures to establish the authenticity and integrity of messages required by the algorithm. Moreover, in many actual systems where there is no intentional malevolence on the part of malfunctioning processes, error-correcting code may suffice in place of the signature mechanism. This and other performance improvements, such as ensuring that processes do not relay the values that they have sent before, have given rise to more efficient solutions to the problem when some reasonable restrictions are imposed.

Summary

Distributed computer systems are generally characterized by the absence of globally shared memory, comparatively long and generally unpredictable internode communication delays, and a practically unobservable global system state.

Potential advantages of distributed processing include resource sharing and load balancing; communication and information sharing; incremental growth; and improved reliability, availability, fault tolerance, and performance. Difficulties with and disadvantages of distributed processing include a rich set of failure modes, reduced ability to pool memory, increased dependence on the network, and security weaknesses.

The three basic resources that may be distributed are hardware, control, and data. Control over any given resource may be centralized at the control node, or fully decentralized and carried out through cooperation and negotiation. Data may be distributed and partially or fully replicated for increased availability and fault tolerance.

Wide-area computer networks may span large geographic areas. Their implementations usually involve a store-and-forward subnetwork with dedicated communication processors. Local-area networks are generally characterized by comparatively high bandwidth and low communication delays. High-speed LANs can approximate the intrabackplane speeds of the component machines, thus offering numerous possibilities for creative placement of devices and services. Popular LAN topologies include ring and bus. Open Systems Interconnect is a seven-layer model of the networking architecture that may be applied to different types of networks.

Time-stamping provides a relatively simple but powerful method for ordering events in distributed systems without the need for synchronization of physical clocks. It is used as a basis of numerous algorithms, including distributed mutual exclusion and transaction concurrency control.

In distributed systems, deadlocks occur for much the same reasons and under similar conditions as in centralized systems. However, their prevention, avoidance, and detection are more complex and expensive, as no global-state information is readily available for analyzing chains of waiting processes that can span multiple sites.

In order to realize the potential for increased availability and fault tolerance, distributed systems must be equipped to detect failures and to recover from them. The potentially catastrophic loss of the synchronizing token in ring-based networks can be ameliorated with the aid of one of the token regeneration algorithms. Likewise, election of the successor node can be vital for many asymmetric algorithms that depend on a coordinator.

Reaching agreement among distributed nodes that communicate over unreliable channels is a challenging problem, especially when nodes do not halt upon failure but continue to communicate potentially false and misleading message.

16

Distributed Operating Systems: Implementation

Implementation of distributed systems raises several issues that either are not present or are much less complex in centralized time-sharing and multiuser operating systems. These include hardware and software heterogeneity, a much richer set of failure modes and security threats, and the need for synchronization and communication between processes that reside on different nodes while accessing network resources. A unique and probably the most difficult problem facing designs of distributed operating systems is the need to support network transparency.

Network transparency generally refers to the hiding of networking aspects of the system from its users. Network-transparent resource usage means that there should be no difference in the manner of access between local and remote resources. Carried to its logical extreme, network transparency implies that an application developed and tested in a single-site environment should run unchanged in a distributed environment. Network transparency thus allows users to enjoy the benefits of distributed processing, such as resource sharing and increased availability, without the penalty of special coding or retrofitting of the existing applications. It also allows the distributed operating system to balance the resource usage, to migrate and replicate processes and files dynamically for increased performance and/or reliability, and to perform a number of other, similar optimizations without affecting the executing applications and user programs. In comparison, nontransparent network applications are inflexible, nonportable, and much more failure-prone due to having a specific network topology and resource distribution hardwired into their code. As a consequence, they generally cannot adapt to changes without recoding.

Network transparency has a number of aspects. Its components and include name transparency, location transparency, access transparency, and many variations and combinations of these. In order to support network transparency, a distributed operating system usually must provide a globally unique and largely location-independent naming of system resources, and a unified file system that spans volume and machine boundaries.

Implementation of network transparency can take place at a number of different system levels. The three major ones are:

1. Transparency via an application system
2. Programming-language-supported transparency
3. Transparency at the operating-system level

Network transparency may be provided within a common application, such as a database—resulting in a distributed database system. Another possibility is to provide distribution in a suitable programming language. In that case, the language compiler and run-time system become responsible for providing the mechanisms and for implementing various forms of transparency. Implementation of the remote procedure call is often of central importance in this approach.

Models of Distributed Systems

The four basic models and configurations of distributed systems are:

- Host-based (minicomputer) model
- Processor pool model
- Workstation model
- Integrated model

The Host-based Model

The host-based model is an outgrowth of time-sharing systems. It is essentially a loose federation of time-sharing systems connected via a network. A popular variation of this model is clustering of processors and disks via a high-speed local interconnect, such as VAX clusters. This model is sometimes called a minicomputer model due to its early implementations in academia, where several departmental minicomputer time-sharing systems were joined to form a campus-wide distributed system. Host-based distributed systems typically retain full local autonomy for the participating nodes and use the network to provide remote log-ins, file transfer, and electronic mail. Transparent networking and distributed file systems are usually not supported at this level. Users of host-based systems typically have to obtain node-specific passwords for each node whose resources they intend to access, except for electronic mail, which typically transcends node boundaries under system control.

The Processor Pool Model

The processor pool model aims to overcome some of these limitations by bringing some processors and their resources into a common pool. Users access the processor pool via their terminals. At log-in time, the system assigns the user to a processor from the pool taking into account considerations such as proximity, system state, and the individual processor utilization. In principle, users may be allowed to designate a specific processor for a log-in. However, such fixed assignments should be an exception rather than the rule in order for the system to exploit its potential benefits, such as resource sharing, load balancing, increased availability, and fault tolerance. Since the processors are pooled together, with proper scheduling it is possible to dynamically assign several processors to the execution of a single user program. Upon completion, the processors are returned to the pool. Although other arrangements are possible, full benefits of the processor pool model are realized in conjunction with a transparent, unified, system-wide file system. Terminals are often serviced by and connected to the network via dedicated front-end processors, sometimes called *terminal interface processors* (TIPs). Separation of terminals from the processors usually requires high-bandwidth TIP-to-processor-pool links and thus restricts this model to implementations of a local-area network.

The Workstation/Server Model

In the workstation/server model, a workstation is dedicated to each user at least for the duration of a log-in session. Common system services and shared resources are provided in the form of specialized servers. Servers and user workstations are connected via a local-area network. Figure 16.1 depicts a typical workstation/server-based distributed system.

In the workstation/server-based model, common services are usually invoked using the client/server model, with servers running the server portion.

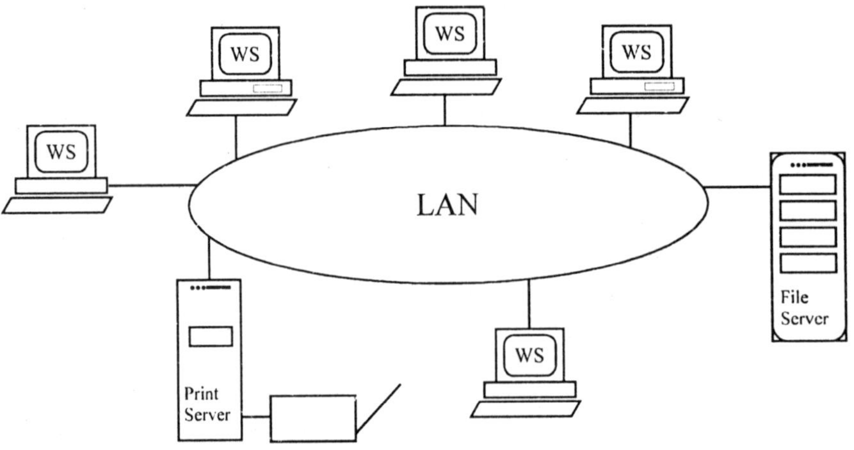

Fig. 16.1. Workstation model of distributed processing.

Each individual workstation operating environment is functionally extended with the client protocols and procedures that allow it to access the shared services remotely.

A *server* is a collection of hardware and software components that provide a common service to a priori unknown clients. Some of the more common server types include file servers, compute servers, print servers, name servers, authentication servers, network gateway servers, terminal servers, and electronic mail servers. For availability and performance reasons, several physical servers of the same type—say, file servers—may exist in a given system. Depending on the size of the system, its workload, and server hardware requirements, servers may be implemented on dedicated machines—such as powerful workstations, minicomputers, or even mainframes.

Graphics is a very attractive aspect of the workstation model. Graphics provide for a rich and powerful user interface in almost any setup, and it is mandatory for certain applications, such as simulations and computer-aided design. Due to its high bandwidth requirements, which often exceed the sustained stream transmission capability of commercial LANs, in many systems it is mandatory to provide graphics display refreshing and manipulation locally within a workstation. Thus, user workstations typically provide the user interface and the processing power to execute some applications and most operating-system commands locally. There is a pronounced drive to standardize this interface across applications and to provide a single, consistent user interface, to make the distributed system truly transparent to its users when desirable. In terms of hardware, a typical workstation contains a processor, memory, graphics engine and monitor, mouse, and keyboard. Optionally, the workstations may also contain local secondary storage such as a hard disk.

In general, local (within the workstation) execution tends to improve response time and reduce its variation when executing applications and common operating-system commands. Applications that require special resources or have computational requirements beyond the ability of a local workstation are executed remotely by one or several cooperating servers. The workstation model is a sound foundation for cooperative processing, where different portions of a single application are executed by different machines. For example, the numerically intensive portion of a modelling application may be executed on a superminicomputer, its files managed by a file server, and the output visualized on the user's workstation. This mode of operation provides considerable flexibility in allocating processing and system resources so as to optimize system availability, response time, performance, and cost. In this way, the workstation model capitalizes on the economy of sharing, facilitates hardware specialization, and allows various optimizations while providing the rich graphical interface to its users.

Hardware specialization of individual servers is viewed by some designers as an attractive alternative to the larger, general-purpose computers. The argument goes that a functionally specialized component, such as a number-crunching supermini acting as a computational server, or a file server with hardware accelerators, can provide a given service more reliably, with higher performance, and at a lower cost than its general-purpose counterparts. By the same argument, the operating system for a specialized server may be streamlined to support only the particular function and thus be relieved of much of the overhead imposed on general-purpose operating systems that must do "all things for all people." Pooling of such specialized services provides the collective general-purpose variety of services to the networked users in workstation/server-based systems. To paraphrase a slogan, with the workstation/server model, the network becomes the computer.

Sharing of resources is generally attractive, especially in high-bandwidth LAN environments. In terms of software, storage at the server of common applications and utilities—such as design packages, editors, and compiler—can reduce disk-capacity requirements at the workstations. When required for execution, these programs may be executed at the server or be brought across the LAN for execution at the workstation. Hardware cost-effectiveness can often be increased by placing expensive resources at the server. For example, it may be attractive to place large, expensive disks on a server and thus enable the workstations to share its benefits. Such disks may have lower cost per megabyte and better performance than workstation disks. Besides, very large files and databases simply may not fit on smaller disks that are suitable for workstations. Similar arguments may be made for other expensive devices, such as high-speed laser and color printers.

The workstation-based model of distributed processing is often implemented by extending, rather than redesigning, the existing hardware and software. Typically, a common baseline workstation operating system, such as Unix, is augmented with a software layer that can distinguish whether a resource requested by an application is local or remote. Local requests are completed as usual, and remote ones are routed to the appropriate server. Cooperative processing is supported to the extent that portions of the processing of locally initiated applications are farmed out to servers. However, mechanisms for support of full distribution transparency in terms of resource distribution and run-time assignment are usually not extensive in the workstation-based systems of the late eighties and early nineties. There is nothing inherent in the workstation model that precludes this possibility; it is the desire to use and retrofit the existing operating systems that introduces limitations.

The Integrated Model

A different approach, sometimes called the integrated model, provides a truly distributed operating system by designing it from scratch. In this model, distribution of resources and services is fully transparent to the application programs. File names are global, and there is a single set of system primitives to access them regardless of their geographic location in relation to the requesting client. Likewise, the use of a uniform procedure call mechanism erases syntactic differences between local and remote calls. As a result of these and other techniques for achieving full distribution transparency, the entire networked system appears to its users as a single computer. All of its services and special devices are available to every authorized user and application. The absence of site-dependent resource access and naming allows application portability across the wide range of system configurations and reduces their sensitivity to individual component unavailability or outages. At the same time, the operating system is free to migrate resources, such as files and processes, in order to optimize the system's performance in response to demand, load, and component availability variations.

Naming

Distributed operating systems manage a number of user-accessible objects, such as files, directories, processes, mailboxes, services, nodes, and I/O devices. Each such object has a name and resides at some location. A mechanism is often provided to allow users to name resources to be operated on in a human-friendly way, such as a string of alphanumeric characters. At the system level, resources are typically identified by numeric tokens. A *naming* mechanism provides the mapping between the symbolic, user-given names and the low-level system identifiers used in operating-system calls. Basically, a name designates the specific object of interest, a location is its address, and a route specifies how to get there.

Naming is essentially a lookup function that takes the symbolic name as input and returns a system-level token (ID). For example, in a Unix file system, the user-level name is mapped into a token that is an index into the system's internal list of open files. Upon opening a file, the system returns the token, which the user program uses in all subsequent references to that file. In this way, directory traversals necessary to perform name-to-taken mapping are bypassed in repeated references to the same file.

In distributed system, each name lookup must return two values: (1) the node address where the target object resides, and (2) a token for referring to the target object at the node where it resides. The object's node address is required for proper directing of user request messages. A token is sent with each request to designate a specific object at the chosen node. A token must be unique at least at the node level. In some distributed systems, low-level tokens are unique globally at the system level. This helps to fully decouple names from locations.

Desirable properties of a name service in a distributed system include:

- Name transparency
- Location transparency
- Replication transparency
- Dynamic adaptability to changes of object residence
- Good performance

Name transparency means that an object name should not reveal any hint as to its location. Location transparency implies that a name or a token should not have to be changed when the related object changes its residence. Replication transparency ensures that replication of an object is hidden from users. Thus, the system may return one appropriate token even when multiple instances of the target object are available. This allows the operating system to vary the degree of object replication dynamically in response to load and usage patterns. Since object migration may be beneficial for load sharing, availability, and fault tolerance, the naming system should support it by handling address changes dynamically and gracefully.

A distributed name service is a mapping that may be multilevel and multivalued. It may be organized as a hierarchy where certain parts of prefixes designate a specific subdomain. The phone service represents an example of a naming hierarchy where the first few digits designate a country, the next few digits represents the area code or the city code, and the remaining digits are the within-area (sub-domain) number. The multivalued possibility is due to replicated objects, in which case the mapping returns one or more of the machine addresses where a copy of the target object resides. Replication is generally useful for important services and files that may be provided by several servers. By locating more than one eligible server, the naming service allows the operating system to choose the most appropriate server in terms of its proximity to the user, server load, availability of the communication paths, or some other consideration.

There is a variety of ways to implement a naming service in a distributed operating system. Some of the common one include:

- Static maps
- Broadcasting
- Name server
- Prefix tables

Static Maps

Static maps represent a fixed mapping of resource names to the respective locations where those resources reside. Static maps can be used in systems where names include the location of the related objects. Such names are typically of the form *hostname: pathname.* For example, the global file name *X:a/b* may be formed by prefixing the file name *a/b* with the name of the host, *X*, where it resides. Static naming systems represent a relatively easy way to extend an existing single-computer operating system for operation in a distributed environment.

A popular variation of the static-map naming scheme is to map remoter files as a virtual extension of the client's local directory hierarchy. In many PC-based networks, remote files are mapped into a logical drive name that is not used by a locally attached physical drive in a given workstation. Assuming that *E* designates such an unused drive letter on a given machine, after executing an initial attach command, the client can refer to remote files in the same manner as the local files by simply prefixing their path names with the drive designation, *E*. Thus, assuming proper authorizations are in place, a user can perform remote file transfer by issuing a standard copy command, such as

```
COPY A: FILELOC E: FILEREM
```

In a PC DOS-like system, this would transfer a local file, FILELOC, from the workstation's drive A and store it in the server under the name FILEREM.

In the more elaborate Unix-like systems, remote files can be mounted to the designated point of the client's directory tree. The remote host name may need to be explicitly used only once when issuing the remote mount command. Thereafter, remote files can be manipulated using the standard Unix syntax and path names.

The remote-mount approach can greatly increase user convenience and provide apparent naming transparency even in the systems where the actual implementation of naming is essentially static and location-dependent.

Broadcasting

Broadcasting can be used to implement the naming function without maintenance of name tables or use of name servers. In this approach, a node simply broadcasts the target object's name to all servers. After looking up their local name tables, one or more of the qualified servers reply. Broadcasting dynamically reacts to changes of object residence and simplifies updating of naming information. Unfortunately, its performance is usually poor due to the disruption and overhead of frequent name lookup imposed on servers that do not contain the desired target object. This problem may be alleviated by caching recent name translations at the workstations as described in the next section.

Name Servers

Name servers can be implemented in its entirely by one or more specialized name servers. In such systems, a client presents the name of the target object to the name service, which then returns the corresponding node address and the token. Depending on the implementation, a name server may completely resolve a name or only partially resolve it and provide a pointer to the client where to proceed.

By providing extra levels of mapping indirection, name servers can easily decouple names from locations and thus support object migration. In effect, name servers maintain system-wide directories of globally accessible resources. However, the use of name servers can adversely affect both the performance and reliability of a distributed system by introducing a third party into client-server interactions. The drawbacks of having to access the third party include increased delays and sensitivity to failures of the name server. Updating of the name-server database can be quite complex in cases when multiple copies of mapping tables are maintained.

Since name resolution in general can be quite lengthy, many distributed systems attempt to improve performance by caching in each workstation a collection of its recently requested name-token translations. The idea, as in file systems, is to avoid the overhead of name translation on repeated references to the same object. Hits into the name cache result in quick translations that bypass the name server and thus improve performance in applications and user environments that exhibit temporal locality of object references. The difficulty with client caching in distributed systems is that object migrations can invalidate the cached names. Since keeping track of the client name caches and their updating is a potentially significant overhead for servers, the common approach is to treat the client entries as merely a hint as to the whereabouts of the target object.

When the client uses a stale entry and the object is not found at the designated location, the cache entry in question is invalidated and optionally updated by invoking the name service.

Prefix Tables

Prefix tables are a naming mechanism in which each client maintains a list of partial or complete path names of a subset of the objects that it has accessed in the past. When accessing an object, a client sends its request to the server designated by the longest matching prefix. Figure 16.2 illustrates the prefix-table approach to naming, which was originally introduced in a paper by Welch and Osterhout (1986).

In the system depicted in Figure 16.2 files are grouped into four domains marked by dotted lines. Two domains, labelled B and C, are stored at servers with the same name. The two remaining domains are stored at the single file server A.

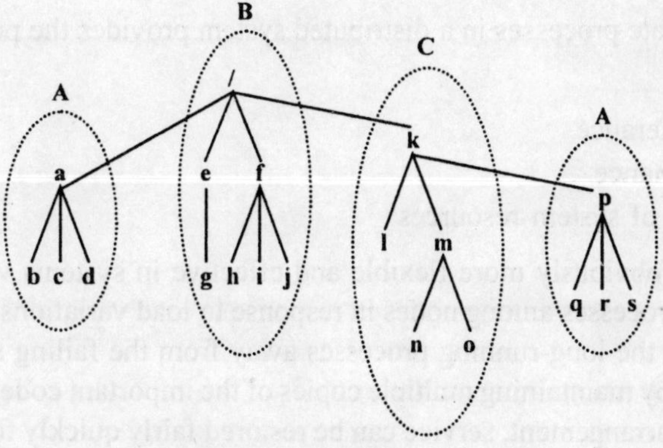

Prefix Table		
Prefix	Server	Token
/	B	12
/a	A	5
/k	C	32
/k/p	A	17

Fig. 16.2. Prefix tables.

A possible appearance of the prefix table constructed by a client is shown in the box in Figure 16.2. As indicated, each entry in the prefix table contains a partial or a complete path name, the corresponding server ID, and the token. When a client needs to resolve a file name in order to direct the request to the appropriate server, it searches the longest matching portion of the path name in the prefix table. In the example presented, requests for the file */a* would be forwarded to server A, requests for */k/m/n* to server C, and requests for files whose path names begin with */k/p* to server A. Clients also send the related tokens that servers use to identify a particular object or a directory subtree of interest.

When a client needs to deal with a path that is not stored in the prefix table, it broadcasts the file name to all servers. The server that stores the subtree of interest returns a message with its ID and the path token. Initially, each client starts with an empty prefix table and fills it up as needed by broadcasting.

Prefix tables are used only as hints. Changes in system configuration and server failures can result in the failure to locate the object at the place designated in the client's prefix table. In case of misdirected requests, it is usually the client's responsibility to attempt to identify the appropriate new server, if any, and to update the prefix table accordingly. This may be accomplished by broadcasting.

Process Migration

Process migration in distributed systems refers to the transfer of an active process from one node to another. Migration entails the transfer of a sufficient amount of a process's state to allow the process to execute on the destination node.

The ability to migrate processes in a distributed system provides the potential to:

- Balance the load
- Increase fault tolerance
- Improve performance
- Make better use of system resources

Load balancing is obviously more flexible and effective in systems where the scheduler can dynamically reassign processes among nodes in response to load variations. Fault tolerance may be increased by migrating the long-running processes away from the failing nodes. In addition, fault tolerance can be aided by maintaining multiple copies of the important code at strategic points in the systems. With such an arrangement, service can be restored fairly quickly following a server failure by migrating the run-time state and reactivating the related process at one of the backup nodes. Performance may be improved by migrating the process to the data site for programs that perform operations on large volumes of data. Both performance and load balancing may be improved in workstation-based systems by distributing certain applications across the idle workstations. Process migration is advantageous in such systems because it allows a remote application to retreat without loss of completed work when the workstation's owner returns. Another possibility availed by process migration is the use of special-purpose system resources that cannot be invoked remotely. In such cases, the requesting process migrates and executes the appropriate access routines locally at the home site of the restricted resource.

The decision of when and where to relocate a process is made by a scheduler. These issues are quite difficult, and few if any general solutions exist. The mechanics of process migration, however, is much better understood.

Process migration basically involves transfer of the process state from one node to another. In general, components of the process state include:

- *Static process image* (executable file) on disk
- *Process state,* which includes the run-time image of process registers, pages in main memory (code, data, and stack), and pages swapped to disk

- *Process execution environment,* including the list of resources in use by the process, such as open files, pending I/O notifications, and IPC, such as signals and messages

Once the decision to move the process to a specific destination is made, process migration consists of some permutation of the following steps:

1. Remove the process from execution at the source node.
2. Negotiate with the destination node to move the process.
3. Allocate space for the process state at the destination.
4. Move the program image (executable file) to the destination.
5. Move the process state to the destination.
6. Activate the process at the destination node.
7. Forward pending messages and IPC to the destination.
8. Update system naming and location structures that involve location of the migrated process.

Some aspects of Steps 4 and 5 are illustrated in Figure 16.3. Lines with arrows indicate clusters of messages that transfer major portions of the process state and environment.

Three major difficulties in implementing process migration are: (1) a large volume of state may need to be moved, (2) the execution environment is quite difficult to move without leaving residual dependencies at a former residence, and (3) communication and invocations of the migrated process have to be redirected to its new residence.

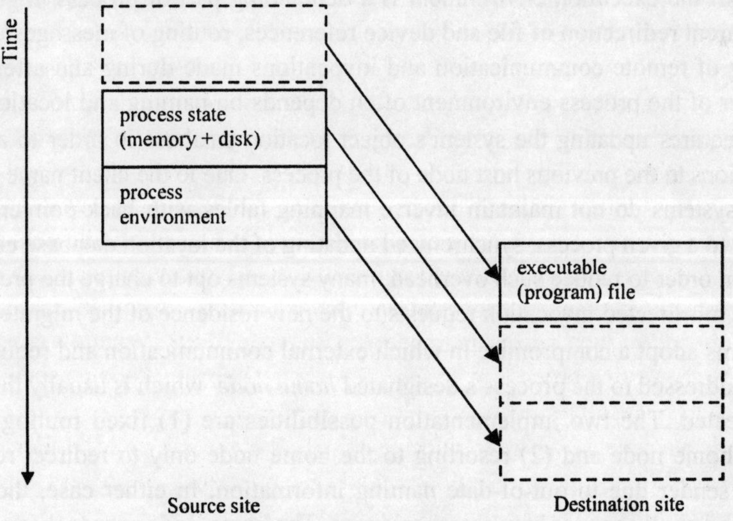

Fig. 16.3. Process migration.

In systems with virtual memory implemented at individual nodes, the size of a process state can be on the order of megabytes. Thus process migration can result in considerable network loading and in prolonged unavailability of the migrating process. The adverse impact of the latter may be alleviated by precopying the program image to the destination while allowing the process to continue running at the source site. Since the program image and swapped pages represent the bulk of the process state, the program's unavailability is reduced to the time it takes to move the comparatively small remainder of the process state.

The volume of data involved in a migration can be reduced in systems that use the network as the backing store for workstation's virtual memory. This approach accelerates process migration by having to move only a skeletal portion of the state. The rest of the state is then page-faulted across the network in the course of process execution at the destination node. The dirty pages from the source node must be flushed to the backing store before the process is reactivated at the destination. In addition, descriptor tables of the swap areas used by the process may have to be moved to the destination. A potential drawback of paging across the network is its increased loading in normal operation caused by the page traffic between the workstations and the backing store.

In general, virtual memory can be quite beneficial for implementations of process migration. Its primary attractions are the built-in mechanism for demand loading of pages and the run-time virtual-to-physical address mapping mechanism. Thus, it is possible to activate a process at the destination after moving only a minimal part of the state and a few pages. The rest of the memory can be page-faulted as needed from the backing store, which can be located at individual nodes or provided as a network-wide function. The primary advantage of virtual memory approaches is that only the actually referenced parts of the state are involved in moving. The extent of the realized savings is a function of the ratio of the total size of a program's virtual memory to the fraction that is actually touched on a given execution.

Relocation of the execution environment is a demanding part of process migration. It entails program-transparent redirection of file and device references, routing of messages and signals, and proper directing of remote communication and invocations made during and after the migration. Efficient transfer of the process environment often depends on naming and location transparency.

Migration requires updating the system's object location database in order to avoid routing of external invocations to the previous host node of the process. Due to the client name caching and the fact that many systems do not maintain inverse mapping tables with back-pointers to all naming entries that refer to a given process, synchronized updating of the location database can be quite slow and expensive. In order to reduce such overhead, many systems opt to charge the previous host node with forwarding misdirected invocation requests to the new residence of the migrated module.

Some systems adopt a compromise in which external communication and requests for process invocation are addressed to the process's designated *home node,* which is usually the site where the process was created. The two implementation possibilities are (1) fixed routing of all external requests to the home node and (2) resorting to the home node only to redirect requests that are returned to the sender due to out-of-date naming information. In either case, the home node is regularly informed of all changes in process residence. The home-node approach is relatively simple to implement. Its drawbacks include an extra level of addressing indirection and reduced fault tolerance due to dependence on the home node.

Remote Procedure Calls

There are basically two ways to distribute execution of a program. One way is to implement the application in question as a set of cooperating but separate processes. Individual processes can then be placed on different nodes and interact by means of various distributed mechanisms for interprocess communication and synchronization.

Another approach is to partition a single monolithic program and allow its pieces to execute on different nodes of a distributed system. Procedures are natural boundaries for program division because they are largely self-contained logical entities that have well-defined interfaces and entry/exit points. In addition, a remote procedure call (RPC) mechanism must be provided to make the partitioned program work in a distributed environment.

Conceptually, the *remote-procedure call* follows the well-understood mechanism for transfer of control and data within a single computer. When a remote procedure is invoked, the calling environment is suspended, and the parameters are passed across the network to the node where the procedure is to execute (callee). When the procedure finishes and produces its results, the callee's node returns them across the network to the caller's node.

Distribution of computation assisted by remote-procedure calls has a number of attractive properties. One is the clean and simple semantics, which facilitates correct implementation of distributed computations. Unlike alternatives discussed earlier, remote-procedure implementations make distribution largely transparent to programmers. By using a familiar model of data and control flow, application programmers are relieved of explicit coding and controlling of distribution-related primitives, such as message passing. Another benefit of distribution transparency that RPC provides is that existing applications developed for a single computer can be comparatively easily ported to a distributed environment. A third advantage is generality: procedures are one of the most common and well understood mechanisms for communication between parts of the algorithm in single-computer systems.

Remote procedures are a natural fit for the client/server model of distributed computing. Client routines can call on the services by remotely invoking the execution of the appropriate procedures on the server. Servers may provide common services by means of the public server procedures that a number of potential clients can call. This concept is similar to shared subroutine libraries in single-computer systems. In both environments, public routines must either be reentrant or protected from preemption by some form of concurrency control, such as mutual exclusion.

Three major issues in implementing the remote-procedure call mechanism are:

- Transfer of control
- Binding
- Transfer of data

We treat these issues in detail in the sections that follow.

Transfer of Control

Presumably, some form of a global shared-memory abstraction could serve as a facility for implementing remote-procedure calls in a distributed system. This approach has two potential difficulties: (1) It may require modification of programming languages in order to support remote addresses. (2) It is hard to implement efficiently enough for the RPC. The methods presented in the rest of this section assume the absence of shared memory.

The program structure for remote-procedure call is often based on the concept of *stubs*. Figure 16.4 illustrates the basic components of an RPC.

In addition to the user (calling) routine, the caller machine contains a user stub and the RPC run-time package. The callee machine has its own RPC run-time routines, server stub, and the called routine, labelled *server*. The user's remote-procedure call is linked on the user machine to the user stub. Thus, the user's invocation of the remote procedure is converted into a local call to teh corresponding procedure in the user stub. The *user stub* is responsible for placing a specification of the target procedure and its arguments into communication packets. The user stub then invokes the local RPC run-time via a local procedure call to transmit those packets reliably to the callee machine.

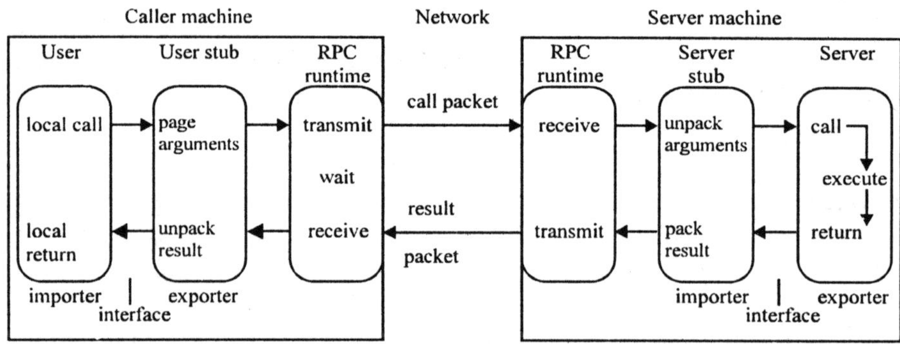

Fig. 16.4. Remote-procedure call.

The server (callee) RPC run-time receives the packets and passes them to the server stub via the local procedure call. The server stub unpacks the packets and acts as an agent of the remote users. In particular, the server stub makes a local call to the appropriate procedure and supplies the received parameters. When the called procedure completes execution, it returns control and results to the server stub. The server stub passes results to the server RPC run-time for transmission to the caller's machine. The caller's RPC run-time passes the result packets to the user stub. Upon unpacking, the user stub completes the process by making a local return to the calling routine.

As the generic implementation indicates, a user's run-time perception of the remote-procedure call is hardly different from the local procedure call. With the caller and server code brought into one machine and bound directly without the stubs, the program would still work. Except for multimachine binding, RPC semantics follows that of the single-machine procedure call.

In terms of flow of control the caller is suspended until the called procedure completes and returns. As expected, there is complete synchrony between the caller and the callee. Upon completion of the call, the caller continues execution from the point immediately following the call. The server procedure is supposed to execute in its entirety prior to returning control. Remote-procedure calls may be nested; that is, a server procedure can call other procedures. The RPC's mimicking of the normal procedure call is intentional. It is the familiar semantics and behaviour that account for much of the appeal of remote procedure calls.

Binding

Part of the added complexity of the RPC is embodied in the need to provide user and server stubs. Many RPC implementations provide automatic tools such as interface languages to facilitate generation of stubs.

In programming languages with support for separate compilation, such as Ada and Modula, procedures that implement an interface are said to *export* that interface (placed in the public part of Ada tasks). A program module that calls procedures from an interface is said to *import* the interface. Type checking across module boundaries during separate compilation may be enforced by requiring a module to be compiled with all interface definitions (exported by their owners) that it imports. In general, the user stub imports the interface, and the server stub exports it.

In a single-computer system binding or linking consists of (1) locating component modules and (2) resolving address references to produce an executable program image. Binding may be performed at compile-time or, at run-time.

An added problem in a distributed system is that an importer and exporter of a module exist in a system-wide global name space, rather than within a single-machine name space. This raises the question of *naming*. That is, given the name of the interface, the object is to find a machine where its exporter resides. An importer may name either a specific *instance* or a type of the interface. If the specification is an instance, the caller is bound to a specific server. If the specification is a type, the caller names the type of the service it desires, and the system is free to provide any suitable server of the appropriate type. This is useful for resource optimization in systems that provide multiple servers of the same type. For example, if the user wishes to use the services of a print server, the system may supply the name of the closest one or of the one that happens to be least busy at the time.

Naming is typically handled by a mechanism separate from the RPC package. However, once the name is resolved, the RPC package is responsible for determining the machine address of the callee and for specifying to it the procedure to be invoked. These operations entail locating of the exporter and local binding therein.

A simple way to identify exporters is to broadcast the interface and then choose among the appropriate respondents. This approach tends to burden the communication links and nodes that do not export the specific interface but must receive and examine each broadcast only to find out that they are not interested.

A more efficient approach is to have exporters advertise their wares by registering them with a broker. For example, exporters can register their interfaces and the intention to serve with a binding server. In such systems, importers forward their requests to the binding server. Binding is completed by having the binding server match the two parties, who then proceed to interact on their own. The server can store both the individual instances as well as types of service providers by forming lists of exporters of the same type. In an analogy with the phone book, individual servers are listed in the white pages, and assorted types of service providers are listed in the yellow pages.

Thus, either at compile-time or at run-time, the caller's node initiates the binding by communicating with the binding server. In general, delayed binding (run-time) is preferable in distributed systems because of its flexibility. Early (compile-time) binding has the drawback of wiring a specific instance of the server into the code too soon. Run-time binding delays this commitment until the call is actually made; as a result, the system can optimize performance by allocating resources on the basis of the system's state encountered during the actual execution of the RPC. For example, the system may choose to employ a lightly loaded server, or to increase robustness by offering suitable substitutes for the crashed servers.

Flow of Data

By extending the notion of a local procedure call, the RPC is supposed to pass all parameters at the time of a call. Given that the caller and the callee execute on different nodes and in separate address spaces, all parameters must be passed explicitly and by value. In systems without shared memory, global variables and calls by reference cannot be supported by the RPC mechanism. Some aspects of call by reference (*var* in Pascal, *out* and *in out* in Ada) can be simulated by outputting the variable in question and having the callee operate on it and return the modified value as a result. Passing arguments that contain pointers is meaningless in systems without global shared memory.

One of the major issues in RPC implementations is support for heterogeneity. Differences in software, hardware, or both can lead to incompatible representations of data types at different machines in a distributed system. Some of the common primitive data-type problems include incompatible byte ordering, floating-point representations, and character encoding (ASCII vs. EBCDIC). Some relief is provided by standards, such as IEEE floating-point, and by some processor vendors who support program-selectable byte ordering in their designs. Yet a viable RPC designed for a heterogeneous environment must provide some means for coping with the problem. One approach is to provide a network-wide uniform data representation format. Each sender converts its local data formats into the uniform representation for subsequent decoding by the receiver. This is obviously wasteful when two homogeneous machines are communicating in a heterogeneous system. Another possibility is to provide a common programming language that bridges the representation differences by compiling into the native machine language of each node and providing the run-time translation routines when necessary.

RPC Server Design Issues

When the RPC model is used as a way to provide services in a client/server environment, server designs must address several implementation issues. These include handling of concurrent client calls, coping with failures, and recovery.

When an RPC is used for bulk data transfers, such as files and pages of virtual memory, the caller/server interaction consists of a series of packet exchanges. One dilemma is how much state should be maintained at each end, and what should be done with that state when either party fails or becomes unreachable.

Custom RPC run-time protocols can further burden server design by requiring it to detect failures, ranging from lost and duplicate messages to client crashes, and to provide some form of recovery.

Client failures can cause orphan processes, created for procedure execution, to linger at the server. With the possibility of failures, RPC semantics can assume one of the following types:

- Exactly once
- At most once
- At least once
- Maybe

Exactly-once semantics corresponds to the single-computer model, but it is extremely difficult to guarantee in the presence of mishaps. For instance, a simple retransmission of the call request following execution of a time-out may cause repeated execution of the procedure if the server is functional but its original reply was delayed. Likewise, when a server crashes, it is very difficult to determine whether it did so an instant before or after invoking the procedure in question.

At-most-once semantics provides a guarantee that the remote procedure is either executed once or not at all. This is desirable for some applications, such as transaction commit.

At-least-once semantics guarantees one or more executions of the remote procedure. It is acceptable only for procedures that are *idempotent,* that is, amenable to repeated executions. An idempotent procedure has the same effect and returns the same result when executed repeatedly.

Maybe semantics does not offer any guarantees. It is the easiest to implement but probably the least desirable.

Process creation is a frequent operation at servers that have to maintain multiple concurrent client sessions. While each client is suspended awaiting a server's response, a number of client sessions may be active at a server at any one time. Typically, each remotely invoked procedure execution is handled by a separate thread or by a separate process at the server. In addition to the complexity and restrictions involved in dealing with concurrent invocations of the same server procedure by different clients, process creation in response to client requests can become a serious bottleneck at the server. Some early RPC implementations that created a separate process for each user session exceeded the number of processes that a major commercial operating system could handle.

A common approach to dealing with this problem is to use threads rather than processes to server individual user request. Threads are lightweight in the sense that they have a much smaller state than processes. As a result., thread creation and context switching are much more efficient. Another, complementary technique is to create and maintain a stock of idle threads (or processes) at the server. These are assigned to specific user as the need arises, thus saving the overhead of threads creation at times when the server is busy handling client requests. Upon termination of a client session, the server returns the worker thread to the idle pool.

RPC versus Message Passing

Remote procedure calls are a mechanism for distributing an application on procedure-call boundaries across multiple machines. Messages, on the other hand, are an interprocess synchronization and communication mechanism suitable for use by cooperating but separate and largely autonomous processes. Thus, the two mechanisms serve somewhat different purposes and are not direct substitutes for each other.

However, when one of these mechanisms is used for other than its primary purpose, some overlap, some overlap exists, and the choice between them may have to be made. For example, this may be the case when the distribution facility is used for bulk data transfers, such as files, or when a programming style and the supporting interprocess communication (IPC) mechanism are contemplated for a new distributed application. Some of the major considerations of interest here are:

- Transfer of control and synchronicity
- Binding
- Transfer of data
- Fault tolerance

These issues are briefly elaborated in the subsequent paragraphs.

Closely following the semantics of a procedure call in a single-computer system, RPCs are synchronous. Messages provide both synchronous and asynchronous varieties of the sender/receiver relationship. Asynchronous messages can improve concurrency at the cost of having to deal with the buffering of messages that are sent but not yet received. Imposing a limit on the number of outstanding messages tends to solve the implementation problem, but it also complicates the semantics of the asynchronous send primitive.

RPCs rely on multimachine binding for proper processing of remote invocations. Message passing generally does not require binding. It only requires a target port or a recipient to be identified by the naming mechanism at run-time. The asymmetric nature of the RPC requires a caller to be bound to one server and to await its reply. This property is not convenient for implementing broadcasts and multicasts, which messages can handle quite naturally.

In terms of data transfers, RPCs impose some sort of parameter typing and typically require all parameters to be furnished at the time of the call. Messages are less structured and allow the sender and the receiver to freely negotiate the data format. Being essentially byte streams, messages tend to be easier to adapt to heterogeneous environments.

Failures are difficult to deal within both environments. However, messages do have the convenient property that a receiver can act on a message that is logically independent of the failure or termination of the sender. If, for instance, the operation is to update a shared variable, it may still complete despite the sender's failure after sending the message. In the RPC model, failure of the client creates an orphan process that is typically aborted by the server.

Distributed Shared Memory

Messages and RPCs pass variables by value and thus implement the *data-passing model* of interprocess communication in distributed systems. An alternative form of interprocess communication is to employ the shared-memory model in a distributed system by providing processes with a commonly accessible shared address space.

Distributes shared memory (DSM) is an abstraction of shared memory implemented in a distributed system. Since distributed systems consist of loosely coupled systems with no physically shared memory, this abstraction may be provided by an additional software layer that uses message passing. This software layer may be a part of the kernel, or it may be a separate run-time subsystem that operates below the application layer. In this way, applications programmers are provided with the familiar abstraction of the (globally) shared memory that is accessed and manipulated by simple read and write operations. Conceptually, distributed shared memory extends the local address across the host boundaries in a distributed compared system. For performance reasons, DSM should be implemented in systems with high-bandwidth and low-latency communication links. Such links are typically available in some types of local-area networks but are rarely found in wide-area networks.

The primary advantage of distributed shared memory is that it implements a simple, familiar model of shared memory that allows unrestricted forms of data passing. In particular, DSM allows sharing and passing of complex data structures by reference. At least in theory, single-site programs developed using the shared-memory model may be "ported" to a distributed environment without recoding if it supports distributed shared memory. Another advantage is that shared data may be allowed to persist beyond the lifetimes of individual participating processes. Proponents of the scheme also argue that DSM may improve performance, relative to direct message passing, in some cases by moving data in blocks and only on demand—when actually referenced by an executing application.

The common algorithms for DSM implementation include:

- Central server
- Migration
- Read replication
- Full replication

The *central-server* approach consists of maintaining a single physical copy of the shared memory at the central server. In this scheme, reads and writes to shared memory performed at any other site are converted to messages and sent to the central server for processing. In the case of reads, the server returns desired values. For writes, the server updates the master copy of shared memory and returns an acknowledgement. This implementation makes it relatively easy to provide the single-site semantics of reads and writes where each returns results of the most recent write to the target memory object.

The *migration* algorithm operates by maintaining a single physical copy of the shared memory and migrating it to the site where access is desired. The floating copy of shared memory may be relatively easily integrated into the virtual-memory addressing scheme of its resident host. This implementation of shared memory is conceptually simple, but it has poor performance when the locus of shared-memory activity tends to move quickly among hosts. When two or more hosts attempt to use shared memory within the same time frame, excessive migration of data may lead to thrashing. This is especially troublesome when the competing hosts are actually accessing nonoverlapping areas of shared memory.

Read replication allows the simultaneous coexistence of multiple read copies of shared memory at different hosts. At most one host is allowed to have write access to shared memory. Thus, this is a multiple-readers, single-writer scheme. A host wishing to read shared memory obtains a local copy with a read access and is thus able to satisfy repeated read queries locally. In order to maintain consistency, active reading must preclude writing by invalidating and temporarily withholding write access right to shared memory elsewhere in the system. Naturally, multiple concurrent read copies are permitted. Read replication is commonly used to implement distributed shared memory. Its operation resembles the readers/writers problem, and consistency is maintained in much the same way as in client cache coherence. In order to improve performance, shared memory is often divided into logical blocks, and an owner host is designated for each block. Consistent reading and writing is then performed as described, but on a per-block basis under coordination of the applicable home host.

Full replication allows simultaneous maintenance of multiple read and write copies of portions of shared memory. Consistency is maintained by means of protocols that broadcast writes to all read and write copies of affected blocks. In order to sequence global writes properly, a global sequence may be used.

The choice of the particular implementation of distributed shared memory that is appropriate for a given system is based on a number of factors, such as frequency of reads versus writes, locality of reference of shared memory, computational complexity, and the expected number of messages.

Distributed File Systems

In distributed systems based on the workstation model, servers provide common services. A *service* is a software entity that implements a well-defined function and executes on one or more machines. A *server* is a subsystem that provides a particular type of service to clients unknown a priori. Not being tied to specific clients at either compile-time or link-time is crucial for flexibility and fault tolerance in server implementations. By establishing communication between interested parties at run-time, the client/server model can accommodate varying system configurations, including dynamic node additions and removals that may occur due to changes, expansions, and node failures.

A given machine becomes a server by running the service, exporting the client interface, and, optionally, announcing the fact by registering with a name service. Depending on the requirements imposed by running the service, the server hardware can range from a more powerfully configured workstation to a dedicated machine optimized for the task at hand.

A file server can provide a number of valuable services, including:

- *Management of shared resources.* Entrusting administration of shared resources, such as files and databases, to a sever usually results in improved efficiency, security, and availability.
- *Management of backup and recovery.* Backup and recovery procedures usually require specialized tools, skills, and daily attention that may be unreasonable to expect from the individual workstation users.
- *User mobility.* User mobility may provide advantages such as continuation of work in cases of workstation failures, working away from the office (when travelling to or from home), pooling of workstations in environments such as universities, and supporting of portable computers. Support for user mobility can be facilitated by maintaining user files on a server rather than on a specific workstation.
- *Diskless workstations.* Diskless workstations are desirable in some situations because they can reduce the cost of low-entry workstations, provide added security by preventing users from copying sensitive system data, and simplify system administration and software standardization by executing all applications from a server. This comes at the potential expense of performance if the network response is substantially greater than the response time of a local disk.

Client/Server Division of Labour

In a workstation-based model of distributed computing, the functions of the file subsystem are partitioned between client and server machines. Some of the functions may be fully entrusted to a single party, and others may be replicated or executed in cooperative fashion. Naturally, all functions delegated to the client need to be replicated in all workstations that are clients of the file service.

In general, the file system may be viewed as consisting of three levels of abstraction that may be implemented in the server, in the client workstation, or in both. The basic functional components of the three levels are:

- *Logical file system.* Includes directory management and performs file-relative to volume-relative translation of logical addresses. This layer also verifies and enforces access rights and, optionally, controls concurrent updating of shared files.

- *Block buffer management.* Includes blocking and deblocking functions, and caching of file blocks that are in active use.
- *Device management.* Provides logical-to-physical address mapping and performs physical I/O.

The trade-off in the client/server division of file-service labour includes considerations such as response time, throughput, resource utilization, load sharing, network loading, fault tolerance, and cost of implementation. File-system layers and major possible paths of client/server interactions in a distributed file system are depicted in Figure 16.5.

As a minimum, the client needs to provide a mechanism for accessing and for flow control of the file-service calls by means of the set of operations called the *application interface* (API) or *system-call interface.* In principle, the client workstation may forward all requests to the server and need not implement any of the file-system layers locally. This mode of access is often referred to as *remote access,* and it is depicted by the like-named arrow in Figure 16.5. With the server having full information about ongoing client activities, it can control concurrent access to shared files.

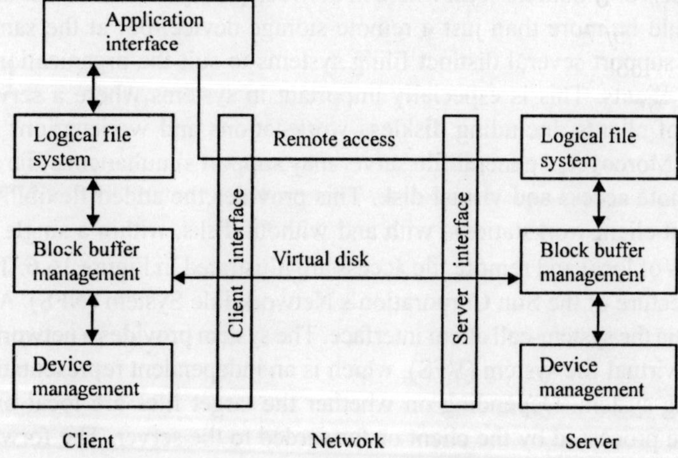

Fig. 16.5. Client/server division of labour.

The mechanics of client/server communication is handled by a software layer labelled *client interface* in Figure 16.5. It may be implemented using remote procedure calls or messages.

With regard to performance, a powerful server equipped with a large cache on a fast LAN can provide workstations with a response time close to that of a local disk. Due to its heavy reliance on the server, the remote-access method tends to increase the load on both the server and on the network. In general, a server of given processing capacity can support fewer diskless workstations than workstations with local disks.

Fault tolerance is generally adversely affected by the increased dependence on the network and on the server. On the other hand, with relatively simple and consequently cheaper workstations, it may be cost-effective to invest in fault tolerance at the server. File backup, software distribution, and system administration tend to be easier in systems with diskless workstations.

At the other extreme, the client can contain most of the layers of the file system, with the server providing only a low-level *virtual-disk* abstraction. In this approach, a client may use the server as an unsophisticated repository of data blocks. The client basically checks out the files of interest, or portions thereof, from the server and performs most of the processing locally. Upon closing or some time thereafter, files are returned to the server for permanent storage and optional sharing. In effect, the working set of files is cached by the client for processing and returned to server for long-term storage. The workstation memory, and even the local disk, can be regarded as the client cache. In such a setup, the server may be accessed only to process the client cache-miss exceptions.

With *client caching,* response time may be improved and server and network loading reduced. Local file processing at the client end also tends to relieve the server. The cost paid for these gains lies in having to use more powerful and costly workstations with large memory and possibly local disks. Moreover, concurrent client caching of shared files can lead to cache consistency problems that may require the use of special algorithms and client/server protocols. These issues are described in the next section. Reduced client dependence on the network and on the server can be beneficial for fault tolerance.

A general file server should lie somewhere in between purely remote access and the virtual-disk abstraction. It should be more than just a remote storage device, but at the same time should be general enough to support several distinct filing systems to suit the organizational and protection needs of different clients. This is especially important in systems where a server is supposed to support a variety of clients, including diskless workstations and workstations that use different operating systems. Moreover, a general file server may support simultaneous file access at different levels, such as remote access and virtual disk. This provides the added flexibility of supporting a mixture of different client workstations, with and without disks, within a single system.

Several aspects of local and remote file access are illustrated in Figure 16.6. The figure presents a simplified architecture of the Sun Corporation's Network File System (NFS). As indicated, client calls are accepted via the system-call client interface. The system provides a network-wide abstraction of files, called the virtual file system (VFS), which is an independent representation not tied to any particular operating system. Depending on whether the target files are local or remote, the file-system requests are processed by the client or forwarded to the server. The forwarding of requests relies on the remote-procedure call mechanism. When heterogeneous machines are involved, the external data representation (XDR) layer provides the necessary format translations. At the server end, the request is presented to the local VFS, which translated it into the corresponding calls of the local file system. When processing is complete, the server returns results via the RPC mechanism. Using the local VFS system, the client machine emulates a local return to its user. Thus, the network is largely hidden from users, who access all files as if they were local (except for the initial remote mount required for remote files). Moreover, the VFS abstraction allows the server to support clients with different operating systems and file types simultaneously. For example, such a system can support both Unix and PC-DOS clients concurrently.

Another important aspect of the file-server design is the granularity of user requests. The three granularity levels of file access are:

- File-level storage and retrieval
- Block level (sometimes called page level)
- Byte level

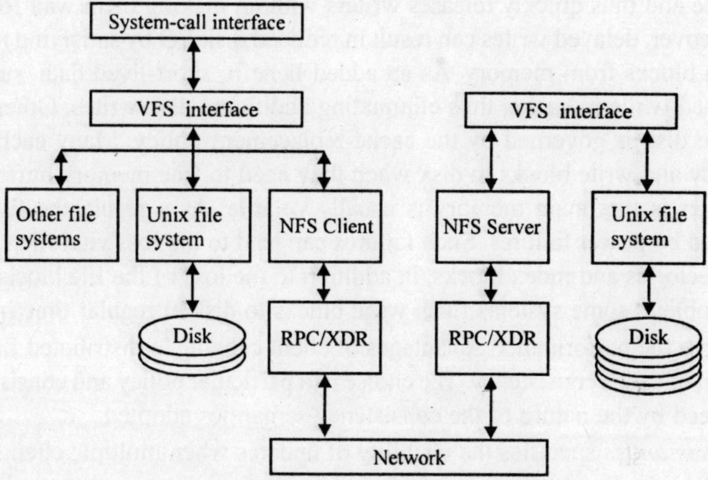

Fig. 16.6. Architecture of the Network File System.

At the file level, clients retrieve and submit entire files. Block-or page-level access can support both files and virtual memory with server facilities used as a backing store. Byte-level access provides the ability to retrieve and update arbitrary fields of variable lengths; this is a common form of user interface in Unix-like file systems and in databases. A general-purpose file server may simultaneously provide different levels of access to different clients. It may be required to provide fast access to raw streams of sequential data, such as full-motion video images, while supporting efficient random access to small fields within a file.

File Caching and Consistency Semantics

In the remote-access model of the file service, the client interface at the workstation intercepts all file-related client requests and forwards them to the server. Requests are processed remotely by the server. This approach tends to off-load the workstation at the expense of burdening the communication network and the file server.

In more balanced systems, clients perform some of the file-related operations locally. While the client performs local operations, some portions of the files and brought to the client and cached there. There are several potential benefits of client caching. As a result of local availability of the cached data, access speed can be significantly improved over the remote access—especially on repeated references to the same data. At the same time, both network and server loads may be decreased.

Clients can cache data in main memory, on local disk, or both. Caches may contain read-only data or both read and write blocks. One possibility is to cache in memory the read-only blocks and to write to disk without delay all modified blocks. This policy is called *write-through.* Due to the general tendency of reads to outnumber writes, write-through can work well in many applications. Depending on the system configuration and design principles, write-throughs can be staged to local disk or sent directly to the server.

Write caching is sometimes referred to as *delayed write.* In this approach, the system performs writes to the cache and thus quickly releases writers without making them wait for the disk writes to complete. Moreover, delayed writes can result in reduced disk I/O by satisfying repeated requests for the same data blocks from memory. As an added benefit, short-lived data, such as temporary files, may be erased while in cache, thus eliminating additional disk writes. Otherwise, writing of data blocks to the disk is governed by the cache-replacement policy. Many caches use the LRU replacement policy and write blocks to disk when they need to free memory buffers. The problem with delayed writes is that main memory is usually volatile. As a result, the file system can be seriously corrupted by power failures. Such failures can lead to the loss vital file system data, such as portions of directories and index blocks, in addition to the loss of the file blocks themselves. To ameliorate the problem, some systems flush write blocks to disk at regular time intervals.

To benefit from the performance advantages of client caching, a distributed file system should enforce some level of cache consistency. The choice of a particular policy and consistency guarantees is largely influenced by the nature of the consistency semantics adopted.

Consistency semantics specifies the visibility of updates when multiple clients are accessing a shared file concurrently. For performance and implementation reasons, the consistency semantics suitable for centralized systems is not necessarily the most appropriate for distributed systems.

In a centralized system, updates made by one client are usually immediately visible to the others that have the file open. Concurrency control, when enforced, is often accomplished by temporarily delaying some of the conflicting writers. This approach essentially revolves around a single physical image of the file that is shared by all active clients. Contention for this single image results in delaying of some clients. This semantics is difficult and often inefficient to implement in a distributed environment. Some researchers argue that it is not necessarily the semantics of choice for distributed systems.

Another possibility is the *open/close consistency semantics,* where a client is guaranteed to obtain the most recent image of the file at the time of opening. Writes to an open file by a client are not immediately visible to other clients that have the file open. Upon closing, changes made to the file are visible to clients that open the file subsequently. In terms of implementation, multiple physical images of the file may exist simultaneously and be used by different clients. This approach is suitable in systems where clients cache entire files locally. However, the open/close semantics can lead to the creation of inconsistent copies of a file that is updated simultaneously by concurrent writers.

Some distributed file systems offer a *transaction-style consistency semantics.* In this approach, the final result of a series of concurrent operations on a file is consistent and equivalent to some serial ordering of transactions. In this context, a transaction may be viewed as a series of operations between the consecutive open and close operations on a given file.

A cache-consistency algorithm should achieve two basic objectives:

1. Provide consistency guarantees adequate for the chosen mode of consistency semantics.
2. Provide a way to determine the usability of residual data left in cache by the previous operations.

Cache consistency is essentially a distributed instance of the concurrent readers/writers problem. The basic strategy is to prevent incompatible forms of sharing, such as multiple concurrent writes. Servers that require clients to report all file openings, which is usually coupled with a declaration of the intended mode of access, can detect the problem early on by keeping track of the number and nature of opens on actively used files. A popular policy is to temporarily disable client caching while incompatible opens on a file are active. In effect, the server forces the clients to switch to the remote-access mode of operation during the time-critical period when incompatible opens are in effect. The performance penalty of remote accessing is thereby limited to the subset of files that are read/write-shareable and only for the duration of incompatible opens. In practice, this policy can be effectively implemented with the aid of a *callback* mechanism, where the server calls back the affected clients and instructs them to flush the blocks and to stop caching of a specific file. Alternatively, cache-consistency checking can be initiated by clients. Frequent checking can be inefficient, as it uses the communication bandwidth and processing cycles of clients and the server. Infrequent checking, on the other hand, can result in inconsistencies or delaying of updates.

System performance can also be improved by facilitating the reuse of residual data in the cache when clients reopen a recently used file. The problem here is that the data left over in the cache may become stale if another client modifies the file in the interim. One way to detect stale cache data is by using the *cache-block version control.* In this approach, the system maintains an internal version number for each modifiable file. The version number can be the number of the last write to the file. The client obtains and records this number with each cached block of the file. Upon reopening the file, the client can verify the validity of the residual data blocks by contacting the server and obtaining the current file-version number. If the version numbers stored in cache blocks and obtained from the server are identical, the blocks are valid and may by reused. Otherwise, the blocks could be stale and must be flushed from cache. New copies of the needed blocks are then obtained from the server.

Statefulness and Performance

Many single-site operating systems keep track of the client state across repeated calls to the file service. This is often referred to as the *stateful* model of file operations. As a typical example, Unix requires client processes to open files per client to accessing them. The operating system maintains a list of open files per client and a system list of open files. Following an open, the system returns a file identifier, which is a pointer to the related file descriptor in the system list of open files. Unix also keeps the access pointer, which indicates the byte offset of the last read or write operation on the file. When reading or writing an open file, the client process supplies only the file identifier and the number of bytes of interest. The stateful approach tends to speed up repeated access to files by keeping the naming and access information in main memory.

Depending on the amount of the client-state information retained between requests, server implementations can be classified as

- *Stateless:* The server keeps no client-state information between requests.
- *Stateful:* The server keeps track of each client's ongoing activity, including the list of open files, the mode in which they are accessed, and file markers.

In the stateless approach, the server keeps no client-state information between requests. Clients keep track of their own state and include complete information with each file-related request to the server, including the file name, the absolute offset within the file, and the nature of the operation (read or write). Open and close operations on files are not necessary since each request is self-contained.

Primary advantages of the stateless approach include reduced load on the server and almost trivial recovery. Following a crash, the server can simply reboot and immediately continue to service the incoming requests. Client crashes are also handled with relative ease, provided that their operations are idempotent, that is, have the same effect and return the same result when executed repeatedly. This is necessary because clients typically repeat requests that fail due to communication errors or server failures. Self-contained read and write requests are idempotent, but some care must be taken in implementing destructive operations, such as delete.

Two primary disadvantages of the stateless-server approach are the difficulty of enforcing consistency and the lower performance potential in comparison with stateful servers. Since a stateless server retains no knowledge of client activity, it cannot detect file sharing and possible conflicts due to incompatible modes of the ongoing file accesses. As a partial remedy, many systems with stateless servers require clients to perform writes in the form of direct write-thoughts to the server disk. Nevertheless, stateless servers cannot guarantee the consistency of a client's read-only caches. This puts system implementers in the awkward situation of having to choose between performance and consistency. The lack of main-memory file-access and state tables also tends to reduce performance by prolonging the service time of individual requests. Stateless file service can be implemented on top of a datagram network service.

Statefulness is much better served by a virtual-circuit type of connection between clients and servers. As discussed in the previous section, stateful servers can maintain consistency of client caches. In-memory access tables and shorter client request messages provide further potential for increased performance in systems with stateful servers. Unfortunately, these very factors contribute to the reduced fault tolerance and complicated crash recovery of stateful servers. Server crashes can lead to prolonged unavailability while the server is engaged in reconstructing the client state lost due to the failure. This is typically accomplished by querying the clients. Client crashes are also a problem because they leave the server with the orphaned state information. The server must expend the added effort to detect client failures and attempt to identify the cause. In case of hard client failures, it may be best to discard the related state and free the server resources. Transient failures, such as communication malfunctions, are a difficult call. On one hand, deapping the state can be too drastic since it may force the client to abort upon reconnecting. On the other hand, retaining the state can burden the server by tying up storage and requiring continued monitoring of the suspect client's health.

Fault Tolerance

Redundancy is a standard method for achieving fault tolerance. One copy, designated as the primary, processes client requests. The other copy, a backup or a hot standby, mimics operations of the primary server by copying and processing all client requests. The backup copy is passive in the sense that it does not give any replies to the clients. If the primary fails, the backup copy takes over. Elaborate techniques, such as incremental database copying and comparison and verification of each other's sanity are employed to keep the two nodes in synchrony and to detect failures.

The inherent broadcast nature of the communication medium in many local-area area networks allows numerous creative variations in implementing fault tolerance in distributed systems. For instance, processes may checkpoint themselves across the network, and a special node may be charged with eavesdropping and recording all interprocess messages. Thus, when a node crashes, the process of interest may be reconstructed from its checkpointed state and brought up to date by having all outstanding messages replayed to it.

Whatever the implementation, a distributed file system should be robust, and failed or incomplete actions should not corrupt it. A file is said to be *recoverable* if it is possible to revert it to an earlier consistent state. A file is said to be *robust* if it survives crashes of the storage devices and decays of the storage medium. In general, robustness does not imply recoverability, and recoverability does not imply robustness. Therefore, different techniques are used to ensure each property.

Distributed systems provide much greater flexibility by allowing for partial redundancy. For example, files and critical server functions may be replicated at different nodes. The remainder of this section briefly discusses some of the relatively simple techniques that can be applied to server implementation.

One way to implement file recoverability is by making transactions atomic. An atomic transaction either completeness successfully and transforms a file into a new consistent state, or fails without changing the state of the target file. In effect, the previous state of the file is recovered in case of transaction file.

A common requirement for making files recoverable is not to perform updates in place. Otherwise, original data can be overwritten and irrecoverably lost unless before-and-after images and trail logs are maintained. As an alternative, updates can be tentatively written into different blocks, called *shadow pages.* If the transaction completes successfully, it commits and makes the tentative updates permanent by updating the directory and index structures to point to the new blocks instead of the old ones.

Stable storage is a complementary technique for surviving server crashes during pointer swaps and other critical operations. Basically, the *stable storage* abstraction is provided by writing the lists of update intentions and the actual updates in duplicate on two separate volumes, preferably on separate controllers. All writes are *careful writes* in the sense that the contents of each block written is read back for verification. A *stable write* consists of a careful write to one volume, followed by a careful write to its matching pair on the other volume. If a write fails, a crash is forced.

At the system level, transaction atomicity can be implemented by extending these notions into a *two-phase commit protocol.* When a distributed transaction completes, its coordinator node broadcast the prepare-to-commit message. Upon receiving the message, each participating node records the list of intended tentative updates using stable storage and informs the coordinator about the outcome. If all responses are affirmative, the coordinator broadcasts the commit message. Otherwise, the transaction needs to be aborted and the coordinator broadcasts the abort message. As a result, individual copies of the tentative updates are discarded, and the database is in effect, rolled back to a previous consistent state.

Summary

Hiding of the networking aspects of the system, called network transparency, is one of the key goals of implementations of distributed operating systems. Network transparency can be implemented at the application level, at the programming language level, or at the operating-system level.

The host-based system, the processor pool, the workstation/serve, and the integrated model are the four primary models of distributed processing. The first three represent evolutionary paths from existing systems, while integrated systems are a native distributed design.

The naming service allows applications to refer to objects of interest by name rather than by node address. Decoupling of names from locations facilitates naming and location transparency, which in turn provides the operating system with the flexibility to dynamically migrate and replicate objects for improved performance, availability, and fault tolerance. Static maps are quite inflexible, and broadcasting is a rather inefficient method of implementing a name service. Name servers provide flexibility at the expense of adding a third party, while prefix tables have a good performance potential with comparatively less overhead.

Process migration generally facilitates resource balancing and offers potential for improved performance and fault tolerance. Its implementation must cope with the overhead of transferring a potentially large volume of state, and with the difficulties of dealing with the execution environment and of rerouting the communication and invocations directed to the migrated process. Virtual memory provides some possibilities for reducing the volume of the state to be transferred in the course of process migration.

The remote-procedure call (RPC) mechanism provides a viable alternative to the distribution of applications on procedure-call boundaries. RPC follows the familiar semantics of procedure calls. Its implementations usually entails production of the client and server stubs, the RPC run-time package, and mechanism for multimachine binding. Some of the RPC limitations include the inability to handle broadcasts and multicasts, passing of parameters by value alone, and potential inefficiency in handling bulk data transfers.

File servers are a key component of many implementations of distributed file systems. They can provide management of shared resources and management of backup and recovery while facilitating user mobility and supporting diskless workstations. File servers can also be instrumental in increasing the fault tolerance of a distributed system and in easing the complexity of administration in systems with a large number of workstations.

A general file server should provide the client/server division of labour, which represents a hybrid between a virtual disk and a purely remote-access approach. In general, system performance can be improved and network loading diminished when clients cache actively used files or portions thereof. Client caching introduces the problem of cache coherence. Stateful servers, by keeping track of client activities, have the ability to support a variety of forms of the file-consistency semantics, can enforce coherence of client caches, and can control concurrent access to files. Stateless servers, on the other hand, do not maintain client-state information and thereby simplify crash recovery.

A distributed file system can provide file recovery and robustness through a combination of hardware and software redundancy, and by means of special mechanisms such as the stable storage and commit protocols.